programming the 6502

RODNAY ZAKS

THIRD EDITION

SYBEX

THE 6502 SERIES:

VOLUME I— PROGRAMMING THE 6502
VOLUME II— PROGRAMMING EXERCISES FOR THE 6502
VOLUME III— 6502 APPLICATIONS BOOK
VOLUME IV— 6502 GAMES

SOFTWARE: 6502 ASSEMBLER IN BASIC
8080 SIMULATOR FOR APPLE
8080 SIMULATOR FOR KIM
6502 GAMES
6502 APPLICATIONS

Cover Art: Daniel Le Noury

Every effort has been made to supply complete and accurate information. However, Sybex assumes no responsibility for its use, nor for any infringements of patents or other rights of third parties which would result. No license is granted by the equipment manufacturers under any patent or patent right. Manufacturers reserve the right to change circuitry at any time without notice.

Copyright © 1980 SYBEX Inc. World Rights reserved. No part of this publication may be stored in a retrieval system, copied, transmitted, or reproduced in any way, including, but not limited to, photocopy, photography, magnetic or other recording, without the prior written permission of the publisher.

ISBN 0-89588-046-6
Library of Congress Card Number: 80-51037
First Edition published 1978. Third Edition 1980.
Printed in the United States of America
Printing 9 8 7 6 5 4 3 2 1

PREFACE

This book has been designed as a complete self-contained text to learn programming, using the 6502. It can be used by a person who has never programmed before, and should also be of value to anyone using the 6502.

For the person who has already programmed, this book will teach specific programming techniques using (or working around) the specific characteristics of the 6502. This text covers the elementary to intermediate techniques required to start programming effectively.

This text aims at providing a true level of competence to the person who wishes to program using this microprocessor. Naturally, no book will teach effectively how to program, unless one actually practices. However, it is hoped that this book will take the reader to the point where he feels that he can start programming by himself and solve simple or even moderately complex problems using a microcomputer.

This book is based on the author's experience in teaching more than 1000 persons how to program microcomputers. As a result, it is strongly structured. Chapters normally go from the simple to the complex. For readers who have already learned elementary programming, the introductory chapter may be skipped. For others who have never programmed, the final sections of some chapters may require a second reading. The book has been designed to take the reader systematically through all the basic concepts and techniques required to build increasingly complex programs. It is, therefore, strongly suggested that the ordering of the chapters be followed. In addition, for effective results, it is important that the reader attempt to solve as many exercises as possible. The difficulty within the exercises has been carefully graduated. They are designed to verify that the material which has been presented is really understood. Without doing the programming exercises, it will not be possible to realize the full value of this book as an educational medium. Several of the exercises may require time, such as the multiplication exercise for example. However, by doing these, you will actually program and *learn by doing*. This is indispensable.

For those who will have acquired a taste for programming when reaching the end of this volume, companion volumes are available:

—"Programming Exercises for the 6502" is a complement to this volume.
—The "6502 Applications Book" covers input/output.
—"6502 Games" covers complex algorithms.

Other books in this series cover programming for other popular microprocessors.

For those who wish to develop their hardware knowledge, it is suggested that the reference books "Microprocessors" (ref. C201) and "Microprocessor Interfacing Techniques" (ref. C207) be consulted.

The contents of this book have been checked carefully and are believed to be reliable. However, inevitably, some typographical or other errors will be found. The author will be grateful for any comments by alert readers so that future editions may benefit from their experience. Any other suggestions for improvements, such as other programs desired, developed, or found of value by readers, will be appreciated.

PREFACE TO THE 2ND AND 3RD EDITIONS

This second edition has increased in size by almost 100 pages, with most of the new material added to Chapters 1 and 9, i.e. at both ends of the spectrum; Chapter 1 is the introductory chapter, and Chapter 9 has advanced information on data structures.

Additional improvements have been made throughout the book, and I would like to thank the many readers of the previous edition who have contributed valuable suggestions for improvement.

Special acknowledgements are due to Eric Novikoff and Chris Williams for their contributions to the complex programming examples in Chapter 9, and to Daniel J. David for his many suggested improvements. A number of changes and enhancements are also due to the valuable analysis and comments proposed by Philip K. Hooper, John Smith, Ronald Long, Charles Curley, N. Harris, John McClenon, Douglas Trusty, and Fletcher Carson.

Support software which will facilitate learning such as a 6502 Assembler in Microsoft Basic, has also been introduced for 6502 users.

CONTENTS

PREFACE 5

I.   BASIC CONCEPTS 7

Introduction. What is Programming? Flowcharting. Information Representation.

II.   6502 HARDWARE ORGANIZATION 38

Introduction. System Architecture. Internal Organization of the 6502. The Instruction Execution Cycle. The Stack. The Paging Concept. The 6502 Chip. Hardware Summary.

III. BASIC PROGRAMMING TECHNIQUES 53

Introduction. Arithmetic Programs. BCD Arithmetic. Important Self-Test. Logical Operations. Subroutines. Summary.

IV.   THE 6502 INSTRUCTION SET 99

*PART 1-OVERALL DESCRIPTION
Introduction. Classes of Instructions. Instructions Available on the 6502.
PART 2-THE INSTRUCTIONS
Abbreviations. Description of Each Instruction.*

V.   ADDRESSING TECHNIQUES 188

Introduction. Addressing Modes. 6502 Addressing Modes. Using the 6502 Addressing Modes. Summary.

VI.   INPUT/OUTPUT TECHNIQUES 211

Introduction. Input/Output. Parallel Word Transfer. Bit Serial Transfer. Basic I/O Summary. Communicating with Input/Output Devices. Peripheral Summary. Input/Output Scheduling. Summary. Exercises.

VII.	**INPUT/OUTPUT DEVICES** 254	

Introduction. The Standard PIO (6520). The Internal Control Register. The 6530. Programming a PIO. The 6522. The 6532. Summary.

VIII.	**APPLICATION EXAMPLES**.....................262	

Introduction. Clear a Section of Memory. Polling I/O Devices. Getting Characters In. Testing a Character. Bracket Testing. Parity Generation. Code Conversion: ASCII to BCD. Find the Largest Element of a Table. Sum of N Elements. A Checksum Computation. Count the Zeroes. A String Search. Summary.

IX.	**DATA STRUCTURES**...........................275	

PART 1-DESIGN CONCEPTS
Introduction. Pointers. Lists. Searching and Sorting. Summary. Data Structures.
PART 2-DESIGN EXAMPLES
Introduction. Data Representation for the List. A Simple List. Alphabetic List. Binary Tree. A Hashing Algorithm. Bubble-Sort. A Merge Algorithm. Summary.

X.	**PROGRAM DEVELOPMENT**.....................343	

Introduction. Basic Programming Choices. Software Support. The Program Development Sequence. The Hardware Alternatives. Summary of Hardware Alternatives. Summary of Hardware Resources. The Assembler. Macros. Conditional Assembly. Summary.

XI.	**CONCLUSION** 368	

Technological Development. The Next Step.

APPENDICES...371

A.	Hexadecimal Conversion Table
B.	6502 Instruction-Set: Alphabetic
C.	6502 Instruction-Set: Binary
D.	6502 Instruction-Set: Hexadecimal and Timing
E.	ASCII Table
F.	Relative Branch Table

INDEX...380

TABLE OF ILLUSTRATIONS

Figure 1-1 :	A Flowchart for Keeping Room Temperature Constant	9
Figure 1-2 :	Decimal - Binary Table	13
Figure 1-3 :	2's Complement Table	21
Figure 1-4 :	BCD Table	27
Figure 1-5 :	Typical Floating-Point Representation	30
Figure 1-6 :	ASCII Conversion Table	32
Figure 1-7 :	Octal Symbols	34
Figure 1-8 :	Hexadecimal Codes	35
Figure 2-1 :	Architecture of a Standard Microprocessor System	39
Figure 2-2 :	Internal Organization of the 6502	42
Figure 2-3 :	Fetching an Instruction from the Memory	44
Figure 2-4 :	Automatic Sequencing	46
Figure 2-5 :	The 2 Stack Manipulation Instructions	49
Figure 2-6 :	The Paging Concept	50
Figure 2-7 :	6502 Pinout	51
Figure 3-1 :	8-Bit Addition Res=OP1+OP2	54
Figure 3-2 :	LDA ADR1: OP1 is Loaded from Memory	55
Figure 3-3 :	ADC ADR2	56
Figure 3-4 :	STA ADR3 (Save Accumulator in Memory)	57
Figure 3-5 :	16 Bit Addition: The Operands	59
Figure 3-6 :	Storing Operands in Reverse Order	61
Figure 3-6a:	Pointing to the High Byte	62
Figure 3-7 :	Storing BCD Digits	65
Figure 3-8 :	The Basic Multiplication Algorithm Flowchart	69
Figure 3-9 :	8 X 8 Multiply	70
Figure 3-10:	Multiplication: The Registers	71
Figure 3-11:	Shift and Rotate	72
Figure 3-12:	Form To Be Filled Out For Exercise 3-12	79
Figure 3-13:	First Instruction of Multiplication	80
Figure 3-14:	First Two Lines of Multiplication	80
Figure 3-15:	Partially Completed Form for Exercise 3-12	81
Figure 3-16:	6502 Registers	83
Figure 3-17:	Registered Allocation (Improved Multiply)	84
Figure 3-18:	Improved Multiply	84
Figure 3-19:	8-Bit Binary Division Flowchart	86
Figure 3-20:	16 by 8 Division Flowchart	88
Figure 3-21:	Program	89
Figure 3-22:	16 by 8 Division Flowchart (non-restoring 8-bit result)	89
Figure 3-23:	Subroutine Calls	91
Figure 3-24:	Nested Calls	93
Figure 3-25:	The Subroutine Calls	94
Figure 3-26:	Stack vs. Time	95
Figure 4-1 :	Shift and Rotate	101
Figure 5-1 :	Addressing	189
Figure 5-2 :	Indirect Indexed Addressing	192
Figure 5-3 :	Indirect Addressing	193
Figure 5-4 :	Indexed Indirect Addressing	199
Figure 5-5 :	Character Searching Table	202
Figure 5-6 :	Memory Organization for Block Transfer	205
Figure 5-7 :	Memory Map for General Block Transfer	205

Figure 6-1 :	Turning on a Relay	213
Figure 6-2 :	A Programmed Pulse	213
Figure 6-3 :	A Delay Flowchart	214
Figure 6-4 :	Parallel Word Transfer: The Memory	218
Figure 6-5 :	Parallel Word Transfer: Flowchart	219
Figure 6-6 :	Serial to Parallel Conversion	222
Figure 6-7 :	Bit Serial Transfer: Flowchart	223
Figure 6-8 :	Handshaking (Output)	228
Figure 6-9 :	Handshaking (Input)	229
Figure 6-10:	Seven Segment LED	230
Figure 6-11:	Characters Generated with a 7-Segment LED	231
Figure 6-12:	Format of a Teletype Word	233
Figure 6-13:	TTY Input with Echo	234
Figure 6-14:	Input from Teletype	235
Figure 6-15:	Teletype Input	236
Figure 6-16:	Teletype Output	237
Figure 6-17:	Print a Memory Block	238
Figure 6-18:	Three Methods of I/O Control	239
Figure 6-19:	Polling Loop Flowchart	240
Figure 6-20:	Reading from a Paper-Tape Reader	241
Figure 6-21:	Printing on a Punch or Printer	241
Figure 6-22:	Interrupt Processing	243
Figure 6-23:	6502 Stack After Interrupt	245
Figure 6-24:	Interrupt Vectors	245
Figure 6-25:	Saving All the Registers	247
Figure 6-26:	Polled vs. Vectored Interrupt	248
Figure 6-27:	Several Devices May Use the Same Interrupt Line	249
Figure 6-28:	Stack During Interrupts	250
Figure 6-29:	Interrupt Logic	253
Figure 7-1 :	Typical PIO	255
Figure 7-2 :	PIA Control Word format	256
Figure 7-3 :	Addressing PIA Registers	256
Figure 7-4 :	6530 Pinout	257
Figure 7-5 :	Using a PIA: Load Control Register	259
Figure 7-6 :	Using a PIA: Load Data Direction	259
Figure 7-7 :	Using a PIA: Read Status	260
Figure 7-8 :	Using a PIA: Read Input	260
Figure 8-1 :	String Search: The Memory	272
Figure 8-2 :	Program Flowchart: String Search	273
Figure 8-3 :	String Search Program	274
Figure 9-1 :	An Indirection Pointer	276
Figure 9-2 :	A Directory Structure	277
Figure 9-3 :	A Linked List	278
Figure 9-4 :	Inserting a New Block	279
Figure 9-5 :	A Queue	279
Figure 9-6 :	Round-Robin is Circular List	281
Figure 9-7 :	Genealogical Tree	282
Figure 9-8 :	Doubly-Linked List	282
Figure 9-9 :	The Table Structure	285
Figure 9-10:	Typical List Entries in the Memory	285
Figure 9-11:	The Simple List	287

Figure 9-12:	Table Search Flow Chart	288
Figure 9-13:	Table Insertion Flow Chart	289
Figure 9-14:	Deleting an Entry (Simple List)	290
Figure 9-15:	Table Deletion Flow Chart	291
Figure 9-16:	Simple List Programs: Search, Enter, Delete	292
Figure 9-17:	Binary Search Flow Chart	294
Figure 9-18:	A Binary Search	296
Figure 9-19:	Insert: "BAC"	299
Figure 9-20:	Delete: "BAC"	300
Figure 9-21:	Deletion Flow Chart (Alphabetic List)	301
Figure 9-22:	Alphabetic List Programs: Binary Search, Delete, Insert	302
Figure 9-23:	Linked List Structure	306
Figure 9-24:	Linked List: A Search	308
Figure 9-25:	Linked List: Example of Insertion	308
Figure 9-26:	Example of Deletion (Linked List)	309
Figure 9-27:	Linked List Program	310
Figure 9-28:	Binary Tree	313
Figure 9-29:	Representation in Memory	314
Figure 9-30:	The Tree Builder Flowchart	315
Figure 9-31:	Tree Traverser Flowchart	317
Figure 9-32:	Tree Traversal Algorithm	318
Figure 9-33:	Data Units, or "Nodes" of Tree	319
Figure 9-34:	Memory Maps	319
Figure 9-35:	Inserting an Element in the Tree	320
Figure 9-36:	Listing the Tree	321
Figure 9-37:	Tree Search Programs	322
Figure 9-38:	Tree in Preorder	325
Figure 9-39:	Access Time vs. Relative Fullness	326
Figure 9-40:	Initialize Subroutine	327
Figure 9-41:	"Store" Routine	327
Figure 9-42:	Retrieve Routine, "Find"	328
Figure 9-43:	Hash Routine	329
Figure 9-44:	Hash Store/Retrieve: Memory Maps	330
Figure 9-45:	Hashing Program	331
Figure 9-46:	Bubble Sort Example	334
Figure 9-47:	Bubble Sort	336
Figure 9-48:	Bubble Sort: Memory Maps	337
Figure 9-49:	Bubble Sort Program	338
Figure 9-50:	"Merge" Flow Chart	339
Figure 9-51:	"Merge" Memory Map	340
Figure 9-52:	Merge Program	341
Figure 10-1:	Programming Levels	345
Figure 10-2:	A Typical Memory Map	351
Figure 10-3:	SYM 1 is a Typical Microcomputer Board	353
Figure 10-4:	Rockwell System 65 is a Development System	353
Figure 10-5:	Microprocessor Programming Form	357
Figure 10-6:	Assembler Output: An Example	359
Figure 10-7:	AIM 65 is a Board with Mini-Printer and Full Keyboard	364
Figure 10-8:	Ohio Scientific is a Personal Microcomputer	364
Figure 11-1:	PET is an Integrated Unit	369
Figure 11-2:	APPLE II uses a Conventional TV	369

Acknowledgements

The author would like to express his appreciation to Rockwell International and, in particular, to Scotty Maxwell, who made available to him one of the very first system 65 development systems. The availability of this powerful development tool, at the time the first version of this book was being written, was a major help for the accurate and efficient check-out of all the programs. I would also like to thank Professor Myron Calhoun for his contributions.

1
BASIC CONCEPTS

INTRODUCTION

This chapter will introduce the basic concepts and definitions relating to computer programming. The reader already familiar with these concepts may want to glance quickly at the contents of this chapter and then move on to Chapter 2. It is suggested, however, that even the experienced reader look at the contents of this introductory chapter. Many significant concepts are presented here including, for example, two's complement, BCD, and other representations. Some of these concepts may be new to the reader; others may improve the knowledge and skills of experienced programmers.

WHAT IS PROGRAMMING?

Given a problem, one must first devise a solution. This solution, expressed as a step-by-step procedure, is called an *algorithm*. An algorithm is a step-by-step specification of the solution to a given problem. It must terminate in a finite number of steps. This algorithm may be expressed in any language or symbolism. A simple example of an algorithm is:

1—insert key in the keyhole
2—turn key one full turn to the left
3—seize doorknob
4—turn doorknob left and push the door

At this point, if the algorithm is correct for the type of lock involved, the door will open. This four-step procedure qualifies as an algorithm for door opening.

Once a solution to a problem has been expressed in the form of an algorithm, the algorithm must be executed by the computer. Unfortunately, it is now a well-established fact that computers cannot understand or execute ordinary spoken English (or any other human language). The reason lies in the *syntactic ambiguity* of all common human languages. Only a well-defined subset of natural language can be "understood" by the computer. This is called a *programming language*.

Converting an algorithm into a sequence of instructions in a programming language is called *programming*. To be more specific, the actual translation phase of the algorithm into the programming language is called *coding*. Programming really refers not just to the coding but also to the overall design of the programs and "data structures" which will implement the algorithm.

Effective programming requires not only understanding the possible implementation techniques for standard algorithms, but also the skillful use of all the computer hardware resources, such as internal registers, memory, and peripheral devices, plus a creative use of appropriate data structures. These techniques will be covered in the next chapters.

Programming also requires a strict documentation discipline, so that the programs are understandable to others, as well as to the author. Documentation must be both internal and external to the program.

Internal program documentation refers to the comments placed in the body of a program, which explain its operation.

External documentation refers to the design documents which are separate from the program: written explanations, manuals, and flowcharts.

FLOWCHARTING

One intermediate step is almost always used between the *algorithm* and the *program*. It is called a *flowchart*. A flowchart is simply a symbolic representation of the algorithm expressed as a sequence of rectangles and diamonds containing the steps of the algorithm. Rectangles are used for *commands*, or "executable statements." Diamonds are used for *tests* such as: If information

BASIC CONCEPTS

X is true, then take action A, else B. Instead of presenting a formal definition of flowcharts at this point, we will introduce and discuss flowcharts later on in the book when we present programs.

Flowcharting is a highly recommended intermediate step between the algorithm specification and the actual coding of the solution. Remarkably, it has been observed that perhaps 10% of the programming population can write a program successfully without having to flowchart. Unfortunately, it has also been observed that 90% of the population believes it belongs to this 10%! The result: 80% of these programs, on the average, will fail the first time they are run on a computer. (These percentages are naturally not meant to be accurate.) In short, most novice programmers seldom see the necessity of drawing a flowchart. This usually results in "unclean" or erroneous programs. They must then spend a long time testing and correcting their program (this is called the

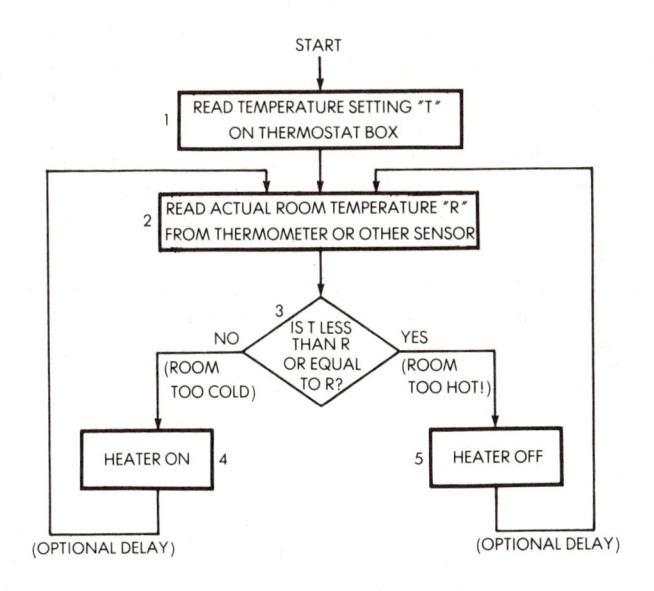

Fig. 1-1: A Flowchart for Keeping Room Temperature Constant

debugging phase). The discipline of flowcharting is therefore highly recommended in all cases. It will require a small amount of additional time prior to the coding, but will usually result in a clear program which executes correctly and quickly. Once flowcharting is well understood, a small percentage of programmers will be able to perform this step mentally without having to do it on paper. Unfortunately, in such cases the programs that they write will usually be hard to understand for anybody else without the documentation provided by flowcharts. As a result, it is universally recommended that flowcharting be used as a strict discipline for any significant program. Many examples will be provided throughout the book.

INFORMATION REPRESENTATION

All computers manipulate information in the form of numbers or in the form of characters. Let us examine here the external and internal representations of information in a computer.

INTERNAL REPRESENTATION OF INFORMATION

All information in a computer is stored as groups of bits. A *bit* stands for a *binary digit*("0" or "1"). Because of the limitations of conventional electronics, the only practical representation of information uses two-state logic (the representation of the state "0" and "1"). The two states of the circuits used in digital electronics are generally "on" or "off", and these are represented logically by the symbols "0" or "1". Because these circuits are used to implement "logical" functions, they are called "binary logic." As a result, virtually all information-processing today is performed in binary format. In the case of microprocessors in general, and of the 6502 in particular, these bits are structured in groups of eight. A group of eight bits is called a *byte*. A group of four bits is called a *nibble*.

Let us now examine how information is represented internally in this binary format. Two entities must be represented inside the computer. The first one is the program, which is a sequence of instructions. The second one is the data on which the program will operate, which may include numbers or alphanumeric text. We will discuss below three representations: program, numbers, and alphanumerics.

BASIC CONCEPTS

Program Representation

All instructions are represented internally as single or multiple bytes. A so-called "short instruction" is represented by a single byte. A longer instruction will be represented by two or more bytes. Because the 6502 is an eight-bit microprocessor, it fetches bytes successively from its memory. Therefore, a single-byte instruction always has a potential for executing faster than a two- or three-byte instruction. It will be seen later that this is an important feature of the instruction set of any microprocessor and in particular the 6502, where a special effort has been made to provide as many single-byte instructions as possible in order to improve the efficiency of the program execution. However, the limitation to 8 bits in length has resulted in important restrictions which will be outlined. This is a classic example of the compromise between speed and flexibility in programming. The binary code used to represent instructions is dictated by the manufacturer. The 6502, like any other microprocessor, comes equipped with a fixed instruction set. These instructions are defined by the manufacturer and are listed at the end of this book, with their code. Any program will be expressed as a sequence of these binary instructions. The 6502 instructions are presented in Chapter 4.

Representing Numeric Data

Representing numbers is not quite straightforward, and several cases must be distinguished. We must first represent integers, then signed numbers, i.e., positive and negative numbers, and finally we must be able to represent decimal numbers. Let us now address these requirements and possible solutions.

Representing integers may be performed by using a *direct binary* representation. The direct binary representation is simply the representation of the decimal value of a number in the binary system. In the binary system, the right-most bit represents 2 to the power 0. The next one to the left represents 2 to the power 1, the next represents 2 to the power 2, and the left-most bit represents 2 to the power $7 = 128$.

$$b_7 b_6 b_5 b_4 b_3 b_2 b_1 b_0$$
represents
$$b_7 2^7 + b_6 2^6 + b_5 2^5 + b_4 2^4 + b_3 2^3 + b_2 2^2 + b_1 2^1 + b_0 2^0$$

The powers of 2 are:

$2^7 = 128, 2^6 = 64, 2^5 = 32, 2^4 = 16, 2^3 = 8, 2^2 = 4, 2^1 = 2, 2^0 = 1$

The binary representation is analogous to the decimal representation of numbers, where "123" represents:

$$
\begin{array}{r}
1 \times 100 = 100 \\
+\ 2 \times 10 = 20 \\
+\ 3 \times 1 = 3 \\
\hline
= 123
\end{array}
$$

Note that $100 = 10^2$, $10 = 10^1$, $1 = 10^0$.
In this "positional notation," each digit represents a power of 10. In the binary system, each binary digit or "bit" represents a power of 2, instead of a power of 10 in the decimal system.

Example: "00001001" in binary represents:

$$
\begin{array}{rll}
1 \times 1 = 1 & (2^0) \\
0 \times 2 = 0 & (2^1) \\
0 \times 4 = 0 & (2^2) \\
1 \times 8 = 8 & (2^3) \\
0 \times 16 = 0 & (2^4) \\
0 \times 32 = 0 & (2^5) \\
0 \times 64 = 0 & (2^6) \\
0 \times 128 = 0 & (2^7) \\
\hline
\end{array}
$$

in decimal: $= 9$

Let us examine some more examples:

"10000001" represents:

$$
\begin{array}{r}
1 \times 1 = 1 \\
0 \times 2 = 0 \\
0 \times 4 = 0 \\
0 \times 8 = 0 \\
0 \times 16 = 0 \\
0 \times 32 = 0 \\
0 \times 64 = 0 \\
1 \times 128 = 128 \\
\hline
\end{array}
$$

in decimal: $= 129$

"10000001" represents, therefore, the decimal number 129.

BASIC CONCEPTS

By examining the binary representation of numbers, you will understand why bits are numbered from 0 to 7, going from right to left. Bit 0 is "b_0" and corresponds to 2^0. Bit 1 is "b_1" and corresponds to 2^1, and so on.

Decimal	Binary	Decimal	Binary
0	00000000	32	00100000
1	00000001	33	00100001
2	00000010	•	
3	00000011	•	
4	00000100	•	
5	00000101	63	00111111
6	00000110	64	01000000
7	00000111	65	01000001
8	00001000	•	
9	00001001	•	
10	00001010	127	01111111
11	00001011	128	10000000
12	00001100	129	10000001
13	00001101		
14	00001110	•	
15	00001111	•	
16	00010000		
17	00010001	•	
•			
•			
•		254	11111110
31	00011111	255	11111111

Fig. 1-2: Decimal-Binary Table

The binary equivalents of the numbers from 0 to 255 are shown in Fig. 1-2.

Exercise 1.1: *What is the decimal value of "11111100"?*

PROGRAMMING THE 6502

Decimal to Binary

Conversely, let us compute the binary equivalent of "11" decimal:

$$11 \div 2 = 5 \text{ remains } 1 \longrightarrow 1 \quad \text{(LSB)}$$
$$5 \div 2 = 2 \text{ remains } 1 \longrightarrow 1$$
$$2 \div 2 = 1 \text{ remains } 0 \longrightarrow 0$$
$$1 \div 2 = 0 \text{ remains } 1 \longrightarrow 1 \quad \text{(MSB)}$$

The binary equivalent is 1011 (read right-most column from bottom to top).

The binary equivalent of a decimal number may be obtained by dividing successively by 2 until a quotient of 0 is obtained.

Exercise 1.2: *What is the binary for 257?*

Exercise 1.3: *Convert 19 to binary, then back to decimal.*

Operating on Binary Data

The arithmetic rules for binary numbers are straightforward. The rules for addition are:

$$0 + 0 = 0$$
$$0 + 1 = 1$$
$$1 + 0 = 0$$
$$1 + 1 = (1)\ 0$$

where (1) denotes a "carry" of 1 (note that "10" is the binary equivalent of "2" decimal). Binary subtraction will be performed by "adding the complement" and will be explained once we learn how to represent negative numbers.

Example:

```
    (2)        10
   +(1)       +01
   ────       ───
   =(3)        11
```

Addition is performed just like in decimal, by adding columns, from right to left:

Adding the right-most column:

```
        10
       +01
       ───
```
$(0 + 1 = 1.$ No carry.$)$

BASIC CONCEPTS

Adding the next column:

$$\begin{array}{r} 10 \\ +01 \\ \hline 11 \end{array} \quad (1 + 0 = 1. \text{ No carry.})$$

Exercise 1.4: *Compute 5 + 10 in binary. Verify that the result is 15.*

Some additional examples of binary addition:

$$\begin{array}{rl} 0010 & (2) \\ +0001 & (1) \\ \hline =0011 & (3) \end{array} \qquad \begin{array}{rl} 0011 & (3) \\ +0001 & (1) \\ \hline =0100 & (4) \end{array}$$

This last example illustrates the role of the carry.

Looking at the right-most bits: $1 + 1 = (1)\,0$
A carry of 1 is generated, which must be added to the next bits:

$$\begin{array}{rl} 001 & - \text{column 0 has just been added} \\ +000 & - \\ +1 & \text{(carry)} \\ \hline =(1)\,0 & - \text{where (1) indicates a new} \\ & \text{carry into column 2.} \end{array}$$

The final result is: 0100

Another example:

$$\begin{array}{rl} 0111 & (7) \\ +0011 & +\ (3) \\ \hline 1010 & =(10) \end{array}$$

In this example, a carry is again generated, up to the left-most column.

Exercise 1.5: *Compute the result of:*

$$\begin{array}{r} 1111 \\ +0001 \\ \hline =? \end{array}$$

PROGRAMMING THE 6502

Does the result hold in four bits?

With eight bits, it is therefore possible to represent directly the numbers "00000000" to "11111111," i.e., "0" to "255". Two obstacles should be visible immediately. First, we are only representing positive numbers. Second, the magnitude of these numbers is limited to 255 if we use only eight bits. Let us address each of these problems in turn.

Signed Binary

In a signed binary representation, the left-most bit is used to indicate the sign of the number. Traditionally, "0" is used to denote a *positive* number while "1" is used to denote a *negative* number. Now "11111111" will represent −127, while "01111111" will represent +127. We can now represent positive and negative numbers, but we have reduced the maximum magnitude of these numbers to 127.

Example: "0000 0001" represents +1 (the leading "0" is "+", followed by "000 0001" = 1).

"1000 0001" is −1 (the leading "1" is "−").

Exercise 1.6: *What is the representation of "−5" in signed binary?*

Let us now address the *magnitude* problem: in order to represent larger numbers, it will be necessary to use a larger number of bits. For example, if we use sixteen bits (two bytes) to represent numbers, we will be able to represent numbers from −32K to +32K in signed binary (1K in computer jargon represents 1,024). Bit 15 is used for the sign, and the remaining 15 bits (bit 14 to bit 0) are used for the magnitude: 2^{15} = 32K. If this magnitude is still too small, we will use 3 bytes or more. If we wish to represent large integers, it will be necessary to use a larger number of bytes internally to represent them. This is why most simple BASICs, and other languages, provide only a limited precision for integers. This way, they can use a shorter internal format for the numbers which they manipulate. Better versions of BASIC, or of these other languages, provide a larger number of significant decimal digits at the expense of a large number of bytes for each number.

Now let us solve another problem, the one of speed efficiency. We are going to attempt performing an addition in the signed

BASIC CONCEPTS

binary representation which we have introduced. Let us add "−5" and "+7".

+7 is represented by   00000111
−5 is represented by   10000101
The binary sum is: 10001100, or −12

This is not the correct result. The correct result should be +2. In order to use this representation, special actions must be taken, depending on the sign. This results in increased complexity and reduced performance. In other words, the binary addition of signed numbers does not "work correctly." This is annoying. Clearly, the computer must not only represent information, but also perform arithmetic on it.

The solution to this problem is called the *two's complement* representation, which will be used instead of the *signed binary* representation. In order to introduce two's complement let us first introduce an intermediate step: *one's complement*.

One's Complement

In the one's complement representation, all positive integers are represented in their correct binary format. For example "+3" is represented as usual by 00000011. However, its complement "−3" is obtained by complementing every bit in the original representation. Each 0 is transformed into a 1 and each 1 is transformed into a 0. In our example, the one's complement representation of "−3" will be 11111100.

Another example:

+2 is 00000010
−2 is 11111101

Note that, in this representation, positive numbers start with a "0" on the left, and negative ones with a "1" on the left.

Exercise 1.7: *The representation of "+6" is "00000110". What is the representation of "−6" in one's complement?*

As a test, let us add minus 4 and plus 6:

```
                              −4 is 11111011
                              +6 is 00000110
                              ─────────────
the sum is:               (1)   00000001   where (1) indicates a
                                                  carry
```

The "correct result" should be "2", or "00000010".

Let us try again:

```
                              −3 is 11111100
                              −2 is 11111101
                              ─────────────
The sum is:              (1)    00000001
```

or "1," plus a carry. The correct result should be "−5." The representation of "−5" is 11111010. It did not work.

This representation does represent positive and negative numbers. However the result of an ordinary addition does not always come out "correctly." We will use still another representation. It is evolved from the one's complement and is called the two's complement representation.

Two's Complement Representation

In the two's complement representation, positive numbers are still represented, as usual, in signed binary, just like in one's complement. The difference lies in the representation of *negative numbers*. A negative number represented in two's complement is obtained by first computing the one's complement, and then *adding one*. Let us examine this in an example:

+3 is represented in signed binary by 00000011. Its one's complement representation is 11111100. The two's complement is obtained by adding one. It is 11111101.

Let us try an addition:

```
                         (3)      00000011
                        +(5)     +00000101
                        ─────    ─────────
                        =(8)     =00001000
```

The result is correct.

BASIC CONCEPTS

Let us try a subtraction:

$$\begin{array}{rr} (3) & 00000011 \\ (-5) & +11111011 \\ \hline & =11111110 \end{array}$$

Let us identify the result by computing the two's complement:

the one's complement of 11111110 is   00000001
                          Adding 1 +   1
                                      ─────────────
therefore the two's complement is   00000010 or +2

Our result above, "11111110" represents "−2". It is correct.

We have now tried addition and subtraction, and the results were correct (ignoring the carry). It seems that two's complement works!

Exercise 1.8: *What is the two's complement representation of "+127"?*

Exercise 1.9: *What is the two's complement representation of "−128"?*

Let us now add +4 and −3 (the subtraction is performed by adding the two's complement):

$$\begin{array}{r} +4 \text{ is } 00000100 \\ -3 \text{ is } 11111101 \\ \hline \end{array}$$

The result is: (1)   00000001

If we ignore the carry, the result is 00000001, i.e., "1" in decimal. This is the correct result. Without giving the complete mathematical proof, let us simply state that this representation does work. In two's complement, it is possible to add or subtract signed numbers regardless of the sign. Using the usual rules of binary addition, the result comes out correctly, including the sign. The carry is ignored. This is a very significant advantage. If it were not the case, one would have to correct the result for sign every time, causing a much slower addition or subtraction time.

For the sake of completeness, let us state that two's complement is simply the most convenient representation to use for simpler processors such as microprocessors. On complex processors, other representations may be used. For example, one's complement may be used, but it requires special circuitry to "correct the result."

From this point on, all signed integers will implicitly be represented internally in two's complement notation. See Fig. 1-3 for a table of two's complement numbers.

Exercise 1.10: *What are the smallest and the largest numbers which one may represent in two's complement notation, using only one byte?*

Exercise 1.11: *Compute the two's complement of 20. Then compute the two's complement of your result. Do you find 20 again?*

The following examples will serve to demonstrate the rules of two's complement. In particular, C denotes a possible carry (or borrow) condition. (It is bit 8 of the result.)

V denotes a two's complement overflow, i.e., when the sign of the result is changed "accidentally" because the numbers are too large. It is an essentially internal carry from bit 6 into bit 7 (the sign bit). This will be clarified below.

Let us now demonstrate the role of the carry "C" and the overflow "V".

The Carry C

Here is an example of a carry:

```
     (128)         10000000
    +(129)        +10000001
    ───────────────────────
    (257) = (1)   00000001
```

where (1) indicates a carry.

The result requires a ninth bit (bit "8", since the right-most bit is "0"). It is the carry bit.

If we assume that the carry is the ninth bit of the result, we recognize the result as being $100000001 = 257$.

However, the carry must be recognized and handled with care. Inside the microprocessor, the registers used to hold information are generally only eight-bit wide. When storing the result, only bits 0 to 7 will be preserved.

A carry, therefore, always requires special action: it must be detected by special instructions, then processed. Processing the carry means either storing it somewhere (with a special instruction), or ignoring it, or deciding that it is an error (if the largest authorized result is "11111111").

BASIC CONCEPTS

+	2's complement code	−	2's complement code
+127	01111111	−128	10000000
+126	01111110	−127	10000001
+125	01111101	−126	10000010
...		−125	10000011
		...	
+65	01000001	−65	10111111
+64	01000000	−64	11000000
+63	00111111	−63	11000001
...		...	
+33	00100001	−33	11011111
+32	00100000	−32	11100000
+31	00011111	−31	11100001
...		...	
+17	00010001	−17	11101111
+16	00010000	−16	11110000
+15	00001111	−15	11110001
+14	00001110	−14	11110010
+13	00001101	−13	11110011
+12	00001100	−12	11110100
+11	00001011	−11	11110101
+10	00001010	−10	11110110
+9	00001001	−9	11110111
+8	00001000	−8	11111000
+7	00000111	−7	11111001
+6	00000110	−6	11111010
+5	00000101	−5	11111011
+4	00000100	−4	11111100
+3	00000011	−3	11111101
+2	00000010	−2	11111110
+1	00000001	−1	11111111
+0	00000000		

Fig. 1-3: 2's Complement Table

Overflow V

Here is an example of overflow:

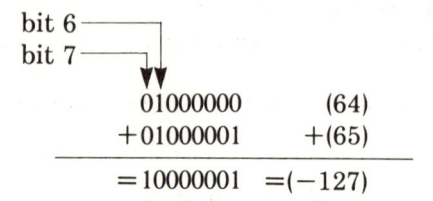

```
bit 6 ─────┐
bit 7 ─────┐│
           ▼▼
      01000000      (64)
     +01000001    +(65)
     ─────────    ──────
     =10000001   =(−127)
```

An internal carry has been generated from bit 6 into bit 7. This is called an overflow.

The result is now negative, "by accident." This situation must be detected, so that it can be corrected.

Let us examine another situation:

```
            11111111     (−1)
           +11111111    +(−1)
           ─────────    ──────
    =(1)    11111110   =(−2)
      ▼
    carry
```

In this case, an internal carry has been generated from bit 6 into bit 7, and also from bit 7 into bit 8 (the formal "Carry" C we have examined in the preceding section). The rules of two's complement arithmetic specify that this carry should be ignored. The result is then correct.

This is because the carry from bit 6 into bit 7 did not change the sign bit.

This is not an *overflow* condition. When operating on negative numbers, the overflow is not simply a carry from bit 6 into bit 7. Let us examine one more example.

```
            11000000     (−64)
           +10111111    (−65)
           ─────────    ──────
    =(1)    01111111   (+127)
      ▼
    carry
```

This time, there has been no internal carry from bit 6 into bit 7, but there has been an external carry. The result is incorrect, as bit 7 has been changed. An overflow condition should be indicated.

BASIC CONCEPTS

Overflow will occur in four situations:

1—adding large positive numbers
2—adding large negative numbers
3—subtracting a large positive number from a large negative number
4—subtracting a large negative number from a large positive number.

Let us now improve our definition of the overflow:

Technically, the overflow indicator, a special bit reserved for this purpose, and called a "flag," will be set when there is a carry from bit 6 into bit 7 and no external carry, or else when there is no carry from bit 6 into bit 7 but there is an external carry. This indicates that bit 7, i.e., the sign of the result, has been accidentally changed. For the technically-minded reader, the overflow flag is set by Exclusive ORing the carry-in and carry-out of bit 7 (the sign bit). Practically every microprocessor is supplied with a special overflow flag to automatically detect this condition, which requires corrective action.

Overflow indicates that the result of an addition or a subtraction requires more bits than are available in the standard eight-bit register used to contain the result.

The Carry and the Overflow

The carry and the overflow bits are called "flags." They are provided in every microprocessor, and in the next chapter we will learn to use them for effective programming. These two indicators are located in a special register called the flags or "status" register. This register also contains additional indicators whose function will be clarified in Chapter 4.

Examples

Let us now illustrate the operation of the carry and the overflow in actual examples. In each example, the symbol V denotes the overflow, and C the carry.

If there has been no overflow, V = 0. If there has been an overflow, V = 1 (same for the carry C). Remember that the rules of two's complement specify that the carry be ignored. (The mathematical proof is not supplied here.)

Positive-Positive

```
   00000110   (+6)
+  00001000   (+8)
─────────────────
=  00001110   (+14)    V:0      C:0
```
(CORRECT)

Positive-Positive with Overflow

```
   01111111   (+127)
+  00000001   (+1)
─────────────────
=  10000000   (−128)   V:1      C:0
```
The above is invalid because an overflow has occurred.

(ERROR)

Positive-Negative (result positive)

```
   00000100   (+4)
+  11111110   (−2)
─────────────────
=(1)00000010  (+2)     V:0      C:1 (disregard)
```
(CORRECT)

Positive-Negative (result negative)

```
   00000010   (+2)
+  11111100   (−4)
─────────────────
=  11111110   (−2)     V:0      C:0
```
(CORRECT)

Negative-Negative

```
   11111110   (−2)
+  11111010   (−4)
─────────────────
=(1)11111010  (−6)     V:0      C:1 (disregard)
```
(CORRECT)

Negative-Negative with Overflow

```
   10000001   (−127)
+  11000010   (−62)
─────────────────
=(1)01000011     (67)  V:1      C:1
```
(ERROR)

BASIC CONCEPTS

This time an "underflow" has occurred, by adding two large negative numbers. The result would be −189, which is too large to reside in eight bits.

Exercise 1.12: *Complete the following additions. Indicate the result, the carry C, the overflow V, and whether the result is correct or not:*

```
  10111111    (___)           11111010    (___)
+ 11000001    (___)         + 11111001    (___)
_____                 _____
= _____   V:___ C:___    = _____   V:___ C:___
□ CORRECT    □ ERROR        □ CORRECT    □ ERROR


  00010000    (___)           01111110    (___)
+ 01000000    (___)         + 00101010    (___)
_____                 _____
= _____   V:___ C:___    = _____   V:___ C:___
□ CORRECT    □ ERROR        □ CORRECT    □ ERROR
```

Exercise 1.13: *Can you show an example of overflow when adding a positive and a negative number? Why?*

Fixed Format Representation

Now we know how to represent signed integers. However, we have not yet resolved the problem of magnitude. If we want to represent larger integers, we will need several bytes. In order to perform arithmetic operations efficiently, it is necessary to use a fixed number of bytes rather than a variable one. Therefore, once the number of bytes is chosen, the maximum magnitude of the number which can be represented is fixed.

Exercise 1.14: *What are the largest and the smallest numbers which may be represented in two bytes using two's complement?*

The Magnitude Problem

When adding numbers we have restricted ourselves to eight bits because the processor we will use operates internally on eight bits at a time. However, this restricts us to the numbers in the range −128 to +127. Clearly, this is not sufficient for many applications.

Multiple precision will be used to increase the number of digits which can be represented. A two-, three-, or N-byte format may then be used. For example, let us examine a 16-bit, "double-precision" format:

```
00000000   00000000   is "0"
00000000   00000001   is "1"

01111111   11111111   is "32767"
11111111   11111111   is "−1"
11111111   11111110   is "−2"
```

Exercise 1.15: *What is the largest negative integer which can be represented in a two's complement triple-precision format?*

However, this method will result in disadvantages. When adding two numbers, for example, we will generally have to add them eight bits at a time. This will be explained in Chapter 4 (Basic Programming Techniques). It results in slower processing. Also, this representation uses 16 bits for any number, even if it could be represented with only eight bits. It is, therefore, common to use 16 or perhaps 32 bits, but seldom more.

Let us consider the following important point: whatever the number of bits N chosen for the two's complement representation, it is fixed. If any result or intermediate computation should generate a number requiring more than N bits, some bits will be lost. The program normally retains the N left-most bits (the most significant) and drops the low-order ones. This is called truncating the result.

Here is an example in the decimal system, using a six digit representation:

```
        123456
     ×     1.2
     ─────────
        246912
        123456
     ─────────
     = 148147.2
```

The result requires 7 digits! The "2" after the decimal point will be dropped and the final result will be 148147. It has been truncated. Usually, as long as the position of the decimal point is not lost, this method is used to extend the range of the operations which may be performed, at the expense of precision.

The problem is the same in binary. The details of a binary multi-

BASIC CONCEPTS

plication will be shown in Chapter 4.

This fixed-format representation may cause a loss of precision, but it may be sufficient for usual computations or mathematical operations.

Unfortunately, in the case of accounting, no loss of precision is tolerable. For example, if a customer rings up a large total on a cash register, it would not be acceptable to have a five figure amount to pay, which would be approximated to the dollar. Another representation must be used wherever precision in the result is essential. The solution normally used is *BCD*, or binary-coded decimal.

BCD Representation

The principle used in representing numbers in BCD is to encode each decimal digit separately, and to use as many bits as necessary to represent the complete number exactly. In order to encode each of the digits from 0 through 9, four bits are necessary. Three bits would only supply eight combinations, and can therefore not encode the ten digits. Four bits allow sixteen combinations and are therefore sufficient to encode the digits "0" through "9". It can also be noted that six of the possible codes will not be used in the BCD representation (see Fig. 1-3). This will result later on in a potential problem during additions and subtractions, which we will have to solve. Since only four bits are needed to encode a BCD

CODE	BCD SYMBOL	CODE	BCD SYMBOL
0000	0	1000	8
0001	1	1001	9
0010	2	1010	unused
0011	3	1011	unused
0100	4	1100	unused
0101	5	1101	unused
0110	6	1110	unused
0111	7	1111	unused

Fig. 1-4: BCD Table

digit, two BCD digits may be encoded in every byte. This is called *"packed BCD."*

As an example, "00000000" will be "00" in BCD. "10011001" will be "99".

A BCD code is read as follows:

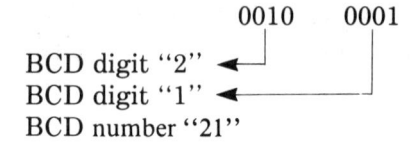

```
              0010    0001
BCD digit "2"   ◄──┘      │
BCD digit "1"   ◄─────────┘
BCD number "21"
```

Exercise 1.16: *What is the BCD representation for "29"? "91"?*

Exercise 1.17: *Is "10100000" a valid BCD representation? Why?*

As many bytes as necessary will be used to represent all BCD digits. Typically, one or more nibbles will be used at the beginning of the representation to indicate the total number of nibbles, i.e., the total number of BCD digits used. Another nibble or byte will be used to denote the position of the decimal point. However, conventions may vary.

Here is an example of a representation for multibyte BCD integers:

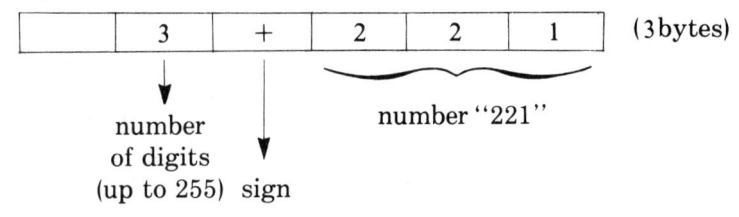

| 3 | + | 2 | 2 | 1 | (3 bytes) |

number of digits (up to 255)   sign   number "221"

This represents +221
(The sign may be represented by 0000 for +, and 0001 for −, for example.)

Exercise 1.18: *Using the same convention, represent "−23123". Show it in BCD format, as above, then in binary.*

Exercise 1.19: *Show the BCD for "222" and "111", then for the result of 222 × 111. (Compute the result by hand, then show it in the above representation.)*

The BCD representation can easily accommodate decimal numbers.

BASIC CONCEPTS

For example, +2.21 may be represented by:

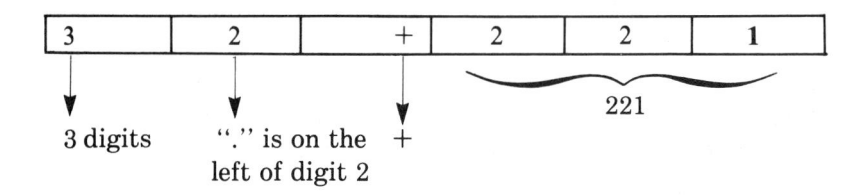

| 3 | 2 | + | 2 | 2 | 1 |

- 3 digits
- "." is on the left of digit 2
- +
- 221

The advantage of BCD is that it yields absolutely correct results. Its disadvantage is that it uses a large amount of memory and results in slow arithmetic operations. This is acceptable only in an accounting environment and is normally not used in other cases.

Exercise 1.20: *How many bits are required to encode '9999" in BCD? And in Two's complement?*

We have now solved the problems associated with the representation of integers, signed integers and even large integers. We have even already presented one possible method of representing decimal numbers, with BCD representation. Let us now examine the problem of representing decimal numbers in a fixed length format.

Floating-Point Representation

The basic principle is that decimal numbers must be represented with a fixed format. In order not to waste bits, the representation will *normalize* all the numbers.

For example, "0.000123" wastes three zeros on the left of the number, which have no meaning except to indicate the position of the decimal point. Normalizing this number results in $.123 \times 10^{-3}$. ".123" is called a *normalized mantissa*, "−3" is called the *exponent*. We have normalized this number by eliminating all the meaningless zeros on the left of it and adjusting the exponent.

Let us consider another example:

22.1 is normalized as $.221 \times 10^2$

or $M \times 10^E$ where M is the mantissa, and E is the exponent.

29

It can be readily seen that a normalized number is characterized by a mantissa less than 1 and greater or equal to .1 in all cases where the number is not zero. In other words, this can be represented mathematically by:

$$.1 \leq M < 1 \text{ or } 10^{-1} \leq M < 10^0$$

Similarly, in the binary representation:

$$2^{-1} \leq M < 2^0 \text{ (or } .5 \leq M < 1)$$

Where M is the absolute value of the mantissa (disregarding the sign).

For example:

$$111.01 \text{ is normalized as: } .11101 \times 2^3.$$

The mantissa is 11101.

The exponent is 3.

Now that we have defined the principle of the representation, let us examine the actual format. A typical floating-point representation appears below.

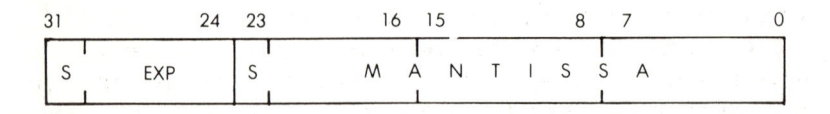

```
31           24 23          16 15            8 7            0
┌─────────────┬──┬──────────────────────────────────────────┐
│ S    EXP    │S │            M A N T I S S A               │
└─────────────┴──┴──────────────────────────────────────────┘
```

Fig. 1-5: Typical Floating-Point Representation

In the representation used in this example, four bytes are used for a total of 32 bits. The first byte on the left of the illustration is used to represent the exponent. Both the exponent and the mantissa will be represented in two's complement. As a result, the maximum exponent will be -128. "S" in Fig. 1-5 denotes the sign bit.

Three bytes are used to represent the mantissa. Since the first bit in the two's complement representation indicates the sign, this leaves 23 bits for the representation of the magnitude of the mantissa.

BASIC CONCEPTS

Exercise 1.21: *How many decimal digits can the mantissa represent with the 23 bits?*

This is only one example of a floating point representation. It is possible to use only three bytes, or it is possible to use more. The four-byte representation proposed above is just a common one which represents a reasonable compromise in terms of accuracy, magnitude of numbers, storage utilization, and efficiency in arithmetic operation.

We have now explored the problems associated with the representation of numbers and we know how to represent them in integer form, with a sign, or in decimal form. Let us now examine how to represent alphanumeric data internally.

Representing Alphanumeric Data

The representation of alphanumeric data, i.e. characters, is completely straightforward: all characters are encoded in an eight-bit code. Only two codes are in general use in the computer world, the ASCII Code, and the EBCDIC Code. ASCII stands for "American Standard Code for Information Interchange," and is universally used in the world of microprocessors. EBCDIC is a variation of ASCII used by IBM, and therefore not used in the microcomputer world unless one interfaces to an IBM terminal.

Let us briefly examine the ASCII encoding. We must encode 26 letters of the alphabet for both upper and lower case, plus 10 numeric symbols, plus perhaps 20 additional special symbols. This can be easily accomplished with 7 bits, which allow 128 possible codes. (See Fig.1-6.) All characters are therefore encoded in 7 bits. The eighth bit, when it is used, is the *parity bit*. Parity is a technique for verifying that the contents of a byte have not been accidentally changed. The number of 1's in the byte is counted and the eighth bit is set to one if the count was odd, thus making the total even. This is called even parity. One can also use odd parity, i.e. writing the eighth bit (the left-most) so that the total number of 1's in the byte is odd.

Example: let us compute the parity bit for "0010011" using even parity. The number of 1's is 3. The parity bit must therefore be a 1 so that the total number of bits is 4, i.e. even. The result is 10010011, where the leading 1 is the parity bit and 0010011 identifies the character.

PROGRAMMING THE 6502

The table of 7-bit ASCII codes is shown in Fig. 1-6. In practice, it is used "as is," i.e. without parity, by adding a 0 in the left-most position, or else with parity, by adding the appropriate extra bit on the left.

Exercise 1.22: *Compute the 8-bit representation of the digits "0" through "9", using even parity. (This code will be used in application examples of Chapter 8.)*

Exercise 1.23: *Same for the letters "A" through "F".*

Exercise 1.24: *Using a non-parity ASCII code (where the left-most bit is "0"), indicate the binary contents of the 4 bytes below:*

HEX	MSD	0	1	2	3	4	5	6	7
LSD	BITS	000	001	010	011	100	101	110	111
0	0000	NUL	DLE	SPACE	0	@	P	—	p
1	0001	SOH	DC1	!	1	A	Q	a	q
2	0010	STX	DC2	"	2	B	R	b	r
3	0011	ETX	DC3	#	3	C	S	c	s
4	0100	EOT	DC4	$	4	D	T	d	t
5	0101	ENQ	NAK	%	5	E	U	e	u
6	0110	ACK	SYN	&	6	F	V	f	v
7	0111	BEL	ETB	'	7	G	W	g	w
8	1000	BS	CAN	(	8	H	X	h	x
9	1001	HT	EM	)	9	I	Y	i	y
A	1010	LF	SUB	*	:	J	Z	j	z
B	1011	VT	ESC	+	;	K	[	k	{
C	1100	FF	FS	,	<	L	\	l	--
D	1101	CR	GS	—	=	M	]	m	}
E	1110	SO	RS	.	>	N	∧	n	~
F	1111	SI	US	/	?	O	←	o	DEL

Fig. 1-6: ASCII Conversion Table
(See Appendix E for abbreviations)

In specialized situations such as telecommunications, other codings may be used such as error-correcting codes. However they are beyond the scope of this book.

BASIC CONCEPTS

We have examined the usual representations for both program and data inside the computer. Let us now examine the possible external representations.

EXTERNAL REPRESENTATION OF INFORMATION

The external representation refers to the way information is presented to the *user*, i.e. generally to the programmer. Information may be presented externally in essentially three formats: binary, octal or hexdecimal, and symbolic.

1. Binary

It has been seen that information is stored internally in *bytes*, which are sequences of eight *bits* (0's or 1's). It is sometimes desirable to display this internal information directly in its binary format and this is called *binary representation*. One simple example is provided by Light Emitting Diodes (LEDs) which are essentially miniature lights, on the front panel of the microcomputer. In the case of an eight-bit microprocessor, a front panel will typically be equipped with eight LEDs to display the contents of any internal register. (A register is used to hold eight bits of information and will be described in Chapter 2). A lighted LED indicates a one. A zero is indicated by an LED which is not lighted. Such a binary representation may be used for the fine debugging of a complex program, especially if it involves input/output, but is naturally impractical at the human level. This is because in most cases, one likes to look at information in symbolic form. Thus "9" is much easier to understand or remember than "1001". More convenient representations have been devised, which improve the person-machine interface.

2. Octal and Hexadecimal

"Octal" and "hexadecimal" encode respectively three and four binary bits into a unique symbol. In the octal system, any combination of three binary bits is represented by a number between 0 and 7.

"Octal" is a format using three bits, where each combination of three bits is represented by a symbol between 0 and 7:

33

binary	octal
000	0
001	1
010	2
011	3
100	4
101	5
110	6
111	7

Fig. 1-7: Octal Symbols

For example, "00 100 100" binary is represented by:
     ▼   ▼   ▼
     0   4   4

or "044" in octal.

Another example: 11 111 111 is:
         ▼   ▼   ▼
         3   7   7

or "377" in octal.

Conversely, the octal "211" represents:

            010   001   001

or "10001001" binary.

Octal has traditionally been used on older computers which were employing various numbers of bits ranging from 8 to perhaps 64. More recently, with the dominance of eight-bit microprocessors, the eight-bit format has become the standard, and another more practical representation is used. This is *hexadecimal*.

In the hexdecimal representation, a group of four bits is encoded as one hexadecimal digit. Hexadecimal digits are represented by the symbols from 0 to 9, and by the letters A, B, C, D, E, F. For example, "0000" is represented by "0", "0001" is represented by "1" and "1111" is represented by the letter "F" (see Fig. 1-8).

BASIC CONCEPTS

DECIMAL	BINARY	HEX	OCTAL
0	0000	0	0
1	0001	1	1
2	0010	2	2
3	0011	3	3
4	0100	4	4
5	0101	5	5
6	0110	6	6
7	0111	7	7
8	1000	8	10
9	1001	9	11
10	1010	A	12
11	1011	B	13
12	1100	C	14
13	1101	D	15
14	1110	E	16
15	1111	F	17

Fig. 1-8: Hexadecimal Codes

Example: 1010 0001 in binary is represented by
           A   1 in hexadecimal.

Exercise 1.25: *What is the hexadecimal representation of "10101010?"*

Exercise 1.26: *Conversely, what is the binary equivalent of "FA" hexadecimal?*

Exercise 1.27: *What is the octal of "01000001"?*

Hexadecimal offers the advantage of encoding eight bits into only two digits. This is easier to visualize or memorize and faster to type into a computer than its binary equivalent. Therefore, on most new microcomputers, hexadecimal is the preferred method of representation for groups of bits.

Naturally, whenever the information present in the memory has a meaning, such as representing text or numbers, hexadecimal is not convenient for representing the meaning of this information when it is brought out for use by humans.

Symbolic Representation

Symbolic representation refers to the external representation of information in actual symbolic form. For example, decimal numbers are represented as decimal numbers, and not as sequences of hexadecimal symbols or bits. Similarly, text is represented as such. Naturally, symbolic representation is most practical to the user. It is used whenever an appropriate display device is available, such as a CRT display or a printer. (A CRT display is a television-type screen used to display text or graphics.) Unfortunately, in smaller systems such as one-board microcomputers, it is uneconomical to provide such displays, and the user is restricted to hexadecimal communication with the computer.

Summary of External Representations

Symbolic representation of information is the most desirable since it is the most natural for a human user. However, it requires an expensive interface in the form of an alphanumeric keyboard, plus a printer or a CRT display. For this reason, it may not be

BASIC CONCEPTS

available on the less expensive systems. An alternative type of representation is then used, and in this case hexadecimal is the dominant representation. Only in rare cases relating to fine de-bugging at the hardware or the software level is the binary representation used. *Binary* directly displays the contents of registers of memory in binary format.

(The utility of a direct binary display on a front panel has always been the subject of a heated emotional controversy, which will not be debated here.)

We have seen how to represent information internally and externally. We will now examine the actual microprocessor which will manipulate this information.

Additional Exercises

Exercise 1.28: *What is the advantage of two's complement over other representations used to represent signed numbers?*

Exercise 1.29: *How would you represent "1024" in direct binary? Signed binary? Two's complement?*

Exercise 1.30: *What is the V-bit? Should the programmer test it after an addition or subtraction?*

Exercise 1.31: *Compute the two's complement of "+16", "+17", "+18", "−16", "−17", "−18".*

Exercise 1.32: *Show the hexadecimal representation of the following text, which has been stored internally in ASCII format, with no parity: = "MESSAGE".*

37

2
6502 HARDWARE ORGANIZATION

INTRODUCTION

In order to program at an elementary level, it is not necessary to understand in detail the internal structure of the processor that one is using. However, in order to do efficient programming, such an understanding is required. The purpose of this chapter is to present the basic hardware concepts necessary for understanding the operation of the 6502 system. The complete microcomputer system includes not only the microprocessor unit (here the 6502), but also other components. This chapter presents the 6502 proper, while the other devices (mainly input/output) will be presented in a separate chapter (Chapter 7).

We will review here the basic architecture of the microcomputer system, then study more closely the internal organization of the 6502. We will examine, in particular, the various registers. We will then study the program execution and sequencing mechansim. From a hardware standpoint, this chapter is only a simplified presentation. The reader interested in gaining detailed understanding is referred to our book ref. C201 ("Microprocessors," by the same author).

SYSTEM ARCHITECTURE

The architecture of the microcomputer system appears in Figure 2-1. The microprocessor unit (MPU), which will be a 6502 here, appears on the left of the illustration. It implements the functions

6502 HARDWARE ORGANIZATION

of a *central processing unit* (CPU) within one chip: it includes an *arithmetic-logical-unit* (ALU), plus its internal registers, and a *control-unit* (CU) in charge of sequencing the system. Its operation will be explained in this chapter.

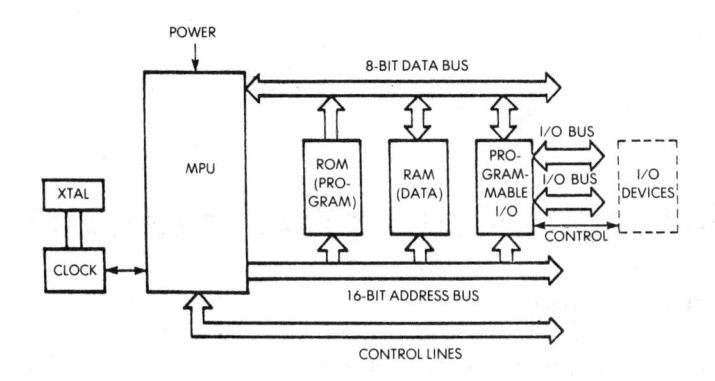

Fig. 2-1: Architecture of a Standard Microprocessor System

The MPU creates three *buses:* an 8-bit bi-directional *data-bus*, which appears at the top of the illustration, a 16-bit mono-directional *address-bus* and a *control-bus* which appears at the bottom of the illustration. Let us describe the function of each of the *buses*.

The *data-bus* carries *data* being exchanged by the various elements of the system. Typically, it will carry data from the memory to the MPU, from the MPU to the memory, or from the MPU to an input/ouput chip. (An input/output chip is a component in charge of communicating with an external device.)

The *address-bus* carries an *address* generated by the MPU, which will select one internal register within one of the chips attached to the system. This address specifies the source, or the destination, of the data which will transit along the data-bus.

The *control-bus* carries the various synchronization signals required by the system.

Having described the purpose of the busses, let us now connect the additional components required by a complete system.

Every MPU requires a precise timing reference, which is supplied by a *clock* and a *crystal*. In most "older" microprocessors, the clock-oscillator is external to the MPU and requires an extra chip. In most recent microprocessors, the clock oscillator is usually incorporated within the MPU. The quartz crystal, however, because of its bulk is always external to the system. The crystal and the clock appear on the left of the MPU box in the illustration.

Let us now turn our attention to the other elements of the system. Going from left to right on the illustration, we distinguish:

The *ROM* is the *read-only-memory* and contains the *program* for the system. The advantage of the ROM is that its contents are permanent and do not disappear whenever the system is turned off. The ROM, therefore, always contains a *bootstrap* or a *monitor* program (their function will be explained later) to permit initial system operation. In a process-control environment, nearly all the programs will reside in ROM as they will probably never be changed. In such case, the industrial user has to protect the system against power failures: programs may not be volatile. They must be in ROM.

However, in a hobbyist environment, or in a program-development environment (when the programmer tests the program), most of the programs will reside in RAM so that they can easily be changed. Later, they may remain in RAM, or be transferred into ROM, if desired. RAM, however, is volatile. Its contents are lost when power is turned off.

The *RAM (random-access-memory)* is the read/write memory for the system. In the case of a control system, the amount of RAM will typically be small (for data only). On the other hand, in a program-development environment, the amount of RAM will be large, as it will contain programs plus development software. All RAM contents must be loaded prior to use from an external device.

Finally, the system will contain one or more interface chips so that it may communicate with the external world. The most frequently used interface chip is the *"PIO"* or parallel-input-output chip. It is the one shown in the illustration. This PIO, like all other chips in the system, connects to all three busses and provides at least two 16-bit *ports* for communication with the outside world. For more details on how an actual PIO works, refer to book C201 or else, for specifics of the 6502 system, refer to Chapter 7 (Input/Output devices).

6502 HARDWARE ORGANIZATION

All these chips are connected to all three busses, including the control bus. However, to clarify the illustration, the connections between the control bus and these various chips are not shown on the diagram.

The functional modules which have been described need not necessarily reside on a single LSI chip. In fact, we will use *combination chips* which include both a PIO and a limited amount of ROM or RAM. For more details refer to Chapter 7.

Still more components will be required to build a real system. In particular, the busses usually need to be *buffered*. Also *decoding logic* may be used for the memory RAM chips, and finally some signals may need to be amplified by *drivers*. These auxiliary circuits will not be described here as they are not relevant to programming. The reader interested in specific assembly and interfacing techniques is referred to book C207 "Microprocessor Interfacing Techniques."

INTERNAL ORGANIZATION OF THE 6502

A simplified diagram of the internal organization of the 6502 appears in Figure 2-2.

The arithmetic logical unit (ALU) appears on the right of the illustration. It can easily be recognized by its characteristic "V" shape. The function of the ALU is to perform arithmetic and logical operations on the data which is fed to it via its two input ports. The two input ports of the ALU are respectively the "left input" and the "right input." They correspond to the top extremities of the "V" shape. After performing an arithmetic operation such as an addition or subtraction, the ALU outputs its contents at the bottom of the illustration.

The ALU is equipped with a special register, the *accumulator* (A). The accumulator is on the left input. The ALU will automatically reference this accumulator as one of the inputs. (However, a bypass also exists.) This is a classic accumulator-based design. In arithmetic and logical operations, one of the operands will be the accumulator, and the other will typically be a memory location. The result will be deposited in the accumulator. Referencing the accumulator as both the source and the destination for data is the reason for its name: it accumulates results. The advantage of this accumulator-based approach is the possibility of using very short instructions-just a single byte (8 bits) to specify the "opcode" i.e.

41

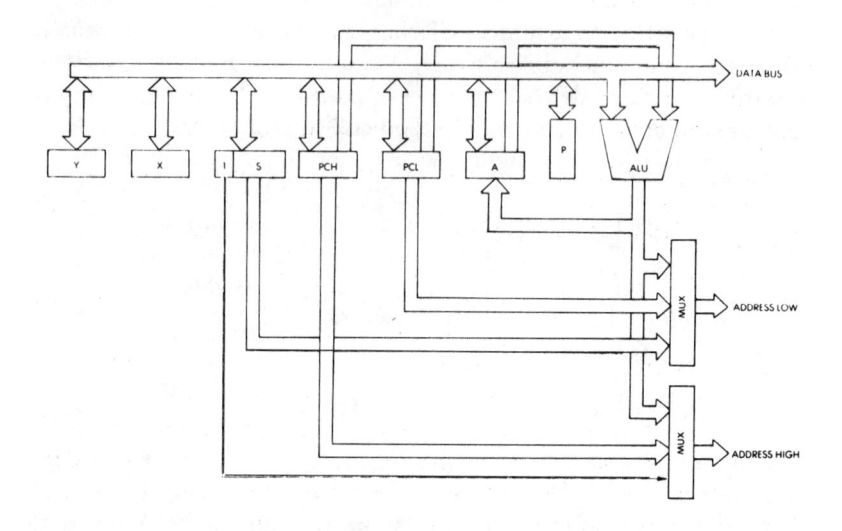

Fig. 2-2: Internal Organization of the 6502

the nature of the operation performed. If the operand had to be fetched from one of the other registers (other than an accumulator), it would be necessary to use a number of extra bits to designate this register within the instruction. The accumulator architecture therefore, results in improved execution speed. The disadvantage is that the accumulator must always be loaded with the desired data prior to its use. This may result in some inefficiency.

Let us go back to the illustration. By the side of the ALU, to its left, appears a special 8-bit register, the processor *status-flags* (P). This register contains 8 status bits. Each of these bits, physically implemented by a flip-flop inside the register is used to denote a special condition. The function of the various status bits will be explained progressively during the programming examples presented in the next chapter, and will be described completely in Chapter 4, which presents the complete instruction set. As an example, three such status flags are the N, Z, and C bits.

N stands for "negative." It is bit 7 (i.e., the left-most) of register P. Whenever this bit is one it indicates that the result of the operation through the ALU is negative.

Bit Z stands for zero. Whenever this bit (bit position 1) is a one, it denotes that a zero result was obtained.

Bit C, in the right-most position (position 0), is a *carry* bit. Whenever two 8-bit numbers are added and the result cannot be contained in 8 bits, bit C is the ninth bit of the result. The carry is used extensively during arithmetic operations.

These status bits are automatically set by the various instructions. A complete list of the instructions and the way in which they affect the status bits of the system appears in Appendix A, as well as in Chapter 4. These bits will be used by the programmer to test various special or exceptional conditions, or else to test quickly for some erroneous result. As an example, testing bit Z may be accomplished with special instructions and will immediately tell whether the result of a previous operation was 0 or not. All decisions in an assembly language program, i.e. in all the programs that will be developed in this book, will be based on the testing of bits. These bits will be either bits that will be read from the outside world, or else the status bits of the ALU. It is therefore very important to understand the function and use of all status bits in the system. The ALU here is equipped with a status register containing these bits. All other input/output chips in the system will also be equipped with status bits. These will be studied in Chapter 7.

Let us now move leftwards of the ALU on illustration 2-2. The horizontal rectangles represent the internal registers of the 6502.

PC is the *program counter*. It is a 16-bit register and is physically implemented as two 8-bit registers: PCL and PCH. PCL stands for the low half of the program counter, i.e., bits 0 through 7. PCH stands for the high part of the program counter, i.e., bits 8 through 15. The program counter is a 16-bit register which contains the address of the next instruction to be executed. Every computer is equipped with a program counter so that it knows which instruction to execute next. Let us review briefly the memory access mechanism in order to illustrate the role of the program counter.

PROGRAMMING THE 6502

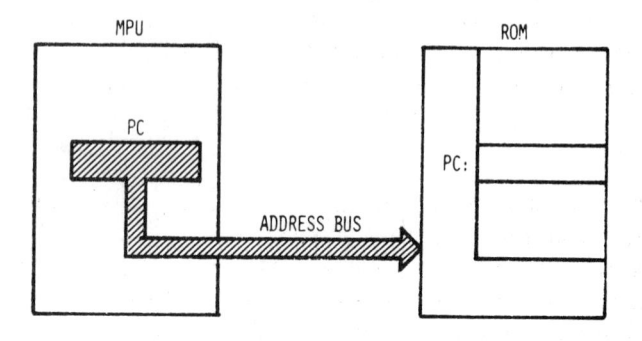

Fig. 2-3: Fetching an Instruction from the Memory

THE INSTRUCTION EXECUTION CYCLE

Let us refer now to Figure 2-3. The microprocessor unit appears on the left, and the memory appears on the right. The memory chip may be a ROM or a RAM, or any other chip which happens to contain memory. The memory is used to store instructions and data. Here, we will fetch one instruction from the memory to illustrate the role of the program counter. We assume that the program counter has valid contents. It now holds a 16-bit address which is the address of the next instruction to fetch in the memory. Every processor proceeds in three cycles:

1 — Fetch the next instruction
2 — Decode the instruction
3 — Execute the instruction

Fetch

Let us now follow the sequence. In the first cycle, the contents of the program counter are deposited on the address bus and gated to the memory (on the address bus). Simultaneously, a read signal may be issued on the control bus of the system, if required. The memory will receive the address. This address is used to specify one location within the memory. Upon receiving the read signal, the memory will decode the address it has received, through internal decoders, and will select the location specified by the address. A few hundred nanoseconds later, the memory will deposit the 8-bit data corresponding to the specified address on its data-bus. This 8-bit word is the instruction that we want to fetch. In our illustration, this instruction will be deposited on top of the data bus.

Let us briefly summarize the sequencing. The contents of the program counter are output on the address bus. A read signal is generated. The memory cycles. Perhaps 300 nanoseconds later, the instruction at the specified address is deposited on the data-bus. The microprocessor then reads the data-bus and deposits its contents into a specialized internal register, the IR register. The IR register is the *instruction-register*. It is 8 bits wide and is used to contain the instruction just fetched from the memory. The fetch cycle is now completed. The 8 bits of the instruction are now physically in the special internal register of the 6502, the IR register. This IR register appears on the left of Figure 2-4.

Decoding and Execution

Once the instruction is contained in IR, the control-unit of the microprocessor will decode the contents and will be able to generate the correct sequence of internal and external signals for the execution of the specified instruction. There is, therefore, a short decoding delay followed by an execution phase, the length of which depends on the nature of the instruction specified. Some instructions will execute entirely within the MPU. Other instructions will fetch or deposit data from or into the memory. This is why the various instructions of the 6502 require various lengths of time to execute. This duration is expressed as a number of (clock) cycles. Refer to the Appendix for the number of cycles required by each instruction. A typical 6502 uses one-megahertz clock. The length of each cycle is therefore 1 microsecond. Since various clock rates may be used with different components, speed of execution is normally expressed in number of cycles rather than in number of nanoseconds.

In the case of the 6502, its *clock* is internal, represented by the internal oscillator (see Fig. 2-1).

Fetching the Next Instruction

We have now described how, using the program counter, an instruction can be fetched from the memory. During the execution of a program, instructions are fetched *in sequence* from the memory. An automatic mechanism must therefore be provided to fetch instructions in sequence. This task is performed by a simple incrementor attached to the program counter. This is illustrated in Figure 2-4. Every time that the contents of the program counter (at the bottom of the illustration) are placed on the address-bus, its contents will be incremented and written back into the program counter. As an example, if the program counter did contain the value 0, the value 0 would be output in the address bus. Then the contents of the program counter would be incremented and the value 1 would be written back into the program counter. In this way, the next time that the program counter is used, it is the instruction at address 1 that will be fetched. We have just implemented an automatic mechanism for sequencing instructions.

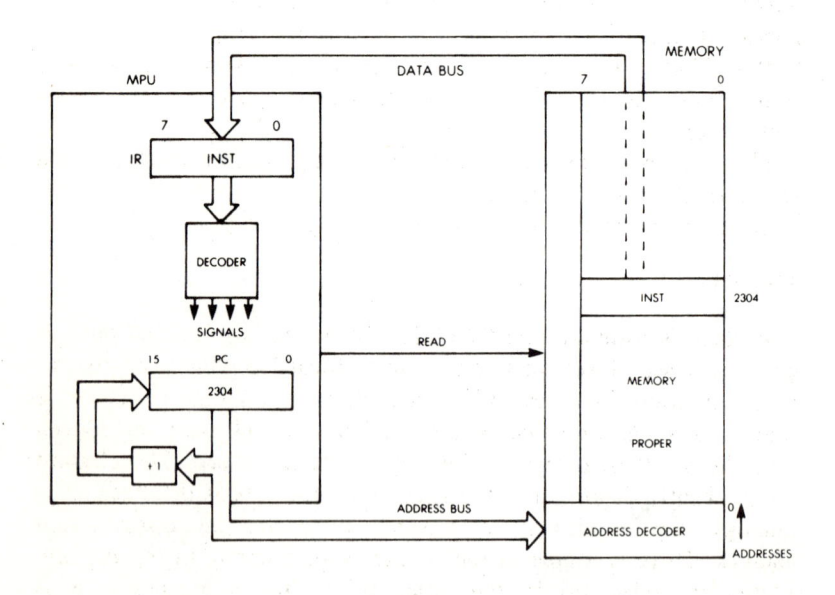

Fig. 2-4: Automatic Sequencing

6502 HARDWARE ORGANIZATION

It must be stressed that the above descriptions are simplified. In reality, some instructions may be 2- or even 3-bytes long so that successive bytes will be fetched in this manner from the memory. However, the mechanism is identical. The program counter is used to fetch successive bytes of an instruction, as well as to fetch successive instructions themselves. The program counter, together with its incrementer, provides an automatic mechanism for pointing to successive memory locations.

Other 6502 Registers

One last area on Figure 2-2 has not yet been explained. It is the set of three registers labeled X, Y and S. Registers X and Y are called index registers. They are 8 bits wide. They may be used to contain data on which the program will operate. However, they normally are used as index registers.

The role of index registers will be described in Chapter 5 on addressing techniques. Briefly, the contents of these two index registers may be added in several ways to any specified address within the system to provide an automatic offset. This is an important facility for retrieving data efficiently when it is stored in tables. These two registers are not completely symmetrical, and their roles will be differentiated in the chapter on addressing techniques.

The stack register S is used to contain a pointer to the top of the stack area within the memory.

Let us now introduce the formal concept of a stack.

THE STACK

A stack is formally called an LIFO structure (last-in, first-out). A stack is a set of registers, or memory locations, allocated to this data structure. The essential characteristic of this structure is that it is a *chronological* structure. The first element introduced into the stack is always at the bottom of the stack. The element most recently deposited in the stack is on the top of the stack. The analogy can be drawn to a stack of plates on a restaurant counter. There is a hole in the counter with a spring in the bottom. Plates are piled up in the hole. With this organization, it is guaranteed that the plate which has been put first in the stack (the oldest) is always at the bottom. The one that has been placed most recently on the stack is the one which is on top of it. This example also illustrates another characteristic of the stack. In normal use, a stack is only accessible via two instructions: "push" and "pop" (or "pull"). The *push* operation results in depositing one element on top of the stack. The *pull* operation consists of removing one element from the stack. In practice, in the case of a microprocessor, it is the *accumulator* that will be deposited on top of the stack. The *pop* will result in a transfer of the top element of the stack into the accumulator. Other specialized instructions may exist to transfer the top of the stack between other specialized registers, such as the status register.

The availability of a stack is required to implement three programming facilities within the computer system: subroutines, interrupts, and temporary data storage. The role of the stack during subroutines will be explained in Chapter 3 (Basic Programming Techniques). The role of the stack during interrupts will be explained in Chapter 6 (Input/Output Techniques). Finally, the role of the stack to save data at high speed will be explained during specific application programs.

We will simply assume at this point that the stack is a required facility in every computer system. A stack may be implemented in two ways:

1. A fixed number of registers may be provided within the microprocessor itself. This is a "hardware stack." It has the advantage of high speed. However, it has the disadvantage of a limited number of registers.

2. Most general-purpose microprocessors choose another approach, the software stack, in order not to restrict the stack to a very small number of registers. This is the approach chosen in the 6502. In the software approach, a dedicated register within the microprocessor, here register S, stores the stack pointer, i.e., the address of the top element of the stack (or more precisely, the address of the top element of the stack plus one). The stack is then implemented as an area of memory. The stack pointer will therefore require 16 bits to point anywhere in the memory.

However, in the case of the 6502, the stack pointer is restricted to 8 bits. It includes a 9th bit, in the left-most position, always set to 1. In other words, the area allocated to the stack in the case of the 6502 ranges from address 256 to address 511. In binary, this is "100000000" to "111111111." The stack always starts at address 111111111 and may have up to 255 words. This may be viewed

6502 HARDWARE ORGANIZATION

as a limitation of the 6502 and will be discussed later in this book. In the 6502, the stack is at the high address, and grows "backwards"; the stack pointer is decremented by a PUSH.

In order to use the stack, the programmer will simply initialize the S register. The rest is automatic.

The stack is said to reside in *page 1* of the memory. Let us now introduce the *paging* concept.

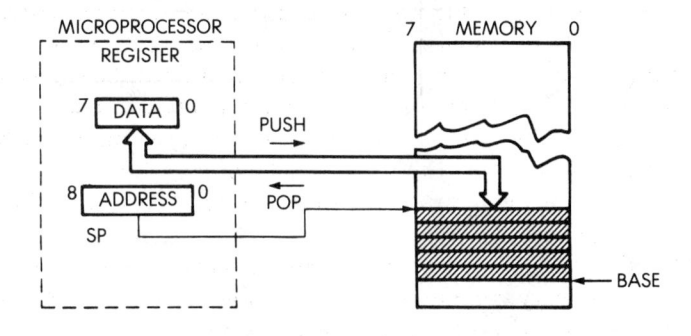

Fig. 2-5: The 2 Stack Manipulation Instructions

THE PAGING CONCEPT

The 6502 microprocessor is equipped with a 16-bit address-bus. 16 binary bits may be used to create up to $2^{16} = 64K$ combinations (1K equals 1,024). Because of addressing features of the 6502 which will be presented in Chapter 5, it is convenient to partition the memory into logical *pages*. A page is simply a block of 256 words. Thus, memory locations 0 to 255 are page 0 of the memory. It will be used for "page zero" addressing. Page 1 of the memory includes memory locations 256 through 511. We have just established that page 1 is normally reserved for the stack area. All other pages in the system are unconstrained by the design and may be used in any way. In the case of the 6502, it is important to keep in mind the page organization of the memory. Whenever a page boundary has to be crossed, it will often introduce an extra cycle delay in the execution of an instruction.

PROGRAMMING THE 6502

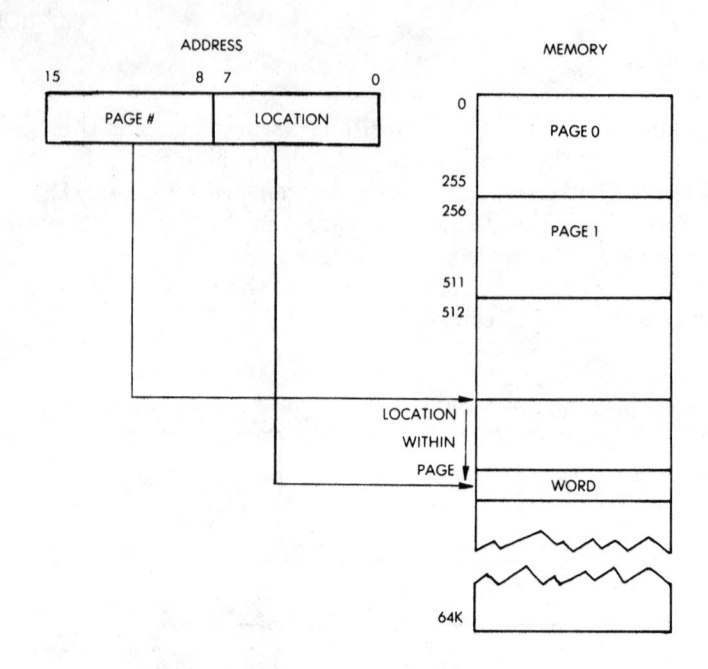

```
           ADDRESS                        MEMORY
      15        8 7         0
      ┌─────────┬───────────┐      0  ┌──────────────┐
      │ PAGE #  │ LOCATION  │         │   PAGE 0     │
      └─────────┴───────────┘         │              │
                                 255  │              │
                                 256  ├──────────────┤
                                      │   PAGE 1     │
                                      │              │
                                 511  │              │
                                 512  ├──────────────┤
                                      │              │
                              LOCATION │              │
                              WITHIN   │              │
                              PAGE     ├──────────────┤
                                      │   WORD       │
                                      └──────────────┘

                                 64K
```

Fig. 2-6: The Paging Concept

THE 6502 CHIP

To complete our description of the diagram, the data bus at the upper part of Figure 2-2 represents the external data bus. It will be used to communicate with the external devices, and the memory in particular. A0-7 and A8-15 represent respectively the low-order and the high-order part of the address-bus created by the 6502.

For completeness, we present here the actual pin-out of the 6502 microprocessor. You need not read it to understand the rest of this book. However, if you intend to connect devices to a system, this description will be valuable.

The actual pin-out of the 6502 appears in Figure 2-7. The data bus is labeled DB0-7 and is easily recognizable on the right of the illustration. The address bus is labeled A0-11 and A12-15. It comes

50

6502 HARDWARE ORGANIZATION

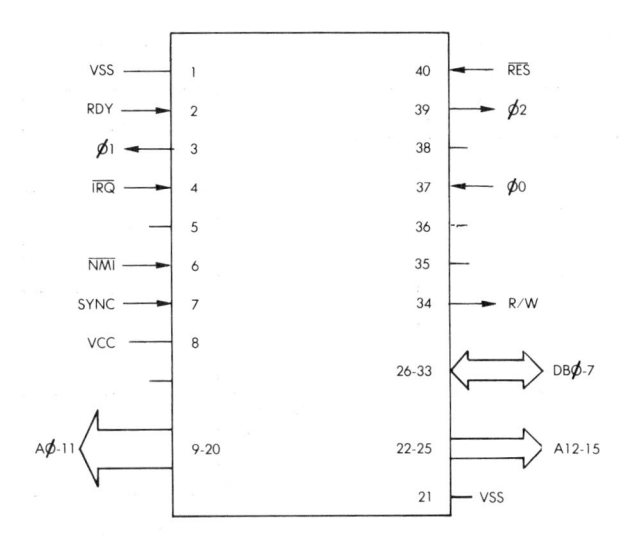

Fig. 2-7: 6502 Pinout

from pins 9 to 20 on the left of the chip, and pins 22 to 25 on its right.

The rest of the signals are power and control signals.

The control signals

—R/W: the READ/WRITE line controls the direction of data transfers on the data-bus.

—IRQ and NMI are "Interrupt Request" and "Non-Maskable Interrupt". They are two interrupt lines and will be used in Chapter 7.

—SYNC is a signal which indicates an opcode fetch to the external world.

—RDY is normally used to synchronize with a slow memory: it will stop the processor.

—SO sets the overflow flag. It is normally not used.

—ϕ_0, ϕ_1 and ϕ_2 are clock signals.

—RES is RESET, used to initialize.

—V_{SS} and V_{CC} are for power (5V).

51

HARDWARE SUMMARY

This completes our hardware description of the internal organization of the 6502. The exact internal bussing structure of the 6502 is not important at this point. However, the exact role of each of the registers is important and should be fully understood before the reader proceeds. If you are familiar with the concepts that have been presented, read on. If you do not feel sure about some of them, it is suggested that you read again the relevant sections of this chapter, as they will be needed in the next chapters. It is suggested that you look again at Figure 2-2 and make sure that you understand the function of every register in the illustration.

3
BASIC PROGRAMMING TECHNIQUES

INTRODUCTION

The purpose of this chapter is to present all the basic techniques necessary to write a program using the 6502. This chapter will introduce additional concepts such as register management, loops, and subroutines. It will focus on programming techniques using only the *internal* 6502 resources, i.e., the registers. Actual programs will be developed such as arithmetic programs. These programs will serve to illustrate the various concepts presented so far and will use actual instructions. Thus, it will be seen how instructions may be used to manipulate the information between the memory and the MPU, as well as manipulate information within the MPU itself. The next chapter will then discuss in complete detail the instructions available on the 6502. Chapter 6 will present the techniques available to manipulate information *outside* the 6502: the input/output techniques.

In this chapter, we will essentially learn by "doing." By examining programs of increasing complexity, we will learn the role of the various instructions and of the registers and will apply the concepts developed so far. However, one important concept will not be presented here; it is the concept of addressing techniques. Because of its apparent complexity, it will be presented separately in chapter 5.

Let us immediately start writing some programs for the 6502. We will start with arithmetic programs.

ARITHMETIC PROGRAMS

Arithmetic programs cover addition, subtraction, multiplication, and division. The programs that will be presented here will operate on integers. These integers may be positive binary integers or may be expressed in two's complement notation, in which case the left-most bit is the sign bit (See Chapter 1 for a reminder of the two's complement notation.)

8-Bit Addition

We will add two 8-bit operands called OP1 and OP2, respectively stored at memory address ADR1 and ADR2. The sum will be called RES and will be stored at memory address ADR3. This is illustrated in Figure 3-1. The program which will perform this addition is the following:

```
LDA     ADR1     LOAD OP1 IN A
ADC     ADR2     ADD OP2 TO OP1
STA     ADR3     SAVE RES AT ADR3
```

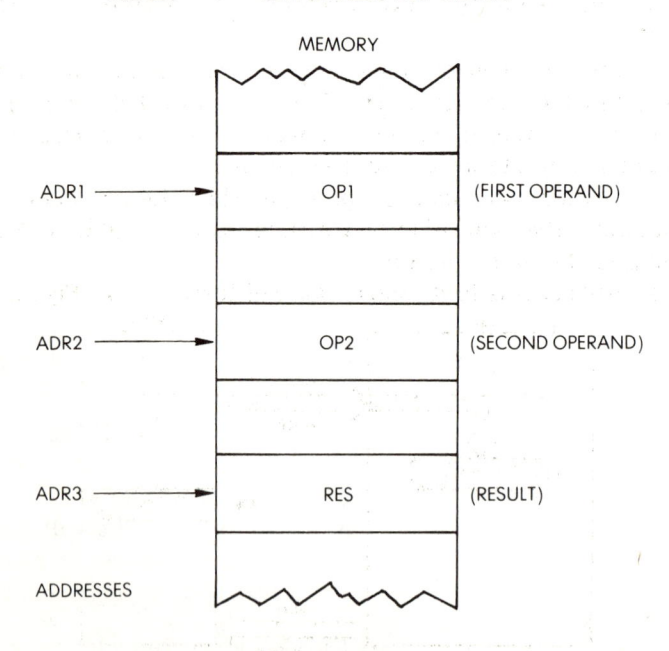

Fig. 3-1: 8-Bit Addition Res = OP1 + OP2

BASIC PROGRAMMING TECHNIQUES

This is a three-instruction program. Each line is one instruction, in symbolic form. Each such instruction will be translated by the assembler program into 1, 2, or 3 binary bytes. We will not concern ourselves with the translation here and only look at the symbolic representation. The first line specifies an LDA instruction. LDA means "load the accumulator A from the address which follows."

The address specified on the first line is ADR1. ADR1 is a symbolic representation for an actual 16-bit address. Somewhere else in the program, the ADR1 symbol will be defined. It could be, for example, address 100.

The instruction LDA specifies "load accumulator A" (inside the 6502) from memory location 100. This will result in a read operation from address 100, the contents of which will be transmitted along the data-bus and deposited inside the accumulator. You will recall that arithmetic and logical operations operate on the accumulator as one of the source operands. (Refer to the previous chapter for more details.) Since we wish to add the two values OP1 and OP2 together, we first load OP1 into the accumulator. Then we will be able to add the contents of the accumulator (OP1) to OP2.

The right-most field of this instruction is called a *comment field*. It is ignored by the processor, but it is provided for program readability. In order to understand what the program does, it is of paramount importance to use good comments.

This is called *documenting* a program. Here the comment is self explanatory: the value of OP1, which is located at address ADR1, is being loaded in accumulator A.

The result of this first instruction is illustrated by Figure 3-2.

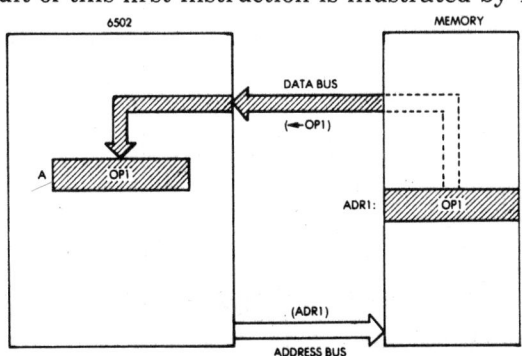

Fig. 3-2: LDA ADR1: OP1 is Loaded from Memory

The second instruction of our program is:

    ADC   ADR2

It specifies "add the contents of memory location ADR2 to the accumulator." Referring to Figure 3-1, the contents of memory location ADR2 are OP2, our second operand. The actual contents of the accumulator now OP1, our first operand. As a result of the execution of the second instruction, OP2 will be fetched from the memory and added to OP1. The sum will be deposited in the accumulator. The reader will remember that the results of an arithmetical operation, in the case of the 6502, are deposited back into the accumulator. In other microprocessors, it may be possible to deposit these results in other registers or back into the memory.

The sum of OP1 and OP2 is now in the accumulator. We have just to transfer the contents of the accumulator into memory location ADR3 in order to store the results at the specified location. Again, the right-most field of the second instruction is simply a comment field which explains the role of the instruction (add OP2 to A).

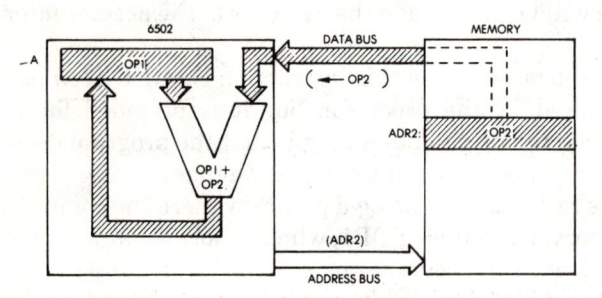

Fig. 3-3: ADC ADR2

The effect of the second instruction is illustrated by Figure 3-3.

It can be verified in Figure 3-3 that, initially the accumulator contained OP1. After the addition, a new result has been written into the accumulator. It is OP1 + OP2. The contents of any register within the system, as well as any memory location, remain the same when a read operation is performed. In other words, *reading the contents of a register or a memory location does not change its contents*. It is only, and exclusively, a write operation that will

BASIC PROGRAMMING TECHNIQUES

change the contents of a register. In this example, the contents of memory locations ADR1 and ADR2 are unchanged. However, after the second instruction of this program, the contents of the accumulator have been modified because the output of the ALU has been written into the accumulator. Its previous contents are then lost.

Let us now save this result at address ADR3 and we will have completed our simple addition.

The third instruction specifies: STA ADR3. This means "Store the contents of accumulator A at the address ADR3." This is self-explanatory and is illustrated in Figure 3-4.

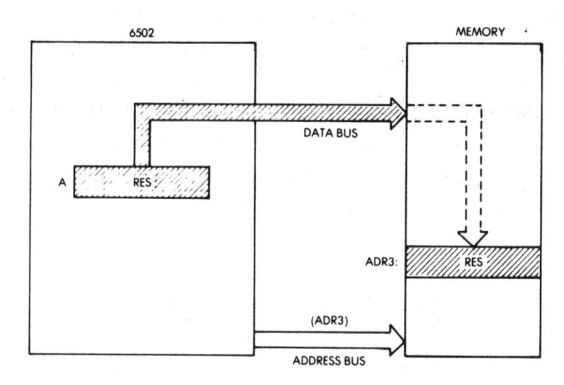

Fig. 3-4: STA ADR3 (Save Accumulator in Memory)

6502 Peculiarities

The above three-instruction program would indeed by the complete program for most microprocessors. However, two peculiarities of the 6502 exist, which will normally require two additional instructions.

First, the ADC instruction really means "add *with carry*," rather than "add." The difference is that a regular add instruction adds two numbers together. An add-with-carry adds two numbers together plus the value of the carry bit. Since we are adding here 8-bit numbers, no carry should be used, and at the time we start the addition we do not necessarily know the condition of the carry bit (it may have been set by a previous instruction), so we must clear it, i.e., set it to zero. This will be accomplished by the CLC instruction: "clear carry."

57

Unfortunately, the 6502 does not have both types of addition operations. It has only an ADC operation. As a result, for single 8-bit additions, a necessary precaution is to always clear the carry bit. This is no significant disadvantage but should not be forgotten.

The second peculiarity of the 6502 lies with the fact that it is equipped with powerful decimal instructions, which will be used in the next section on BCD arithmetic. The 6502 always operates in one of two modes: binary or decimal. The state it is in is conditioned by a status bit, the "D" bit (of register P). Since we are operating in binary mode in this example, it is necessary to make sure that the D bit is correctly set. This will be done by a CLD instruction, which will clear the D bit. Naturally, if all arithmetic within the system is done in binary, the D bit will be cleared once and for all at the beginning of the program, and it will not be necessary to set it every time. Therefore, this instruction may, in fact, be omitted in most programs. However, the reader, who will practice these exercises on a computer, may go back and forth between BCD and binary exercises, and this extra instruction has been included here as it must appear at least once before any binary addition is performed.

To summarize: our complete, and safe, 8-bit program is now:

```
CLC              CLEAR CARRY BIT
CLD              CLEAR DECIMAL BIT
LDA    ADR1      LOAD OP1 IN A
ADC    ADR2      ADD OP2 TO OP1
STA    ADR3      SAVE RES AT ADR3
```

Actual physical addresses may be used instead of ADR1, ADR2, and ADR3. If one wishes to keep symbolic addresses, it will be necessary to use so-called "pseudo-instructions" which specify the value of these symbolic addresses so that the assembly program may, during translation, substitute the actual physical addresses. Such pseudo-instructions would be, for example:

```
ADR1 = $100
ADR2 = $120
ADR3 = $200
```

Exercise 3.1: *Now close this book. Refer only to the list of instructions at the end of the book. Write a program which will add two*

BASIC PROGRAMMING TECHNIQUES

numbers stored at memory locations LOC1 and LOC2. Deposit the results at memory location LOC3. Then, compare your program to the one above.

16-Bit Addition

An 8-bit addition will only allow the addition of 8-bit numbers, i.e., numbers between 0 and 255, if absolute binary is used. For most practical applications it is necessary to use *multipleprecision* and to add numbers having 16 bits or more. We will present here examples of arithmetic on 16-bit numbers. They can be readily extended to 24, 32 bits, or more. (One always uses multiples of 8 bits.) We will assume that the first operand is stored at memory locations ADR1 and ADR1-1. Since OP1 is a 16-bit number this time, it will require two 8-bit memory locations. Similarly, OP2 will be stored at ADR2 and ADR2-1. The result is to be deposited at memory addresses ADR3 and ADR3-1. This is illustrated in Figure 3-5.

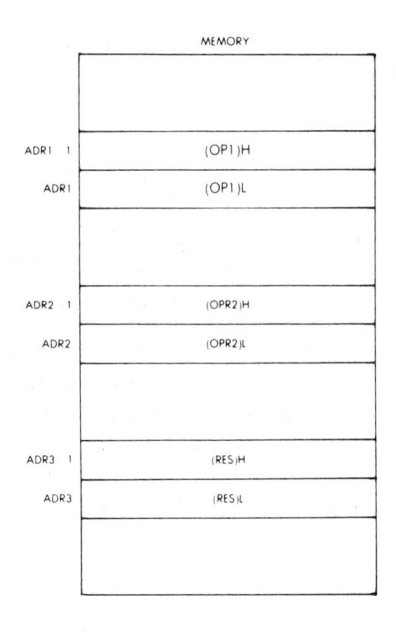

```
                    MEMORY
          ┌──────────────────────┐
          │                      │
          ├──────────────────────┤
ADR1 1    │        (OP1)H        │
          ├──────────────────────┤
ADR1      │        (OP1)L        │
          ├──────────────────────┤
          │                      │
          ├──────────────────────┤
ADR2 1    │        (OPR2)H       │
          ├──────────────────────┤
ADR2      │        (OPR2)L       │
          ├──────────────────────┤
          │                      │
          ├──────────────────────┤
ADR3 1    │        (RES)H        │
          ├──────────────────────┤
ADR3      │        (RES)L        │
          ├──────────────────────┤
          │                      │
          └──────────────────────┘
```

Fig. 3-5: 16 Bit Addition: The Operands

PROGRAMMING THE 6502

The logic of this program is exactly analogous to the previous one. First, the lower half of the two operands will be added, since the microprocessor can only add on 8 bits at a time. Any carry generated by the addition of these low order bytes will be automatically stored in the internal carry bit ("C"). Then, the high order half of the two operands will be added together along with any carry, and the result will be saved in the memory. The program appears below:

```
CLC
CLD
LDA     ADR1      LOW HALF OF OP1
ADC     ADR2      (OP1 + OP2) LOW
STA     ADR3      SAVE LOW HALF OF RES
LDA     ADR1-1    HIGH HALF OF OP1
ADC     ADR2-1    (OP1 + OP2) HIGH + CARRY
STA     ADR3-1    SAVE HIGH HALF OF RES
```

The first two instructions of this program are used to be safe: CLC, CLD. Their roles have been explained in the previous section. Let us examine the program. The next three instructions are essentially identical to the ones for the 8-bit addition. They result in adding the least significant half (bits 0 through 7) of OP1 and OP2. The sum, called RES, is stored at memory location ADR3.

Automatically, whenever an addition is performed, any resulting carry is saved in the carry bit of the flags register (register P). If the two 8-bit numbers do not generate any carry, the value of the carry bit will be zero. If the two numbers do generate a carry, then the C bit will be equal to 1.

The next three instructions of the program are also essentially identical to the previous 8-bit addition program. They add together the most significant half (bits 8 through 15) of OP1 and OP2, plus any carry, and store the results at address ADR3-1. After this program has been executed, the 16-bit result is stored at memory locations ADR3 and ADR3-1.

It is assumed here that no carry will result from this 16-bit addition. It is assumed that the result is, indeed, a 16-bit number. If the programmer suspects for any reason that the result might have 17 bits, then additional instructions should be inserted that would test the carry bit after this addition.

BASIC PROGRAMMING TECHNIQUES

The location of the operands in the memory is illustrated in Figure 3-5.

Note that we have assumed here that the high part of the operand is stored "on top of" the lower part, i.e., at the lower memory address. This need not necessarily be the case. In fact, addresses are stored by the 6502 in the reverse manner: the low part is first saved in the memory, and the high part is saved in the next memory location. In order to use a common convention for both addresses and data, it is recommended that data also be kept with the low part on top of the high part. This is illustrated in Figure 3-6.

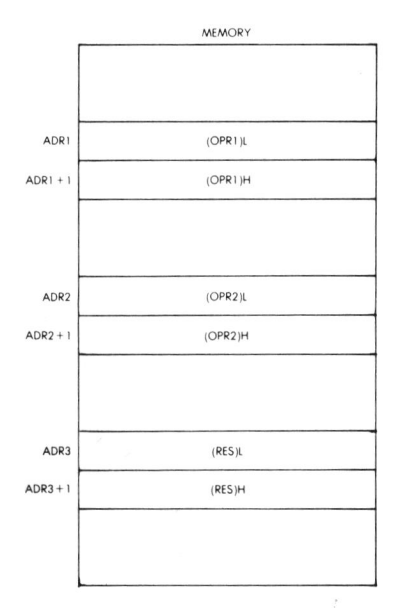

```
                        MEMORY
                  ┌─────────────────┐
                  │                 │
                  ├─────────────────┤
         ADR1     │    (OPR1)L      │
                  ├─────────────────┤
         ADR1+1   │    (OPR1)H      │
                  ├─────────────────┤
                  │                 │
                  │                 │
                  ├─────────────────┤
         ADR2     │    (OPR2)L      │
                  ├─────────────────┤
         ADR2+1   │    (OPR2)H      │
                  ├─────────────────┤
                  │                 │
                  │                 │
                  ├─────────────────┤
         ADR3     │    (RES)L       │
                  ├─────────────────┤
         ADR3+1   │    (RES)H       │
                  ├─────────────────┤
                  │                 │
                  └─────────────────┘
```

Fig. 3-6 Storing Operands in Reverse Order

Exercise 3.2: *Rewrite the 16-bit addition program above with the memory layout indicated in Figure 3-6.*

Exercise 3.3: *Assume now that ADR1 does not point to the lower half of OPR1 (see Figure 3-6), but points to the higher part of OPR1. This is illustrated in Figure 3-6. Again, write the corresponding program.*

61

PROGRAMMING THE 6502

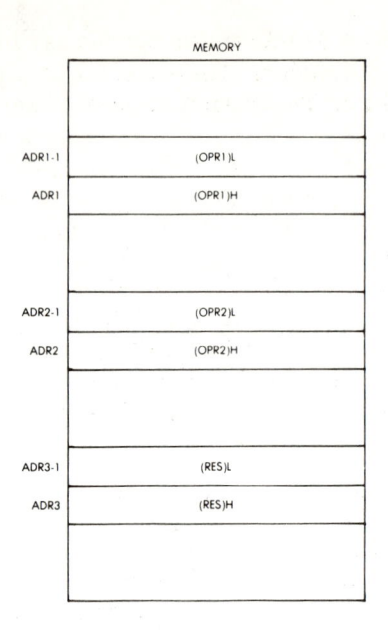

```
                              MEMORY
                     ┌────────────────────┐
                     │                    │
                     │                    │
            ADR1-1   │      (OPR1)L       │
              ADR1   │      (OPR1)H       │
                     │                    │
                     │                    │
                     │                    │
            ADR2-1   │      (OPR2)L       │
              ADR2   │      (OPR2)H       │
                     │                    │
                     │                    │
                     │                    │
            ADR3-1   │      (RES)L        │
              ADR3   │      (RES)H        │
                     │                    │
                     │                    │
                     └────────────────────┘
```

Fig. 3-6[1]: Pointing to the High Byte

It is the programmer, i.e., you, who must decide how to store 16-bit numbers (low part or high part first) and also whether your address references point to the lower or to the higher half of such numbers. This is the first of many choices which you will learn to make when designing algorithms or data structures.

We have now learned to perform a binary addition. Let us turn to the subtraction.

Subtracting 16-Bit Numbers

Doing an 8-bit subtract would be too simple. Let us keep it as an exercise and directly perform a 16-bit subtract. As usual, our two numbers, OPR1 and OPR2, are stored at addresses ADR1 and ADR2. The memory layout will be assumed to be that of Figure 3-6. In order to subtract, we will use a subtact operation (SBC) instead of an add operation (ADC). The only other change, when comparing it to the addition, is that we will use an SEC instruction at the beginning of the

BASIC PROGRAMMING TECHNIQUES

program instead of a CLC. SEC means "set carry to 1." This indicates a "no-borrow" condition. The rest of the program is identical to the one for addition. The program appears below:

```
CLD
SEC                         SET CARRY TO 1
LDA     ADR1                (OPR1) L INTO A
SBC     ADR2                (OPR1) L -(OPR2)L
STA     ADR3                STORE (RESULT)L
LDA     ADR1 + 1            (OPR1) H INTO A
SBC     ADR2 + 1            (OPR1) H -(OPR2)H
STA     ADR3 + 1            STORE (RESULT)H
```

Exercise 3.4: *Write the subtraction program for 8-bit operands.*

It must be remembered that in the case of two's complement arithmetic, the final value of the carry flag has no meaning. If an overflow condition has occurred as a result of the subtraction, then the overflow bit (bit V) of the flags register will have been set. It can then be tested.

The examples just presented are simple binary additions. However, another type of addition may be necessary; it is the BCD addition.

BCD Arithmetic

8-Bit BCD Addition

The concept of BCD arithmetic has been presented in Chapter 1. It is used essentially for business applications where it is imperative to retain every significant digit in a result. In the BCD notation, a 4-bit nibble is used to store one decimal digit (0 through 9). As a result, every 8-bit byte may store two BCD digits. (This is called *packed BCD*.) Let us now add two bytes containing two BCD digits each.

In order to identify the problems, let us try some numeric examples first.

Let us add "01" and "02":

"01" is represented by 0000 0001.

PROGRAMMING THE 6502

"02" is represented by 0000 0010.
The result is   0000 0011.

This is the BCD representation for "03". (If you feel unsure of the BCD equivalent, refer to the conversion table at the end of the book.) Everything worked very simply in this case. Let us now try another example.

"08" is represented by 0000 1000.
"03" is represented by 0000 0011.

Exercise 3.5: *Compute the sum of the two numbers above in the BCD representation. What do you obtain? (answer follows)*

If you obtain 0000 1011, you have computed the *binary* sum of "8" and "3". You have indeed obtained "11" in *binary*. Unfortunately, "1011" is an *illegal code in BCD*. You should obtain the *BCD* representation of "11", i.e., "0001 0001"!

The problem stems from the fact that the BCD representation uses only the first ten combinations of 4 digits in order to encode the decimal symbols "0" through "9". The remaining six possible combinations of 4 digits are unused, and illegal "1011" is one such combination. In other words, whenever the sum of two binary digits is greater than "9", then one must add "6" to the result in order to skip over the unused 6 codes. Add the binary representation for "6" to "1011":

```
      1011    (illegal binary result)
    + 0110    (+ 6)
    ――――――
```

The result is: 0001 0001.

This is, indeed, "11" in the BCD notation! We now have the correct result.

This example illustrates one of the basic difficulties of the BCD mode. One must compensate for the six missing codes. On most microprocessors, a special instruction, called "decimal adjust," must be used to adjust the result of the binary addition (add 6 if result greater than 9). In the case of the 6502, the ADC instruction does it automatically. This is a clear advantage of the 6502 when doing BCD arithmetic.

The next problem is illustrated by the same example. In our example, the carry will be generated from the lower BCD digit

BASIC PROGRAMMING TECHNIQUES

(the right-most one) into the left-most one. This internal carry must be taken into account and added to the second BCD digit. The addition instruction for the 6502 takes care of this automatically. However, it is often convenient to detect this internal carry from bit 3 to bit 4 (the "half-carry"). No flag is provided in the 6502.

Finally, just as in the case of the binary addition, the usual SED and CLC instructions must be used prior to executing the BCD addition proper. As an example, a program to add the BCD numbers "11" and "22" appears below:

```
CLC             CLEAR CARRY
SED             SET DECIMAL MODE
LDA    #$11     LITERAL BCD "11"
ADC    #$22     LITERAL BCD "22"
STA    ADR
```

In this program, we are using two new symbols: "#" and "$". The "#" symbol denotes that a "literal" (or constant) follows. The "$" sign within the operand field of the instruction specifies that

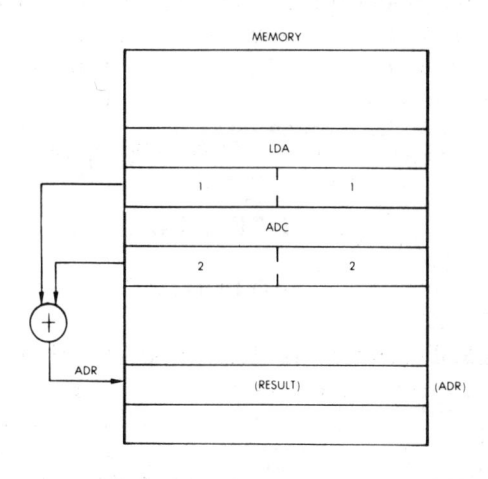

Fig. 3-7: Storing BCD Digits

the data which follows is expressed in hexadecimal notation. The hexadecimal and the BCD representations for digits "0" through "9" are identical. Here we wish to add the literals (or constants) "11" and "22". The result is stored at the address ADR. When the operand is specified as part of the instruction, as it is in the above example, this is called *immediate addressing*. (The various addressing modes will be discussed in detail in Chapter 5.) Storing the result at a specified address, such as STA ADR, is called *absolute addressing* when ADR represents a regular 16-bit address.

Exercise 3.6: *Could we move the CLC instruction in the program below the instruction LDA?*

BCD Subtraction

BCD subtraction appears to be complex. In order to perform a BCD subtraction, one must add the *10's complement* of the number, just like one adds the 2's complement of a number to perform a binary subtract. The 10's complement is obtained by computing the complement to 9, then adding 1. This typically requires three to four operations on a standard microprocessor. However, the 6502 is equipped with a special BCD subtraction instruction which performs this in a single instruction! Naturally, and just as in the binary example, the program will be preceded by the instructions SED, which sets the decimal mode, unless it has been previously set, and SEC, which sets the carry to 1. Thus, the program to subtract BCD "25" from BCD "26" is the following:

```
SED                SET DECIMAL MODE
SEC                SET CARRY
LDA    #$26        LOAD BCD 26
SBC    #$25        MINUS BCD 25
STA    ADR         STORE RESULT
```

16-Bit BCD Addition

16-bit addition is performed just as simply as in the binary case. The program for such an addition appears below:

```
CLC
SED
LDA        ADR1
```

BASIC PROGRAMMING TECHNIQUES

```
ADC     ADR2
STA     ADR3
LDA     ADR1-1
ADC     ADR2-1
STA     ADR3-1
```

Exercise 3.7: *Compare the program above to the one for the 16-bit binary addition. What is the difference?*

Exercise 3.8: *Write the subtraction program for a 16-bit BCD. (Do not use CLC and ADC!)*

BCD Flags

In BCD mode, the carry flag during an addition indicates the fact that the result is larger than 99. This is not like the two's complement situation, since BCD digits are represented in true binary. Conversely, the absence of the carry flag during a subtraction indicates a borrow.

Programming Hints for Add and Subtract

—Always clear the carry flag before performing an addition.
—Always set the carry flag to 1 before performing a subtraction.
—Set the appropriate mode: binary or decimal.

Instruction Types

We have now used three types of microprocessor instructions. We have used LDA and STA, which respectively load the accumulator from the memory address and store its contents at the specified address. These two instructions are *data transfer* instructions.

Next, we have used *arithmetic* instructions, such as ADC and SBC. They perform respectively an addition and a subtraction operation. More ALU instructions will be introduced in this chapter soon.

Finally, we have used instructions such as CLC, SEC and others, which manipulate the flag bits (respectively the carry and the decimal bits in our examples). They are *status manipulation* or control instructions. A comprehensive description of the 6502 instruc-

67

tions will be presented in Chapter 4.

Still other types of instructions are available within the microprocessor which we have not yet used. They are in particular the "branch" and "jump" instructions, which will modify the order in which the program is being executed. This new type of instruction will be introduced in our next example.

Multiplication

Let us now examine a more complex arithmetic problem: the multiplication of binary numbers. In order to introduce the algorithm for a binary multiplication, let us start by examining a usual decimal multiplication: We will multiply 12 by 23.

```
     12    (Multiplicand)
   ×23    (Multiplier)
   ____
     36    (Partial Product)
   + 24
   ____
   =276   Final Result
```

The multiplication is performed by multiplying the right-most digit of the multiplier by the multiplicand, i.e., "3" × "12". The partial product is "36." Then one multiplies the next digit of the multiplier, i.e., "2," by "12." "24" is then added to the partial product.

But there is one more operation: 24 is *offset to the left* by one position. We will say that 24 is being *shifted left* by one position. Equivalently, we could have said that the partial product (36) had been *shifted one position to the right* before adding.

The two numbers, correctly shifted, are then added and the sum is 276. This is simple. Let us now look at the binary multiplication. The binary multiplication is performed in exactly the same way.

Let us look at an example. We will multiply 5 × 3:

```
    (5)      101     (MPD)
    (3)    ×011     (MPR)
           ____
             101     (PP)
            101
           000
           _____
   (15)    01111    (RES)
```

BASIC PROGRAMMING TECHNIQUES

In order to perform the multiplication, we operate exactly as we did above. The formal representation of this algorithm appears in Figure 3-8. It is a flowchart for the algorithm, our first flowchart. Let us examine it more closely.

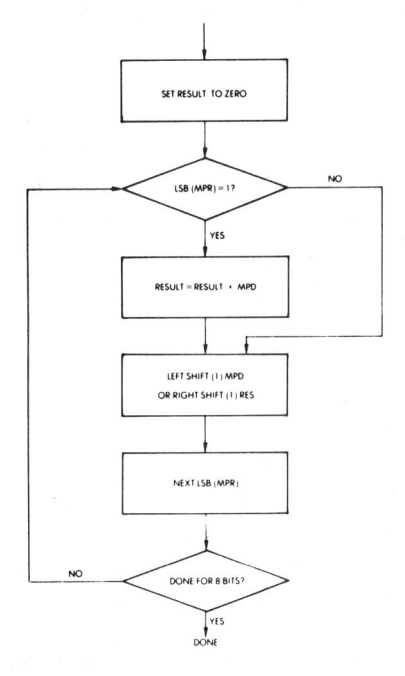

```
         │
         ▼
  ┌─────────────────┐
  │ SET RESULT TO ZERO │
  └─────────────────┘
         │
         ▼
       ╱   ╲        NO
      ╱ LSB ╲──────────┐
      ╲(MPR)=1?╱        │
       ╲   ╱           │
         │ YES         │
         ▼             │
  ┌─────────────────┐  │
  │ RESULT=RESULT+MPD│  │
  └─────────────────┘  │
         │             │
         ▼             │
  ┌─────────────────┐  │
  │ LEFT SHIFT (1) MPD │◄┘
  │ OR RIGHT SHIFT (1) RES │
  └─────────────────┘
         │
         ▼
  ┌─────────────────┐
  │  NEXT LSB (MPR)  │
  └─────────────────┘
         │
         ▼
   NO  ╱   ╲
  ◄───╱ DONE  ╲
      ╲FOR 8 BITS?╱
       ╲   ╱
         │ YES
         ▼
       DONE
```

Fig. 3-8: The Basic Multiplication Algorithm: Flowchart

This flow-chart is a symbolic representation of the algorithm we have just presented. Every rectangle represents an order to be carried out. It will be translated into one or more program instructions. Every diamond-shaped symbol represents a test being performed. This will be a branching point in the program. If the test succeeds, we will branch to a specified location. If the test does not succeed, we will branch to another location. The concept of branching will be explained later in the program itself. The reader should now examine this flow-chart and ascertain that it does indeed represent the algorithm exactly. Note that there is an arrow coming out of the last diamond at the bottom of the flow-chart, back to the first diamond on top. This is because the same portion of the flow-chart will be executed eight times, once for every bit of the multiplier. Such a situation where execution will restart at the same point is called a *program loop*, for obvious reasons.

Exercise 3.9: *Multiply "4" by "7" in binary using the flow chart, and verify that you obtain "28." If you do not, try again. It is only if you obtain the correct result that you are ready to translate this flow chart into a program.*

Let us now translate this flow-chart into a program for the 6502. The complete program appears in Figure 3.9. We are now going to study it in detail. As you will recall from Chapter 1, programming consists here of translating the flowchart of Figure 3-8 into the program of Figure 3-9. Each of the boxes in the flowchart will be translated by one or more instructions.

It is assumed that MPR and MPD already have a value.

```
           LDA    #0          ZERO ACCUMULATOR
           STA    TMP         CLEAR THIS ADDRESS
           STA    RESAD       CLEAR
           STA    RESAD+1     CLEAR
           LDX    #8          X IS COUNTER
   MULT    LSR    MPRAD       SHIFT MPR RIGHT
           BCC    NO ADD      TEST CARRY BIT
           LDA    RESAD       LOAD A WITH LOW RES
           CLC                PREPARE TO ADD
           ADC    MPDAD       ADD MPD TO RES
           STA    RESAD       SAVE RESULT
           LDA    RESAD+1     ADD REST OF SHIFTED MPD
           ADC    TMP
           STA    RESAD+1
   NOADD   ASL    MPDAD       SHIFT MPD LEFT
           ROL    TMP         SAVE BIT FROM MPD
           DEX                DECREMENT COUNTER
           BNE    MULT        DO IT AGAIN IF COUNTER #0
```

Fig. 3-9: 8x8 Multiply

The first box of the flow-chart is an *initialization* box. It is necessary to set a number of registers or memory locations to "0," as this program will require their use. The registers which will be used by the multiplication program appear in Figure 3-10. On the left of the illustration appears the relevant portion of the 6502 microprocessor. On the right of the illustration appears the rele-

BASIC PROGRAMMING TECHNIQUES

vant section of the memory. We will assume here that memory addresses increase from the top to the bottom of the illustration. Naturally, the reverse convention could be used. The X register on the far left (one of the two index registers of the 6502) will be used as a *counter*. Since we are doing an 8-bit multiplication, we will have to test 8 bits of the multiplier. Unfortunately, there is no instruction in the 6502 which allows us to test those bits in sequence. The only bits that can conveniently be tested are the flags in the status register. As a result of this limitation of most microprocessors, in order to test successively all the bits of the multiplier, it will be necessary to transfer the multiplier value into the accumulator. Then, the contents of the accumulator will be shifted right. A shift instruction moves every bit in the register by one position to the right or to the left. The bit which falls off the register drops into the carry bit of the status register. The effect of a shift operation is illustrated in Figure 3-11. There are many variations possible depending upon the bit that comes into the register, but these differences will be discussed in Chapter 4 (6502 instruction set).

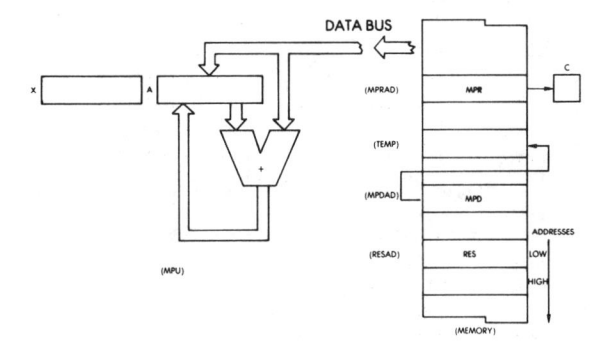

Fig. 3-10: Multiplication: The Registers

Let us go back to the successive testing of each of the 8 bits of the multiplier. Since one can easily test the carry bit, the multiplier will be shifted by one position 8 times. Every time its rightmost bit will fall into the carry bit, where it will be tested.

The next problem to be solved is that the partial product which is accumulated during the successive additions will require 16 bits. Multiplying two 8-bit numbers may yield a 16-bit re-

PROGRAMMING THE 6502

sult. This is because $2^8 \times 2^8 = 2^{16}$. We need to reserve 16 bits for this result. Unfortunately, the 6502 has very few internal registers, so that this partial product cannot be stored within the 6502 itself. In fact, because of the limited number of registers, we are unable to store the multiplier, the multiplicand, or the partial product within the 6502. They will all be stored in the memory. This will result in a slower execution than if it were possible to store them all in internal registers. This is a limitation inherent in the 6502. The memory area used for the multiplication appears on the right of Figure 3-10. On top one can see the memory word allocated for the multiplier. We will assume, for example, that it contains "3" in binary. The address of this memory location is MPRAD. Below it, we find a "temporary" whose address is TMP. The role of this location will be clarified below. We will shift the multiplicand left into this location prior to adding it to the partial product. The multiplicand is next and will be assumed to contain the value "5" in binary. Its address is MPDAD.

Finally, at the bottom of the memory, we find the two words allocated for the partial product or the result. Their address is RESAD.

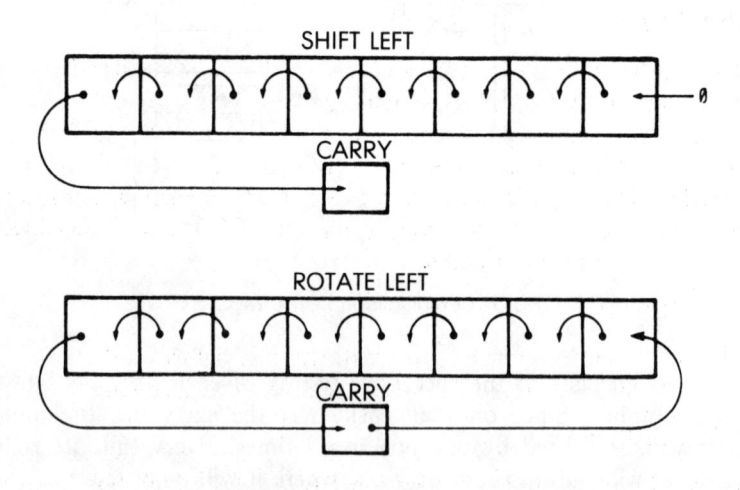

Fig. 3-11: Shift and Rotate

BASIC PROGRAMMING TECHNIQUES

These memory locations will be our "working registers," and the word "register" may be used interchangeably with "location" in this context.

The arrow which appears on the top right of the illustration coming out of MPR into bit C is a symbolic way of showing how the multiplier will be shifted in the carry bit. Naturally, this carry bit is physically contained within the 6502 and not within the memory.

Let us now go back to the program of Figure 3-9. The first five instructions are initialization instructions:

The first four instructions will clear the contents of "registers" TMP, RESAD, and RESAD+1. Let us verify this.

LDA #0

This instruction loads the accumulator with the literal value "0." As a result of this instruction, the accumulator will contain "00000000."

The contents of the accumulator will now be used to clear the three "registers" in the memory. It must be remembered that reading a value out of a register does not empty it. It is possible to read as many times as necessary out of a register. Its contents are not changed by the read operation. Let us proceed:

STA TMP

This instruction stores the contents of the accumulator in memory location TMP. Refer to Figure 3-10 to understand the flow of data in the system. The accumulator contains "00000000." The result of this instruction will be to write all zeroes in memory location TMP. Remember that the contents of the accumulator remain 0 after a read operation on the accumulator. It is unchanged. We are going to use it again.

STA RESAD

This instruction operates just like the one before and clears the contents of address RESAD. Let us do it one more time:

STA RESAD+1

We finally clear memory location RESAD+1 which has been reserved to store the high part of the result. (The high half is bits 8–15; the low part is bits 0–7.)

Finally, in order to able to stop shifting the multiplier bits at the right time, it is necessary to count the number of shifts that have to be performed. Eight shifts are necessary. Register X will be used as a counter and initialized to the value "8." Every time that the shift will have been performed, the contents of this counter will be decremented by 1. Whenever the value of this counter reaches "0," the multiplication is finished. Let us initialize this register to "8":

LDX #8

This instruction loads the literal "8" into register X.

Referring back to the flow chart of Figure 3-8, we must test the least significant bit of the multiplier. It has been indicated above that this test cannot be performed in a single instruction. Two instructions must be used. First the multiplier will be shifted right, then the bit which fell out of it will be tested. It is the carry bit. Let us perform these operations:

LSR MPRAD

This instruction is a "Logical Shift Right" of the contents of memory location MPRAD.

Exercise 3.10: *Assuming that the multiplier in our example is "3," which bit falls off the right end of memory location MPRAD? (In other words, which will be the value of the carry after this shift?)*

The next instruction tests the value of the carry bit:

BCC NOADD

This instruction means "Branch if Carry Clear" (i.e. equals zero) to the address NOADD.

This is the first time we encounter a branch instruction. All the programs we have considered so far have been strictly sequential. Each instruction was executed after the previous one. In order to be able to use logical tests such as testing the carry bit, one must be able to execute instructions anywhere in the program after the test. The branch instruction performs just such a function. It will test the value of the carry bit. If the carry was "0," i.e., if it was cleared, then the program will branch to address NOADD. This means that the next instruction executed after the BCC will be the instruction at address NOADD if the test succeeds.

BASIC PROGRAMMING TECHNIQUES

Otherwise, if the test fails, no branch will occur and the instruction following BCC NOADD will be normally executed.

One more explanation is in order about NOADD: this is a *symbolic label*. It represents an actual physical address within the memory. For the convenience of the programmer, the assembler program allows using symbolic names instead of actual addresses. During the assembly process, the assembler will substitute the real physical address instead of the symbol "NOADD." This improves the readability of the program substantially and also allows the programmer to insert additional instructions between the branch point and NOADD, without having to rewrite everything. These merits will be studied in more detail in Chaper 10 on the assembler.

If the test fails, the next sequential instruction in the program is executed. We will now study both alternatives:

Alternative 1: the carry was "1."
If the carry was 1, the test specified by BCC has failed and the next instruction after BCC is executed.

LDA RESAD

Alternative 2: the carry was "0."
The test succeeds, and the next instruction is the one at label "NOADD."

Referring to Figure 3-8, the flow-chart specifies that if the carry bit was 1, the multiplicand must be added to the partial product (here, the RES registers). Also, a shift must be performed. The partial product must be moved by one position to the right or else the multiplicand must be moved by one position to the left. We will adopt here the usual convention in performing multiplications by hand, and we will move the multiplicand by one position to the left.

The multiplicand is contained in registers TMP and MPDAD. (To simplify, we call memory locations "registers," a usual term.) The 16 bits of the partial product are contained in memory addresses RESAD and RESAD + 1.

In order to illustrate this, let us assume that the multiplicand was "5." The various registers appear in Figure 3-10.

We simply have to add two 16-bit numbers. This is a problem that we have learned to solve. (If you have any doubts, refer to the section on 16-bit addition above.) We are going to add the low-

PROGRAMMING THE 6502

order bytes first, and then the high-order bytes. Let us proceed:

LDA RESAD

The accumulator is loaded with the low part of RES.

CLC

Prior to any addition, the 6502 requires that the carry bit be cleared. It is important to do so here as we know that the carry bit had been set to 1. It must be cleared.

ADC MPDAD

The multiplicand is added to the accumulator, which contains (RES)LOW.

STA RESAD

The result of the addition is saved at the appropriate memory location, (RES)LOW. The second half of the addition is then performed. When checking execution of this program later by hand, do not forget that the addition will set the carry bit. The carry will be set to either "0" or "1" depending on the results of the addition. Any carry that might have been generated will automatically be carried forward into the high-order part of the result.

Let us now finish the addition:

```
LDA   RESAD+1
ADC   TMP
STA   RESAD+1
```

These three instructions complete our 16-bit add. We have now added the multiplicand to RES. We still have to shift it by one position to the left in anticipation of the next addition. We could also have considered shifting the multiplicand by one position to the left *before* adding, except for the first time. This is one of many programming options which are always open to the programmer.

Let us shift the multiplicand to the left:

NOADD ASL MPDAD

This instruction is an "Arithmetic Shift Left." It will shift by one position to the left the contents of memory location MPDAD which happens to contain the low part of the multiplicand. This is not enough. We cannot afford to lose the bit which falls off the left

BASIC PROGRAMMING TECHNIQUES

end of the multiplicand. This bit will fall into the carry bit. It should not be stored there permanently since it can be destroyed by any arithmetic operation. This bit should be saved in a "permanent" register. It should be shifted into memory location TMP. This is precisely accomplished by the next instruction:

ROL TMP

This specifies: "Rotate Left" the contents of TMP.

One interesting observation can be made here. We just used two different kinds of shift instructions to shift a register by one position to the left. The first one is ASL. The second one is ROL. What is the difference?

The ASL instruction shifts the contents of the register. The ROL instruction is a rotate instruction. It does shift the contents of the register by one position to the left, and the bit falling off the left end goes into the carry bit, as usual. The difference is that the *previous contents of the carry bit are forced into the right-most position*. This is called a circular rotation in mathematics (a 9-bit rotation). This is exactly what we want. As a result of the ROL, the bit which had been shifted out of TMP on the left and preserved in the carry bit C will land in the right-most position of register TMP. It works.

We are now finished with the arithmetic portion of this program. We still have to test whether we have performed the operation eight times, i.e., whether we are finished. As usual in most microprocessors, this test will require two instructions:

DEX

This instruction decrements the contents of register X. If it contained 8, its contents will be 7 after execution of this instruction.

BNE MULT

This is another test-and-branch instruction. It specifies "branch if result is not equal to 0 to location MULT." As long as our counter-register decrements to a non-zero integer, there will be an automatic branch back to label MULT. This is called the multiplication loop. Referring back to the multiplication flow-chart, this correponds to the arrow coming out of the last box. This loop will be executed 8 times.

Exercise 3.11: *What happens when X decrements to 0? What is*

77

the next instruction to be executed?

In most cases, the program that we just developed will be a subroutine and the final instruction in the subroutine will be RTS. The subroutine mechanism will be explained later in this chapter.

IMPORTANT SELF-TEST

If you wish to learn how to program, it is extremely important that you understand such a typical program in complete detail. We have introduced many new instructions. The algorithm is reasonably simple, but the program is much longer than the previous programs that we have developed so far. *It is very strongly suggested that you do the following exercise completely and correctly before you proceed in this chapter.* If you do it correctly, you will have really understood the mechanism by which instructions manipulate the contents of memory and of the microprocessor registers and how the carry flag is being used. If you do not, it is likely that you will experience difficulties in writing programs yourself. Learning to program does involve actually programming. Please pause to take a piece of paper and do the following exercise.

Exercise 3.12: *Every time that a program is written, one should verify it by hand, in order to ascertain that its results will be correct. We are going to do just that: the purpose of this exercise is to fill in the table of Figure 3-12.*

You can write directly on it or else make a copy of it. The purpose is to determine the contents of every relevant register and memory location in the system after each instruction is executed by this program, from beginning to end. You will find horizontally on Figure 3-12 all the register locations used by the program: X, A, MPR, C (the carry bit flag), TMP, MPD, RESADL, RESADH. On the left part of the illustration you must fill in the label, if applicable, and the instruction being executed. At the right of the illustration you must write the contents of every register after execution of that instruction. Whenever the contents of a register are indefinite, we will use dashes. Let us start filling

BASIC PROGRAMMING TECHNIQUES

LABEL	INSTRUCTION	X	A	MPR	C	TEMP	MPD	(RESAD)L	(RESAD)H

Fig. 3-12: Form To Be Filled Out For Exercise 3-12

PROGRAMMING THE 6502

in this table together. You will have to fill in the remainder alone. The first line appears below:

LABEL	INSTRUCTION	X	A	MPR	C	TEMP	MPD	(RES)L	(RES)H
	LDA #0	-----	00000000	00000011	--	-----	00000101	-----	-----

Fig. 3-13: First Instruction of Multiplication

The first instruction to be executed is LDA #0.

After execution of this instruction, the contents of register X are unknown. This is indicated by dashes. The contents of the accumulator are all zeroes. We also assume that the multiplier and the multiplicand had been loaded by the programmer prior to execution of this program. (Otherwise, additional instructions would be needed to set the contents of MPR and MPD.) We find in MPR the binary value for "3." We find in MPD the binary value for "5." The carry bit is undefined. Register TMP is undefined. And both registers used for RESAD are undefined. Let us now fill the next line. It appears below; the only difference is that the contents of register TMP have been set to "0." The next instruction will set the contents of RESAD to "0" and the one after will set the contents of RESAD +1 to "0."

LABEL	INSTRUCTION	X	A	MPR	C	TEMP	MPD	(RES)L	(RES)H
	LDA #0	-----	00000000	00000011	--	-----	00000101	-----	-----
	STA TEMP					00000000			

Fig. 3-14: First Two Lines of Multiplication

The fifth instruction, #8, will set the contents of X to "8." Let us do one more instruction set (see Figure 3-15).

The LSR MPRAD instruction will shift the contents of MPRAD right by one position. You can see that after the shift the contents of MPR are "0000 0001." The right-most "1" of MPR has fallen

BASIC PROGRAMMING TECHNIQUES

LABEL	INSTRUCTION	X	A	MPR	C	TEMP	MPD	(RES)L	(RES)H
000	LDA #0	----	00000000	00000011	--	----	00000101	----	----
	STA TEMP					00000000			
	STA RESAD							00000000	
	STA RESAD + 1								00000000
	LDX #8	00001000							
MULT	LSR MPRAD			00000001	1				
	BCC NOADD								
	LDA RESAD								
	CLC				0				
	ADC MPDAD		00000101						
101	STA RESAD							00000101	
	LDA RESAD + 1		00000000						
	ADC TEMP								
	STA RESAD + 1								
NOADD	ASL MPDAD						00001010		
	ROL TEMP								
	DEX	00000111							
	BNE MULT								
MULT	LSR MPRAD			00000000	1				
	(2nd ITERATION)								

Fig. 3-15: Partially Completed Form For Exercise 3-12

into the carry bit. Bit C is now set to 1. Other registers are unchanged.

It is now your turn. Please fill in the rest of this table completely. It is not difficult, but it does require attention. If you have doubts about the role of some instructions, you may want to refer to Chapter 4 where you will find each of them listed and described, or else to the Appendix section of this book where they are listed in table form.

The final result of your multiplication should be "15" in binary form, contained in registers RESAD low and high. RESAD high should be set to "0000 0000." RESAD low should be "0000 1111." If you obtained this result, you won. If you did not, try one more time. The most frequent source of errors is a mishandling of the carry bit. Make sure that the carry bit is changed every time you perform an arithmetic instruction. Do not forget that the ALU will set the carry bit after each addition operation.

Programming Alternatives

The program that we have just developed is one of many ways in which it could have been written. Every programmer can find ways to modify and sometimes improve a program. For example, we have shifted the multiplicand left before adding. It would have been mathematically equivalent to shift the result by one position to the right before adding it to the multiplicand. The advantage is that we would not have required register TMP, thus saving one memory location. This would be a preferred method in a microprocessor equipped with enough internal registers so that

MPR, MPD, and RESAD could be contained within the microprocessor. Since we were obliged to use the memory to perform these operations, saving one memory location is not relevant. The question is, therefore, whether the second method might result in a somewhat faster multiplication. This is an interesting exercise:

Exercise 3.13: *Now write an 8×8 multiply, using the same algorithm, but shifting the result by one position to the right instead of shifting the multiplicand by one position to the left. Compare it to the previous program and determine whether this different approach would be faster or slower than the preceding one.*

One more problem may come up: In order to determine the speed of the program, you may want to refer to the tables in the Appendix section which list the number of cycles required by each instruction. However, the number of cycles required by some instructions depends on where they are located. A special addressing mode exists for the 6502 called the *Direct Addressing Zero Page* Mode, where the first page (memory location 0 to 255) is reserved for fast execution. This will be explained in Chapter 5 on addressing techniques. Briefly, all programs that require a fast execution time will use variables located in page 0 so that instructions require only two bytes to address memory locations (addressing 256 locations requires only one byte), whereas instructions located anywhere else in the memory will typically require 3-byte instructions. Let us defer this analysis until after Chapter 5.

An Improved Multiplication Program

The program we have just developed is a straightforward translation of the algorithm into code. However, effective programming requires close attention to detail so that the length of the program can be reduced and so that its execution speed can be improved. We are now going to present an improved implementation of the same algorithm.

One of the tasks which consume instructions and time is the shifting of the result and the multiplier. A standard "trick" used in the multiply algorithm is based on the following observation: every time that the multiplier is shifted by one bit position to the right, a bit position becomes available on the left. Simultaneously, we can observe that the first result (or partial product) will

BASIC PROGRAMMING TECHNIQUES

use, at most, 9 bits. After the next multiply shift, the size of the partial product will be increased by one bit again. In other words, we can just reserve, initially, one memory location for the partial product and then use the bit positions which are being freed by the multiplier as it is being shifted.

We are now going to shift the multiplier right. It will free one bit position to the left. We are going to enter the left-most bit of the partial product into this bit position that has been freed. Let us now consider the program.

Let us now also consider the optimal use of registers. The internal registers of the 6502 appear in Fig. 3-16. X is best used as a counter. We will use it to count the number of bits shifted. The accumulator is (unfortunately) the only internal register which can be shifted. In order to improve efficiency, we should store in it either the multiplier or the result.

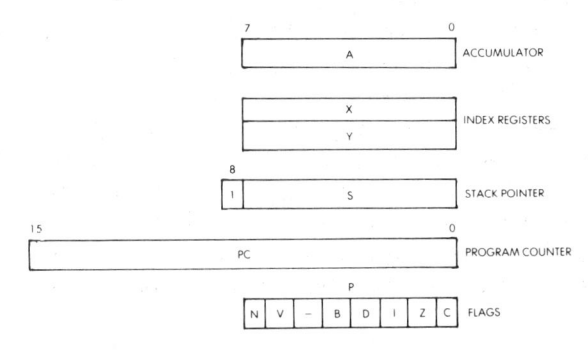

Fig. 3-16: 6502 Registers

Which one should we put in the accumulator? The result must be added to the multiplicand every time a 1 is shifted out. Since the 6502 also always adds something to the accumulator only, it is the result which will reside in the accumulator.

The other numbers will have to reside in the memory (see Figgure 3-17).

A and B will hold the result. A will hold the high part of the result, and B will hold the low part of the result. A is the accumulator, and B is a memory location, preferably in page 0. C will hold the multiplier (a memory location). D holds the multipli-

83

PROGRAMMING THE 6502

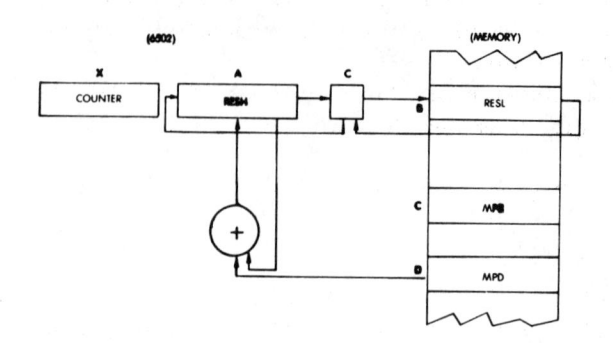

Fig. 3-17: Register Allocation (Improved Multiply)

cand (a memory location). The program appears below:

```
MULT    LDA  #0        INITIALIZE RESULT TO ZERO (HIGH)
        STA  B         INITIALIZE RESULT (LOW)
        LDX  #8        X IS SHIFT COUNTER
LOOP    LSR  C         SHIFT MPR
        BCC  NOADD
        CLC            CARRY WAS ONE. CLEAR IT
        ADC  D         A = A + MPD
NOADD   ROR  A         SHIFT RESULT
        ROR  B         CATCH BIT INTO B
        DEX            DECREMENT COUNTER
        BNE  LOOP      LAST SHIFT?
```

Fig. 3-18: Improved Multiply

Let us examine the program. Since A and B will hold the result, they must be initialized to the value 0. Let us do it:

MULT LDA #0
     STA B

We will then use register X as a shift counter and initialize it to the value 8:

LDX #8

We are now ready to enter the main multiplication loop as before. We will first shift the multiplier, then test the carry bit which holds the right-most bit of the multiplier, which has fallen off. Let us do it:

LOOP LSR C
     BCC NOADD

BASIC PROGRAMMING TECHNIQUES

Here we shift the multiplier right as before. This is equivalent to the previous algorithm because the addition operation is said to be communicative.

Two possibilities exist: if the carry was 0, we will branch to NOADD. Let us assume that the carry was 1. We will proceed:

    CLC
    ADC D

Since the carry was 1, it must be cleared, and we then add the multiplicand to the accumulator. (The accumulator holds the results, 0 so far.)

Let us now shift the partial product:

NOADD ROR A
         ROR B

The partial product in A is shifted right by one bit. The rightmost bit falls into the carry bit. The carry bit is captured and rotated into register B, which holds the low part of the result.

We simply have to test whether we are finished:

    DEX
    BNE LOOP

If we now examine this new program, we see that it has been written in about half the number of instructions of the previous program. It will also execute much faster. This shows the value of selecting the correct registers to contain the information.

A straightforward design will result in a program that works. It will not result in a program that is optimized. It is, therefore, of significant importance to use the available registers and memory locations in the best possible way. This example illustrates a rational approach to register selection for maximum efficiency.

Exercise 3.14: *Compute the speed of a multiplication operation using this last program. Assume that a branch will occur in fifty percent of the cases. Look up the number of cycles required by every instruction in the table at the end of the book. Assume a clock rate of one cycle = 1 microsecond.*

Binary Division

The algorithm for binary division is analogous to the one which has been used for multiplication. The divisor is successively subtracted from the high order bits of the dividend. After each subtraction, the result is used instead of the initial dividend. The value of the quotient is simultaneously increased by 1 every time. Eventually, the result of the subtraction is negative. This is called an overdraw. One must then restore the partial result by adding the divisor back to it. Naturally, the quotient must be simultaneously decremented by 1. Quotient and dividend are then shifted by one bit position to the left and the algorithm is repeated.

The method just described is called the *restoring method*. A variation of this method which yields an improved speed of execution is called *non-restoring* method.

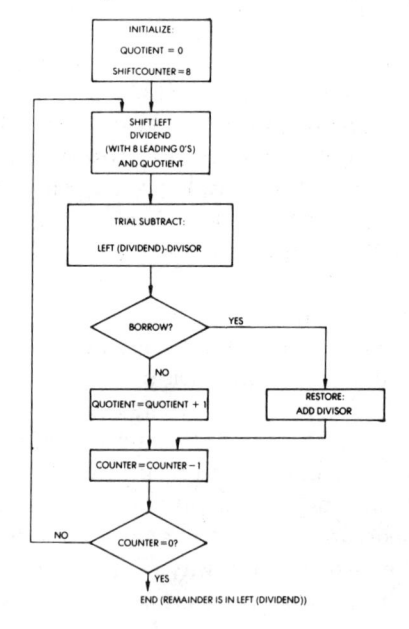

Fig. 3-19: 8 Bit Binary Division Flowchart

The 16-bit Division

The non-restoring division for a 16-bit dividend, and an 8-bit divisor will now be described. The result will have 8 bits. The reg-

BASIC PROGRAMMING TECHNIQUES

ister and memory location for this program are shown in Fig. 3-20. The dividend is contained in the accumulator (high part) and in memory location 0, called B here. The result is contained in Q (memory location 1). The divisor is contained in D (memory location 2). The result will be contained in Q and A (A will contain the remainder).

The program appears on Fig. 3-21, the corresponding flow chart is shown on Fig. 3-22.

Exercise 3.15: *Verify the correct operation of this program by performing the division by hand and exercising the program, as you did in Exercise 3.12. Divide 33 by 3. The result naturally should be 11, with a remainder of 0.*

LOGICAL OPERATIONS

The other class of instructions that the ALU inside the microprocessor can execute is the set of logical instructions. They include: AND, OR and exclusive OR (EOR). In addition, one can also include there the shift operations which have already been utilized, and the comparison instruction, called CMP for the 6502. The individual use of AND, ORA, EOR, will be described in Chapter 4 on the 6502 instruction set. Let us now develop a brief program which will check whether a given memory location called LOC contains the value "0," the value "1," or something else. The program appears below:

```
                LDA     LOC       READ CHARACTER IN LOC
                CMP     #$00      COMPARE TO ZERO
                BEQ     ZERO      IS IT A 0?
                CMP     #$01      1?
                BEQ     ONE
NONE FOUND      ...
                ...
ZERO            ...
                ...
ONE             ...
```

The first instruction: LDA LOC reads the contents of memory location LOC. This is the character we want to test.

CMP #$00

PROGRAMMING THE 6502

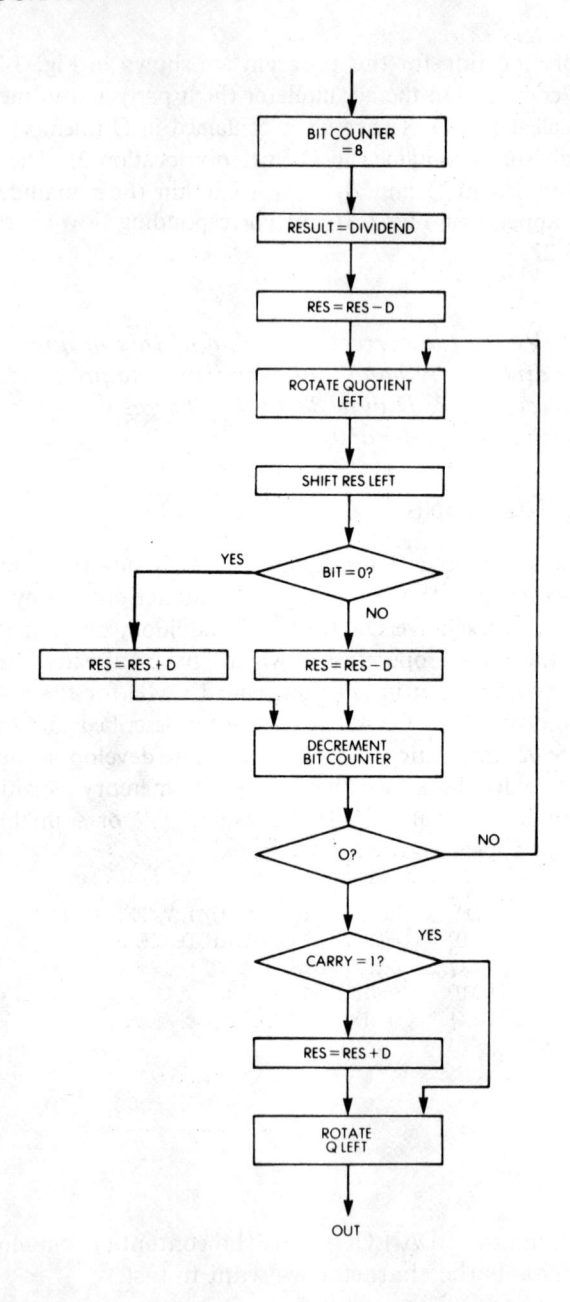

Fig. 3-20: 16 by 8 Division Flowchart

BASIC PROGRAMMING TECHNIQUES

LINE #	LOC	CODE	LINE	
0002	0000			* = $0
0003	0000		B	* = * + 1
0004	0001		Q	* = * + 1
0005	0002		D	* = * + 1
0006	0003			* = $200
0007	0200	A0 08	DIV	LDY #8
0008	0202	38		SEC
0009	0203	E5 02		SBC D
0010	0205	08	LOOP	PHP
0011	0206	26 01		ROL Q
0012	0208	06 00		ASL B
0013	020A	2A		ROL A
0014	020B	28		PLP
0015	020C	90 05		BCC ADD
0016	020E	E5 02		SBC D
0017	0210	4C 15 02		JMP NEXT
0018	0213	65 02	ADD	ADC D
0019	0215	88	NEXT	DEY
0020	0216	D0 ED		BNE LOOP
0021	0218	B0 03		BCS LAST
0022	021A	65 02		ADC D
0023	021C	18		CLC
0024	021D	26 01	LAST	ROL Q
0025	021F	00		BRK
0026	0220			.END

Fig. 3-21: Program

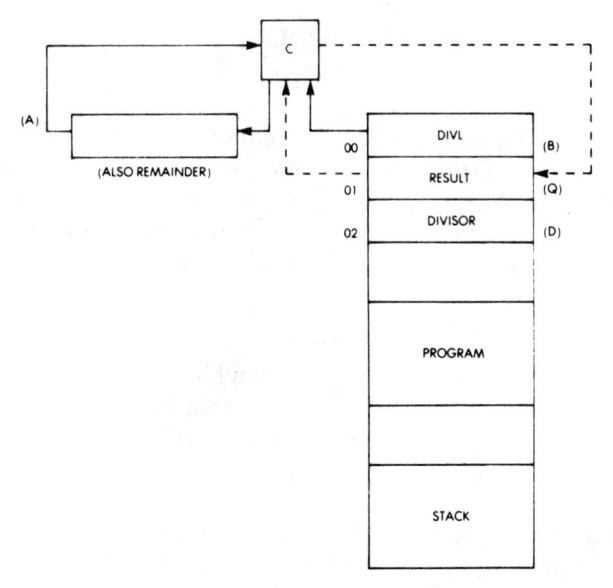

Fig. 3-22: 16 by 8 Division Flowchart (non-restoring 8-bit result)

89

This instruction compares the contents of the accumulator with the literal hexadecimal value "00" (i.e., the bit pattern "00000000"). This comparison instruction will set the Z bit in the flags register, which will then be tested by the next instruction:

BEQ ZERO

The BEQ instruction specifies "branch if equal." The branch instruction will determine whether the test succeeds by examining the Z bit. If set, the program will branch to ZERO. If the test fails, then the next sequential instruction will be executed:

CMP #$01

The process will be repeated against the new pattern. If the test succeeds, the next instruction will result in a branch to location one. If it fails, the next sequential instruction will be executed.

Exercise 3.16: *Write a program which will read the contents of memory location "24" and branch to the address called "STAR" if there were a "*" in memory location 24. The bit pattern for a "*" in assembly language notation is represented by "00101010".*

SUMMARY

We have now studied most of the important instructions of the 6502 by using them. We have transferred values between the memory and the registers. We have performed arithmetic and logical operations on such data. We have tested it, and depending on the results of these tests, we have executed various portions of the program. We have also introduced a structure called the loop, in the multiplication program. An important programming structure will be introduced now: the subroutine.

SUBROUTINES

In concept, a subroutine is simply a block of instructions which has been given a name by the programmer. From a practical standpoint, a subroutine must start with a special instruction called the subroutine declaration, which identifies it as such for the assembler. It is also terminated by another special instruction called a *return*. Let us first illustrate the use of subroutines in the program in order to demonstrate its value. Then, we will examine how it is actually implemented.

BASIC PROGRAMMING TECHNIQUES

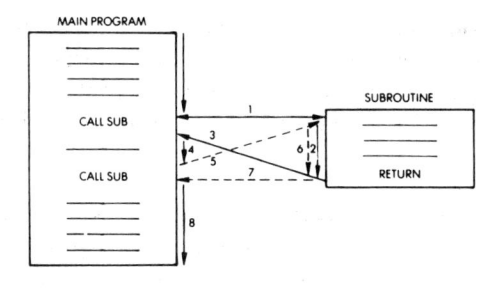

Fig. 3-23: Subroutine Calls

The use of a subroutine is illustrated in Figure 3-23. The main program appears on the left of the illustration. The subroutine is represented symbolically on the right. Let us examine the subroutine mechanism. The lines of the main program are executed succesively until a new instruction, CALL SUB, is met. This special instruction is the *subroutine call* and results in a transfer to the subroutine. This means that the next instruction to be executed after the CALL SUB is the first instruction within the subroutine. This is illustrated by arrow 1 in the illustration.

Then, the subprogram within the subroutine executes just like any other program. We will assume that the subroutine does not contain any other calls. The last instruction of this subroutine is a RETURN. This is a special instruction which will cause a return to the main program. The next instruction to be executed after the RETURN is the one following the CALL SUB. This is illustrated by arrow 3 in the illustration. Program execution continues then as illustrated by arrow 4.

In the body of the main program a second CALL SUB appears. A new transfer occurs, shown by arrow 5. This means that the body of the subroutine is again executed following the CALL SUB instruction.

Whenever the RETURN within the subroutine is encountered, a return occurs to the instruction following the CALL SUB in question. This is illustrated by arrow 7. Following the return to the main program, program execution proceeds normally, as illustrated by arrow 8.

The role of the two special instructions CALL SUB and RE-

TURN should now be clear. What is the value of the subroutine?

The essential value of the subroutine is that it can be called from any number of points in the main program and used repeatedly without rewriting it. A first advantage is that this approach saves memory space and there is no need to rewrite the subroutine every time. A second advantage is that the programmer can design a specific subroutine only once and then use it repeatedly. This is a significant simplification in program design.

Exercise 3.17: *What is the main disadvantage of a subroutine?*

The disadvantage of the subroutine should be clear just from examining the flow of execution between the main program and the subroutine. A subroutine results in a slower execution, since extra instructions must be executed: the CALL SUB and the RETURN.

Implementation of the Subroutine Mechanism

We will examine here how the two special instructions, CALL SUB and RETURN, are implemented internally within the processor. The effect of the CALL SUB instruction is to cause the next instruction to be fetched at a new address. You will remember (or else read Chapter 1 again) that the address of the next instruction to be executed in a computer is contained in the program counter (PC). This means that the effect of the CALL SUB is to substitute new contents in register PC. Its effect is to load the start address of the subroutine in the program counter. *Is that really enough?*

To answer this question, let us consider the other instruction which has to be implemented: the RETURN. The RETURN must cause, as its name indicates, a return to the instruction that follows the CALL SUB. This is possible only if the address of this instruction has been preserved somewhere. This address happens to be the value of the program counter at the time that the CALL SUB was encountered. This is because the program counter is automatically incremented every time it is used (read Chapter 1 again?). This is precisely the address that we want to preserve so that we can later perform RETURN.

The next problem is: where can we save this return address?

BASIC PROGRAMMING TECHNIQUES

This address must be saved in a reasonable location where it is guaranteed that it will not be erased. However, let us now consider the following situation, illustrated by Figure 3-24: in this example, subroutine 1 contains a call to SUB2. Our mechanism should work in this case as well. Naturally, there might even be more than two subroutines, say N "nested" calls. Whenever a new CALL is encountered, the mechanism must therefore store the program counter again. This implies that we need at least 2N memory locations for this mechanism. Additionally, we will need to return from SUB2 first and SUB1 next. In other words, we need a structure which can preserve the chronological order in which data will have been saved.

The structure has a name. We have already introduced it. It is *the stack*. Figure 3-26 shows the actual contents of the stack during successive subroutine calls. Let us look at the main program first. At address 100, the first call is encountered: CALL SUB1. We will assume that, in this microprocessor, the subroutine call uses 3 bytes. The next sequential address is therefore not

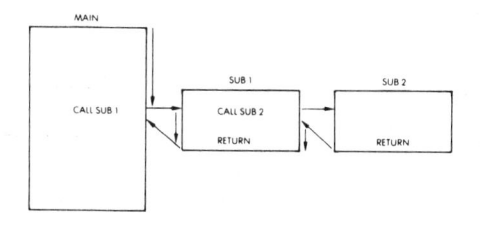

Fig. 3-24: Nested Calls

"101", but "103." The CALL instruction uses addresses "100", "101", and "102". Because the control unit of the 6502 "knows' that it is a 3-byte instruction, the value of the program counter when the call has been completely decoded will be "103". The effect of the call will be to load the value "280" in the program counter. "280" is the starting address of SUB1.

The second effect of the CALL will be to push into the stack (to preserve) the value "103" of the program counter. This is illustrated at the bottom left of the illustration which shows that at time 1, the value "103" is preserved in the stack. Let us move to the right of the illustration. At location 300, a new call is encountered. Just as in the preceding case, the value "900" will be loaded in the program counter. This is the starting address of SUB2. Simultaneously, the value "303" will be pushed into the stack. This is illustrated at the bottom left of the illustration where the entry at time 2 is "303". Execution will then proceed to the right of the illustration within SUB2.

We are now ready to demonstrate the effect of the RETURN instruction and the correct operation of our stack mechanism. Execution proceeds within SUB2 until the RETURN instruction is encountered at time 3. The effect of the RETURN instruction is simply to pop the top of the stack into the program counter. In other words, the program counter is restored to its value prior to the entry into the subroutine. The top of the stack in our example is "303." Figure 3-26 shows that, at time 3, value "303" has been removed from the stack and has been put back into the program counter. As a result, instruction execution proceeds from address "303." At time 4, the RETURN of SUB1 is encountered. The value on top of the stack is "103." It is popped and is installed in the program counter. As a result, the program execution will proceed from location "103" on within the main program. This is, indeed,

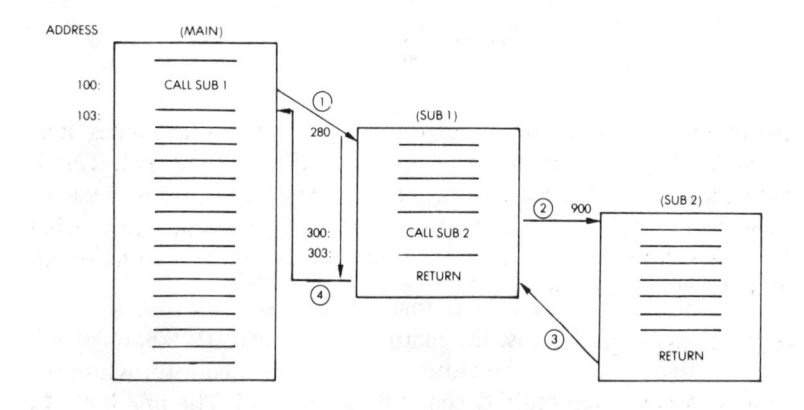

Fig. 3-25: The Subroutine Calls

the effect that we wanted. Figure 3-26 shows that at time 4 the stack is again empty. The mechanism works.

BASIC PROGRAMMING TECHNIQUES

The subroutine call mechanism works up to the maximum dimension of the stack. This is why early microprocessors, which had a 4 or 8-register stack, were essentially limited to 4 or 8 levels of subroutine calls. In theory, the 6502, which is restricted to 256 memory locations for the stack (Page 1), can therefore accommodate up to 128 successive subroutine calls. This is true only if there are no interrupts, if the stack is used for no other purpose, and if no register needs be stored within the stack. In practice, fewer subroutine levels will be used.

Note that, on illustrations 3-24 and 3-25, the subroutines have been shown to the right of the main program. This is only for the clarity of the diagram. In reality, the subroutines are typed by the user as regular instructions of the program. On a sheet of

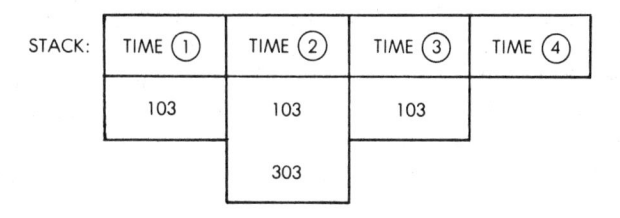

STACK:	TIME ①	TIME ②	TIME ③	TIME ④
	103	103	103	
		303		

Fig. 3-26: Stack vs. Time

paper, in a listing of the complete program, the subroutines may be at the beginning of the text, in its middle, or at the end. This is why they are preceded by a subroutine declaration: they must be identified. The special instructions tell the assembler that what follows should be treated as a subroutine. Such assembler *directives* will be presented in Chapter 9.

6502 Subroutines

We have now described the subroutine mechanism, and how the stack is used to implement it. The subroutine call instruction for the 6502 is called JSR (jump to subroutine). It is, indeed, a 3-byte instruction. Unfortunately, it is an unconditional jump: it does not test bits. Explicit branches must be inserted prior to a JSR if a test need be performed.

The return from subroutine is the RTS instruction (Return from subroutine). It is a 1-byte instruction.

Exercise 3.18: *Why is the return from a subroutine as long as the CALL? (Hint: if the answer is not obvious, look again at the stack implementation of the subroutine mechanism and analyze the internal operations that must be performed.)*

Subroutine Examples

Most of the programs that we have developed and are going to develop would usually be written as subroutines. For example, the multiplication program is likely to be used by many areas of the program. In order to facilitate program development and clarify it, it is therefore convenient to define a subroutine whose name would be, for example, MULT. At the end of this subroutine we would simply add the instruction, RTS.

Exercise 3.19: *If MULT is used as a subroutine, would it "damage" any internal flags or registers?*

Recursion

Recursion is a word used to indicate that a subroutine is calling itself. If you have understood the implementation mechanism, you should now be able to answer the following question:

Exercise 3.20: *Is it legal to let a subroutine call itself? (In other words, will everything work even if a subroutine calls itself?) If you are not sure, draw the stack and fill it with the successive addresses. You will physically verify whether it works or not. This will answer the question. Then, look at the registers and memory (see Exercise 3.19) and determine if a problem exists.*

Subroutine Parameters

When calling a subroutine, one normally expects the subroutine to work on some data. For example, in the case of the multiplication, one wants to transmit two numbers to the subroutine which will perform the multiplication. We saw in the case of the multiplication routine that this subroutine expected to find the multiplier and the multiplicand in given memory locations. This illustrates the first method of passing parameters: through memory. Two other techniques are used, and parameters can be passed in three ways:
    1. Through registers

2. Through memory
3. Through the stack

—*Registers* can be used to pass parameters. This is an advantageous solution, provided that registers are available, since one does not need to use a fixed memory location. The subroutine remains memory-independent. If a fixed memory location is used, any other user of the subroutine must be very careful that he uses the same convention and that the memory location is indeed available (look at Exercise 3-20 above). This is why, in many cases, a block of memory locations is reserved, simply to pass parameters between various subroutines.

—*Using memory* has the advantage of greater flexibility (more data), but results in poorer performance and also in tying up the subroutine to a given memory area.

—Depositing parameters in *the stack* has the same advantage as using registers: it is memory-independent. The subroutine simply knows that it is supposed to receive, say, two parameters which are stored on top of the stack. Naturally, it has a disadvantage: it clutters the stack with data and, therefore, reduces the number of possible levels of subroutine calls.

The choice is up to the programmer. In general, one wishes to remain independent from actual memory locations as long as possible.

If registers are not available, the next best solution is usually the stack. However, if a large quantity of information should be passed to a subroutine, then this information will have to reside in the memory. An elegant way around the problem of passing a block of data is to simply transmit a pointer to the information. A *pointer* is the address at the beginning of the block. A pointer can be transmitted in a register (in the case of the 6502, this limits the pointer to 8 bits), or else in the stack (two-stack locations can be used to store a 16-bit address).

Finally, if neither of the two solutions is applicable, then an agreement may be made with the subroutine that the data will be at some fixed memory location (the "mailbox").

Exercise 3.21: *Which of the three methods above is best for recursion?*

Subroutine Library

There is a strong advantage to structuring portions of a program into identifiable subroutines: they can be debugged independently and can have a mnemonic name. Provided that they will be used in other areas of the program, they become shareable, and one can thus build a library of useful subroutines. However, there is no general panacea in computer programming. Using subroutines systematically for any set of instructions that can be grouped by function may also result in poor efficiency. The alert programmer will have to weigh the advantages vs. the disadvantages.

SUMMARY

This chapter has presented the way information is manipulated inside the 6502 by instructions. Increasingly complex algorithms have been introduced, and translated into programs. The main types of instructions have been used.

Important structures such as loops, stacks and subroutines have been defined.

You should now have acquired a basic understanding of programming, and of the major techniques used in standard applications. Let us study the instructions available.

4
THE 6502 INSTRUCTION SET

PART 1 - OVERALL DESCRIPTION

INTRODUCTION

This chapter will first analyze the various classes of instructions which should be available in a general purpose computer. It will then analyze one by one all of the instructions available for the 6502, and explain in detail their purpose and the manner in which they affect flags, or can be used in conjunction with the various addressing modes. A detailed discussion of addressing techniques will be presented in Chapter 5.

CLASSES OF INSTRUCTIONS

Instructions may be classified in many ways, and there is no standard. We will distinguish here five main categories of instructions:

1. data transfers
2. data processing
3. test and branch
4. input/output
5. control

Let us now examine in turn each of these classes of instructions.

Data transfers

Data transfer instructions will transfer 8-bit data between two registers, or between a register and memory, or between a register and an input/output device. Specialized transfer instructions may exist for registers which play a special role, for example, a push and pull operation, for efficient stack implementation. They will move a word of data between the top of the stack and the accumulator in a single instruction, while automatically updating the stack-pointer register.

Data Processing

Data processing instructions fall into four general categories:

- arithmetic operations (such as plus/minus)
- logical operations (such as AND, OR, exclusive OR)
- skew and shift operations (such as shift, rotate, swap)
- increment and decrement

It should be noted that for efficient data processing, it is desirable to have powerful arithmetic instructions, such as multiply and divide. Unfortunately, this is not available on most microprocessors. It is also desirable to have powerful shift and skew instructions, such as shift n bits, or a nibble exchange, where the right half and the left half of the byte are exchanged. These are also unavailable on most microprocessors.

Before examining the actual 6502 instructions, let us recall the difference between a *shift* and a *rotation*. The shift will move the contents of a register or a memory location by one bit location to the left or to the right. The bit falling out of the register will go into the carry bit. The bit coming in on the other side will be a "0."

In the case of a rotation, the bit coming out still goes in the carry. However, the bit coming in is the previous value which was in the carry bit. This corresponds to a 9-bit rotation. It would often be desirable to have a true 8-bit rotation where the bit coming in on one side is the one falling off on the other side. This is not usually provided on microprocessors. Finally, when shifting a word to the right, it is convenient to have one more type of shift called a sign-extension or an "arithmetic shift right". When doing operations on two's complement numbers, particularly when implementing floating-point routines, it is often necessary to shift a negative number to the right. When shifting a two's complement number to the right, the bit which must come in on the left side should be a 1 (the sign bit should get repeated as many times as needed by the suc-

6502 INSTRUCTION SET

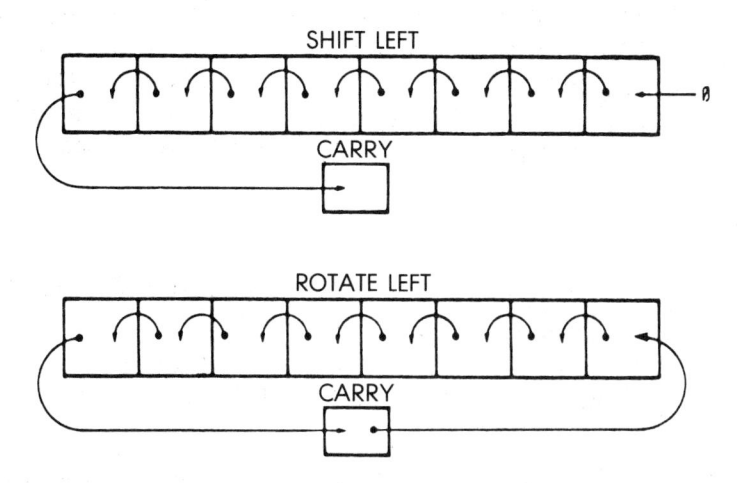

```
                    SHIFT LEFT
  ┌──┬──┬──┬──┬──┬──┬──┬──┐
  │↑ │↑ │↑ │↑ │↑ │↑ │↑ │↑ │── 0
  └──┴──┴──┴──┴──┴──┴──┴──┘
              CARRY
              ┌──┐
              └──┘

                    ROTATE LEFT
  ┌──┬──┬──┬──┬──┬──┬──┬──┐
  │↑ │↑ │↑ │↑ │↑ │↑ │↑ │↑ │←─
  └──┴──┴──┴──┴──┴──┴──┴──┘
              CARRY
              ┌──┐
              └──┘
```

Fig. 4-1: Shift and Rotate

cessive shifts). Unfortunately, this type of shift does not exist in the 6502. It exists in other microprocessors.

Test and Branch

The test instructions will test all bits of the flags register of "0" or "1," or combinations. It is, therefore, desirable to have as many flags as possible in this register. In addition, it is convenient to be able to test for combinations of such bits with a single instruction. Finally, it is desirable to be able to test any bit position in any register, and to test the value of a register compared to the value of any other register (greater than, less than, equal). Microprocessor test instructions are usually limited to testing single bits of the flags register.

The jump instructions that may be available generally fall into three categories:

- the jump proper, which specifies a full 16-bit address,
- the branch, which often is restricted to an 8-bit displacement field,
- the call, which is used with subroutines.

It is convenient to have two- or even three-way branches, depending, for example, on whether the result of a comparison is "greater than," "less than," or "equal." It is also convenient to have skip operations, which will jump forward or backwards by a few instructions. Finally, in most loops, there is usually a decrement or increment operation at the end, followed by a test and branch. The availability of a single-instruction increment/decrement plus test and branch is, therefore, a significant advantage for efficient loop implementation. This is not available in most microprocessors. Only simple branches, combined with simple tests, are available. This naturally complicates programming, and reduces efficiency.

Input/Output

Input/output instructions are specialized instructions for the handling of input/output devices. In practice, nearly all microprocessors use *memory-mapped I/O*. This means that input/output devices are connected to the address-bus, just like memory chips, and addressed as such. They appear to the programmer as memory locations. All memory-type operations can then be applied to desired devices. This has the advantage of providing a wide variety of instructions which can be applied. The disadvantage is that memory-type operations normally require 3 bytes and are, therefore, slow. For efficient input/output handling in such an environment, it is desirable to have a short addressing mechanism available so that I/O devices whose handling speed is crucial may reside in page 0. However, if page 0 addressing is available, it is usually used for RAM memory, and therefore prevents its effective use for input/output devices.

Control Instructions

Control instructions supply synchronization signals and may suspend or interrupt a program. They can also function as a break or a simulated interrupt. (Interrupts will be described in Chapter 6 on Input/Output Techniques.)

INSTRUCTIONS AVAILABLE ON THE 6502

Data Transfer Instructions

The 6502 has a complete set of data transfer instructions, except for the loading of the stack pointer, which is restricted in flexiblility. The contents of the accumulator may be exchanged with a memory location with the instructions LDA (load) and STA (store). The same applies to registers X and Y. These are, respectively, instructions LDX LDY, and STX STY. There is no direct loading for S. Inter-register transfers are naturally provided: the instructions are TAX (transfer A to X), TAY, TSX, TXA, TXS, TYA. There is a slight asymmetry, since the stack contents may be exchanged with X, but not with Y.

There is no 2-address memory to memory operation, such as "add contents of LPC1 and LOC2."

Stack Operations

Two "push" and "pop" operations are available. They transfer register A or the status register (P) to the top of the stack in the memory while updating the stack pointer S. They are PHA and PHP. The reverse instructions are PLA and PLP (pull A and pull P), which transfer the top of the stack respectively into A or P.

Data Processing

Arithmetic

The usual (restricted) complement of arithmetic, logical and shift functions is available. Arithmetic operations are: ADC, SBC. ADC is an addition with carry, and there is no addition without carry. This is a minor nuisance as it requires a CLC instruction prior to any addition. The subtraction is performed by SBC.

A special decimal mode is available which allows the direct addition and subtraction of numbers expressed in BCD. In many other microprocessors only one of these BCD instructions is available as a separate instruction code. The presence of the decimal flag multiplies by two the effective number of arithmetic operations available.

Increment/Decrement

Increment and decrement operations are available on the memory, and on index registers X and Y, but not on the accumulator. They are respectively: INC and DEC, which operate on the memory; INX, INY and DEX, DEY, which operate on index registers X and Y.

Logical Operations

The logical operations are the classic ones: AND, ORA, EOR. The role of each of these instructions will be clarified.

AND

Each logical operation is characterized by a truth table, which expresses the logical value of the result in function of the inputs. The truth table for AND appears below:

$$0 \text{ AND } 0 = 0$$
$$0 \text{ AND } 1 = 0$$
$$1 \text{ AND } 0 = 0$$
$$1 \text{ AND } 1 = 1$$

The AND operation is characterized by the fact that the output is "1" only if both inputs are "1." In other words, if one of the inputs is "0," it is guaranteed that the result is "0." This feature is used to zero a bit position in a word. This is called "masking."

One of the important uses of the AND instruction is to clear or mask out one or more specified bit positions in a word. Assume, for example, that we want to zero the right-most four-bit positions in a word. This will be performed by the following program:

```
LDA   WORD              WORD CONTAINS '10101010'
AND   #%11110000        '11110000' IS MASK
```

Let us assume that WORD is equal to '10101010.' The result of this program is to leave in the accumulator the value '1010 0000.' "%" is used to represent a binary number.

Exercise 4.1: *Write a three-line program which will zero bits 1 and 6 of WORD.*

Exercise 4.2: *What happens with a mask: MASK = '11111111'?*

ORA

This instruction is the inclusive OR operation. It is charac-

6502 INSTRUCTION SET

terized by the following truth table:

$$0 \text{ OR } 0 = 0$$
$$0 \text{ OR } 1 = 1$$
$$1 \text{ OR } 0 = 1$$
$$1 \text{ OR } 1 = 1$$

The logical OR is characterized by the fact that if any one of the operands is "1", the result is to set any bit in a word to="1".

```
LDA #WORD
ORA #%00001111
```

Let us assume that WORD did contain '10101010.' The final value of the accumulator will be '10101111.'

Exercise 4.3: *What would happen if we were to use the instruction ORA #%10101111?*

Exercise 4.4: *What is the effect of ORing with "FF" hexadecimal?*

EOR

EOR stands for "exclusive OR." The exclusive OR differs from the inclusive OR, that we have just described, in one respect: the result is "0" only if one, and only one, of the operands is equal to "1." If both operands are equal to "1," the normal OR would give a "1" result. The exclusive OR gives a "0" result. The truth table is:

$$0 \text{ EOR } 0 = 0$$
$$0 \text{ EOR } 1 = 1$$
$$1 \text{ EOR } 0 = 1$$
$$1 \text{ EOR } 1 = 0$$

The exclusive OR is used for comparisons. If any bit is different, the exclusive OR of two words will be non-zero. In addition, in the case of the 6502, the exclusive OR is used to *complement* a word, since there is no specific complement instruction. This is done by performing the EOR of a word with all 1's. The program appears below:

```
LDA     #WORD
EOR     #%11111111
```

Let us assume that WORD did contain "10101010." The final value of the accumulator will be "01010101." We can verify that this is the complement of the original value.

Exercise 4.5:   *What is the effect of EOR #$00?*

Shift Operations

The standard 6502 is equipped with a left shift, called ASL (arithmetic shift left), and a right shift, called LSR (logical shift right). They will be described below.

However, the 6502 has only one rotate instruction, to the left (ROL).

Warning: newer versions of the 6502 have an extra rotate instruction. Check the manufacturer's data to verify this fact. (ROR = rotate right)

Comparisons

Registers X, Y, A can be compared to the memory with instructions CPX, CPY, CMP.

Test and Branch

Since testing is almost exclusively performed on the flags register, let us examine now the flags available in the 6502. The contents of the flags register appear in Figure 4-2 below.

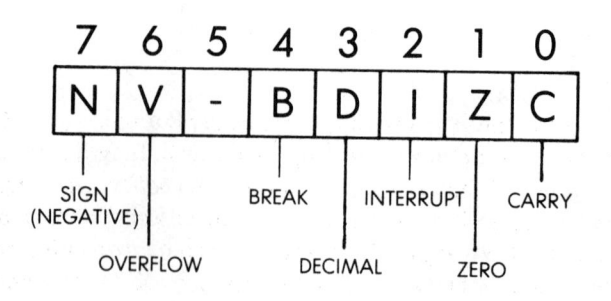

```
   7   6   5   4   3   2   1   0
 ┌───┬───┬───┬───┬───┬───┬───┬───┐
 │ N │ V │ - │ B │ D │ I │ Z │ C │
 └───┴───┴───┴───┴───┴───┴───┴───┘
   │   │       │   │   │   │
  SIGN │     BREAK │ INTERRUPT CARRY
(NEGATIVE)         │
       │           │       │
    OVERFLOW    DECIMAL   ZERO
```

Fig. 4-2: The Flags Register

6502 INSTRUCTION SET

Let us examine the function of the flags from left to right.

Sign

The left-most bit is the sign bit, or negative bit. Whenever N is 1, it indicates that the value of a result is negative in two's complement representation. In practice, flag N is identical to bit 7 of a result. It is set, or reset, by all data transfers and data processing instructions.

The N flag is identical to bit 7 of the accumulator, in most cases. As a result, bit 7 of the accumulator is the only bit that one can test conveniently with a single instruction. To test any other bit of the accumulator, it is necessary to shift its contents. In all cases where one wants to test the contents of the word quickly, the preferred bit position will, therefore, be bit 7. This is why input/output status bits are normally connected to position 7 of the data-bus. When reading the status of an I/O device, one will simply read the contents of the external status register into the accumulator and then test bit N.

The bit within the accumulator which is the next easiest to test is bit Z (zero). However, it requires a right shift by 1 into the carry bit so that it can be tested. It indicates whether a result is zero. Bit Z may not be set by the programmer. It is automatically set by instructions.

Instructions that set N are: ADC, AND, ASL, BIT, CMP, CPY, CPX, DEC, DEX, DEY, EOR, INC, INX, INY, LDA, LDX, LDY, LSR, ORA, PLA, PLP, ROL, ROR, TAX, TAY, TXS, TXA, TYA.

Overflow

The role of the overflow has already been discussed in Chapter 3 in the section on arithmetic operations. It is used to indicate that the result of the addition or subtraction of two's complement numbers might be incorrect because of an overflow from bit 6 to bit 7, i.e., into the sign bit. A special correction routine must be used whenever this bit is set. If one does not use two's complement representation, but direct binary, the overflow bit is equivalent to a carry from bit 6 into bit 7.

A special use of this bit is made by the BIT instruction. A result of this instruction is to set the "V" bit identical to bit 6 of the data being tested.

The V flag is conditioned by ADC, BIT, CLV, PLP, RTI, SBC.

Break

This break flag is automatically set by the processor if an interrupt is caused by the BRK command. It differentiates between a programmed break and a hardware interrupt. No other user instruction will modify it.

Decimal

The use of this flag has already been discussed in Chapter 3 in the section on arithmetic programs. Whenever D is set to "1", the processor operates in *BCD mode*, and whenever it is set to "0", it operates in *binary mode*. This flag is conditioned by four instructions: CLD, PLP, RTI, SED.

Interrupt

This interrupt-mask bit may be set explicitly by the programmer with the CLI or PLP instructions, or by the microprocessor during the reset or during an interrupt.

Its effect is to inhibit any further interrupt.

Instructions which condition this bit are: BRK, CLI, PLP, RTI, SEI.

Zero

The Z flag indicates, when set (equal to "1"), that the result of a transfer or an operation is a zero. It is also set by the comparison instruction. There is no specific instruction which will set or clear

6502 INSTRUCTION SET

the Z bit. However, the same result can easily be accomplished. In order to set the zero bit, one can, for example, execute the following instruction:

LDA #0

The Z bit is conditioned by many instructions: ADC, AND, ASL, BIT, CMP, CPY, CPX, DEC, DEX, DEY, EOR, INC, INX, INY, LDA, LDX, LDY, LSR, ORA, PLA, PLP, ROL, ROR, RTI, SBC, TAX, TAY, TXA, TYA.

Carry

It has been seen that the carry bit is used for a dual purpose. Its first purpose is to indicate an arithmetic carry or borrow during arithmetic operations. Its second purpose is to store the bit "falling out" of a register during the shift or rotate operations. The two roles do not necessarily need be confused, and they are not on larger computers. However, this approach saves time in the microprocessor, in particular for the implementation of a multiplication or a division. The carry bit can be set or cleared explicitly.

Instructions which will condition the carry bit are: ADC, ASL, CLC, CMP, CPX, CPY, LSR, PLP, ROL, ROR, RTI, SBC, SEC.

Test and Branch Instructions

In the 6502, it is not possible to test every bit of the flags register for one or zero. There are 6 bits which can be tested, and there are, therefore, 12 different branch instructions. They are:

— BMI (branch on minus), BPL (branch on plus). These two instructions, naturally, test the N bit.
— BCC (branch on carry clear) and BCS (branch on carry set): they test C.
— BEQ (branch when result is null) and BNE (branch on result not zero). They test Z.
— BVS (branch when overflow is set) and BVC (branch on overflow clear). They test V.

These instructions test and branch within the same instruction. All branches specify a displacement relative to the current instruction. Since the displacement field is 8 bits, this allows a displacement of -128 to $127 (in two's complement). The displacement is added to the address of the first instruction following the branch.

Since all branches are 2 bytes long, this results in an effective displacement of $-128 + 2 = $ -126 to $127 + 2 = +129$.

Two more unconditional instructions are available: JMP and JSR. JMP is a jump to a 16-bit address. JSR is a subroutine call. It jumps to a new address and automatically preserves the program counter into the stack. Being unconditional, these two instructions are usually preceded by a "test and branch" instruction.

Two returns are available: RTI, a return from interrupt, which will be discussed in the interrupt section, and RTS, a return from subroutine, which pulls a return address from the stack (and increments it).

Two special instructions are provided especially for bit-testing and for comparisons.

The BIT instruction performs an AND between the memory location and the accumulator. One important aspect is that *it does not change the contents of the accumulator*. The flag N is set to the value of bit 7 of the location tested, while the V flag is set to bit 6 of the memory location being tested. Finally, bit Z indicates the result of the AND operation. Z is set to "1" if the result is "0". Typically a mask will be loaded in the accumulator, and successive memory values will then be tested using the BIT instruction. If the mask contains a single "1" for example, this will test whether any given memory word does contain a "1" in that position. In practice, this means that a mask should be used only when one is testing memory bit locations "0" to "5". The reader will remember that bit locations "6" and "7" are automatically stored respectively in the "V" flag and in the "N" flag. They do not need to be masked.

The CMP instruction will compare the contents of the memory location to those of the accumulator by subtracting it from the accumulator. The result of the comparison will be indicated, therefore, by bits Z and N. One can detect equality, greater than, or less than. The value of the accumulator is not changed by the comparison. CPX and CPY will compare to X and Y respectively.

Input/Output Instructions

There are no specialized input/output instructions in the 6502.

Control Instructions

Control instructions include specialized instructions to set or clear the flags. They are: CLC, CLD, CLI, CLV, which clear respectively bits C, D, I and V; and SEC, SED, SEI, which set respectively in bits C, D, and I.

The BRK instruction is the equivalent of a software interrupt and will be described in Chapter 7 in the interrupt section.

The NOP instruction is an instruction which has no effect and is commonly used to extend the timing of a loop. Finally, two special pins on the 6502 will trigger an interrupt mechanism, and this will be explained in Chapter 6 on input/output techniques. It is a hardware control facility (IRQ and NMI pins).

Let us now examine each instruction in detail.

In order to truly understand the various addressing modes, the reader is encouraged to read the following section quickly the first time, and then in more detail the second time after studying Chapter 5 on Addressing Techniques.

PART 2 - THE INSTRUCTIONS

ABBREVIATIONS

A	Accumulator
M	Specified address (memory)
P	Status register
S	Stack pointer
X	Index register
Y	Index register
DATA	Specified data
HEX	Hexadecimal
PC	Program counter
PCH	Program counter high
PCL	Program counter low
STACK	Contents of top of stack
V	Logical or
$\wedge$	Logical and
$\forall$	Exclusive or
•	Change
$\leftarrow$	Receives the value of (assignment)
( )	Contents of
(M6)	Bit position 6 at address M

6502 INSTRUCTION SET

ADC Add with carry

Function: A ← (A) + DATA + C

Format:

| 011bbb01 | ADDR/DATA | ADDR |

Description:
Add the contents of memory address or literal to the accumulator, plus the carry bit. The result is left in the accumulator.

Remarks:

—ADC may operate either in decimal or binary mode: flags must be set to the correct value
—To ADD without carry, flag C must be cleared (CLC).

Data Paths:

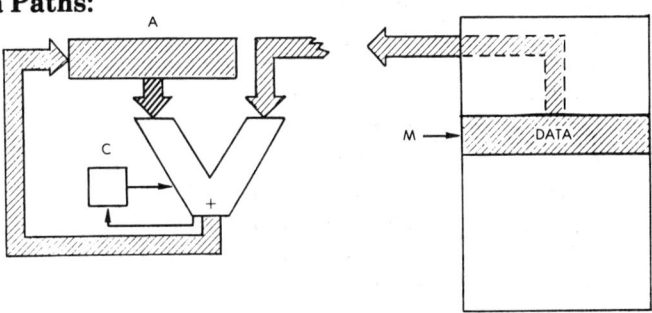

Addressing Modes:

	IMPLIED	ACCUMULATOR	ABSOLUTE	0-PAGE	IMMEDIATE	ABS. X	ABS. Y	(IND. X)	(IND). Y	0-PAGE. X	0-PAGE. Y	RELATIVE	INDIRECT
HEX			6D	65	69	7D	79	61	71	75			
BYTES			3	2	2	3	3	2	2	2			
CYCLES			4	3	2	4*	4*	6	5*	4			
bbb			011	001	010	111	110	000	100	101			

*: PLUS 1 CYCLE IF CROSSING PAGE BOUNDARY.

Flags:

N	V	B	D	I	Z	C
●	●				●	●

113

PROGRAMMING THE 6502

Instruction Codes:

ABSOLUTE	01101101	16-BIT ADDRESS	
	bbb = 011	HEX = 6D	CYCLES = 4
ZERO-PAGE	01100101	ADDR	
	bbb = 001	HEX = 65	CYCLES = 3
IMMEDIATE	01101001	DATA	
	bbb = 010	HEX = 69	CYCLES = 2
ABSOLUTE, X	01111101	16-BIT ADDRESS	
	bbb = 111	HEX = 7D	CYCLES = 4*
ABSOLUTE, Y	01111001	16-BIT ADDRESS	
	bbb = 110	HEX = 79	CYCLES = 4*
(IND, X)	01100001	ADDR	
	bbb = 000	HEX = 61	CYCLES = 6
(IND), Y	01110001	ADDR	
	bbb = 100	HEX = 71	CYCLES = 5*
ZERO-PAGE, X	01110101	ADDR	
	bbb = 101	HEX = 75	CYCLES = 4

*: PLUS 1 CYCLE IF CROSSING PAGE BOUNDARY.

6502 INSTRUCTION SET

AND   Logical AND

Function: A ← (A) ∧ DATA

Format: | 001bbb01 | ADDR/DATA | ADDR |

Description:

Perform the logical AND of the accumulator and specified data. The result is left in the accumulator.

The truth table is:

A\M	0	1
0	0	0
,1	0	1

Data Paths:

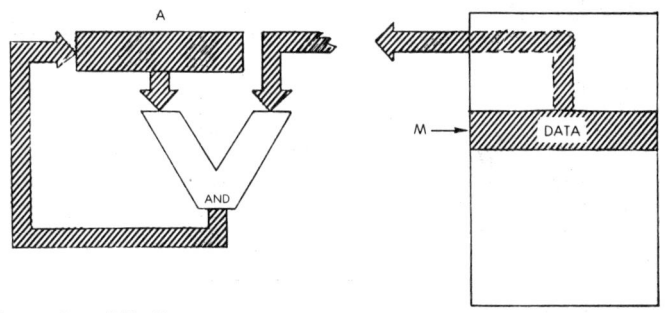

Addressing Modes:

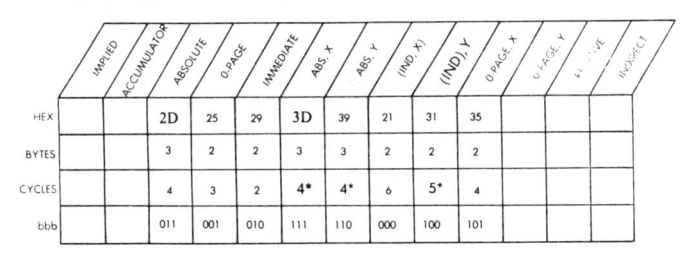

	IMPLIED	ACCUMULATOR	ABSOLUTE	0-PAGE	IMMEDIATE	ABS. X	ABS. Y	(IND, X)	(IND), Y	0-PAGE, X	0-PAGE, Y	RELATIVE	INDIRECT
HEX			2D	25	29	3D	39	21	31	35			
BYTES			3	2	2	3	3	2	2	2			
CYCLES			4	3	2	4*	4*	6	5*	4			
bbb			011	001	010	111	110	000	100	101			

*: PLUS 1 CYCLE IF CROSSING PAGE BOUNDARY.

Flags:

N	V	B	D	I	Z	C
●					●	

115

PROGRAMMING THE 6502

Instruction Codes:

Mode	Opcode	bbb	Operand	HEX	Cycles
ABSOLUTE	00101101	bbb = 011	16-BIT ADDRESS	HEX = 2D	CYCLES = 4
ZERO-PAGE	00100101	bbb = 001	ADDR	HEX = 25	CYCLES = 3
IMMEDIATE	00101001	bbb = 010	DATA	HEX = 29	CYCLES = 2
ABSOLUTE, X	00111101	bbb = 111	16-BIT ADDRESS	HEX = 3D	CYCLES = 4*
ABSOLUTE, Y	00111001	bbb = 110	16-BIT ADDRESS	HEX = 39	CYCLES = 4*
(IND, X)	00100001	bbb = 000	ADDR	HEX = 21	CYCLES = 6
(IND), Y	00110001	bbb = 100	ADDR	HEX = 31	CYCLES = 5*
ZERO-PAGE, X	00110101	bbb = 101	ADDR	HEX = 35	CYCLES = 4

*: PLUS 1 CYCLE IF CROSSING PAGE BOUNDARY.

6502 INSTRUCTION SET

ASL — Arithmetic shift left

Function:

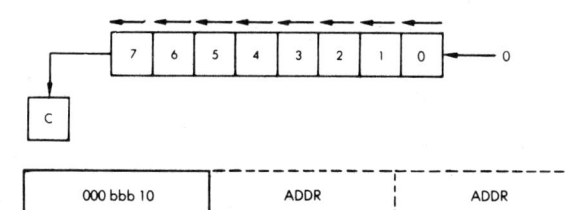

```
     ┌──────────────────────────┐
  ┌──┤ 7 | 6 | 5 | 4 | 3 | 2 | 1 | 0 │◄── 0
  │  └──────────────────────────┘
  ▼
  C
```

Format:

| 000 bbb 10 | ADDR | ADDR |

Description:

Move the contents of the accumulator or of the memory location left by one bit position. 0 comes in on the right. Bit 7 falls into the carry. The result is deposited in the source, i.e. either accumulator or memory.

Data paths:

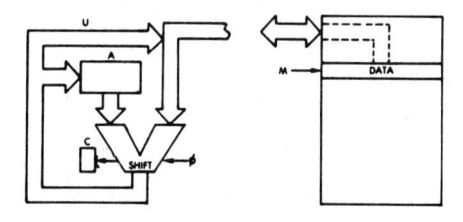

Addressing Modes:

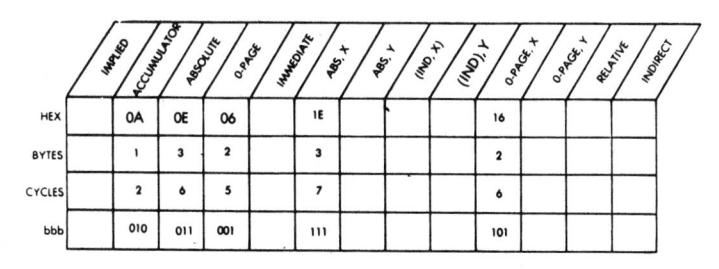

	IMPLIED	ACCUMULATOR	ABSOLUTE	0-PAGE	IMMEDIATE	ABS. X	ABS. Y	(IND, X)	(IND), Y	0-PAGE, X	0-PAGE, Y	RELATIVE	INDIRECT
HEX		0A	0E	06	1E				16				
BYTES		1	3	2	3				2				
CYCLES		2	6	5	7				6				
bbb		010	011	001	111				101				

Flags:

N	V	B	D	I	Z	C
●					●	●

117

PROGRAMMING THE 6502

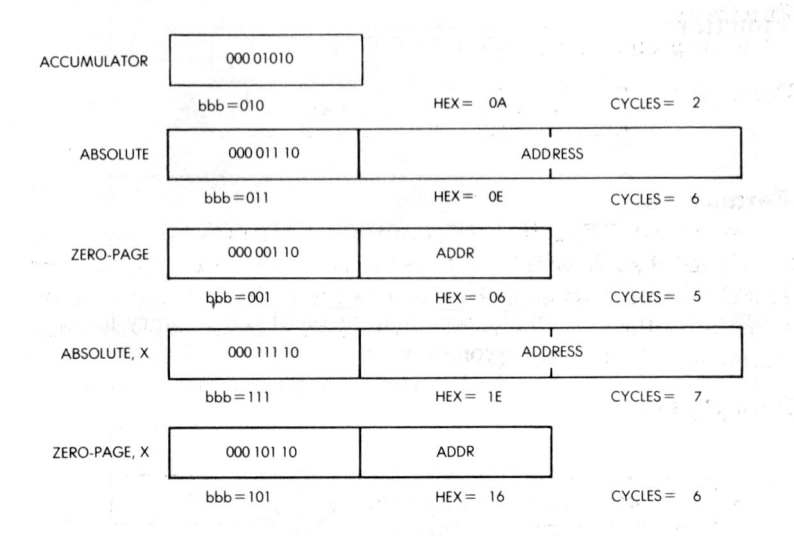

Instruction Codes:

ACCUMULATOR	000 01010	HEX = 0A	CYCLES = 2
	bbb = 010		
ABSOLUTE	000 011 10 / ADDRESS	HEX = 0E	CYCLES = 6
	bbb = 011		
ZERO-PAGE	000 001 10 / ADDR	HEX = 06	CYCLES = 5
	bbb = 001		
ABSOLUTE, X	000 111 10 / ADDRESS	HEX = 1E	CYCLES = 7
	bbb = 111		
ZERO-PAGE, X	000 101 10 / ADDR	HEX = 16	CYCLES = 6
	bbb = 101		

6502 INSTRUCTION SET

BCC   Branch on carry clear

Function:
Go to specified address if C = 0

Format:

1001000	DISPLACEMENT

Description:
Test the carry flag. If C = 0, branch to the current address plus the signed displacement (up to +127 or −128). If C = 1, take no action. The displacement is added to the address of the first instruction following the BCC. This results in an effective displacement of +129 to −126.

Data Paths:

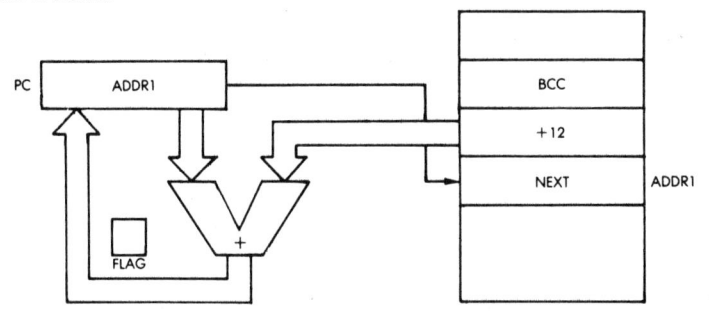

Addressing Mode:

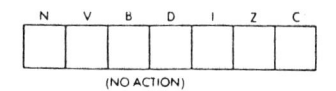

Relative only:
HEX = 90, bytes = 2, cycles = 2   + 1 if branch succeeds
                                                         + 2 if into another page

Flags:

(NO ACTION)

119

BCS   Branch on carry set

Function:
 Go to specified address if C = 1

Format: | 10110000 | DISPLACEMENT |

Description:
 Test the carry flag. If C = 1, branch to the current address plus the signed displacement (up to +127 or −128). If C = 0, take no action. The displacement is added to the address of the first instruction following the BCS. This results in an effective displacement of +129 to −126.

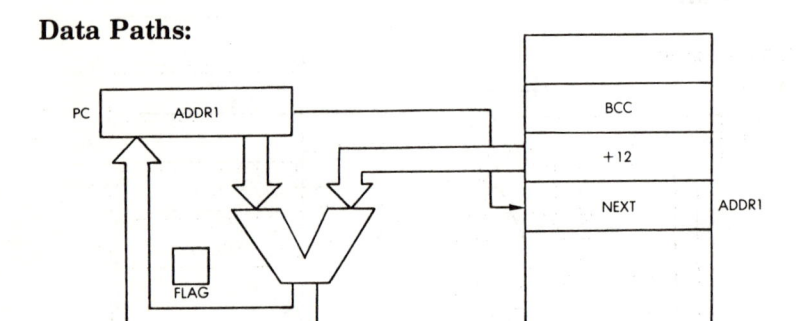

Data Paths:

Addressing Mode:
 Relative only:
 HEX = B0, bytes = 2, cycles = 2   +1 if branch succeeds
                                                   +2 if into another page

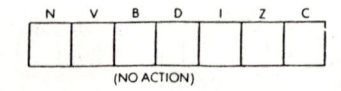

Flags:

N	V	B	D	I	Z	C

(NO ACTION)

6502 INSTRUCTION SET

BEQ — Branch if equal to zero

Function:
Go to specified address if Z = 1 (result = 0).

Format:

11110000	DISPLACEMENT

Description:
Test the Z flag. If Z = 1, branch to the current address plus the signed displacement (up to +127 or −128). If Z = 0, take no action.

The displacement is added to the address of the first instruction following the BEQ. This results in an effective displacement of +129 to −126.

Data Paths:

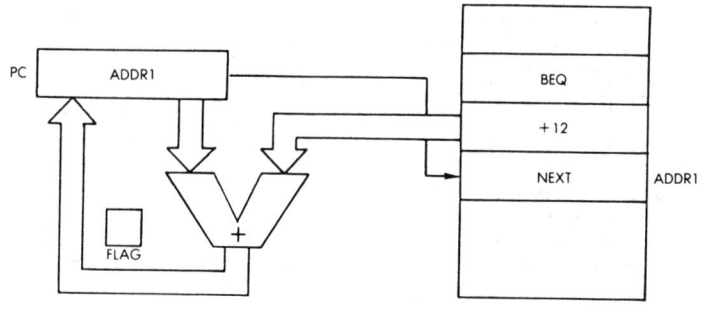

```
   PC  ┌─────ADDR1──────┐                    ┌──────────┐
       │                │─────────────┐      │   BEQ    │
       │                │             │      ├──────────┤
       ▲                ▼             │      │   +12    │
       │               ▽▽             │      ├──────────┤
       │                +             └─────▶│   NEXT   │  ADDR1
       │              FLAG                   │          │
       └────────────────┘                    └──────────┘
```

Addressing Mode:
Relative only:
HEX = F0, bytes = 2, cycles = 2   +1 if branch succeeds
                                   +2 if into another page

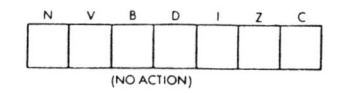

Flags:

N	V	B	D	I	Z	C

(NO ACTION)

121

BIT — Compare memory bits with accumulator

Function:
$Z \leftarrow \overline{(A) \land (M)}$, $N \leftarrow (M^7)$, $V \leftarrow (M^6)$

Format:

0010b100	ADDR	ADDR

Description:

The logical AND of A and M is performed, but not stored. The result of the comparison is indicated by Z. Z = 1 if the comparison succeeds; 0 otherwise. In addition, bits 6 and 7 of the memory data are transferred into V and N of the status register. It does not modify the contents of A.

Data Paths:

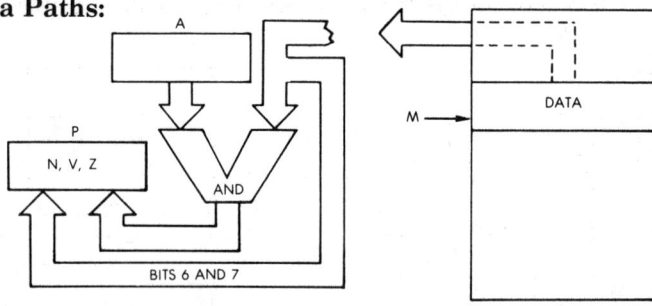

Addressing Modes:

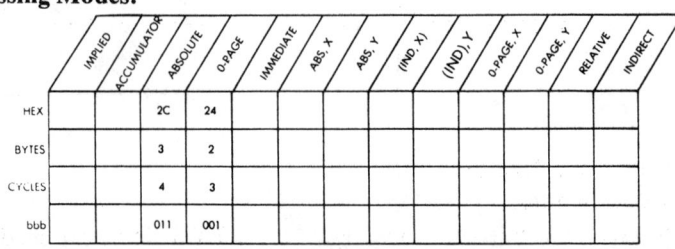

	IMPLIED	ACCUMULATOR	ABSOLUTE	O-PAGE	IMMEDIATE	ABS, X	ABS, Y	(IND, X)	(IND), Y	O-PAGE, X	O-PAGE, Y	RELATIVE	INDIRECT
HEX			2C	24									
BYTES			3	2									
CYCLES			4	3									
bbb			011	001									

Flags:

N	V	B	D	I	Z	C
M₇	M₆				●	

Instruction Codes:

ABSOLUTE | 00101100 | 16-BIT ADDRESS
HEX = 2C   CYCLES = 4

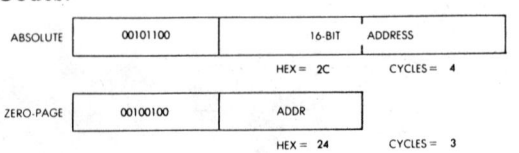

ZERO-PAGE | 00100100 | ADDR
HEX = 24   CYCLES = 3

6502 INSTRUCTION SET

BMI   Branch on minus

Function:
Go to specified address if N = 1 (result < 0).

Format:

00110000	DISPLACEMENT

Description:
Test the N flag (sign). If N = 1, branch to the current address plus the signed displacement (up to +127 or −128). If N = 0, take no action.

The displacement is added to the address of the first instruction following the BMI. This results in an effective displacement of +129 to −126.

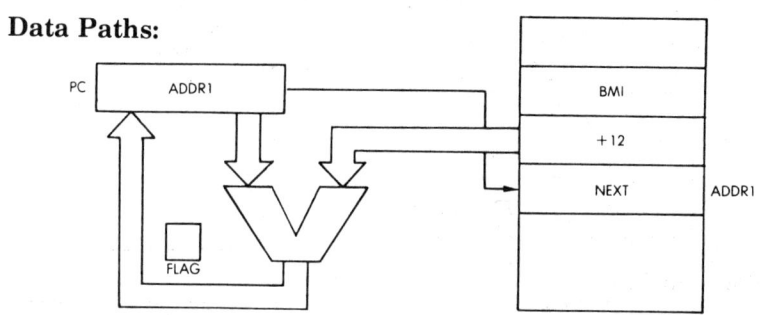

Data Paths:

```
PC ─ ADDR1 ──────────────┐
    ▲   │                │   BMI
    │   ▼                │
    │  ╲╱                │   +12
    │  FLAG              │
    │                    │   NEXT    ADDR1
```

Addressing Mode:
Relative only:
HEX = 30, bytes = 2, cycles = 2   +1 if branch succeeds
                                                              +2 if into another page

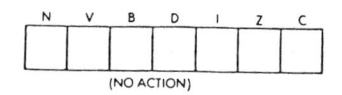

Flags:

N	V	B	D	I	Z	C

(NO ACTION)

BNE Branch on not equal to zero

Function:
Go to specified address if Z = 0 (result ≠ 0).

Format:

11010000	DISPLACEMENT

Description:
Test the result (Z flag). If the result is not equal to 0 (Z = 0), branch to the current address plus the signed displacement (up to +127 to −128). If Z = 1, take no action.

The displacement is added to the address of the first instruction following the BNE. This results in an effective displacement of +129 to −126.

Data Paths:

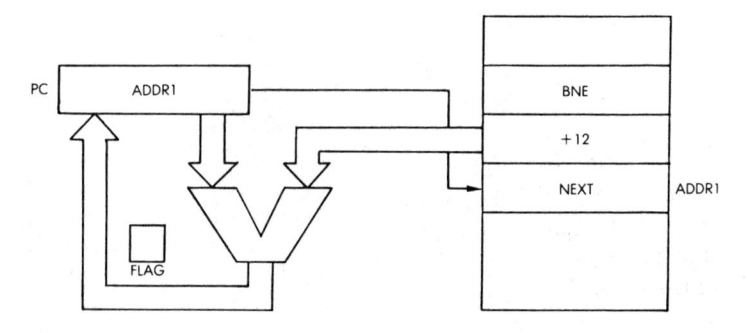

Addressing Mode:
Relative only:
HEX = D0, bytes = 2, cycles = 2   +1 if branch succeeds
                                    +2 if into another page

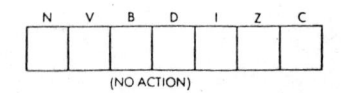

Flags:

N	V	B	D	I	Z	C

(NO ACTION)

BPL Branch on plus

Function:
Go to specified address if N = 0 (result ≥ 0).

Format:

| 00010000 | DISPLACEMENT |

Description:
Test the N flag (sign). If N = 0 (result positive), branch to the current address plus the signed displacement (up to +127 or −128). If N = 0, take no action.

The displacement is added to the address of the first instruction following the BPL. This results in an effective displacement of +129 to −126.

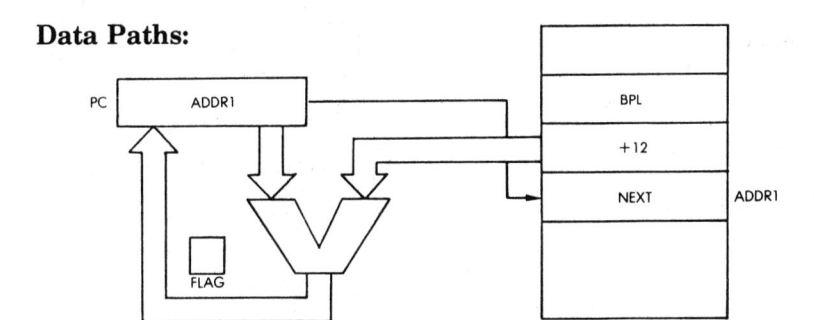

Data Paths:

Addressing Mode:
Relative only:
HEX = 10, bytes = 2, cycles = 2 +1 if branch succeeds
                                 +2 if into another page

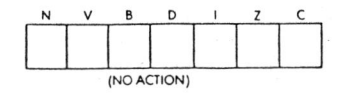

Flags:

N	V	B	D	I	Z	C

(NO ACTION)

BRK   Break

Function:
   STACK (PC) + 2, STACK (P), PC ◄─(FFFE,FFFF)

Format: | 00000000 |

Description:
Operates like an interrupt: the program counter is pushed on the stack, then the status register P. The contents of memory locations FFFE and FFFF are then deposited respectively in PCL and PCH. The value of P stored in the stack has the B flag set to 1, to differentiate a BRK from an IRQ.

Important: unlike an interrupt, PC + 2 is saved. This may not be the next instruction, and a correction may be necessary. This is due to the normal use of BRK to patch existing programs where BRK replaces a 2-byte instruction.

Data Paths:

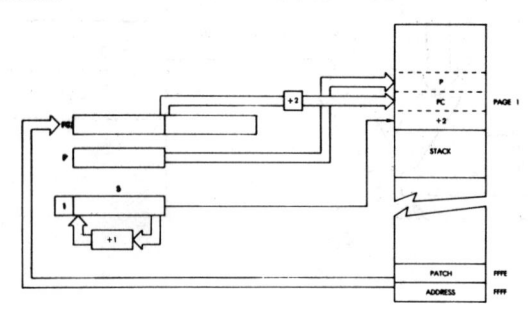

Addressing Mode:
   Implied only:
   HEX = 00 , byte = 1, cycles = 7

Flags:

N	V	B	D	I	Z	C
		★		1		

Note: B is set in before P is pushed in the stack.

6502 INSTRUCTION SET

BVC Branch on overflow clear

Function:
Go to specified address if V = 0.

Format:

0101000	DISPLACEMENT

Description:
Test the overflow flag (V). If there is no overflow (V = 0), branch to the current address plus the signed displacement (up to +127 or −128). If V = 1, take no action.

The displacement is added to the address of the first instruction following the BVC. This results in an effective displacement of +129 to −126.

Data Paths:

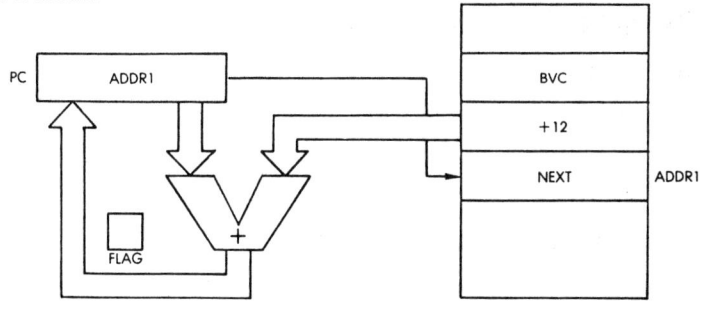

Addressing Mode:
Relative only:
Hex = 50, bytes = 2, cycles = 2   +1 if branch succeeds
                                   +2 if into another page

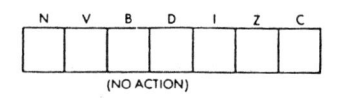

Flags:

N	V	B	D	I	Z	C

(NO ACTION)

127

BVS Branch on overflow set

Function:
Go to specified address if V = 1.

Format:

01110000	DISPLACEMENT

Description:
Test the overflow flag (V). If an overflow has occurred (V = 1), branch to the current address plus the signed displacement (up to +127 or −128). If V = 0, take no action.

The displacement is added to the address of the first instruction following the BVS. This results in an effective displacement of +129 to −126.

Data Paths:

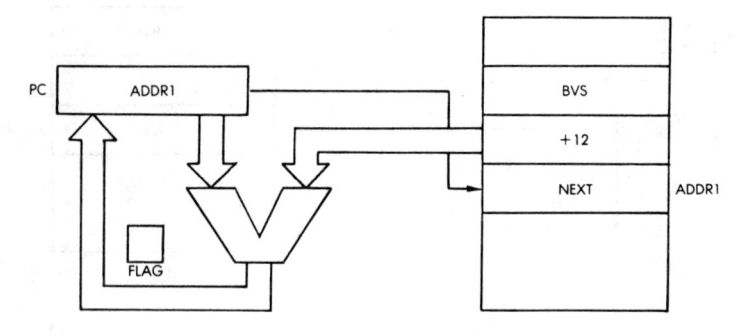

Addressing Mode:
Relative only:
HEX = 70, bytes = 2, cycles = 2   +1 if branch succeeds
+2 if into another page

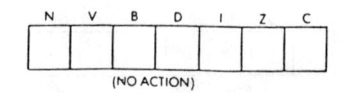

Flags:

(NO ACTION)

CLC   Clear carry

Function:
  C ← ∅

Format:
  ` 00011000 `

Description:
  The carry bit is cleared. This is often necessary before an ADC.

Addressing Mode:
  Implied only
  HEX = 18, byte = 1, cycles = 2

Flags:

N	V	B	D	I	Z	C
						∅

CLD   Clear decimal flag

Function:
D ← ∅

Format:

11011000

Description:

The D flag is cleared, setting the binary mode for ADC and SBC.

Addressing Mode:
Implied only:
HEX = D8, byte = 1, cycles = 2

Flags:

N	V	B	D	I	Z	C
			∅			

CLI

Clear interrupt mask

Function:
I ← ∅

Format:

01011000

Description:

The interrupt mask bit is set to 0. This enables interrupts. An interrupt handling routine must always clear the I bit, or else other interrupts may be lost.

Addressing Mode:
Implied only:
HEX = 58, byte= 1, cycles= 2

Flags:

N	V	B	D	I	Z	C
				∅		

CLV — Clear overflow flag

Function:
V ← ∅

Format: `10111000`

Description:
The overflow flag is cleared.

Addressing Mode:
Implied only:
HEX = B8, byte = 1, cycles = 2

Flags:

N	V	B	D	I	Z	C
	∅					

6502 INSTRUCTION SET

CMP — Compare to accumulator

Function:
(A) − DATA → NZC:

+ (A > DATA)	=	− (A < DATA)
−01	011	−00

Format:

110bbb01	ADDR/DATA	ADDR

Description:

The specified contents are subtracted from A. The result is not stored, but flags NZC are conditioned, depending on whether the result is positive, null or negative. The value of the accumulator is not changed. Z is set by an equality, reset otherwise; N is set; reset by the sign (bit 7), C is set when (A) ⩾ DATA. CMP is usually followed by a branch: BCC detects A < DATA, BEQ detects A = DATA, BCS detects A ⩾ DATA, and BEQ followed by BCS detects A ⩾ DATA.

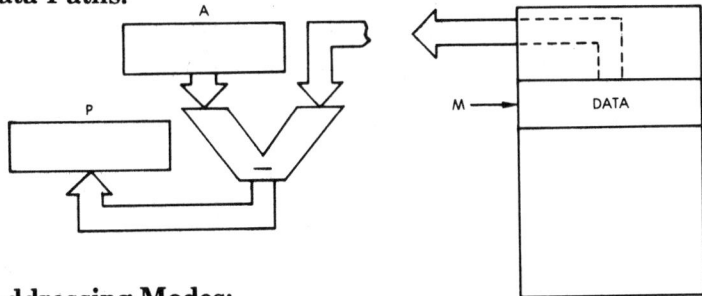

Data Paths:

Addressing Modes:

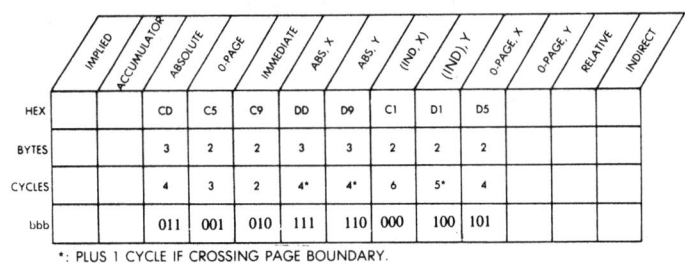

	IMPLIED	ACCUMULATOR	ABSOLUTE	0-PAGE	IMMEDIATE	ABS, X	ABS, Y	(IND, X)	(IND), Y	0-PAGE, X	0-PAGE, Y	RELATIVE	INDIRECT
HEX			CD	C5	C9	DD	D9	C1	D1	D5			
BYTES			3	2	2	3	3	2	2	2			
CYCLES			4	3	2	4*	4*	6	5*	4			
bbb			011	001	010	111	110	000	100	101			

*: PLUS 1 CYCLE IF CROSSING PAGE BOUNDARY.

Flags:

N	V	B	D	I	Z	C
●					●	●

PROGRAMMING THE 6502

Instruction Codes:

ABSOLUTE	11001101	16-BIT ADDRESS
	bbb = 011	HEX = CD CYCLES = 4

ZERO-PAGE	11000101	ADDR
	bbb = 001	HEX = C5 CYCLES = 3

IMMEDIATE	11001001	DATA
	bbb = 010	HEX = C9 CYCLES = 2

ABSOLUTE, X	11011101	16-BIT ADDRESS
	bbb = 111	HEX = DD CYCLES = 4*

ABSOLUTE, Y	11011001	16-BIT ADDRESS
	bbb = 110	HEX = D9 CYCLES = 4*

(IND, X)	11000001	ADDR
	bbb = 000	HEX = C1 CYCLES = 6

(IND), Y	11010001	ADDR
	bbb = 100	HEX = D1 CYCLES = 5*

ZERO-PAGE, X	11010101	ADDR
	bbb = 101	HEX = D5 CYCLES = 4

*: PLUS 1 CYCLE IF CROSSING PAGE BOUNDARY.

6502 INSTRUCTION SET

CPX — Compare to register X

Function:
X − DATA → NZC:

+(X > DATA)	=	−(X < DATA)
−01	011	−00

Format:

1110bb00	ADDR/DATA	ADDR

Description:

The specified contents are subtracted from X. The result is not stored, but flags NZC are conditioned, depending on whether the result is positive, null or negative. The value of the accumulator is not changed. CMP is usually followed by a branch: BCC detects (X) < DATA, BEQ detects (X) = DATA, and BEQ followed by BCS detects (X) > DATA. BCS detects (X) ≥ DATA.

Data Paths:

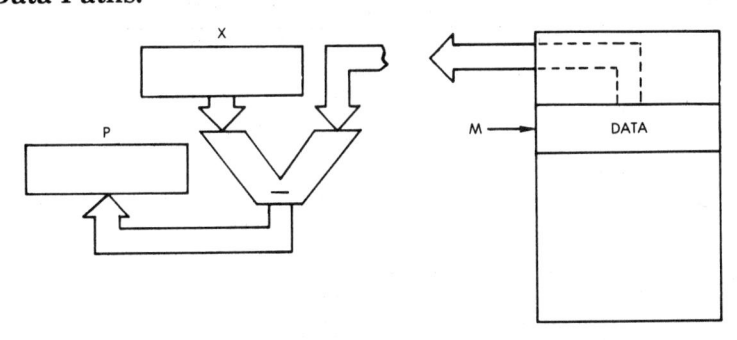

Addressing Modes:

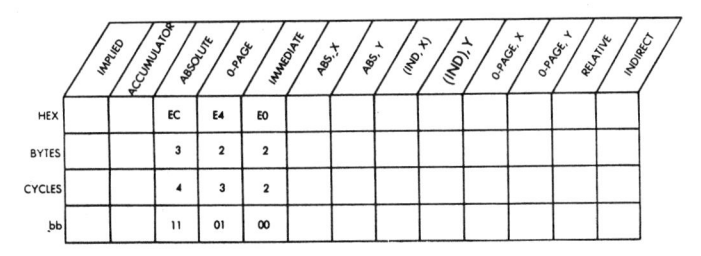

	IMPLIED	ACCUMULATOR	ABSOLUTE	0-PAGE	IMMEDIATE	ABS. X	ABS. Y	(IND, X)	(IND), Y	0-PAGE, X	0-PAGE, Y	RELATIVE	INDIRECT
HEX			EC	E4	E0								
BYTES			3	2	2								
CYCLES			4	3	2								
bb			11	01	00								

Flags:

N	V	B	D	I	Z	C
●					●	●

PROGRAMMING THE 6502

Instruction Codes:

ABSOLUTE	11101100	16-BIT ADDRESS	
	bb = 11	HEX = EC	CYCLES = 4

ZERO-PAGE	11100100	ADDR	
	bb = 01	HEX = E4	CYCLES = 3

IMMEDIATE	11100000	DATA	
	bb = 00	HEX = E0	CYCLES = 2

6502 INSTRUCTION SET

CPY   Compare to register Y

Function:
(Y) – DATA ➤ NZC:

+(Y > DATA)	=	–(Y < DATA)
–01	011	–00

Format:

| 1100bb00 | ADDR/DATA | ADDR |

Description:

The specified contents are subtracted from Y. The result is not stored, but flags NZC are conditioned, depending on whether the result is positive, null or negative. The value of the accumulator is not changed. CMP is usually followed by a branch: BCC detects Y < data, BEQ detects Y = data, and BEQ followed by BCS detects Y > data. BCS detects Y ≥ data.

Data Paths:

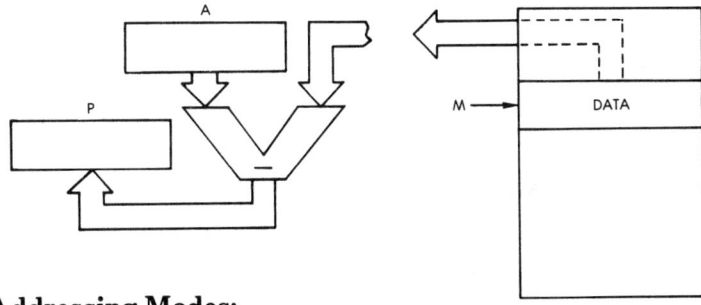

Addressing Modes:

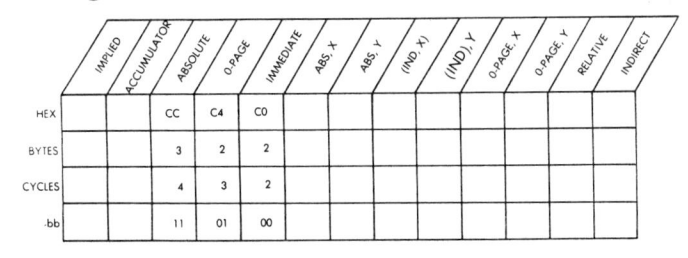

	IMPLIED	ACCUMULATOR	ABSOLUTE	O.PAGE	IMMEDIATE	ABS, X	ABS, Y	(IND, X)	(IND), Y	O.PAGE, X	O.PAGE, Y	RELATIVE	INDIRECT
HEX			CC	C4	C0								
BYTES			3	2	2								
CYCLES			4	3	2								
.bb			11	01	00								

Flags:

N	V	B	D	I	Z	C
●					●	●

137

Instruction Codes:

ABSOLUTE	11001100	16-BIT ADDRESS	
	bb = 11	HEX = CC	CYCLES = 4
ZERO-PAGE	11000100	ADDR	
	bb = 01	HEX = C4	CYCLES = 3
IMMEDIATE	11000000	DATA	
	bb = 00	HEX = C0	CYCLES = 2

DEC Decrement

Function:
M ← (M) − 1

Format:

110bb110	ADDR	ADDR

Description:
The contents of the specified memory address are decremented by 1. The result is stored back at the specified memory address.

Data Paths:

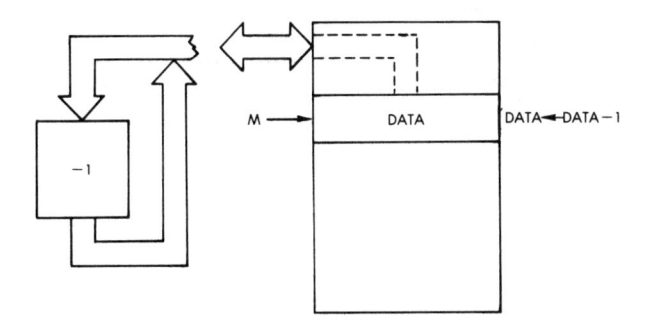

Addressing Modes:

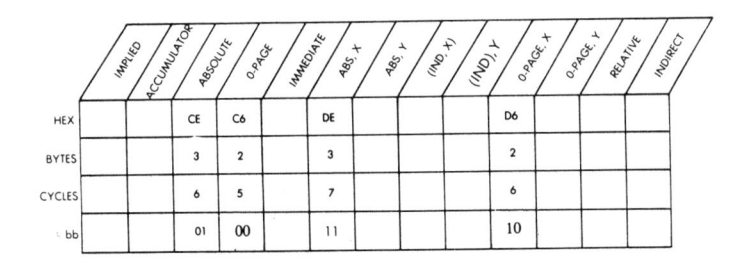

	IMPLIED	ACCUMULATOR	ABSOLUTE	O-PAGE	IMMEDIATE	ABS, X	ABS, Y	(IND, X)	(IND), Y	O-PAGE, X	O-PAGE, Y	RELATIVE	INDIRECT
HEX			CE	C6		DE				D6			
BYTES			3	2		3				2			
CYCLES			6	5		7				6			
bb			01	00		11				10			

Flags:

N ● V B D I Z ● C

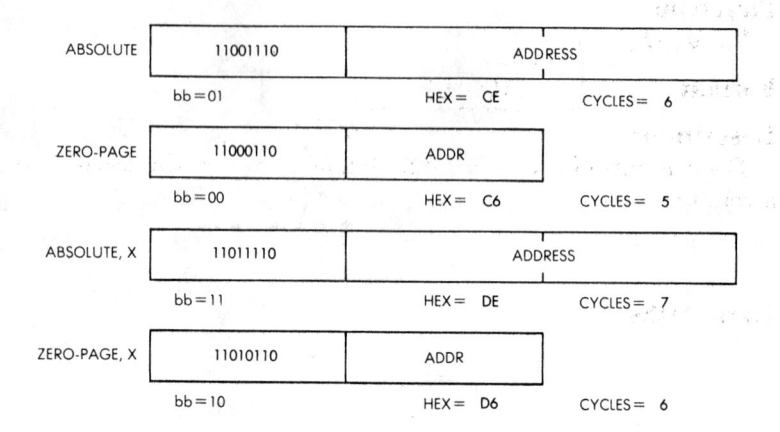

PROGRAMMING THE 6502

Instruction Codes:

ABSOLUTE	11001110	ADDRESS
	bb = 01 HEX = CE CYCLES = 6	
ZERO-PAGE	11000110	ADDR
	bb = 00 HEX = C6 CYCLES = 5	
ABSOLUTE, X	11011110	ADDRESS
	bb = 11 HEX = DE CYCLES = 7	
ZERO-PAGE, X	11010110	ADDR
	bb = 10 HEX = D6 CYCLES = 6	

DEX   Decrement X

Function:
$X \leftarrow (X) - 1$

Format: | 11001010 |

Description:
The contents of X are decremented by 1. Allows the use of X as a counter.

Data Paths:

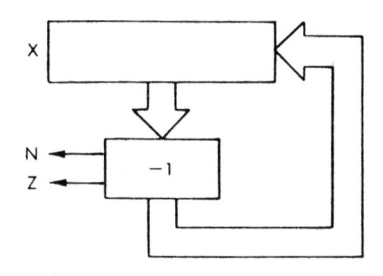

Addressing Mode:
Implied only:
HEX = CA, byte = 1, cycles = 2

Flags:

N ●, V, B, D, I, Z ●, C

DEY Decrement Y

Function:
Y ← (Y) −1

Format: | 10001000 |

Description:
The contents of Y are decremented by 1. Allows the use of Y as a counter.

Data Paths:

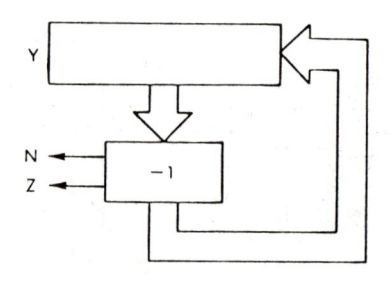

```
        ┌─────────────────┐
      Y │                 │◄─────┐
        └────────┬────────┘      │
                 ▼               │
        ┌─────────────────┐      │
      N◄┤      −1         │      │
      Z◄┤                 ├──────┘
        └─────────────────┘
```

Addressing Mode:
Implied only:
HEX = 88, byte = 1, cycles = 2

Flags:

N	V	B	D	I	Z	C
●					●	

EOR — Exclusive—OR with accumulator

Function:
A ← (A) ∀ DATA

Format:

010bbb01	ADDR/DATA	ADDR

Description:

The contents of the accumulator are exclusive–ORed with the specific data. The truth table is:

	0	1
0	0	1
1	1	0

Note: EOR with "-1" may be used to complement.

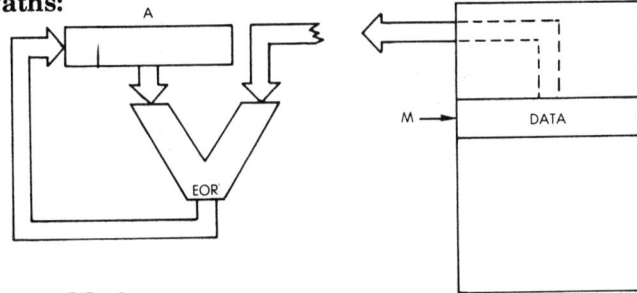

Data Paths:

Addressing Modes:

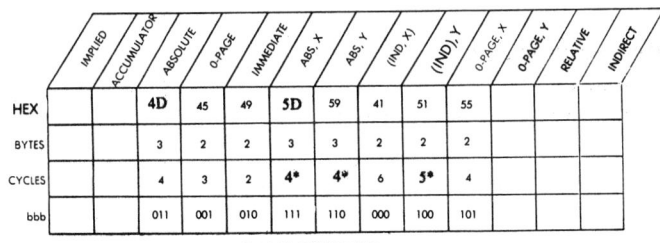

	IMPLIED	ACCUMULATOR	ABSOLUTE	O-PAGE	IMMEDIATE	ABS. X	ABS. Y	(IND, X)	(IND), Y	O-PAGE, X	O-PAGE, Y	RELATIVE	INDIRECT
HEX			4D	45	49	5D	59	41	51	55			
BYTES			3	2	2	3	3	2	2	2			
CYCLES			4	3	2	4*	4*	6	5*	4			
bbb			011	001	010	111	110	000	100	101			

*: PLUS 1 CYCLE IF CROSSING PAGE BOUNDARY.

Flags:

N	V	B	D	I	Z	C
●					●	

143

PROGRAMMING THE 6502

Instruction Codes:

Mode	Opcode	Operand		
ABSOLUTE	01001101	16-BIT ADDRESS		
	bbb = 011	HEX = 4D	CYCLES = 4	
ZERO-PAGE	01000101	ADDR		
	bbb = 001	HEX = 45	CYCLES = 3	
IMMEDIATE	01001001	DATA		
	bbb = 010	HEX = 49	CYCLES = 2	
ABSOLUTE, X	01011101	16-BIT ADDRESS		
	bbb = 111	HEX = 5D	CYCLES = 4*	
ABSOLUTE, Y	01011001	16-BIT ADDRESS		
	bbb = 110	HEX = 59	CYCLES = 4*	
(IND, X)	01000001	ADDR		
	bbb = 000	HEX = 41	CYCLES = 6	
(IND), Y	01010001	ADDR		
	bbb = 100	HEX = 51	CYCLES = 5*	
ZERO-PAGE, X	01010101	ADDR		
	bbb = 101	HEX = 55	CYCLES = 4	

*: PLUS 1 CYCLE IF CROSSING PAGE BOUNDARY.

6502 INSTRUCTION SET

INC   Increment memory

Function:
  M ← (M) +1

Format: | 111bb110 | ADDR | ADDR |

Description:
The contents of the specified memory location are incremented by one, then redeposited into it.

Data Paths:

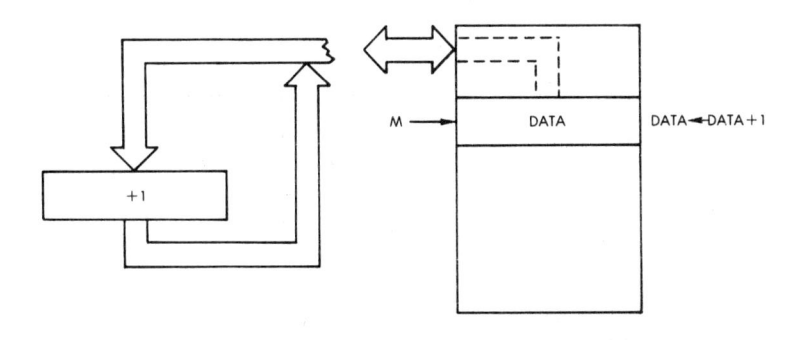

M → DATA   DATA ← DATA +1

Addressing Modes:

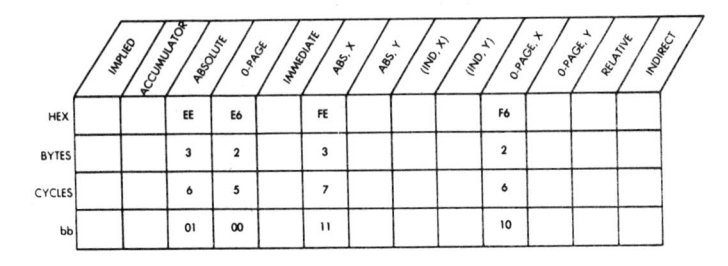

	IMPLIED	ACCUMULATOR	ABSOLUTE	0-PAGE	IMMEDIATE	ABS. X	ABS. Y	(IND. X)	(IND. Y)	0-PAGE. X	0-PAGE. Y	RELATIVE	INDIRECT
HEX			EE	E6	FE					F6			
BYTES			3	2	3					2			
CYCLES			6	5	7					6			
bb			01	00	11					10			

Flags:

N ●   V ○   B ○   D ○   I ○   Z ●   C ○

145

PROGRAMMING THE 6502

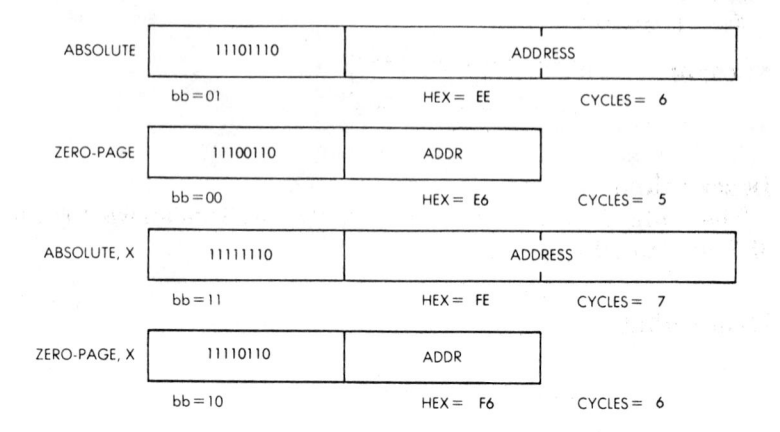

Instruction Codes:

ABSOLUTE	11101110	ADDRESS
bb = 01	HEX = EE	CYCLES = 6

ZERO-PAGE	11100110	ADDR
bb = 00	HEX = E6	CYCLES = 5

ABSOLUTE, X	11111110	ADDRESS
bb = 11	HEX = FE	CYCLES = 7

ZERO-PAGE, X	11110110	ADDR
bb = 10	HEX = F6	CYCLES = 6

INX   Increment X

Function:
  X ← (X) +1

Format:

11101000

Description:
  The contents of X are incremented by one. This allows the use of X as counter.

Data Paths:

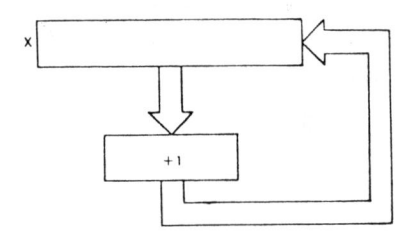

Addressing Mode:
  Implied only:
  HEX = E8, byte = 1, cycles = 2

Flags:

N	V	B	D	I	Z	C
●					●	

INY   Increment Y

Function:
Y ← (Y) + 1

Format:

11001000

Description:
The contents of Y are incremented by one. This allows the use of Y as counter.

Data Paths:

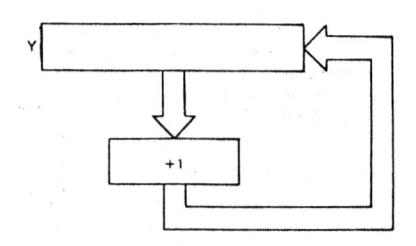

```
    ┌─────────────────┐
    │        Y        │←──┐
    └────────┬────────┘   │
             ▼            │
         ┌──────┐         │
         │  +1  │─────────┘
         └──────┘
```

Addressing Mode:
Implied only:
HEX = C8, byte = 1, cycles = 2

Flags:

N	V	B	D	I	Z	C
●					●	

6502 INSTRUCTION SET

JMP Jump to address

Function:
  PC ← ADDRESS

Format: | 01b01100 | ADDRESS |

Description:
A new address is loaded in the program counter, causing a jump to occur in the program sequence. The address specification may be absolute or indirect.

Data Paths:

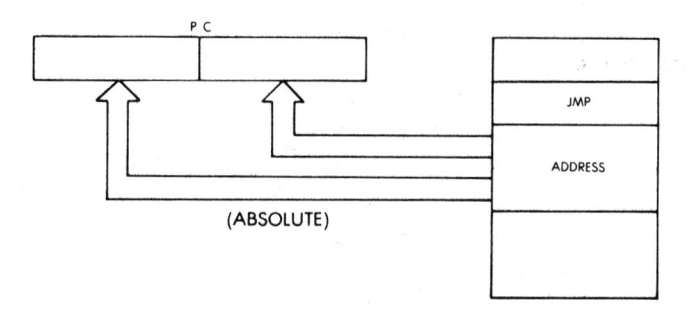

(ABSOLUTE)

JMP
ADDRESS

Addressing Modes:

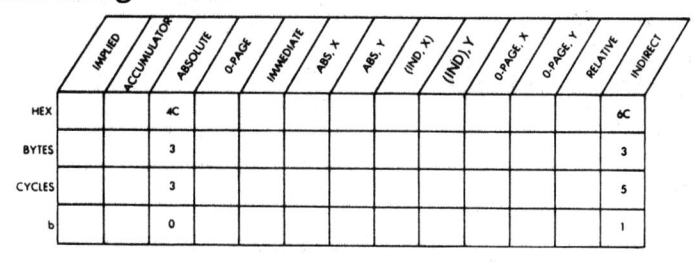

	IMPLIED	ACCUMULATOR	ABSOLUTE	O-PAGE	IMMEDIATE	ABS. X	ABS. Y	(IND. X)	(IND), Y	O-PAGE, X	O-PAGE, Y	RELATIVE	INDIRECT
HEX			4C										6C
BYTES			3										3
CYCLES			3										5
b			0										1

Flags:

N	V	B	D	I	Z	C

(NO EFFECT)

149

PROGRAMMING THE 6502

Instruction Codes:

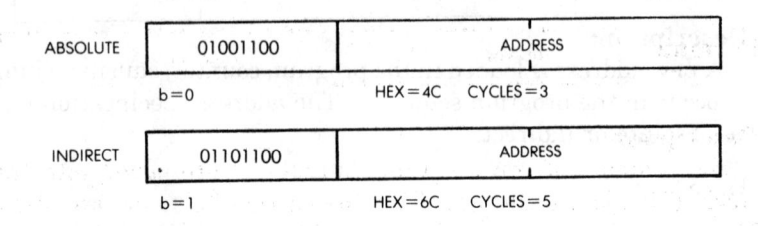

ABSOLUTE	01001100	ADDRESS

b=0   HEX=4C   CYCLES=3

INDIRECT	01101100	ADDRESS

b=1   HEX=6C   CYCLES=5

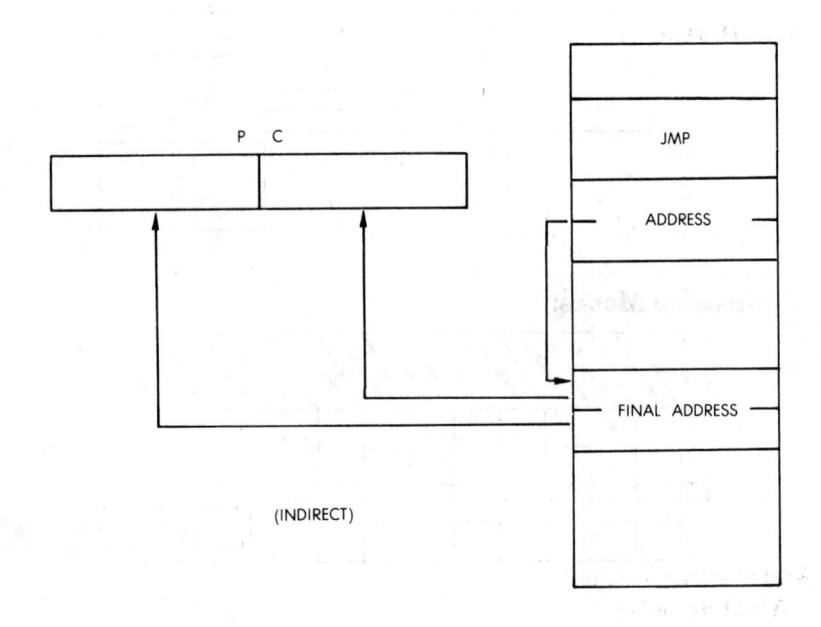

```
              P  C
       ┌─────────┬─────────┐           ┌──────────────┐
       │         │         │           │              │
       └─────────┴─────────┘           │     JMP      │
            ▲         ▲                │              │
            │         │                │   ADDRESS    │
            │         │                │              │
            │         └────────────────│              │
            │                          │              │
            │                          │ FINAL ADDRESS│
            └──────────────────────────│              │
                                       │              │
              (INDIRECT)               └──────────────┘
```

6502 INSTRUCTION SET

JSR Jump to subroutine

Function:
STACK ← (PC) +2
PC ← ADDRESS

Format:

00100000	ADDRESS

Description:

The contents of the program counter +2 are saved into the stack. (This is the address of the instruction following the JSR). The subroutine address is then loaded into PC. This is also called a "subroutine CALL."

Data Paths:

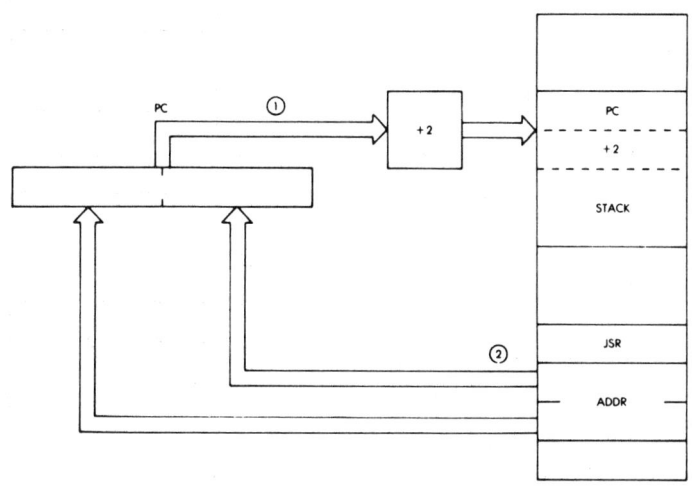

Addressing Mode:
Absolute only:
HEX = 20, bytes = 3, cycles = 6

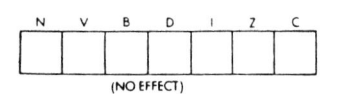

Flags:

N V B D I Z C
(NO EFFECT)

PROGRAMMING THE 6502

LDA   Load accumulator

Function:
 A ← DATA

Format:

101bbb01	ADDR/DATA	ADDR

Description:
 The accumulator is loaded with new data.

Data Paths:

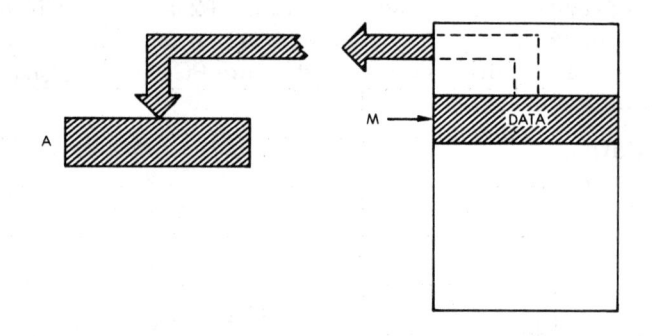

Addressing Modes:

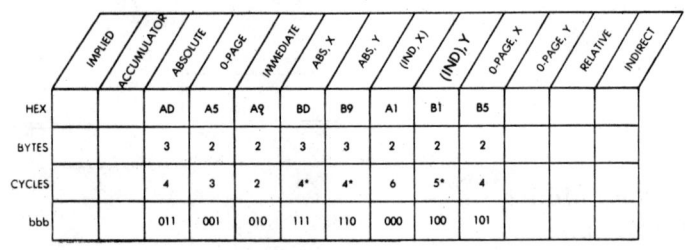

	IMPLIED	ACCUMULATOR	ABSOLUTE	0-PAGE	IMMEDIATE	ABS. X	ABS. Y	(IND, X)	(IND), Y	0-PAGE, X	0-PAGE, Y	RELATIVE	INDIRECT
HEX			AD	A5	A9	BD	B9	A1	B1	B5			
BYTES			3	2	2	3	3	2	2	2			
CYCLES			4	3	2	4*	4*	6	5*	4			
bbb			011	001	010	111	110	000	100	101			

*: PLUS 1 CYCLE IF CROSSING PAGE BOUNDARY.

Flags:

N	V	B	D	I	Z	C
●					●	

152

6502 INSTRUCTION SET

Instruction Codes:

Mode	Opcode (binary)	Operand		
ABSOLUTE	10101101	16-BIT ADDRESS		
	bbb = 011	HEX = AD	CYCLES = 4	
ZERO-PAGE	10100101	ADDR		
	bbb = 001	HEX = A5	CYCLES = 3	
IMMEDIATE	10101001	DATA		
	bbb = 010	HEX = A9	CYCLES = 2	
ABSOLUTE, X	10111101	16-BIT ADDRESS		
	bbb = 111	HEX = BD	CYCLES = 4*	
ABSOLUTE, Y	10111001	16-BIT ADDRESS		
	bbb = 110	HEX = B9	CYCLES = 4*	
(IND, X)	10100001	ADDR		
	bbb = 000	HEX = A1	CYCLES = 6	
(IND), Y	10110001	ADDR		
	bbb = 100	HEX = B1	CYCLES = 5*	
ZERO-PAGE, X	10110101	ADDR		
	bbb = 101	HEX = B5	CYCLES = 4	

*: PLUS 1 CYCLE IF CROSSING PAGE BOUNDARY.

PROGRAMMING THE 6502

LDX   Load register X

Function:
X ← DATA

Format: | 101bbb10 | ADDR/DATA | ADDR |

Description:
Index register X is loaded with data from the specified address.

Data Paths:

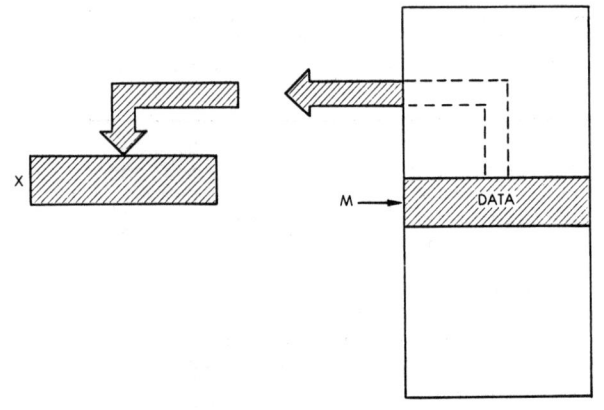

Addressing Modes:

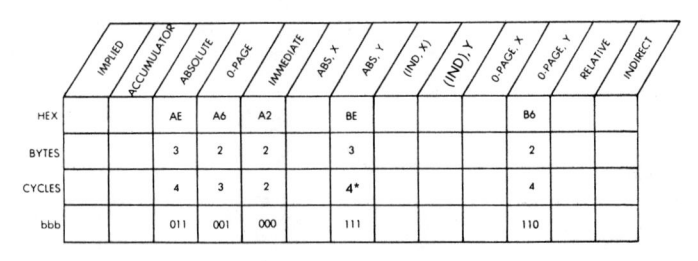

	IMPLIED	ACCUMULATOR	ABSOLUTE	O.PAGE	IMMEDIATE	ABS. X	ABS. Y	(IND, X)	(IND), Y	O.PAGE, X	O.PAGE, Y	RELATIVE	INDIRECT
HEX			AE	A6	A2		BE				B6		
BYTES			3	2	2		3				2		
CYCLES			4	3	2		4*				4		
bbb			011	001	000		111				110		

*: PLUS 1 CYCLE IF CROSSING PAGE BOUNDARY.

Flags:

N	V	B	D	I	Z	C
●					●	

154

6502 INSTRUCTION SET

Instruction Codes:

Mode	Opcode (binary)	Operand		
ABSOLUTE	10101110	16-BIT ADDRESS		
	bbb = 011	HEX = AE	CYCLES = 4
ZERO-PAGE	10100110	ADDR		
	bbb = 001	HEX = A6	CYCLES = 3
IMMEDIATE	10100010	DATA		
	bbb = 000	HEX = A2	CYCLES = 2
ABSOLUTE, Y	10111110	16-BIT ADDRESS		
	bbb = 111	HEX = BE	CYCLES = 4*
ZERO PAGE, Y	10111010	ADDR		
	bbb = 110	HEX = B6	CYCLES = 4

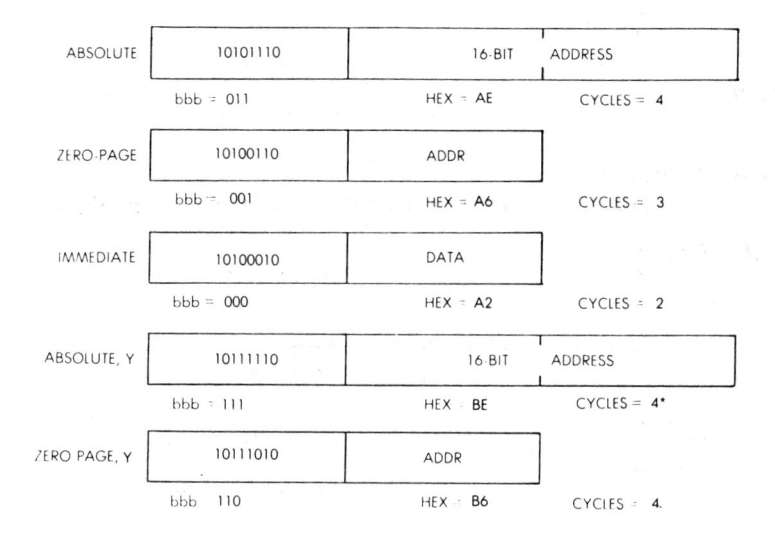

*: PLUS 1 CYCLE IF CROSSING PAGE BOUNDARY.

PROGRAMMING THE 6502

LDY   Load register Y

Function:
Y ← DATA

Format: | 101bbb00 | ADDR/DATA | ADDR |

Description:
Index register Y is loaded with data from the specified address.

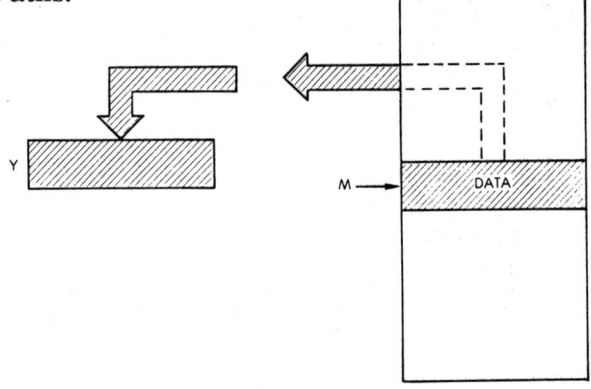

Data Paths:

Addressing Modes:

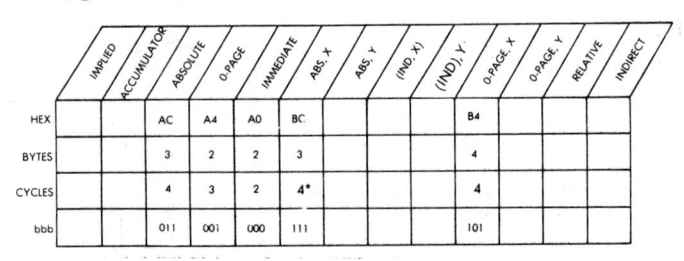

	IMPLIED	ACCUMULATOR	ABSOLUTE	0-PAGE	IMMEDIATE	ABS, X	ABS, Y	(IND, X)	(IND), Y	0-PAGE, X	0-PAGE, Y	RELATIVE	INDIRECT
HEX			AC	A4	A0	BC				B4			
BYTES			3	2	2	3				4			
CYCLES			4	3	2	4*				4			
bbb			011	001	000	111				101			

*: PLUS 1 CYCLE IF CROSSING PAGE BOUNDARY.

Flags:

N ●   V   B   D   I   Z ●   C

6502 INSTRUCTION SET

Instruction Codes:

Mode	Opcode (binary)	Operand		
ABSOLUTE	10101100	16-BIT ADDRESS		
	bbb = 011	HEX = AC	CYCLES = 4	
ZERO-PAGE	10100100	ADDR		
	bbb = 001	HEX = A4	CYCLES = 3	
IMMEDIATE	10100000	DATA		
	bbb = 000	HEX = A0	CYCLES = 2	
ABSOLUTE, X	10111100	16-BIT ADDRESS		
	bbb = 111	HEX = BC	CYCLES = 4*	
ZERO-PAGE, X	10110100	ADDR		
	bbb = 101	HEX = B4	CYCLES = 4	

*: PLUS 1 CYCLE IF CROSSING PAGE BOUNDARY.

LSR Logical shift right

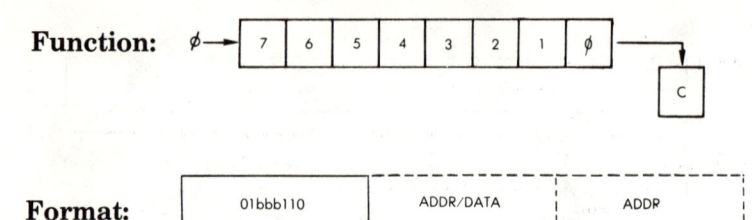

Function: ∅ → [7][6][5][4][3][2][1][∅] → C

Format: | 01bbb110 | ADDR/DATA | ADDR |

Description:

Shift the specified contents (accumulator or memory) right by one bit position. A "0" is forced into bit 7. Bit 0 is transferred to the carry. The shifted data is deposited in the source, i.e., either accumulator or memory.

Data Paths:

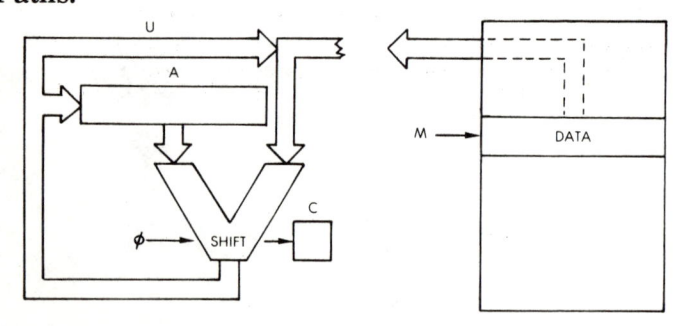

Addressing Modes:

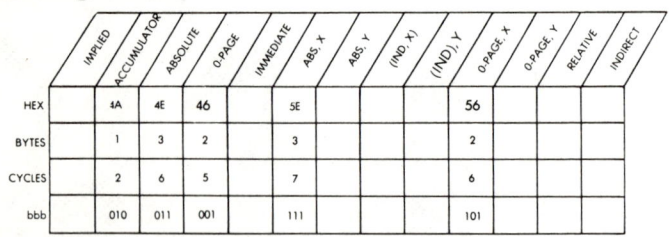

	IMPLIED	ACCUMULATOR	ABSOLUTE	0-PAGE	IMMEDIATE	ABS. X	ABS. Y	(IND, X)	(IND), Y	0-PAGE, X	0-PAGE, Y	RELATIVE	INDIRECT
HEX		4A	4E	46	5E					56			
BYTES		1	3	2	3					2			
CYCLES		2	6	5	7					6			
bbb		010	011	001	111					101			

Flags:

N	V	B	D	I	Z	C
∅					●	●

6502 INSTRUCTION SET

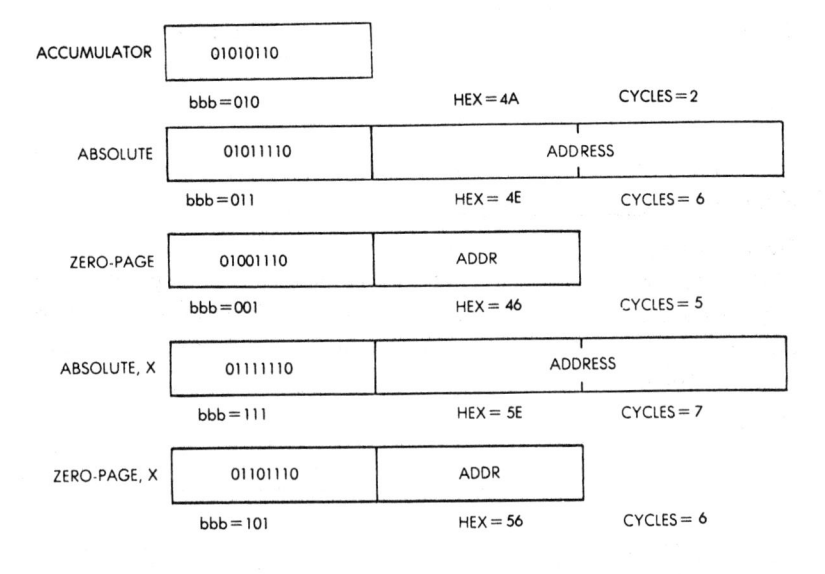

Instruction Codes:

Mode	Opcode	bbb	HEX	CYCLES
ACCUMULATOR	01010110	bbb=010	HEX=4A	CYCLES=2
ABSOLUTE	01011110 + ADDRESS	bbb=011	HEX=4E	CYCLES=6
ZERO-PAGE	01001110 + ADDR	bbb=001	HEX=46	CYCLES=5
ABSOLUTE, X	01111110 + ADDRESS	bbb=111	HEX=5E	CYCLES=7
ZERO-PAGE, X	01101110 + ADDR	bbb=101	HEX=56	CYCLES=6

NOP No operation

Function:
  None

Format: | 11101010 |

Description:
  Does nothing for 2 cycles. May be used to time a delay loop or to fill patches in a program.

Addressing Mode:
  Implied only:
  HEX = EA, byte = 1, cycles = 2

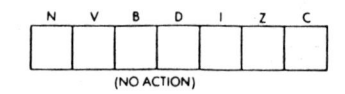

Flags:

N	V	B	D	I	Z	C

(NO ACTION)

ORA Inclusive OR with accumulator

Function:
A ← (A) V DATA

Format:

| 000bbb01 | ADDR/DATA |

Description:

Performs the logical (inclusive) OR of A and the specified data. The result is stored in A. May be used to force a "1" at selected bit locations.

Truth table:

	0	1
0	0	1
1	1	1

Data Paths:

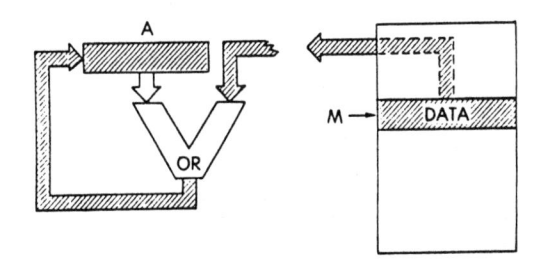

Addressing Modes:

	IMPLIED	ACCUMULATOR	ABSOLUTE	0-PAGE	IMMEDIATE	ABS, X	ABS, Y	(IND, X)	(IND), Y	0-PAGE, X	0-PAGE, Y	RELATIVE	INDIRECT
HEX			0D	05	09	1D	19	01	11	15			
BYTES			3	2	2	3	3	2	2	2			
CYCLES			4	3	2	4*	4*	6	5*	4			
bbb			011	001	010	111	110	000	100	101			

*: PLUS 1 CYCLE IF CROSSING PAGE BOUNDARY.

Flags:

N V B D I Z C
● ○ ○ ○ ○ ● ○

PROGRAMMING THE 6502

Instruction Codes:

ABSOLUTE	00001101	16-BIT ADDRESS	
	bbb = 011	HEX = 0D	CYCLES = 4
ZERO-PAGE	00000101	ADDR	
	bbb = 001	HEX = 05	CYCLES = 3
IMMEDIATE	00001001	DATA	
	bbb = 010	HEX = 09	CYCLES = 2
ABSOLUTE, X	00011101	16-BIT ADDRESS	
	bbb = 111	HEX = 1D	CYCLES = 4*
ABSOLUTE, Y	00011001	16-BIT ADDRESS	
	bbb = 110	HEX = 19	CYCLES = 4*
(IND, X)	00000001	ADDR	
	bbb = 000	HEX = 01	CYCLES = 6
(IND), Y	00010001	ADDR	
	bbb = 100	HEX = 11	CYCLES = 5*
ZERO-PAGE, X	00010101	ADDR	
	bbb = 101	HEX = 15	CYCLES = 4

*: PLUS 1 CYCLE IF CROSSING PAGE BOUNDARY.

PHA Push A

Function:
 STACK ← (A)
 S ← (S) − 1

Format: | 01001000 |

Description:
The contents of the accumulator are pushed on the stack. The stack pointer is updated. A is unchanged.

Data Path:

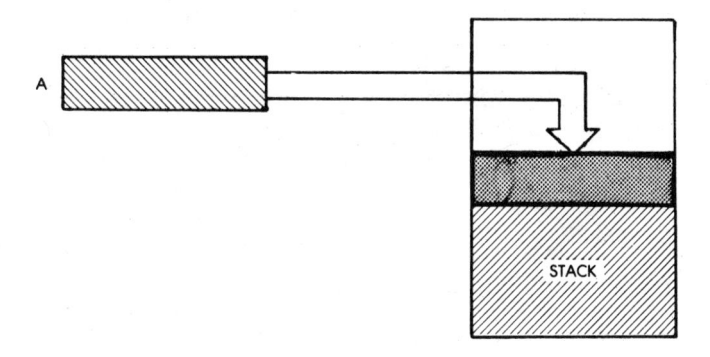

Addressing Mode:
 Implied only:
 HEX = 48, byte = 1, cycles = 3

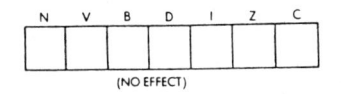

Flags:

N V B D I Z C
(NO EFFECT)

PHP Push processor status

Function:
STACK ← (P)
S ← (S) − 1

Format: | 00001000 |

Description:
The contents of the status register P are pushed on the stack. The stack pointer is updated. A is unchanged.

Data Path:

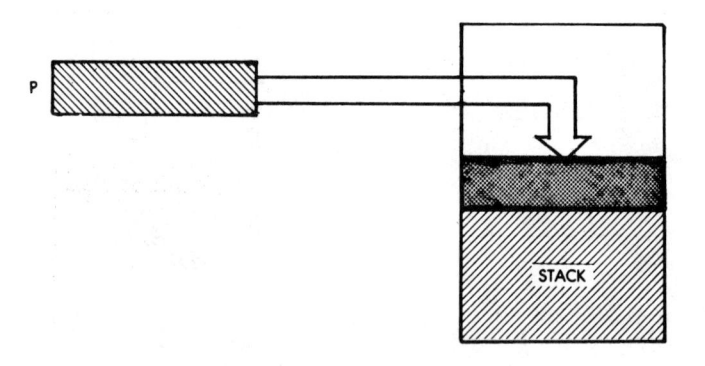

Addressing Mode:
Implied only
Hex = 08, byte = 1, cycles= 3

Flags:

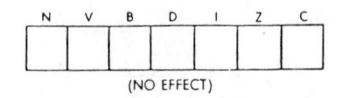

N V B D I Z C
(NO EFFECT)

PLA Pull accumulator

Function:
A ← (STACK)
S ← (S) +1

Format: | 01101000 |

Description:
Pop the top word of the stack into the accumulator. Increment the stack pointer.

Data Paths:

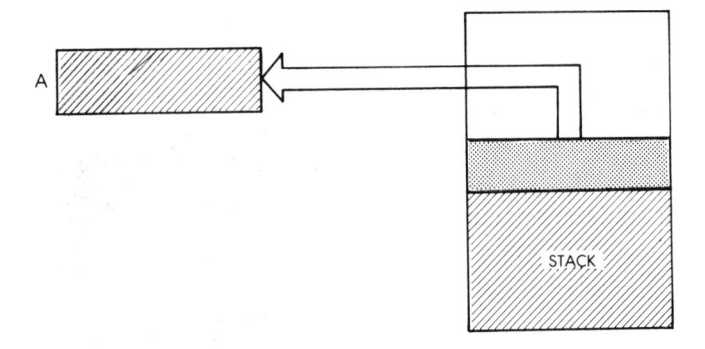

Addressing Mode:
Implied only:
HEX = 68, byte = 1, cycles = 4

Flags:

N V B D I Z C
● ●

PROGRAMMING THE 6502

PLP Pull processor status from stack

Function:
P ← (STACK)
S ← (S) +1

Format: | 00101000 |

Description:
The top word of the stack is popped (transferred) into the status register P. The stack pointer is incremented.

Data Paths:

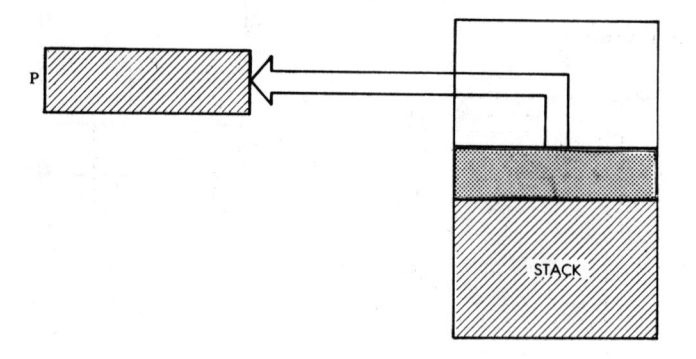

Addressing Mode:
Implied only:
HEX = 28, byte = 1, cycles = 4

Flags:

N V B D I Z C
● ● ● ● ● ● ●

6502 INSTRUCTION SET

ROL — Rotate left one bit

Function:

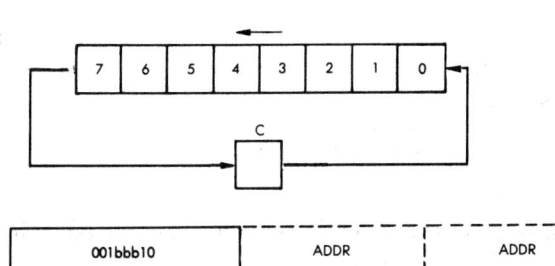

```
 ┌─→ 7 6 5 4 3 2 1 0 ─┐
 │                    │
 │         C          │
 └─────── □ ──────────┘
```

Format: `001bbb10` ADDR ADDR

Description:

The contents of the specified address (accumulator or memory) are rotated left by one position. The carry goes into bit 0. Bit 7 sets the new value of the carry. This is a 9-bit rotation.

Data Paths:

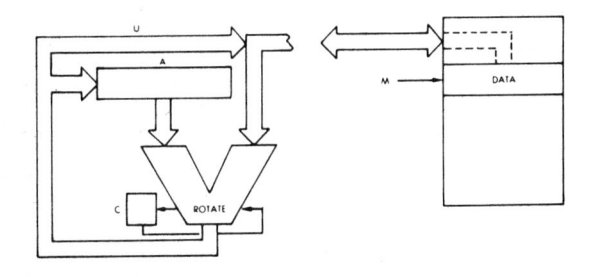

Addressing Modes:

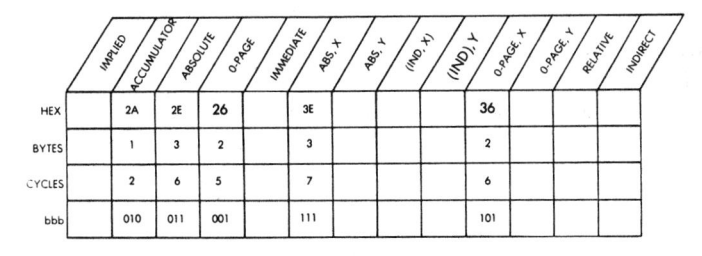

	IMPLIED	ACCUMULATOR	ABSOLUTE	0-PAGE	IMMEDIATE	ABS, X	ABS, Y	(IND, X)	(IND), Y	0-PAGE, X	0-PAGE, Y	RELATIVE	INDIRECT
HEX		2A	2E	26		3E				36			
BYTES		1	3	2		3				2			
CYCLES		2	6	5		7				6			
bbb		010	011	001		111				101			

Flags:

N	V	B	D	I	Z	C
●					●	●

167

PROGRAMMING THE 6502

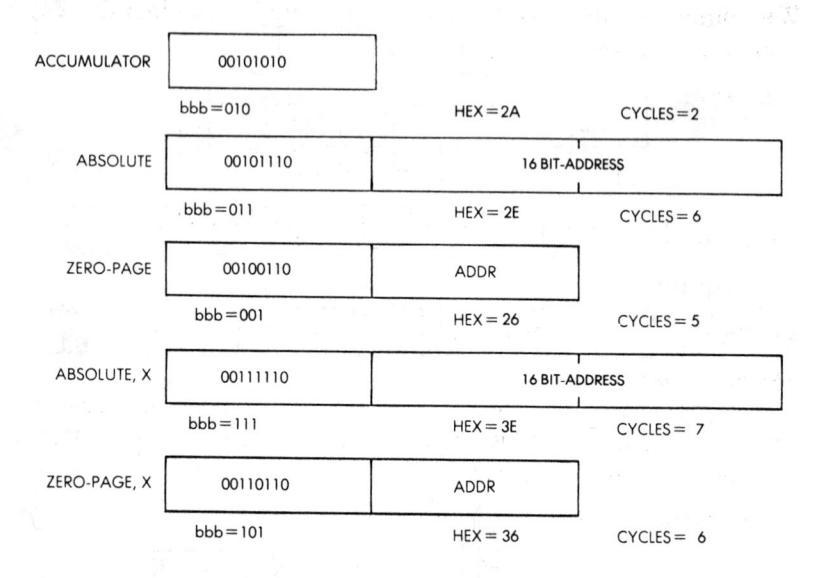

Instruction Codes:

Mode	Opcode			
ACCUMULATOR	00101010		HEX = 2A	CYCLES = 2
	bbb = 010			
ABSOLUTE	00101110	16 BIT-ADDRESS	HEX = 2E	CYCLES = 6
	bbb = 011			
ZERO-PAGE	00100110	ADDR	HEX = 26	CYCLES = 5
	bbb = 001			
ABSOLUTE, X	00111110	16 BIT-ADDRESS	HEX = 3E	CYCLES = 7
	bbb = 111			
ZERO-PAGE, X	00110110	ADDR	HEX = 36	CYCLES = 6
	bbb = 101			

6502 INSTRUCTION SET

ROR   Rotate right one bit

Warning: This instruction may not be available on older 6502's; also, it may exist but not be listed.

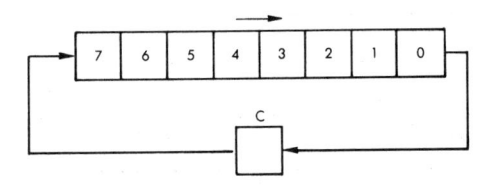

Function:

```
 ┌─────────────────────────────┐
 │ 7 │ 6 │ 5 │ 4 │ 3 │ 2 │ 1 │ 0 │
 └─────────────────────────────┘
                    C
                   □
```

Format: | 011bbb10 | ADDR | ADDR |

Description:

The contents of the specified address (accumulator or memory) are rotated right by one bit position. The carry goes into bit 7. Bit 0 sets the new value of the carry. This is a 9-bit rotation.

Data Paths:

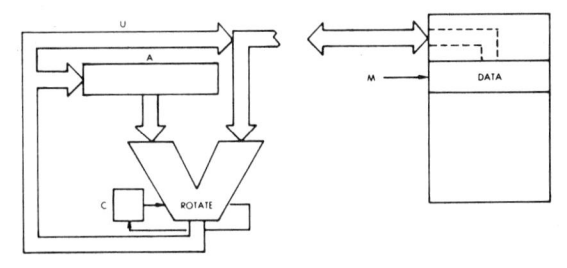

Addressing Modes:

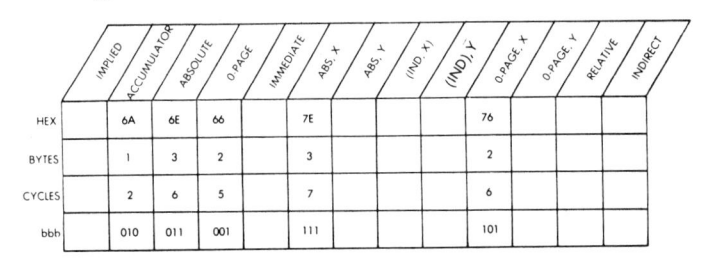

	IMPLIED	ACCUMULATOR	ABSOLUTE	0-PAGE	IMMEDIATE	ABS.X	ABS.Y	(IND,X)	(IND),Y	0-PAGE,X	0-PAGE,Y	RELATIVE	INDIRECT
HEX		6A	6E	66	7E					76			
BYTES		1	3	2	3					2			
CYCLES		2	6	5	7					6			
bbb		010	011	001	111					101			

Flags:

N	V	B	D	I	Z	C
●					●	●

169

PROGRAMMING THE 6502

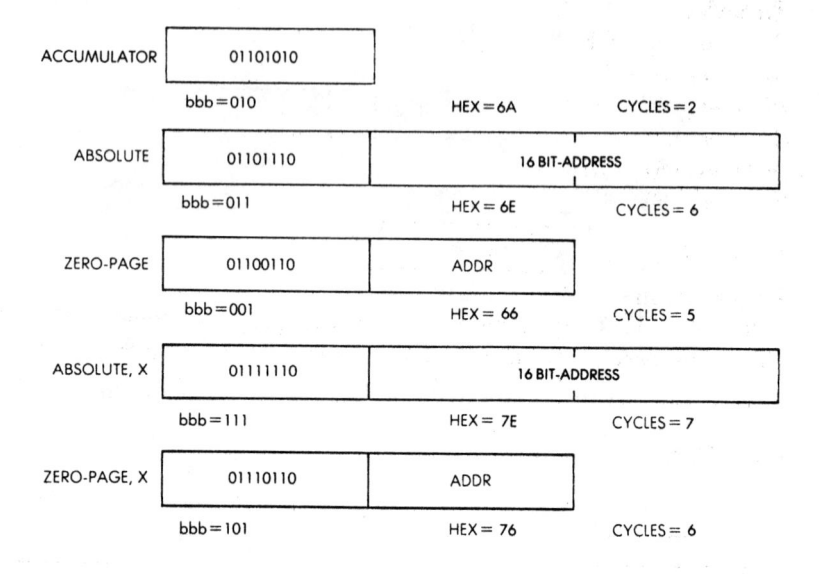

Instruction Codes:

ACCUMULATOR: 01101010
bbb=010   HEX=6A   CYCLES=2

ABSOLUTE: 01101110 | 16 BIT-ADDRESS
bbb=011   HEX=6E   CYCLES=6

ZERO-PAGE: 01100110 | ADDR
bbb=001   HEX=66   CYCLES=5

ABSOLUTE, X: 01111110 | 16 BIT-ADDRESS
bbb=111   HEX=7E   CYCLES=7

ZERO-PAGE, X: 01110110 | ADDR
bbb=101   HEX=76   CYCLES=6

6502 INSTRUCTION SET

RTI   Return from interrupt

Function:
P ← (STACK)
S ← (S) +1
PCL ← (STACK)
S ← (S) +1
PCH ← (STACK)
S ← (S) +1

Format: | 01000000 |

Description:
Restore the status register P and the program counter (PC) which had been saved in the stack. Adjust the stack pointer.

Data Paths:

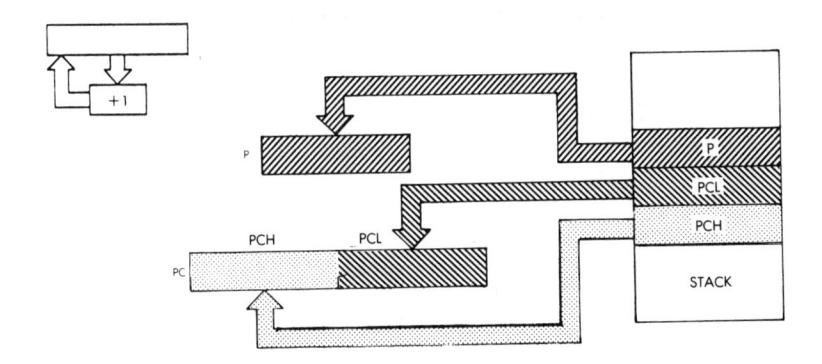

Addressing Mode:
Implied only:
HEX = 40, byte = 1, cycles = 6

Flags:

N V B D I Z C
● ● ● ● ● ● ●

171

PROGRAMMING THE 6502

RTS   Return from subroutine

Function:
PCL ← (STACK)
S   ← (S)+1
PCH ← (STACK)
S   ← (S)+1
PC ← (PC + 1)

Format: | 01100000 |

Description:
Restore the program counter from the stack and increment it by one. Adjust the stack pointer.

Data Paths:

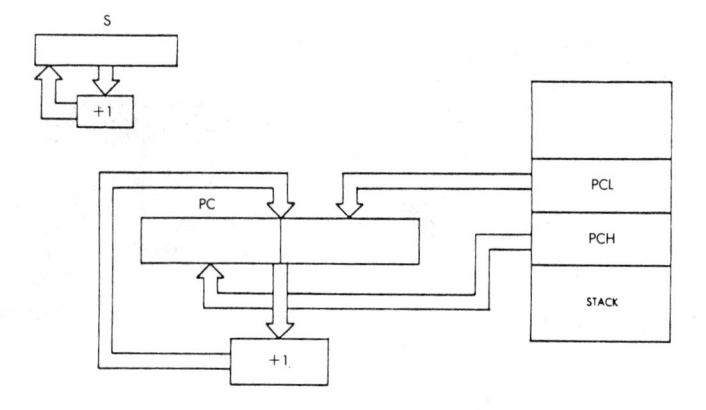

Addressing Mode:
Implied only:
HEX = 60, byte = 1, cycles = 6

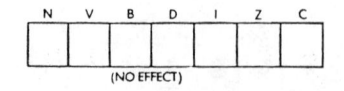

Flags:

(NO EFFECT)

172

6502 INSTRUCTION SET

SBC Subtract with carry

Function:
$A \leftarrow (A) - DATA - \overline{C}$ ($\overline{C}$ is borrow)

Format:

111bbb01	ADDR/DATA	ADDR

Description:
Subtract from the accumulator the data at the specified address, with borrow. The result is left in A. Note: SEC is used for a subtract without borrow.

SBC may be used in decimal or binary mode, depending on bit D of the status register.

Data Paths:

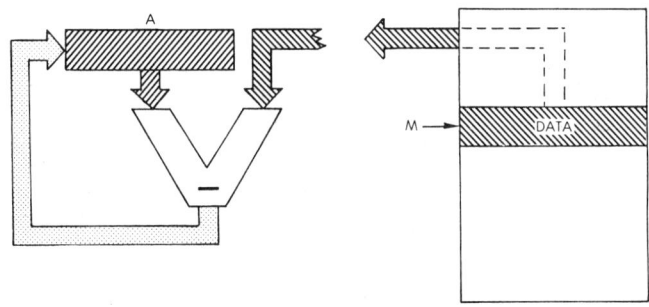

Addressing Modes:

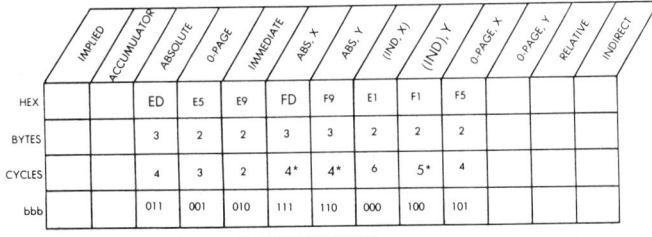

	IMPLIED	ACCUMULATOR	ABSOLUTE	O.PAGE	IMMEDIATE	ABS. X	ABS. Y	(IND, X)	(IND), Y	O.PAGE, X	O.PAGE, Y	RELATIVE	INDIRECT
HEX			ED	E5	E9	FD	F9	E1	F1	F5			
BYTES			3	2	2	3	3	2	2	2			
CYCLES			4	3	2	4*	4*	6	5*	4			
bbb			011	001	010	111	110	000	100	101			

*: PLUS 1 CYCLE IF CROSSING PAGE BOUNDARY.

Flags:

N	V	B	D	I	Z	C
●	●				●	●

173

PROGRAMMING THE 6502

Instruction Codes:

Mode	Opcode (binary)	Operand	
ABSOLUTE	11101101	16-BIT ADDRESS	
	bbb = 011	HEX = ED	CYCLES = 4
ZERO-PAGE	11100101	ADDR	
	bbb = 001	HEX = E5	CYCLES = 3
IMMEDIATE	11101001	DATA	
	bbb = 010	HEX = E9	CYCLES = 2
ABSOLUTE, X	11111101	16-BIT ADDRESS	
	bbb = 111	HEX = FD	CYCLES = 4*
ABSOLUTE, Y	11111001	16-BIT ADDRESS	
	bbb = 110	HEX = F9	CYCLES = 4*
(IND, X)	11100001	ADDR	
	bbb = 000	HEX = E1	CYCLES = 6
(IND), Y	11110001	ADDR	
	bbb = 100	HEX = F1	CYCLES = 5*
ZERO-PAGE, X	11110101	ADDR	
	bbb = 101	HEX = F5	CYCLES = 4

*: PLUS 1 CYCLE IF CROSSING PAGE BOUNDARY.

SEC   Set carry

Function:
C ← 1

Format: | 00111000 |

Description:
The carry bit is set to 1. This is used prior to an SBC to perform a subtract without carry.

Addressing Modes:
Implied only:
HEX = 38, byte = 1, cycles= 2

Flags:

N	V	B	D	I	Z	C
						1

SED Set decimal mode

Function:
D ← 1

Format:

```
11111000
```

Description:
The decimal bit of the status register is set to 1. When it is 0, the mode is binary. When it is 1, the mode is decimal for ADC and SBC.

Addressing Modes:
Implied only:
HEX = F8, byte = 1, cycles = 2

Flags:

N	V	B	D	I	Z	C
			1			

SEI Set interrupt disable

Function:
I ← 1

Format: | 01111000 |

Description:
   The interrupt mask is set to 1. Used during an interrupt or a system reset.

Addressing Modes:

Implied only:

HEX = 78, byte = 1, cycles = 2

Flags:

N	V	B	D	I	Z	C
				1		

STA — Store accumulator in memory

Function:
M ← (A)

Format:

100bbb01	ADDRESS

Description:
The contents of A are copied at the specified memory location. The contents of A are not changed.

Data Paths:

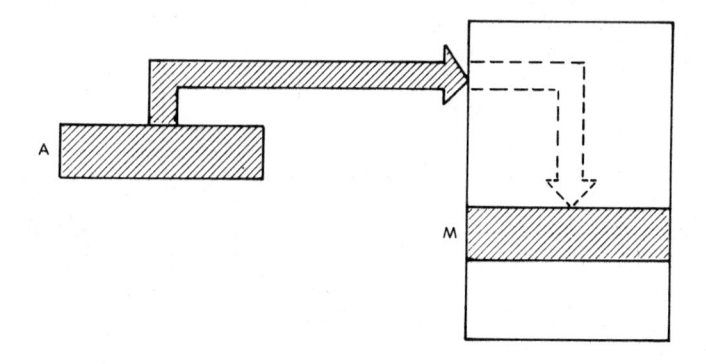

Addressing Modes:

	IMPLIED	ACCUMULATOR	ABSOLUTE	0-PAGE	IMMEDIATE	ABS. X	ABS. Y	(IND, X)	(IND), Y	0-PAGE, X	0-PAGE, Y	RELATIVE	INDIRECT
HEX			8D	85		9D	99	81	91	95			
BYTES			3	2		3	3	2	2	2			
CYCLES			4	3		5	5	6	6	4			
bbb			011	001		111	110	000	100	101			

Flags:

N	V	B	D	I	Z	C

(NO EFFECT)

6502 INSTRUCTION SET

Instruction Codes:

Mode	Opcode		Operand	
ABSOLUTE	10001101 bbb = 011		16-BIT ADDRESS HEX = 8D	CYCLES = 4
ZERO-PAGE	10000101 bbb = 001		ADDR HEX = 85	CYCLES = 3
ABSOLUTE, X	10011101 bbb = 111		16-BIT ADDRESS HEX = 9D	CYCLES = 5
ABSOLUTE, Y	10011001 bbb = 110		16-BIT ADDRESS HEX = 99	CYCLES = 5
(IND, X)	10000001 bbb = 000		ADDR HEX = 81	CYCLES = 6
(IND), Y	10010001 bbb = 100		ADDR HEX = 91	CYCLES = 6
ZERO-PAGE, X	10010101 bbb = 101		ADDR HEX = 95	CYCLES = 4

STX Store X in memory

Function:
M ← (X)

Format:

100bb110	ADDRESS

Description:
Copy the contents of index register X at the specified memory location. The contents of X are left unchanged.

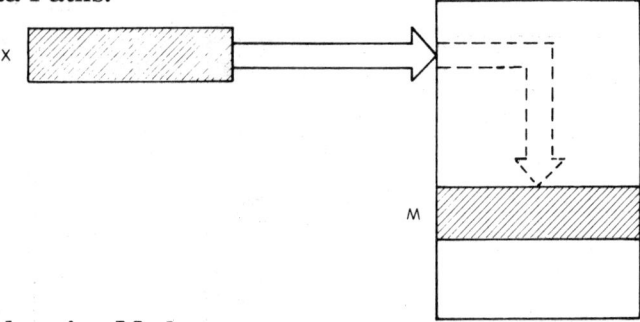

Data Paths:

Addressing Modes:

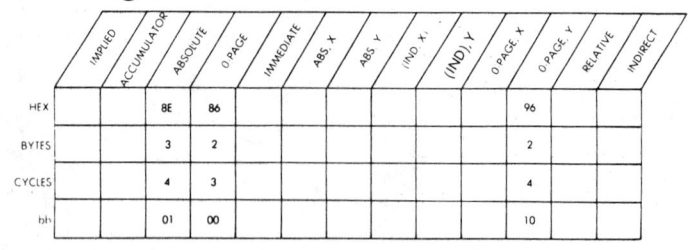

	IMPLIED	ACCUMULATOR	ABSOLUTE	0-PAGE	IMMEDIATE	ABS, X	ABS, Y	(IND, X)	(IND), Y	0-PAGE, X	0-PAGE, Y	RELATIVE	INDIRECT
HEX			8E	86							96		
BYTES			3	2							2		
CYCLES			4	3							4		
bb			01	00							10		

Flags:

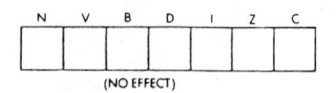

N	V	B	D	I	Z	C

(NO EFFECT)

Instruction Codes:

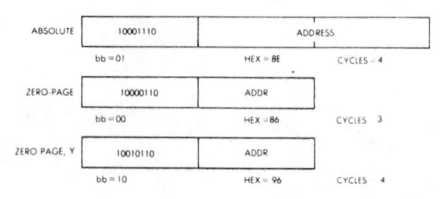

ABSOLUTE	10001110	ADDRESS	
	bb = 01	HEX = 8E	CYCLES = 4

ZERO-PAGE	10000110	ADDR	
	bb = 00	HEX = 86	CYCLES = 3

ZERO PAGE, Y	10010110	ADDR	
	bb = 10	HEX = 96	CYCLES = 4

6502 INSTRUCTION SET

STY — Store Y in memory

Function:
M ← (Y)

Format:
| 100bb100 | ADDRESS |

Description:
Copy the contents of index register Y at the specified memory location. The contents of Y are left unchanged.

Data Paths:

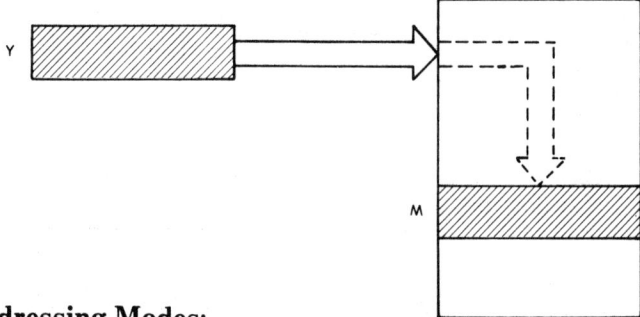

Addressing Modes:

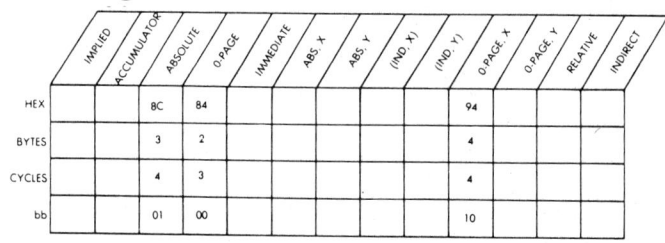

	IMPLIED	ACCUMULATOR	ABSOLUTE	0-PAGE	IMMEDIATE	ABS, X	ABS, Y	(IND, X)	(IND, Y)	0-PAGE, X	0-PAGE, Y	RELATIVE	INDIRECT
HEX			8C	84						94			
BYTES			3	2						4			
CYCLES			4	3						4			
bb			01	00						10			

Flags:

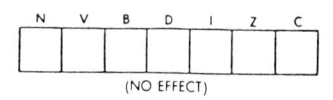

N V B D I Z C
(NO EFFECT)

Instruction Codes:

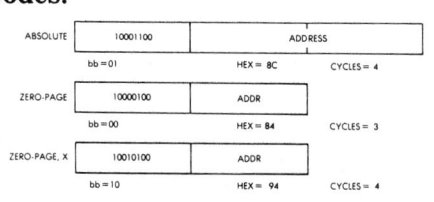

| ABSOLUTE | 10001100 | ADDRESS |
bb = 01   HEX = 8C   CYCLES = 4

| ZERO-PAGE | 10000100 | ADDR |
bb = 00   HEX = 84   CYCLES = 3

| ZERO-PAGE, X | 10010100 | ADDR |
bb = 10   HEX = 94   CYCLES = 4

TAX — Transfer accumulator into X

Function:
 X ← (A)

Format: | 10101010 |

Description:
Copy the contents of the accumulator into index register X. The contents of A are left unchanged.

Data Paths:

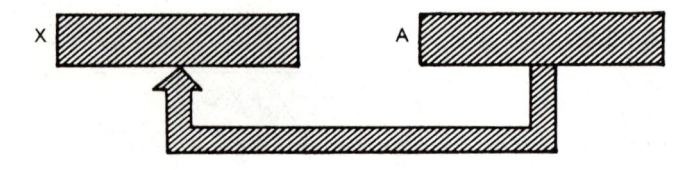

Addressing Mode:
Implied only:
HEX = AA, byte = 1, cycles = 2

Flags:

N ● (set), Z ● (set); V, B, D, I, C unaffected.

TAY

Transfer accumulator into Y

Function:
  Y ← (A)

Format: `10101000`

Description:
Transfer the contents of the accumulator into index register Y. The contents of A are left unchanged.

Data Paths:

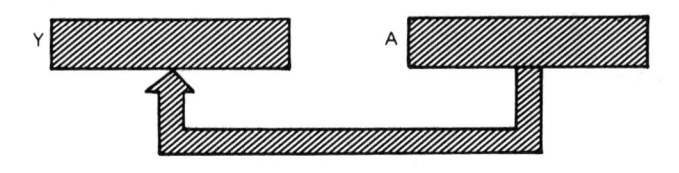

Addressing Mode
  Implied only:
  HEX = A8, byte = 1, cycles = 2

Flags:

N	V	B	D	I	Z	C
●					●	

TSX Transfer S into X

Function:
 X ← (S)

Format:

| 10111010 |

Description:
The contents of the stack pointer S are transferred into index register X. The contents of S are unchanged.

Data Paths:

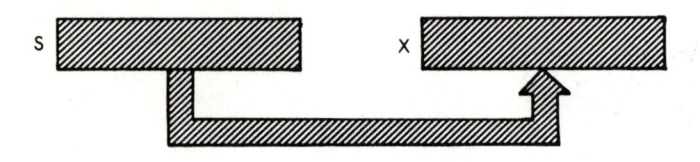

Addressing Mode:
 Implied only:
 HEX = BA, byte = 1, cycles = 2

Flags:

N ●, V, B, D, I, Z ●, C

TXA Transfer X into accumulator

Function:
A ← (X)

Format: | 10001010 |

Description:
The contents of index register X are transferred into the accumulator. The contents of X are unchanged.

Data Paths:

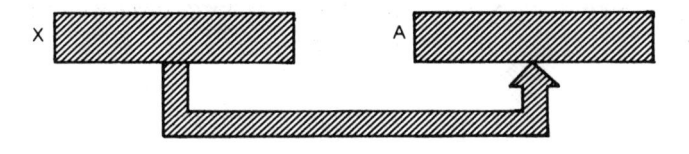

Addressing Mode:
Implied only:
HEX = 8A, byte = 1, cycles = 2

Flags:

N ●, Z ●

TXS   Transfer X into S

Function:
S ← (X)

Format: | 10011010 |

Description:
The contents of index register S are transferred into the stack pointer. The contents of X are unchanged.

Data Paths:

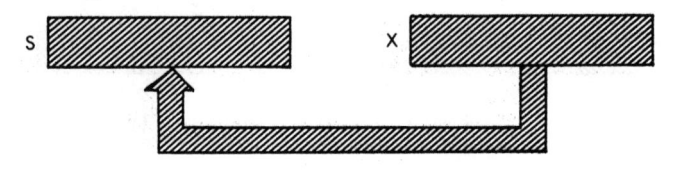

Addressing Mode:
Implied only:
HEX = 9A, byte = 1, cycles = 2

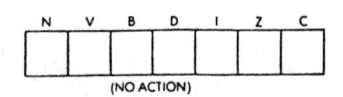

Flags:

(NO ACTION)

6502 INSTRUCTION SET

TYA   Transfer Y into A

Function:
A ← (Y)

Format: | 10011000 |

Description:
The contents of index register Y are transferred into the accumulator. The contents of Y are unchanged.

Data Paths:

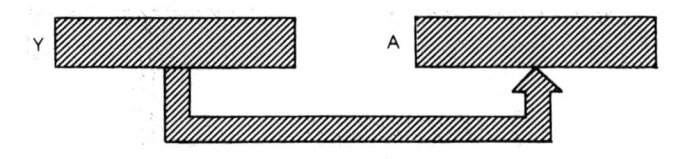

Addressing Mode:
Implied only:
HEX = 98, byte = 1, cycles = 2

Flags:

N V B D I Z C
● · · · · ● ·

187

5
ADDRESSING TECHNIQUES

INTRODUCTION

This chapter will present the general theory of addressing, with the various techniques which have been developed to facilitate the retrieval of data. In a second section, the specific addressing modes which are available in the 6502 will be reviewed, along with their advantages and limitations, where they exist. Finally, in order to familiarize the reader with the various trade-offs possible, an applications section will show possible trade-offs between the various addressing techniques by studying specific application programs.

Because the 6502 has no 16-bit register, other than the program counter, which can be used to specify an address, it is necessary that the 6502 user understand the various addressing modes, and in particular, the use of the index registers. Complex retrieval modes, such as a combination of indirect and indexed, may be omitted at the beginning stage. However, all the addressing modes are useful in developing programs for this microprocessor. Let us now study the various alternatives available.

ADDRESSING MODES

Addressing refers to the specification, within an instruction of the location of the operand on which the instruction will operate. The main methods will now be examined.

ADDRESSING TECHNIQUES

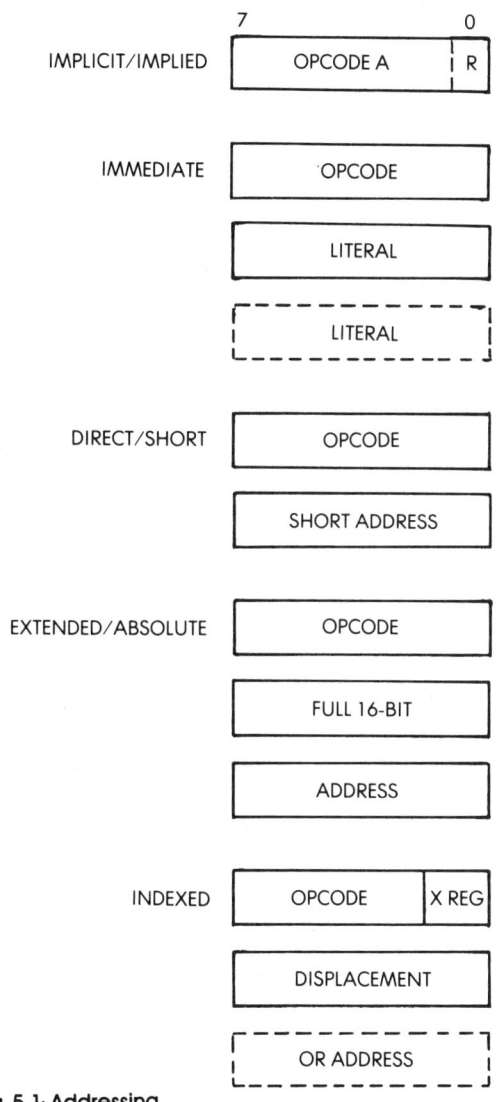

```
                          7                    0
IMPLICIT/IMPLIED      ┌──────────────┬───┐
                      │   OPCODE A   │ R │
                      └──────────────┴───┘

IMMEDIATE             ┌──────────────────┐
                      │     OPCODE       │
                      └──────────────────┘
                      ┌──────────────────┐
                      │     LITERAL      │
                      └──────────────────┘
                      ┌ ─ ─ ─ ─ ─ ─ ─ ─ ─┐
                           LITERAL
                      └ ─ ─ ─ ─ ─ ─ ─ ─ ─┘

DIRECT/SHORT         ┌──────────────────┐
                     │     OPCODE       │
                     └──────────────────┘
                     ┌──────────────────┐
                     │  SHORT ADDRESS   │
                     └──────────────────┘

EXTENDED/ABSOLUTE    ┌──────────────────┐
                     │     OPCODE       │
                     └──────────────────┘
                     ┌──────────────────┐
                     │   FULL 16-BIT    │
                     └──────────────────┘
                     ┌──────────────────┐
                     │     ADDRESS      │
                     └──────────────────┘

INDEXED              ┌──────────────┬─────┐
                     │    OPCODE    │X REG│
                     └──────────────┴─────┘
                     ┌──────────────────┐
                     │   DISPLACEMENT   │
                     └──────────────────┘
                     ┌ ─ ─ ─ ─ ─ ─ ─ ─ ─┐
                          OR ADDRESS
                     └ ─ ─ ─ ─ ─ ─ ─ ─ ─┘
```

Fig. 5-1: Addressing

Implicit Addressing

Instructions which operate exclusively on registers normally use *implicit addressing*. This is illustrated in Figure 5-1. An implicit instruction derives its name from the fact that it does not specifically contain the address of the operand on which it operates. Instead, its opcode specifies one or more registers, usually the accumulator, or else any other register(s). Since internal registers are usually few in number (say a maximum of 8), this will require a small number of bits. As an example, three bits within the instruction will point to 1 out of 8 internal registers. Such instructions can, therefore, normally be encoded within 8 bits. This is an important advantage, since an 8-bit instruction normally executes faster than any two- or three-byte instruction.

An example of an implicit instruction for the 6502 is TAX which specifies "transfer the contents of A to X."

Immediate Addressing

Immediate addressing is illustrated in Figure 5-1. The 8-bit opcode is followed by an 8- or a 16-bit literal (a constant). This type of instruction is needed, for example, to load an 8-bit value to an 8-bit register. If the microprocessor is equipped with 16-bit registers, it may be necessary to load 16-bit literals. This depends upon the internal architecture of the processor. An example of an immediate instruction is ADC #0.

The second word of this instruction contains the literal "0", which is added to the accumulator.

Absolute Addressing

Absolute addressing refers to the way in which data is usually retrieved from memory, where an opcode is followed by a 16-bit address. Absolute addressing, therefore, requires 3-byte instructions. An example of absolute addressing is STA $1234.

It specifies that the contents of the accumulator are to be stored at the memory location "1234" hexadecimal.

The disadvantage of absolute addressing is to require a 3-byte instruction. In order to improve the efficiency of the microprocessor, another addressing mode may be made available, where only one word is used for the address: direct addressing.

Direct Addressing

In this addressing mode, the opcode is followed by an 8-bit address. This is illustrated in Figure 5-1. The advantage of this approach is to require only 2 bytes instead of 3 for absolute addressing. The disadvantage is to limit all addressing within this mode to addresses 0 to 255. This is page 0. This is also called short addressing, or 0-page addressing. Whenever short addressing is available, absolute addressing is often called *extended addressing* by contrast.

Relative Addressing

Normal jump or branch instructions require 8 bits for the opcode, plus the 16-bit address which is the address to which the program has to jump. Just as in the preceding example, this has the inconvenience of requiring 3 words, i.e., 3 memory cycles. To provide more efficient branching, relative addressing uses only a two-word format. The first word is the branch specification, usually along with the test it is implementing. The second word is a displacement. Since the displacement must be positive or negative, a relative branching instruction allows a branch forward to 128 locations (7-bits) or a branch backwards to 128 locations (plus or minus 1, depending on the conventions). Because most loops tend to be short, relative branching can be used most of the time and results in significantly improved performance for such short routines. As an example, we have already used the instruction BCC, which specifies a "branch on carry clear" to a location within 127 words of the branch instruction.

Indexed Addressing

Indexed addressing is a technique specifically useful to access successively the elements of a block or of a table. This will be illustrated by examples later in this chapter. The principle of indexed addressing is that the instruction specifies both an index register and an address. In the most general scheme, the contents of the register are added to the address to provide the final address. In this way, the address could be the beginning of a table in the memory. The index register would then be used to access successively all the elements of the table in an efficient way. In practice, restrictions often exist and may limit the size of the

PROGRAMMING THE 6502

index register, or the size of the address or displacement field.

Pre-indexing and Post-indexing

Two modes of indexing may be distinguished. Pre-indexing is the usual indexing mode where the final address is the sum of a displacement or address and the contents of the index register.

Post-indexing treats the contents of the displacement field like the *address* of the actual displacement, rather than the displacement itself. This is illustrated in Figure 5-2. In post-indexing, the final address is the sum of the contents of the index register plus the contents of the memory word *designated by the displacement field.* This feature utilizes, in fact, a combination of indirect addressing and pre-indexing. But we have not defined indirect addressing yet, so let us do that now.

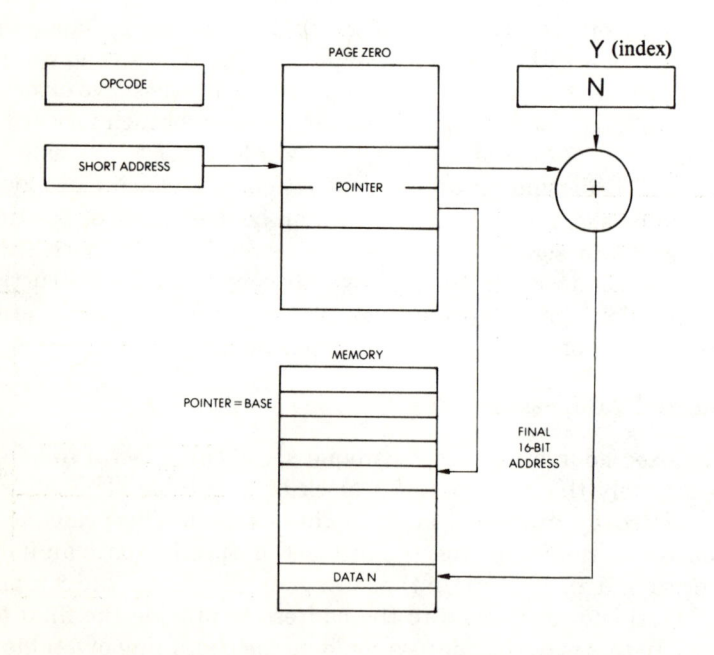

Fig. 5-2: **Indirect** Post-Indexed Addressing

ADDRESSING TECHNIQUES

Indirect Addressing

We have already seen the case where two subroutines may wish to exchange a large quantity of data stored in the memory. More generally, several programs, or several subroutines, may need access to a common block of information. To preserve the generality of the program, it is desirable not to keep such a block at a fixed memory location. In particular, the size of this block might grow or shrink dynamically, and it may have to reside in various areas of the memory, depending on its size. It would, therefore, be impractical to try to have access to this block using absolute addresses.

The solution to this problem lies in depositing the starting address of the block at a fixed memory location. This is analogous to a situation in which several persons need to get into a house,

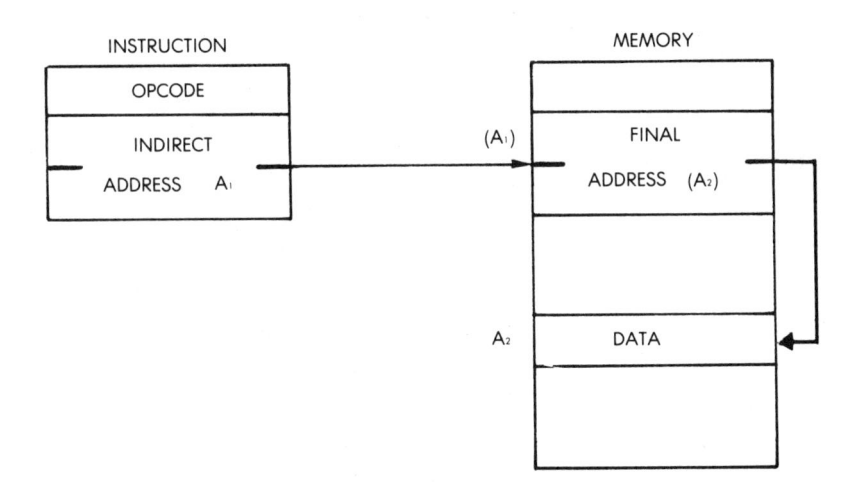

Fig. 5-3: Indirect Addressing

and only one key exists. By convention, the key to the house will be hidden under the mat. Every user will then know where to look (under the mat) to find the key to the house (or, perhaps, to find the address of a scheduled meeting, to have a more correct analogy). Indirect addressing, therefore, uses an 8-bit opcode followed by a 16-bit address. Simply, this address is used to retrieve a word from the memory. Normally, it will be a 16-bit word (in our case, two bytes) within the memory. This is illustrated by Figure 5-3. The two bytes at the specified address, A1, contain A2. A2 is then interpreted as the actual address of the data that one wishes to access.

Indirect addressing is particularly useful any time that pointers are used. Various areas of the program can then refer to these pointers to access conveniently and elegantly a word or a block of data.

Combinations of Modes

The above addressing modes may be combined. In particular, it should be possible in a completely general addressing scheme to use many levels of indirection. The address A2 could be interpreted as an indirect address again, and so on.

Indexed addressing can also be combined with indirect access. That allows the efficient access to word n of a block of data, provided one knows where the pointer to the starting address is.

We have now become familiar with all usual addressing modes that can be provided in a system. Most microprocessor systems, because of the limitation on the complexity of an MPU, which must be realized within a single chip, do not provide all possible modes but only a small subset of these. The 6502 provides an unusually large subset of possibilities. Let us examine them now.

6502 ADDRESSING MODES

Implied Addressing (6502)

Implied addressing is used by a single byte instruction which operates on internal registers. Whenever implicit instructions operate exclusively in internal registers, they require only two clock cycles to execute. Whenever they access memory, they require three cycles.

Instructions **which operate exclusively inside the 6502**

are: CLC, CLD, CLI, CLV, DEX, DEY, INX, INY, NOP, SEC, SED, SEI, TAX, TAY, TSX, TXA, TXS, TYA.

Instructions which require memory access are: BRK, PHA, PHP, PLA, PLP, RTI, RTS.

These instructions have been described in the preceding chapter, and their mode of operation should be clear.

Immediate Addressing (6502)

Since the 6502 has only 8-bit working registers (the PC is not a working register), immediate addressing in the case of the 6502 is limited to 8-bit constants. All instructions in immediate addressing mode are, therefore, two bytes in length. The first byte contains the opcode, and the second byte contains the constant or literal which is to be loaded in a register or used in conjunction with one of the registers for an arithmetic or logical operation.

Instructions using this addressing mode are: ADC, AND, CMP, CPX, CPY, EOR, LDA, LDX, LDY, ORA, SBC.

Absolute Addressing (6502)

By definition, absolute addressing requires three bytes. The first byte is the opcode and the next two bytes are the 16-bit address specifying the location of the operand. Except in the case of a jump absolute, this address mode requires four cycles.

Instructions which may use absolute addressing are: ADC, AND, ASL, BIT, CMP, CPX, CPY, DEC, EOR, INC, JMP, JSR, LDA, LDX, LDY, LSR, ORA, ROL, ROR, SBC, STA, STX, STY.

Zero-Page Addressing (6502)

By definition zero-page addressing requires two bytes: the first one is for the opcode; the second one is for the 8-bit, or short address.

Zero-page addressing requires three cycles. Because zero-page addressing offers significant speed advantages as well as shorter code, it should be used whenever possible. This requires careful memory management by the programmer. Generally speaking, the first 256 locations of memory may be viewed as the set of working registers for the 6502. Any instruction will essentially execute on these 256 "registers" in just three cycles. This space should, therefore, be carefully reserved for essential data that needs to be retrieved at high speed.

Instructions which can use zero-page addressing are those which can use absolute addressing, except for JMP and JSR (which require a 16-bit address).

The list of legal instructions is: ADC, AND, ASL, BIT, CMP, CPX, CPY, DEC, EOR, INC, LDA, LDX, LDY, LSR, ORA, ROL, ROR, SBC, STA, STX, STY.

Relative Addressing (6502)

By definition, relative addressing uses two bytes. The first one is a jump instruction, whereas the second one specifies the displacement and its sign. In order to differentiate this mode from the jump instruction, they are here labeled *branches*. Branches, in the case of the 6502, always use the relative mode. Jumps always use the absolute mode (plus, naturally, the other submodes which may be combined with those, such as indexed and indirect). From a timing standpoint, this instruction should be examined with caution. Whenever a test fails, i.e., whenever there is no branch, this instruction requires only two cycles. This is because the next instruction to be executed is pointed to by the program counter. However, whenever the test succeeds, i.e., whenever the branch must take place this instruction requires three cycles: a new effective address must be computed. The updating of the program counter requires an extra cycle. However, if a branch occurs through a page boundary, one more updating is necessary for the program counter, and the effective length of the instruction becomes four cycles.

From a logical standpoint, the user does not need to worry about crossing a page boundary. The hardware takes care of it. However, because an extra carry or borrow is generated whenever one crosses a page boundary, the execution time of the branch will be changed. If this branch was part of an exact timing loop, caution must be exercised.

A good assembler will normally tell the programmer at the time the program is assembled that a branch is crossing a page boundary, in case timing might be critical.

Whenever one is not sure whether the branch will succeed, one must take into consideration the fact that sometimes the branch will require two cycles, and sometimes three. Often an average time is computed.

The only instructions which implement relative addressing are the branch instructions. There are 8 branch instructions which test flags within the status register for value "0" or "1". The list is: BCC, BCS, BEQ, BMI, BNE, BPL, BVC, BVS.

Indexed Addressing (6502)

The 6502 does not provide a completely general capability, but only a limited one. It is equipped with two index registers. However, these registers are limited to 8 bits. The contents of an index register are added to the address field of the instruction. Usually, the index register is used as a counter in order to access elements of a block or a table successively. This is why specialized instructions are available to increment or decrement each one of the index registers separately. In addition, two specialized instructions exist to compare the contents of the index registers against a memory location, an important facility for the effective use of the index registers to test against limits.

In practice, because most user tables are normally shorter than 256 words, the limitation of the index registers to 8 bits is usually not a significant limitation.

The indexed addressing mode can be used not only with regular absolute addressing, i.e., with 16-bit address fields, but also with the zero-page addressing mode, i.e., with 8-bit address fields.

There is only one restriction. Register X can be used with both types of addressing. However, register Y allows only *absolute* indexed addressing and *not zero-page* indexed addressing (except for LDX and STX instructions, which can be modified by register Y).

Absolute indexed addressing will require four cycles, unless the page boundary is being crossed, in which case five cycles will be required.

Absolute indexed instructions can use either registers X or Y to provide the displacement field. The list of instructions which may use this mode are:

— with X: ADC, AND, ASL, CMP, DEC, EOR, INC, LDA, LDY, LSR, ORA, ROL, ROR, SBC, STA, (not STY).

—with Y: ADC, AND, CMP, EOR, LDA, LDX, ORA, SBC, STA (not ASL, DEC, LSR, ROL, ROR).

In the case of zero-page indexed addressing, register X is the legal displacement register, except for LDX and STX. Legal instructions are: ADC, AND, ASL, CMP, DEC, EOR, INC, LDA, LDY, LSR, ORA, ROL, ROR, SBC, STA, STY.

Indirect Addressing (6502)

The 6502 does not have a fully general indirect addressing capability. It restricts the address field to 8 bits. In other words, all indirect addressing uses the sub-mode of zero page addressing. The effective address on which the opcode is to operate is then the 16 bits specified by the zero-page address of the instruction. Also, no further indirection may occur. This means that an address retrieved from page zero must be used as is, and cannot be used as a further indirection.

Finally, all indirect accesses must be indexed, except for JMP.

For fairness, it should be noted that very few microprocessors provide any indirect addressing at all. Further, it is possible to implement a more general indirect addressing using a macro definition.

Two modes of indirect addressing are possible: indexed indirect addressing, and indirect indexed addressing (except with JMP, which uses pure indirect).

Indexed Indirect Addressing

This mode adds the contents of index register X to the zero-page address to compute the final 16-bit address. This is an efficient way to retrieve one of several possible data pointed to by pointers whose number is contained in index register X. This is illustrated in Figure 5-4.

In this illustration, page zero contains a table of pointers. The first pointer is at the address A, which is part of the instruction. If the contents of X are 2N, then this instruction will access pointer number N of this table and retrieve the data it is pointing to.

Indexed indirect addressing requires 6 cycles. It is naturally less efficient time-wise than any direct addressing mode. Its advantage is the flexibility which may result in coding, or the overall speed improvement.

ADDRESSING TECHNIQUES

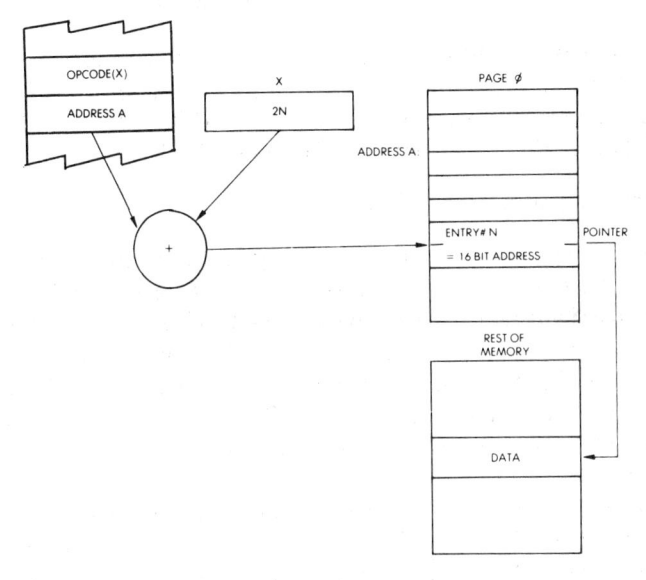

Fig. 5-4: Indexed Indirect Addressing

Permissible instructions are: ADC, AND, CMP, EOR, LDA, ORA, SBC, STA.

Indirect Indexed Addressing

This corresponds to the post-indexing mechanism which has been described in the preceding section. There, the indexing is performed after the indirection, rather than before. In other words, the short address which is part of the instructions is used to access a 16-bit pointer in page zero. The contents of index register Y are then added as a displacement to this pointer. The final data are then retrieved. (see Fig. 5-2.)

In this case, the pointer contained in page zero indicates the base of a table in the memory. Index register Y provides a displacement. It is a true index within a table. This instruction is particularly powerful for referring to the nth element of a table, provided that the start address of the table is saved in page zero.

It can do so in just two bytes.
Legal instructions are: ADC, CMP, EOR, LDA, ORA, SBC, STA.

Exception: Jump Instruction

The jump instruction may use indirect absolute. It is the only instruction that may use this mode.

USING THE 6502 ADDRESSING MODES

Long and Short Addressing

We have already used branch instructions in various programs that we have developed. They are self explanatory. One interesting question is: what can we do if the permissible range for branching is not sufficient for our needs? One simple solution is to use a so-called *long branch*. This is simply a branch to a location which contains a jump specification:

```
BCC +3              BRANCH TO CURRENT ADDRESS
                    +3 IF C CLEAR
JMP FAR             OTHERWISE JUMP TO FAR
(NEXT INSTRUCTION)
```

The two-line program above will result in branching to location **FAR** whenever the carry is set. This solves our long branch problem. Let us therefore now consider the more complex addressing modes, i.e. indexing and indirection.

Use of indexing for sequential block accesses

Indexing is primarily used to address successive locations within a table. The restriction is that the maximum displacement must be less than 256 so that it can reside in an 8-bit index register.

We have learned to check for the character '*'. Now we will search a table of 100 elements for the presence of a '*'. The starting address for this table is called BASE. The table has only 100 elements. It is less than 256 and we can use an index register. The program appears below:

ADDRESSING TECHNIQUES

```
SEARCH      LDX   #0
NEXT        LDA   BASE, X
            CMP   '*
            BEQ   STARFOUND
            INX
            CPX   #100
            BNE   NEXT
NOTFOUND          ...
STARFOUND         ...
```

The flowchart for this program appears in Figure 5-5. The equivalence between the flowchart and the program should be verified. The logic of the program is quite simple. Register X is used to point to the element within the table. The second instruction of the program:

NEXT LDA BASE, X

uses absolute indexed addressing. It specifies that the accumulator is to be loaded from the address BASE (16-bit absolute address) plus contents of X. At the beginning, the contents of X are "0." The first element to be accessed will be the one at address BASE. It can be seen that after the next iteration, X will have the value "1," and the next sequential element of the table will be accessed, at address BASE + 1.

The third instruction of the program, CMP '* compares the value of the character which has been read in the accumulator with the code for "*." The next instruction tests the results of the comparison. If a match has been found, the branch occurs to the label STARFOUND:

BEQ STARFOUND

Otherwise, the next sequential instruction is executed:

INX

201

The index counter is incremented by 1. We find by inspecting the bottom of the flow-chart of Figure 5.5 that the value of our index register at this point must be checked to make sure that we are not going beyond the bounds of the table (here 100 elements). This is implemented by the following instruction:

CPX #100

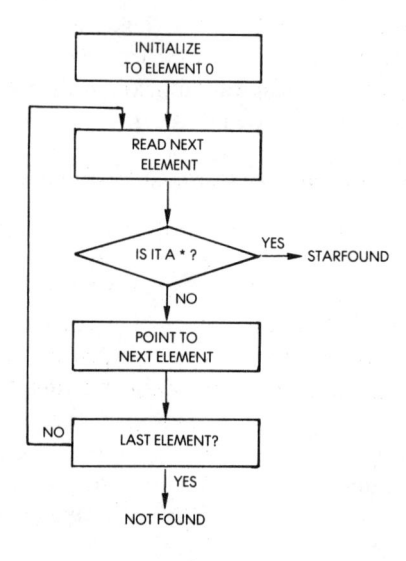

```
        INITIALIZE
        TO ELEMENT 0
             │
             ▼
    ┌──► READ NEXT
    │    ELEMENT
    │        │
    │        ▼
    │     IS IT A * ?  ──YES──► STARFOUND
    │        │ NO
    │        ▼
    │     POINT TO
    │     NEXT ELEMENT
    │        │
    │        ▼
    └─NO── LAST ELEMENT?
             │ YES
             ▼
          NOT FOUND
```

Fig. 5-5: Character Searching Table

This instruction compares register X to the value $100. If the test fails we must again fetch the next character. This is what occurs with:

BNE NEXT

This instruction specifies a branch to the label NEXT if the test has failed (the second instruction in our program). This loop will be executed as long as a "*" is not found, or as long as the value "100" is not reached in the index. Then the next sequential in-

ADDRESSING TECHNIQUES

struction to be executed will be "NOT FOUND". It corresponds to the case where a "*" has not been found.

The actions taken for "*" found and not found are irrelevant here and would be specified by the programmer.

We have learned to use the indexed addressing mode to access successive elements in a table. Let us now use this new skill and slightly increase the difficulty. We will develop an important utility program, capable of copying a block from one area of the memory into another. We will initially assume that the number of the elements within the block is less than 256 so that we can use index register X. Then we will consider the general case where the number of elements in the block is greater than 256.

A Block Transfer Routine for less than 256 elements

We will call "NUMBER" the number of elements in the block to be moved. The number is assumed to be less than 256. BASE is the base address of the block. DESTINATION is the base of the memory area where it should be moved. The algorithm is quite simple: we will move a word at a time, keeping track of which word we are moving by storing its position in index register X. The program appears below:

```
            LDX  #NUMBER
NEXT        LDA  BASE, X
            STA  DEST, X
            DEX
            BNE  NEXT
```

Let us examine it:

LDX # NUMBER

This line of the program loads the number N of words to be transferred in the index register. The next instruction loads word #N of the block within the accumulator and the third instruction deposits it into the destination area. See Figure 5-6.

CAUTION: this program will work correctly only if the base pointer is assumed to point just *below* the block, just like the destination register. Otherwise a small adjustment to this program is needed.

203

After a word has been transferred from the origin to the destination area, the index register must be updated. This is performed by the instruction DEX, which decrements it. Then the program simply tests whether X has decremented to 0. If so, the program terminates. Otherwise, it loops again by going back to location NEXT.

You will notice that when X = 0, the program *does not* loop. Therefore, it will not transfer the word at location BASE. The last word to be transferred will be at BASE+1. This is why we have assumed that the base was just *below* the block.

Exercise 5.1: *Modify the program above, assuming that BASE and DEST point to the first entry in the block.*

This program also illustrates the use of loop counters. You will notice that X has been loaded with the *final* value, then *decremented* and tested. At first sight, it might seem simpler to start with "0" in X, and then increment it until it reaches the maximum value. However, in order to test whether X has attained its maximum value, one extra instruction would be needed (the comparison instruction). This loop would then require 5 instructions instead of 4. Since this transfer program will normally be used for large numbers of words, it is important to reduce the number of instructions for the loop. This is why, at least for short loops, the index register is normally *decremented rather than incremented.*

A Block Transfer Routine (more than 256 elements)

Let us now consider the general case of moving a block which may contain more than 256 elements. We can no longer use a single index register as 8 bits do not suffice to store a number greater than 256. The memory organization for this program is illustrated in Figure 5-7. The length of the memory-block to be transferred requires 16 bits, and therefore is stored in memory. The high-order part represents the number of 256-word blocks: "BLOCKS". The rest is called "REMAIN" and is the number of words to be transferred after all the blocks have been transferred. The address for the source and the destination will be memory locations FROM and TO. Let us first assume that REMAIN is

ADDRESSING TECHNIQUES

Fig. 5-6: Memory Organization for Block Transfer

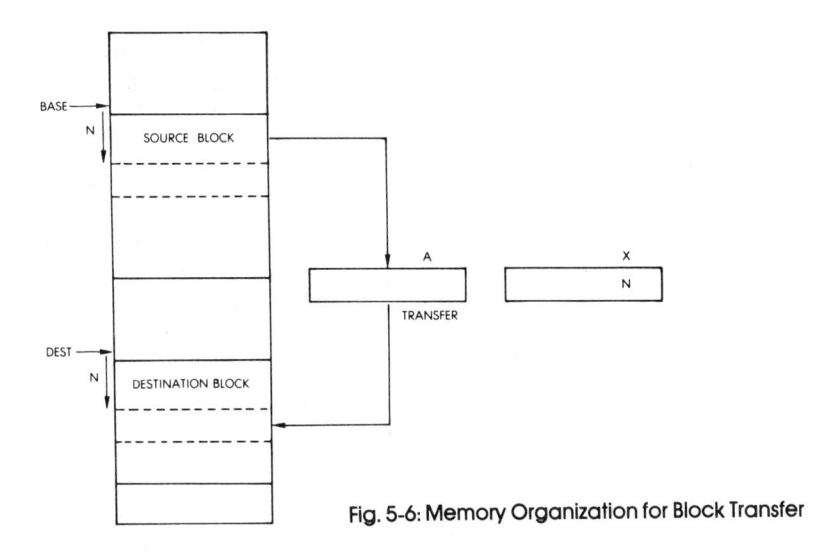

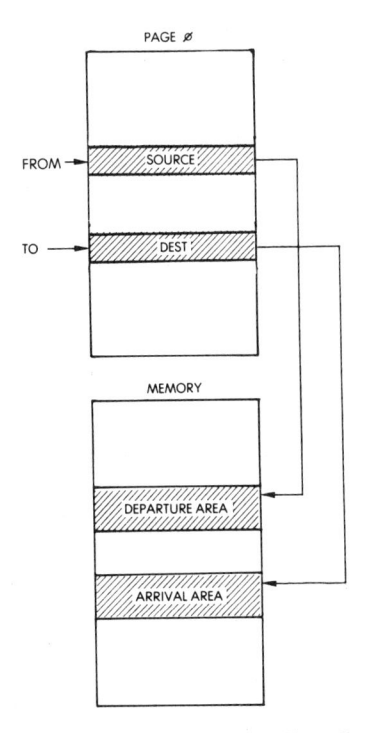

Fig. 5-7: Memory Map for General Block Transfer

PROGRAMMING THE 6502

zero, i.e., that we are transferring 256 word blocks. The program appears below:

```
        LDA  #SOURCELO
        STA  FROM
        LDA  #SOURCEHI
        STA  FROM+1     STORE SOURCE ADDRESS
        LDA  #DESTLO
        STA  TO
        LDA  #DESTHI
        STA  TO+1       STORE DEST ADDRESS
        LDX  #BLOCKS    HOW MANY BLOCKS
        LDY  #0         BLOCK SIZE
NEXT    LDA  (FROM),Y   READ ELEMENT
        STA  (TO),Y     TRANSFER IT
        DEY             UPDATE WORD POINTER
        BNE  NEXT       FINISHED?
NEXBLK  INC  FROM+1     INCREMENT BLOCK POINTER
        INC  TO+1       SAME
        DEX             BLOCK COUNTER
        BMI  DONE
        BNE  NEXT
        LDY  #REMAIN
        BNE  NEXT
```

The 16-bit source address is stored by the first four instructions at memory address "FROM." The next four instructions do the same thing for the destination, which is stored at address "TO". Since we have to transfer a number of words greater than 256, we will simply use two 8-bit index registers. The next instruction loads register X with the number of blocks to be transferred. This is instruction 9 in the program. The next instruction loads the value zero in index register Y in order to initialize it for the transfer of 256 words. We will now use indexed indirect addressing. It should be remembered that indexed indirect will result first in an indirection within page zero, then an indexed access to the 16-bit address specified by the index register. Look at the program:

NEXT LDA (FROM), Y

The instruction loads the accumulator with the contents of the memory location whose address is the source plus the index register Y's contents. Look at Figure 5-7 for the memory map. Here, the content of register Y is initially 0. "A" will therefore be loaded from memory address "SOURCE." Note that here, unlike in our

ADDRESSING TECHNIQUES

previous example, we assume that "SOURCE" is the address of the first word within the block.

Using the same technique, the next instruction will deposit the contents of the accumulator (the first word of the block we want to transfer) at the appropriate destination location:

STA (TO), Y

Just as in the preceding case, we simply decrement the index register, then we loop 256 times. This is implemented by the next two instructions:

DEY

BNE NEXT

Caution: a programming trick is used here for compact programming. The alert reader will notice that the index register Y is *decremented*. The first word to be transferred will, therefore, be the word in position 0. The next one will be word 255. This is because decrementing 0 yields all 1's in the register (or 255). The reader should also ascertain that there is no error. Whenever register Y decrements to 0, a transfer *will not* occur. The next instruction to be executed will be: NEXBLK. Therefore, exactly 256 words will have been transferred. Clearly this trick could have been used in the previous program to write a shorter program.

Once a complete block has been transferred, it is simply a matter of pointing to the next page within our original block and our destination block. This is accomplished by adding "1" to the higher order part of the address for source and destination. This is performed by the next two instructions in the program:

NEXBLK INC   FROM+1
       INC   TO+1

After having incremented the page pointer, we simply check whether or not we should transfer one more block by decrementing the block counter contained in X. This is performed by:

DEX

If all blocks have been transferred, we exit from the program by branching to location DONE:

207

BMI DONE

Otherwise, we have two possibilities: Either we have not decremented to 0 or else we have exactly decremented to zero. If we have not yet decremented to 0, we branch to location NEXT:

BNE NEXT

If we have decremented exactly to 0, we still have to transfer the words specified by REMAIN. This is the last part of our transfer. This is accomplished by:

LDY #REMAIN

which loads index Y with the transfer count.
We then branch back to location NEXT:

BNE NEXT

The reader should ascertain that, during this last loop where the branch instruction to NEXT will be executed, the next time we re-enter NEXBLK, we will, indeed, exit for good from this program. This is because the index X had the value 0 prior to entering NEXBLK. The third instruction of NEXBLK will change it to -1, and we will exit to DONE.

Adding Two Blocks

This example will provide a simple illustration of the use of an index register for the addition of two blocks of less than 256 elements. Then, the next program will make use of the indirect indexed feature to address blocks whose address is known to reside at the given location, but whose actual absolute address is not known. The program appears below:

```
BLKADD  LDY   #NBR -1 ———LOAD COUNTER
NEXT    CLC
        LDA   PTR1, Y  ———READ NEXT ELEMENT
        ADC   PTR2, Y     ADD THEM
        STA   PTR3, Y     STORE RESULT
        DEY               DECREMENT COUNTER
        BPL   NEXT        FINISHED?
```

Index Y is used as an index counter and is loaded with the number of elements minus one. We assume that pointer PTR1 points to the first element of Block 1, PTR2 to the first element of

ADDRESSING TECHNIQUES

Block 2, and PTR3 points to the destination area where the results should be stored.

The program is self-explanatory. The last element of Block 1 is read in the accumulator, then added to the last element of Block 2. It is then stored at the appropriate location of Block 3. The next sequential element is added, and so on.

Same Exercise Using Indexed Indirect Addressing

We assume here that the addresses PTR1, PTR2, PTR3 are not known initially. However, we know that they are stored in Page 0 at addresses LOC1, LOC2, LOC3. This is a common mechanism for passing information between subroutines. The corresponding program appears below:

```
BLKADD  LDY   #NBR-1
NEXT    CLC
        LDA   (LOC1), Y
        ADC   (LOC2), Y
        STA   (LOC3), Y
        DEY
        BPL   NEXT
```

The correspondence between this new program and the previous one should now be obvious. It illustrates clearly the use of the indexed indirect mechanism whenever the absolute address is not known at the time that the program is written, but the location of the information is known. It can be noted that the two programs have exactly the same number of instructions. An interesting exercise is now to determine which one will execute faster.

Exercise 5.2: *Compute the number of bytes and the number of cycles for each of these two programs, using the tables in the Appendix section.*

SUMMARY

A complete description of addressing modes has been presented. It has been shown that the 6502 offers most of the possible mechanisms, and its features have been analyzed. Finally, several application programs have been presented to demonstrate the value of each of the addressing mechanisms. Programming the 6502 requires an understanding of these mechanisms.

EXERCISES

5.3: *Write a program to add the first 10 bytes of a table stored at location "BASE." The result will have 16 bits. (This is a checksum computation).*

5.4: *Can you solve the same problem without using the indexing mode?*

5.5: *Reverse the order of the 10 bytes of this table. Store the result at address "REVER."*

5.6: *Search the same table for its largest element. Store it at memory address "LARGE."*

5.7: *Add together the corresponding elements of three tables, whose bases are BASE1, BASE2, BASE3. The length of these tables is stored in page zero at address "LENGTH."*

6
INPUT/OUTPUT TECHNIQUES

INTRODUCTION

We have learned so far how to exchange information between the memory and the various registers of the processor. We have learned to manage the registers and to use a variety of instructions to manipulate the data. We must now learn to communicate with the external world. This is called the input/output.

Input refers to the capture of data from outside peripherals (keyboard, disk, or physical sensor). *Output* refers to the transfer of data from the microprocessor or the memory to external devices such as a printer, a CRT, a disk, or actual sensors and relays.

We will proceed in two steps. First, we will learn to perform the input/output operations required by common devices. Second, we will learn to manage several input/output devices simultaneously, i.e., to *schedule* them. This second part will cover, in particular, polling vs. interrupts.

INPUT/OUTPUT

In this section we will learn to sense or to generate simple signals, such as pulses. Then we will study techniques for enforcing or measuring correct timing. We will then be ready for more complex types of input/output, such as high-speed serial and parallel transfers.

Generate a Signal

In the simplest case, an output device will be turned off (or on) from the computer. In order to change the state of the output device, the programmer will merely change a level from a logical "0" to a logical "1", or from "1" to "0". Let us assume that an external relay is connected to bit "0" of a register called "OUT1." In order to turn it on, we will simply write a "1" into the appropriate bit position of the register. We assume here that OUT1 represents the address of this output register within our system. The program which will turn the relay on is:

```
TURNON   LDA    #%00000001
         STA    OUT1
```

We have assumed that the state of the other 7 bits of the register OUT1 is irrelevant. However, this is often not the case. These bits might be connected to other relays. Let us, therefore, improve this simple program. We want to turn the relay on, without changing the state of any other bit within this register. We will assume that it is possible to read and write the contents of this register. Our improved program now becomes:

```
TURNON  LDA  OUT1          READ CONTENTS OF OUT1
        ORA  #%00000001    FORCE BIT 0 TO "1"
        STA  OUT1
```

The program first reads the contents of location OUT1, then performs an inclusive OR on its contents. This changes only bit position 0 to "1", and leaves the rest of the register intact. (For more details on the ORA operation, refer to Chapter 4). This is illustrated by Figure 6-1.

Pulses

Generating a *pulse* is accomplished exactly as in the case of the *level* above. An output bit is first turned on, then later turned off. This results in a pulse. This is illustrated in Figure 6-2. This time, however, an additional problem must be solved: one must generate the pulse for the correct length of time. Let us, therefore, study the generation of a computed delay.

INPUT/OUTPUT TECHNIQUES

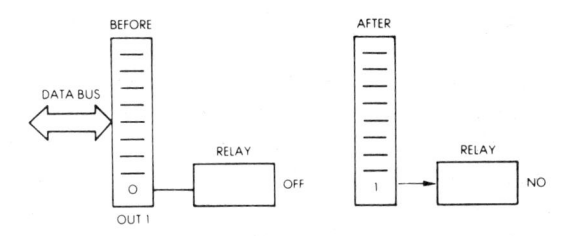

Fig. 6-1: Turning on a Relay

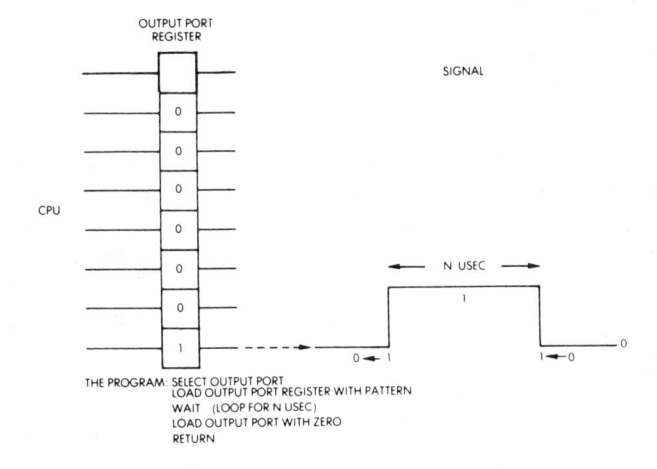

Fig. 6-2: A Programmed Pulse

Delay Generation and Measurement

A delay may be generated by software or by hardware methods. We will study here the way to perform it by program, and later show how it can also be accomplished with a hardware counter, called a programmable interval timer (PIT).

Programmed delays are achieved by counting. A counter register is loaded with a value, then is decremented. The program loops on itself and keeps decrementing until the counter reaches the value "0". The total length of time used by this process will implement the required delay. As an example, let us generate a delay of 37 microseconds.

213

```
DELAY    LDY  #07        Y IS COUNTER
NEXT     DEY             DECREMENT
         BNE  NEXT       TEST
```

This program loads index register Y with the value 7. The next instruction decrements Y, and the next instruction will cause a branch to NEXT to occur as long as Y does not decrement to "0." When Y finally decrements to zero, the program will exit from this loop and execute whatever instruction follows. The logic of the program is simple and appears in the flow chart of Figure 6-3.

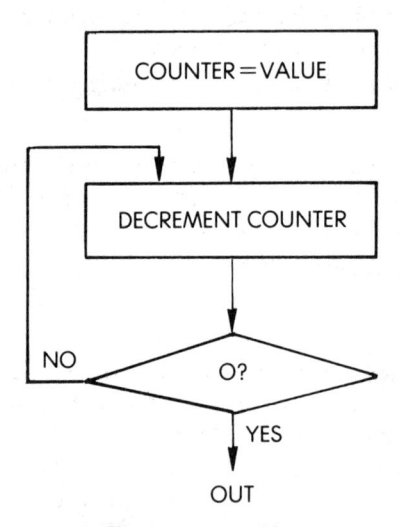

Fig. 6-3: A Delay Flowchart

Let us now compute the effective delay which will be implemented by the program. Looking at the Appendix section of the book, we will look up the number of cycles required by each of these instructions:

LDY, in the immediate mode, requires 2 cycles. DEY will use 2 cycles. Finally, BNE will use 3 cycles. When looking up the number of cycles for BNE in the table, verify that 3 possibilities exist: if the branch does not occur, BNE will only require 2 cycles. If the branch does succeed, which will be the normal case during the loop, then one more cycle is required. Finally, if the page boundary is being crossed, then one extra cycle will be required. We assume here that no page boundary will be crossed.

The timing is, therefore, 2 cycles for the first instruction, plus 5

INPUT/OUTPUT TECHNIQUES

cycles for the next 2, multiplied by the number of times the loop will be executed:
Delay = 2 + 5 × 7 = 37.

Assuming a 1-microsecond cycle time, this programmed delay will be 37 microseconds.

We can see that the maximum definition with which we can adjust the length of the delay is 2 microseconds. The minimum delay is 2 microseconds.

Exercise 6.1: *What is the maximum delay which can be implemented with these three instructions? Can you modify the program to obtain a one microsecond delay?*

Exercise 6.2: *Modify the program to obtain a delay of about 100 microseconds.*

If one wishes to implement a longer delay, a simple solution is to add extra instructions in the program, between DEY and BNE. The simplest way to do so is to add NOP instructions. (The NOP does nothing for 2 cycles).

Longer Delays

Generating longer delays by software can be achieved by using a wider counter. Two internal registers, or, better, two words in the memory, can be used to hold a 16-bit count. To simplify, let us assume that the lower count is "0." The lower byte will be loaded with "255," the maximum count, then go through a decrementation loop. Whenever it is decremented to "0," the upper byte of the counter will be decremented by 1. Whenever the upper byte is decremented to the value "0," the program terminates. If more precision is required in the delay generation, the lower count can have a non-null value. In this case, we would write the program just as explained and add at the end the three-line delay generation program, which has been described above.

Naturally, still longer delays could be generated by using more than two words. This is analogous to the way an odometer works on a car. When the right-most wheel goes from "9" to "0," the next wheel to the left is incremented by 1. This is the general principle when counting with multiple discrete units.

However, the main objection is that when one is counting long delays, the microprocessor will be doing nothing else for hundreds of milliseconds or even seconds. If the computer has nothing else to do, this is perfectly acceptable. However, in the general case, the microcomputer should be available for other tasks so that longer delays are normally not implemented by software. In fact, even short delays may be objectionable in a system if it is to provide some guaranteed response time in given situations. Hardware delays must then be used. In addition, if interrupts are used, timing accuracy may be lost if the counting loop can be interrupted.

Exercise 6.3: *Write a program to implement a 100 ms delay (for a Teletype).*

Hardware Delays

Hardware delays are implemented by using a programmable interval timer, or "timer" for short. A register of the timer is loaded with a value. The difference is that, this time, the timer will automatically decrement this counter periodically. The period is usually adjustable or selectable by the programmer. Whenever the timer will have decremented to "0," it will normally send an interrupt to the microprocessor. It may also set a status bit which can be sensed periodically by the computer. The use of interrupts will be explained later in this chapter.

Other timer operating modes may include starting from "0" and counting the duration of the signal, or else counting the number of pulses received. When functioning as an interval timer, the timer is said to operate in a *one-shot* mode. When counting pulses, it is said to operate in a *pulse-counting* mode. Some timer devices may even include multiple registers and a number of optional facilities which are program-selectable. This is the case, for example, with the timers contained in the 6522 component, an I/O chip described in the next chapter.

Sensing Pulses

The problem of sensing pulses is the reverse problem of generating pulses, plus one more difficulty: whereas an output pulse is generated under program control, input pulses occur *asynchronously* with the program. In order to detect a pulse, two methods may be used: *polling* and *interrupts*. Interrupts will be discussed later in this chapter.

Let us consider now the polling technique. Using this technique, the program reads the value of a given input register continu-

INPUT/OUTPUT TECHNIQUES

ously, testing a bit position, perhaps bit 0. It will be assumed that bit 0 is originally "0." Whenever a pulse is received, this bit will take the value "1." The program monitors bit 0 continuously until it takes the value "1." When a "1" is found, the pulse has been detected. The program appears below:

```
POLL    LDA    #$01
AGAIN   BIT    INPUT
        BNE    AGAIN
ON      ...
```

Conversely, let us assume that the input line is normally "1" and that we wish to detect a "0." This is the normal case for detecting a START bit when monitoring a line connected to a Teletype. The program appears below:

```
POLL    LDA    #$01
NEXT    BIT    INPUT
        BEQ    NEXT
START   ...
```

Monitoring the Duration

Monitoring the duration of the pulse may be accomplished in the same way as computing the duration of an output pulse. Either a hardware or a software technique may be used. When monitoring a pulse by software, a counter is regularly incremented by 1, then the presence of the pulse is verified. If the pulse is still present, the program loops upon itself. Whenever the pulse disappears, the count contained in the counter register is used to compute the effective duration of the pulse. The program appears below

```
DURTN    LDX    #0        CLEAR COUNTER
         LDA    #$01      MONITOR BIT 0
AGAIN    BIT    INPUT
         BPL    AGAIN
LONGER   INX
         BIT    INPUT
         BMI    LONGER
```

Naturally, we assume that the maximum duration of the pulse will not cause register X to overflow. If this were the case, the

PROGRAMMING THE 6502

program would have to be longer to take this into account (or else it would be a programming error!)

Since we now know how to sense and generate pulses, let us capture or transfer larger amounts of data. Two cases will be distinguished: serial data and parallel data. Then we will apply this knowledge to actual input/output devices.

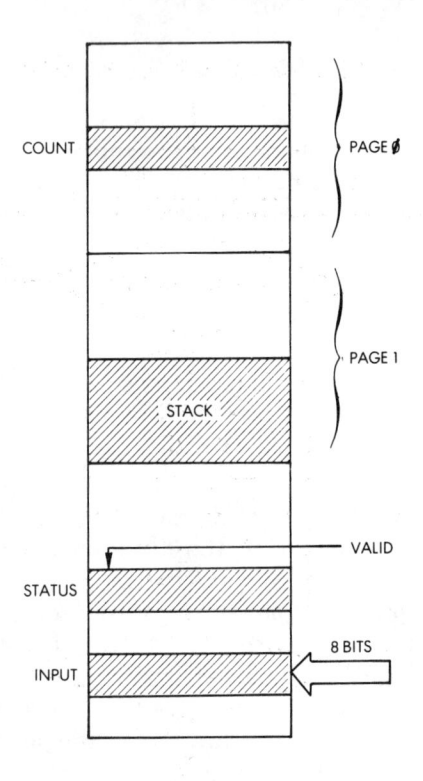

Fig. 6-4: Parallel Word Transfer: The Memory

PARALLEL WORD TRANSFER

It is assumed here that 8 bits of transfer data are available in parallel at address "INPUT." The microprocessor must read the data word at this location whenever a status word indicates that it is valid. The status information will be assumed to be contained in bit 7 of address "STATUS." We will here write a program

INPUT/OUTPUT TECHNIQUES

which will read and automatically save each word of data as it comes in. To simplify, we will assume that the number of words to be read is known in advance and is contained in location "COUNT." If this information were not available, we would test for a so-called *break character*, such as a *rubout*, or perhaps the character "*." We have learned to do this already.

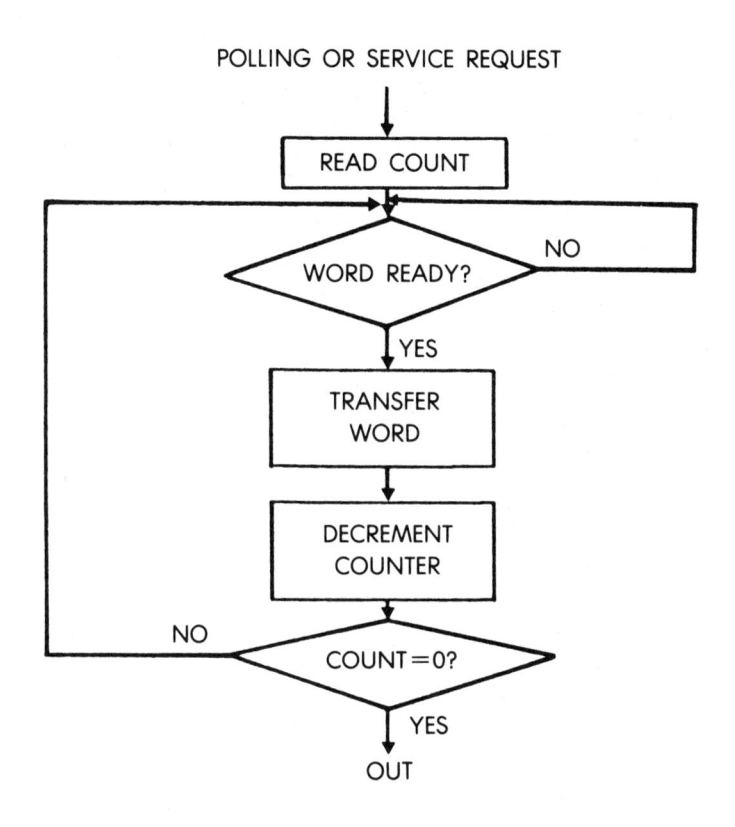

```
        POLLING OR SERVICE REQUEST
                    ↓
              ┌─────────────┐
              │ READ COUNT  │
              └─────────────┘
                    ↓
              ◇ WORD READY? ◇──NO──┐
                    │              │
                   YES             │
                    ↓              │
              ┌─────────────┐      │
              │  TRANSFER   │      │
              │    WORD     │      │
              └─────────────┘      │
                    ↓              │
              ┌─────────────┐      │
              │ DECREMENT   │      │
              │  COUNTER    │      │
              └─────────────┘      │
                    ↓              │
         NO    ◇ COUNT=0? ◇────────┘
                    ↓
                   YES
                    ↓
                   OUT
```

Fig. 6-5: Parallel Word Transfer: Flowchart

The flowchart appears in Figure 6-5. It is quite straightforward. We test the status information until it becomes "1," indicating that a word is ready. When the word is ready, we read it and save it at an appropriate memory location. We decrement the counter and then test whether it has decremented to

PROGRAMMING THE 6502

"0." If so, we are finished; if not, we read the next word. The program which implements this algorithm appears below:

```
PARAL    LDX  COUNT     COUNTER
WATCH    LDA  STATUS    BIT 7 IS "1" IF DATA VALID
         BPL  WATCH     DATA VALID?
         LDA  INPUT     READ IT
         PHA            SAVE IT IN THE STACK
         DEX
         BNE  WATCH
```

The first two instructions of the program read the status information and cause a loop to occur as long as bit 7 of the status register is "0." (It is the sign bit, i.e. bit N).

WATCH LDA STATUS
      BPL WATCH

When BPL fails, data is valid and we can read it:

      LDA INPUT

The word has now been read from address INPUT where it was, and must be saved. Assuming that the number of words to be transferred is small enough, we use:

      PHA

If the stack is full, or the number of words to be transferred is large, we could not push them on the stack and we would have to transfer them to a designated memory area, using, for example, an indexed instruction. However, this would require an extra instruction to increment or decrement the index register. PHA is faster.

The word of data has now been read and saved. We will simply decrement the word counter and test whether we are finished:

      DEX
      BNE WATCH

We keep looping until the counter eventually decrements to "0." This 6-instruction program can be called a *benchmark*. A benchmark program is a carefully optimized program designed to test the capabilities of a given processor in a specific situation. Parallel transfers are one such typical situation. This program has been designed for maximum speed and efficiency. Let us now compute the maximum

INPUT/OUTPUT TECHNIQUES

transfer speed of this program. We will assume that COUNT is contained in page 0. The duration of every instruction is determined by inspecting the table at the end of the book and is found to be the following:

			CYCLES	
	LDX	COUNT	3	
WATCH	LDA	STATUS	4	
	BPL	WATCH	2/3	(FAIL/SUCCEED)
	LDA	INPUT	4	
	PHA		3	
	DEX		2	
	BNE	WATCH	2/3	(FAIL/SUCCEED)

The minimum execution time is obtained by assuming that data is available every time that we sample STATUS. In other words, the first BPL will be assumed to fail every time. Timing is then: $3 + (4+2+4+3+2+3) \times$ COUNT.

Neglecting the first 3 microseconds necessary to initialize the counter register, the time used to transfer one word is 18 microseconds.

The maximum data transfer rate is, therefore,

$$\frac{1}{18(10^{-6})} = 55 \text{ K bytes per second.}$$

Exercise 6.4: *Assume that the number of words to be transferred is greater than 256. Modify the program accordingly and determine the impact on the maximum data transfer rate.*

We have now learned to perform high-speed parallel transfers. Let us consider a more complex case.

BIT SERIAL TRANSFER

A serial input is one in which the bits of information (0's or 1's) come in successively on a line. These bits may come in at regular intervals. This is normally called *synchronous* transmission. Or else, they may come as bursts of data at random intervals. This is called *asynchronous* transmission. We will develop a program which can work in both cases. The principle of the capture of sequential data is simple: we will watch an input line, which will be assumed to be line 0. When a bit of data is detected on this line, we will read the bit in, and shift it into a holding register. Whenever 8 bits have been assembled, we will preserve the

221

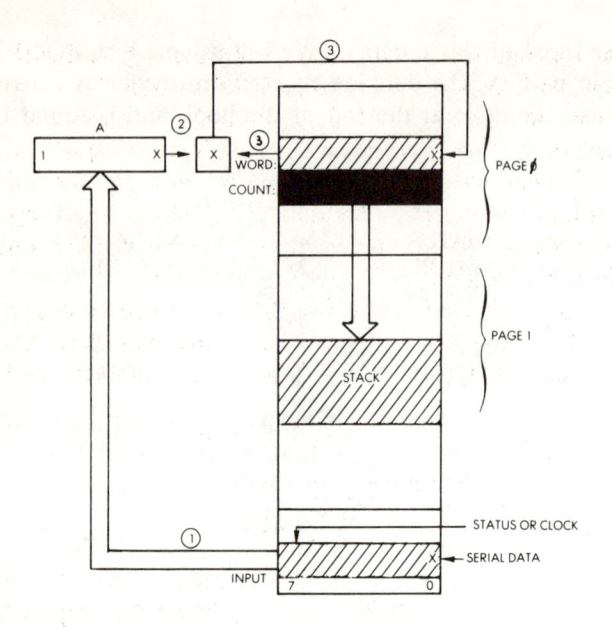

Fig. 6-6: Serial to Parallel Conversion

byte of data into the memory and assemble the next one. In order to simplify, we will assume that the number of bytes to be received is known in advance. Otherwise, we might, for example, have to watch for a special break character, and stop the bit-serial transfer at this point. We have learned to do that. The flow-chart for this program appears in Figure 6-7. The program appears below:

```
SERIAL  LDA  #$00
        STA  WORD
LOOP    LDA  INPUT    BIT 7 IS STATUS, "0" IS DATA
        BPL  LOOP     BIT RECEIVED?
        LSR  A        SHIFT IT INTO C
        ROL  WORD     SAVE BIT IN MEMORY
        BCC  LOOP     CONTINUE IF CARRY = "0"
        LDA  WORD
        PHA           SAVE ASSEMBLED BYTE
        LDA  #$01     RESET BIT COUNTER
        STA  WORD
        DEC  COUNT    DECREMENT WORD COUNT
        BNE  LOOP     ASSEMBLE NEXT WORD
```

INPUT/OUTPUT TECHNIQUES

This program has been designed for efficiency and will use new techniques which we will explain. (See Fig. 6-6.)

The conventions are the following: memory location COUNT is assumed to contain a count of the number of words to be transferred. Memory location WORD will be used to assemble 8 consecutive bits coming in. Address INPUT refers to an input register. It is assumed that bit position 7 of this register is a status flag, or a clock bit. When it is "0," data is not valid. When it is "1," the data is valid. The data itself will be assumed to appear in bit position 0 of this same address. In many instances, the status information will appear on a different register than the data reg-

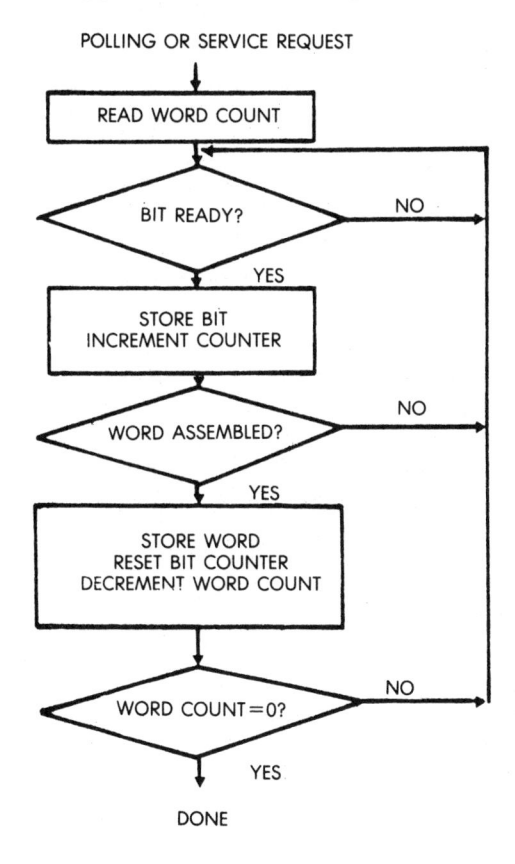

Fig. 6-7: Bit Serial Transfer: Flowchart

ister. It should be a simple task, then, to modify this program accordingly. In addition, we will assume that the first bit of data to be received by this program is guaranteed to be a "1." It indicates that the real data follows. If this were not the case, we will see later an obvious modification to take care of it. The program corresponds exactly to the flowchart of Figure 6-7. The first few lines of the program implement a waiting loop which tests whether a bit is ready. To determine whether a bit is ready, we read the input register then test the sign bit (N). As long as this bit is "0," the instruction BPL will succeed, and we will branch back to the loop. Whenever the status (or clock) bit will become true ("1"), then BPL will fail and the next instruction will be executed.

Remember that BPL means "Branch on Plus," i.e. when bit 7 (the sign bit) is "0." This initial sequence of instructions corresponds to arrow 1 on Figure 6-6.

At this point, the accumulator contains a "1" in bit position 7 and the actual data bit in bit position 0. The first data bit to arrive is going to be a "1." However, the following ones may be either "0" or "1." We now wish to preserve the data bit which has been collected in position 0. The instruction:

LSR A

shifts the contents of the accumulator right by one position. This causes the right-most bit of A, which is our data bit, to fall into the carry bit. We will now preserve this data bit into the memory location WORD (this is illustrated by arrows 2 and 3 in Fig. 6-6):

ROL WORD.

The effect of this instruction is to read the carry bit into the right-most bit position of address WORD. At the same time, the left-most bit of WORD falls into the carry bit. (If you have any doubts about the rotation operation, refer to Chapter 4!)

It is important to remember that a rotation operation will both save the carry bit, here into the right-most bit position, and also recondition the carry bit with the value of bit 7.

Here, a "0" will fall into the carry. The next instruction:

BCC LOOP

tests the carry and branches back to address LOOP as long as the carry is "0." This is our automatic bit counter. It can readily be seen that as a result of the first ROL, WORD will contain "00000001." Eight shifts later, the "1" will finally fall into the carry bit and stop the branching. This is an ingenious way to implement an automatic loop counter without having to waste an instruction to decrement the contents of an index register. This technique is used in order to shorten the program and improve its performance.

Whenever BCC finally fails, 8 bits have been assembled into location WORD. This value should be preserved in the memory. This is accomplished by the next instructions (arrow 4 in Fig. 6-6):

LDA WORD
PHA

We are here saving the WORD of data (8 bits) into the stack. Saving it into the stack is possible only if there is enough room in the stack. Provided that this condition is met, it is the fastest way to preserve a word in the memory. The stack pointer is updated automatically. If we were not pushing a word in the stack, we would have to use one more instruction to update a memory pointer. We could equivalently perform an indexed addressing operation, but that would also involve decrementing or incrementing the index, using extra time.

After the first WORD of data has been saved, there is no longer any guarantee that the first data bit to come in will be a "1." It can be anything. We must, therefore, reset the contents of WORD to "00000001" so that we can keep using it as a bit counter. This is performed by the next two instructions:

LDA #$01
STA WORD

Finally, we will decrement the word counter, since a word has been assembled, and test whether we have reached the end of the transfer. This is accomplished by the next two instructions:

DEC COUNT
BNE LOOP

The above program has been designed for speed, so that one may capture a fast input stream of data bits. Once the program terminates, it is naturally advisable to immediately read away from the stack the words that have been saved there and transfer them elsewhere into the memory. We have already learned to perform such a block transfer in Chapter 2.

Exercise 6.5: *Compute the maximum speed at which this program will be able to read serial bits. To compute this speed, assume that addresses WORD and COUNT are kept in Page 0. Also, assume that the complete program resides within the same page. Look up the number of cycles required by every instruction, in the table at the end of this book, then compute the time which will elapse during execution of this program. To compute the length of time which will be used by a loop, simply multiply the total duration of this loop, expressed in microseconds, by the number of times it will be executed. Also, when computing the maximum speed, assume that a data bit will be ready every time that the input location is sensed.*

This program is more difficult to understand than the previous ones. Let us look at it again (refer to Figure 6-6) in more detail, examining some trade-offs.

A bit of data comes into bit position 0 of "INPUT" from time to time. There might be, for example, three "1's" in succession. We must, therefore, differentiate between the successive bits coming in. This is the function of the "clock" signal.

The clock (or STATUS) signal tells us that the input bit is now valid.

Before reading a bit, we will therefore first test the status bit. If the status is "0", we must wait. If it is "1", then the data bit is good.

We assume here that the status signal is connected to bit 7 of register INPUT.

Exercise 6.6: *Can you explain why bit 7 is used for status, and bit 0 for data?*

Once we have captured a data bit, we want to preserve it in a safe location, then shift it left, so that we can get the next bit.

Unfortunately, the accumulator is used to read and test both data and status in this program. If we were to accumulate data in the accumulator, bit position 7 would be erased by the status bit.

Exercise 6.7: *Can you suggest a way to test status without erasing the contents of the accumulator (a special instruction)? If this*

INPUT/OUTPUT TECHNIQUES

can be done, could we use the accumulator to accumulate the successive bits coming in?

Exercise 6.8: *Re-write the program, using the accumulator to store the bits coming in. Compare it to the previous one in terms of speed and number of instructions.*

Let us address two more possible variations:
  We have assumed that, in our particular example, the very first bit to come in would be a special signal, guaranteed to be "1." However, in the general case, it may be anything.

Exercise 6.9: *Modify the program above, assuming that the very first bit to come in is valid data (not to be discarded), and can be "0" or "1." Hint: our "bit counter" should still work correctly, if you initialize it with the correct value.*

Finally, we have been saving the assembled WORD in the stack, to gain time. We could naturally save it in a specified memory area:

Exercise 6.10: *Modify the program above, and save the assembled WORD in the memory area starting at BASE.*

Exercise 6.11: *Modify the program above so that the transfer will stop when the character "S" is detected in the input stream.*

The Hardware Alternative

As usual for most standard input/output algorithms, it is possible to implement this procedure by hardware. The chip is called a UART. It will automatically accumulate the bits. However, when one wishes to reduce the component count, this program, or a variation of it, will be used instead.

Exercise 6.12: *Modify the program assuming that data is available in bit position 0 of location INPUT, while the status information is available in bit position 0 of address INPUT + 1.*

BASIC I/O SUMMARY

We have now learned to perform elementary input/output operations as well as to manage a stream of parallel data or serial bits. We are ready to communicate with real input/output devices.

COMMUNICATING WITH INPUT/OUTPUT DEVICES

In order to exchange data with input/output devices, we will first have to ascertain whether data is available, if we want to read it, or whether the device is ready to accept data, if we want to send it. Two procedures may be used: handshaking and interrupts. Let us study handshaking first.

Handshaking

Handshaking is generally used to communicate between any two asynchronous devices, i.e., between any two devices which are not synchronized. For example, if we want to send a word to a parallel printer, we must first make sure that the input buffer of this printer is available. We will, therefore, ask the printer: Are you ready? The printer will say "yes" or "no." If it is not ready we will wait. If it is ready, we will send the data. (See Fig. 6-8.)

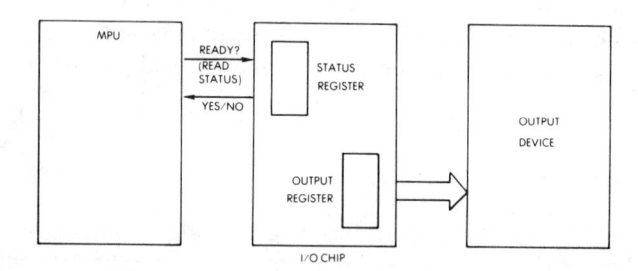

Fig. 6-8: Handshaking (Output)

Conversely, before reading data from an input device, we will verify whether the data is valid. We will ask: "Is data valid?" And the device will tell us "yes" or "no." The "yes" or "no" may be indicated by status bits, or by other means. (See Fig. 6-9.)

INPUT/OUTPUT TECHNIQUES

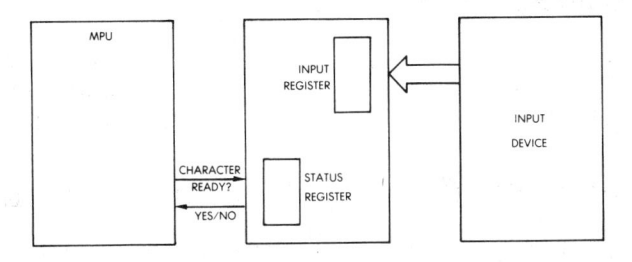

Fig. 6-9: Handshaking (Input)

In short, whenever you wish to exchange information with someone who is independent and might be doing something else at the time, you should ascertain that he is ready to communicate with you. The usual courtesy rule is to shake his hand. Data exchange may then follow. This is the procedure normally used in communicating with input/output devices.

Let us illustrate this procedure now with a simple example:

Sending a Character To The Printer

The character will be assumed to be contained in memory location CHAR. The program to print it appears below:

```
CHARPR   LDX  CHAR      READ CHARACTER
WAIT     LDA  STATUS    BIT 7 IS "READY"
         BPL  WAIT
         TXA
         STA  PRINTD
```

Register X is first loaded from the memory with a character to be printed. Then we test the status bit of the printer to determine that it is ready to accept the character. As long as it is not ready to print, however, we branch back to address WAIT, and we loop. Whenever the printer indicates that it is ready to print by setting its ready-bit (here bit 7 by convention of address STATUS), we can send the character. We transfer the character from register X to register A:

TXA

and we send it to the printer's output register address, called here PRINTD.

STA PRINTD

Exercise 6.13: *Modify the program above to print a string of n characters, where n will be assumed to be less than 255.*

Exercise 6.14: *Modify the above program to print a string of characters until a "carriage-return" code is encountered.*

Let us now complicate the output procedure by requiring a code conversion and by outputting to several devices at a time:

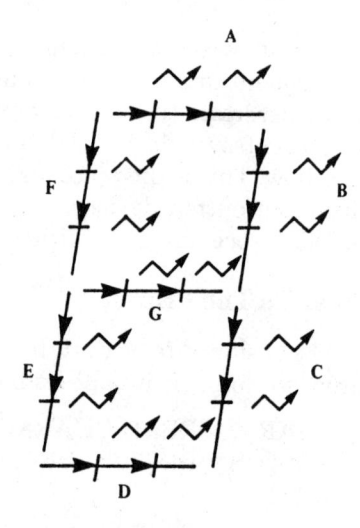

Fig. 6-10: Seven Segment LED

Output to a 7-Segment LED

A traditional 7-segment light-emitting-diode (LED) may display the digits "0" through "9," or even "0" through "F" hexadecimal by lighting combinations of its 7 segments. A 7-segment LED is shown in illustration 6-10. The characters that may be generated with this LED appear in Figure 6-11. The segments of an LED ARE LABELLED "A" through "G" in Figure 6-10.

For example, "0" will be displayed by lighting the segments

INPUT/OUTPUT TECHNIQUES

"ABCDEF." Let us assume, now, that bit "0" of an output port is connected to segment "A," that "1" is connected to segment "B," and so on. Bit 7 is not used. The binary code required to light up "FEDCBA" (to display "0") is, therefore, "0111111." In hexadecimal this is "3F." Do the following exercise.

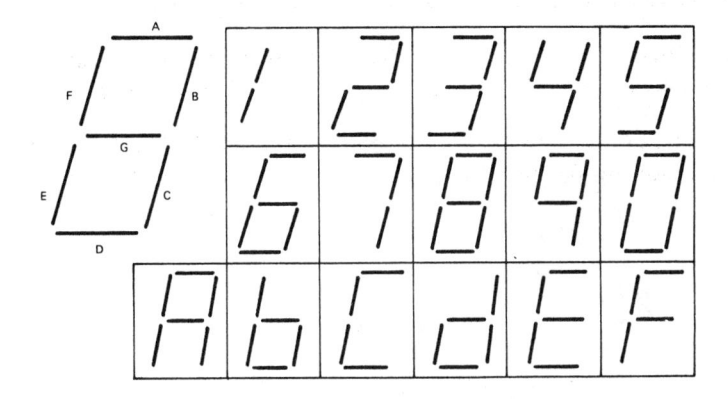

Fig. 6-11: Characters Generated with a 7-Segment LED

Exercise 6.15: *Compute the 7-segment equivalent for the hexadecimal digits "0" through "F." Fill out the table below:*

Hex	LED code	Hex	LED code	Hex	LED code	Hex	LED code
0	3F	4		8		C	
1		5		9		D	
2		6		A		E	
3		7		B		F	

Let us now display hexadecimal values on *several* LEDs.

Driving Multiple LEDs

An LED has no memory. It will display the data only as long as its segment lines are active. In order to keep the cost of an LED display low, the microprocessor will display information in turn on *each of the LEDs*. The rotation between the LEDs must be fast enough so that there is no apparent blinking. This implies that the time spent from one LED to the next is less than 100 milliseconds. Let us design a program which will accomplish this. Register Y will be used to point to the LED on which we want to display a digit. The accumulator is assumed to contain the hexadecimal value to be displayed on the LED. Our first concern is to convert the hexadecimal value into its 7-segment representation. In the preceding section, we have built the equivalence table. Since we are accessing a table, we will use the indexed addressing mode, where the displacement index will be provided by the hexadecimal value. This means that the 7-segment code for hexadecimal digit #3 is obtained by looking up the third element of the table after the base. The address of the base will be called SEGBAS. The program appears below:

```
LEDS     TAX                  USE HEX VALUE AS INDEX
         LDA    SEGBAS,X      READ CODE IN A
         LDX    #$00
         STX    SEGDAT        TURN OFF SEGMENT DRIVERS
         STA    SEGDAT        DISPLAY DIGIT
         LDX    #$70          ANY LARGE NUMBER
         STY    SEGADR
DELAY    DEX
         BNE    DELAY
         DEY                  POINT TO NEXT LED
         BNE    OUT
         LDY    LEDNBR
OUT      RTS
```

The program assumes that register Y contains the number of the LED to be illuminated next, and that register X contains the digit to be displayed.

The program first looks up the 7-segment code corresponding to the hexadecimal value contained in the accumulator with its first two instructions. The next two instructions load "00" as the value of the segments to be displayed, i.e., turn them off. The next instruction then selects the appropriate LED segments for display: STY SEGADR.

A three-instruction loop delay is then implemented before switching to the next LED. Finally, the LED pointer is decremented. (It could be incremented).

If the LED pointer decrements to "0," it must be reloaded with the highest LED number. This is accomplished by the next two instructions. It is assumed here that this is a subroutine and the last instruction is an RTS: "return from subroutine."

INPUT/OUTPUT TECHNIQUES

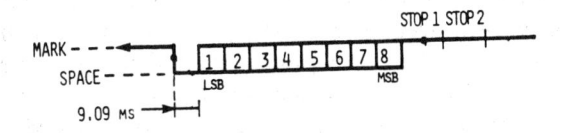

Fig. 6-12: Format of a Teletype Word

Exercise 6.16: *Assuming that the above program is a subroutine, you will notice that it uses registers X and Y internally and modifies their contents. Assuming that the subroutine may freely use the memory area designated by address T1, T2, T3, T4, T5, could you add instructions at the beginning and at the end of this program which will guarantee that, when the subroutine returns, the contents of registers X and Y will be the same as when the subroutine was entered?*

Exercise 6.17: *Same exercise as above, but assume that the memory area T1, etc. is not available to the subroutine. (Hint: remember that there is a built-in mechanism in every computer for preserving information in a chronological order).*

We have now solved common input/output problems. Let us consider the case of a real peripheral: the Teletype.

Teletype Input/Output

The Teletype is a serial device. It both sends and receives words of information in a serial format. Each character is encoded in an 8-bit ASCII format (the ASCII table appears at the end of this

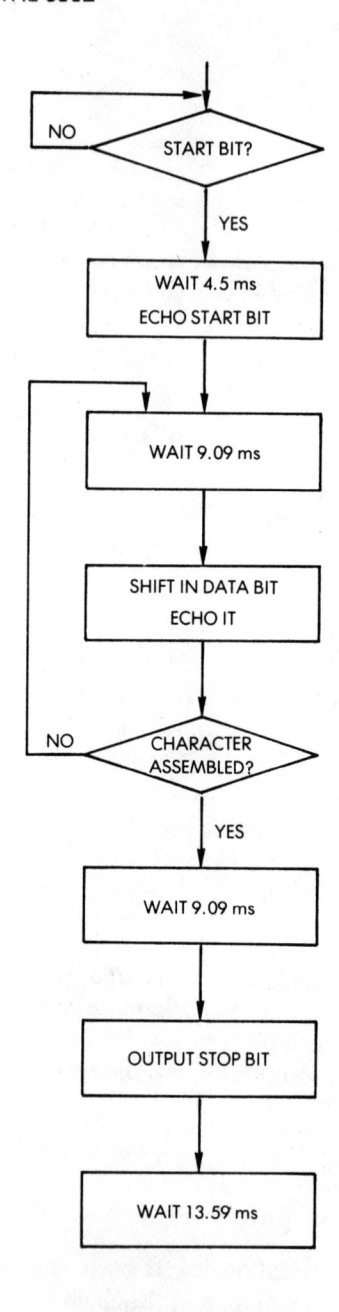

Fig. 6-13: TTY Input with Echo

INPUT/OUTPUT TECHNIQUES

book). In addition, every character is preceded by a "start" bit, and terminated by two "stop" bits. In the so-called 20-milliamp current loop interface, which is most frequently used, the state of the line is normally a "1." This is used to indicate to the processor that the line has not been cut. A start is a "1"-to-"0" transition. It indicates to the receiving device that data bits follow. The standard Teletype is a 10-characters-per-second device. We have just established that each character requires 11 bits. This means that the Teletype will transmit 110 bits per second. It is said to be a 110-baud device. We will design a program to serialize bits in from the Teletype at the correct speed.

One hundred and ten bits per second implies that bits are separated by 9.09 milliseconds. This will have to be the duration of the delay loop to be implemented between successive bits. The format of a Teletype word appears in Figure 6-12. The flowchart for bit input appears in Figure 6-13. The program follows:

```
TTYN    LDA   STATUS
        BPL   TTYIN     USUAL STATUS POLL
        JSR   DELAY     WAIT 9.09 MS
        LDA   TTYBIT    START BIT
        STA   TTYBIT    ECHO BACK
        JSR   DELAY
        LDX   #$08      BIT COUNTER
NEXT    LDA   TTYBIT    SAVE INPUT
        STA   TTYBIT    ECHO BACK
        LSR   A         SAVE BIT IN CARRY
        ROL   CHAR      SAVE BIT IN CHAR
        JSR   DELAY
        DEX             NEXT BIT
        BNE   NEXT
        LDA   TTYBIT    STOP BIT
        STA   TTYBIT
        JSR   DELAY
        RTS
```

Fig. 6-14: Input from Teletype

Note that this program differs slightly from the flowchart of Fig. 6-13.

235

PROGRAMMING THE 6502

The program should be examined with attention. The logic is quite simple. The new fact is that, whenever a bit is read from the Teletype (at address TTYBIT), it is echoed back to the Teletype. This is a standard feature of the Teletype. Whenever a user presses a key, the information is transmitted to the processor and then back to the printing mechanism of the Teletype. This verifies that the transmission lines are working and that the processor is operating when a character is, indeed, printing correctly on the paper.

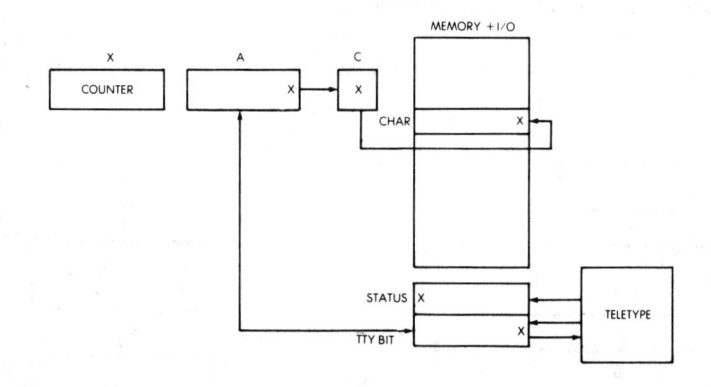

Fig. 6-15: Teletype Input

The first two instructions are the waiting loop. The program waits for the status bit to become true before it starts reading bits in. As usual, the status bit is assumed to come in bit position 7, since this position can be tested in one instruction by BPL (Branch on Plus-this is the sign bit).

JSR is the subroutine jump. We use a DELAY subroutine to implement the 9.09 ms on delay. Note that DELAY can be a delay loop, or can use the hardware timer, if our system has one.

The first bit to come in is the start bit. It should be echoed to the Teletype, but otherwise ignored. This is done by instructions 4 and 5.

Again, we wait for the next bit. But, this time, it is a true data bit, and we must save it. Since all shift instructions will drop a bit in the carry flag, we need two instructions to preserve our data bit (the X in Figure 6-15): one to drop it into C (LSR A),

INPUT/OUTPUT TECHNIQUES

and one to preserve it into memory location CHAR (ROL).

Beware of one problem: the "ROL" will destroy the contents of C. If we want to echo the data bit back, a precaution must be taken to preserve it before it disappears into CHAR. Finally, we echo the data bit (STA TTYBIT) and wait for the next one (JSR DELAY) until we accumulate all eight data bits (DEX).

Whenever we decrement to zero, all 8 bits are in CHAR. We just have to echo the STOP bits, and we are finished.

Exercise 6.18: *Write the delay routine which results in the 9.09 millisecond delay. (DELAY subroutine)*

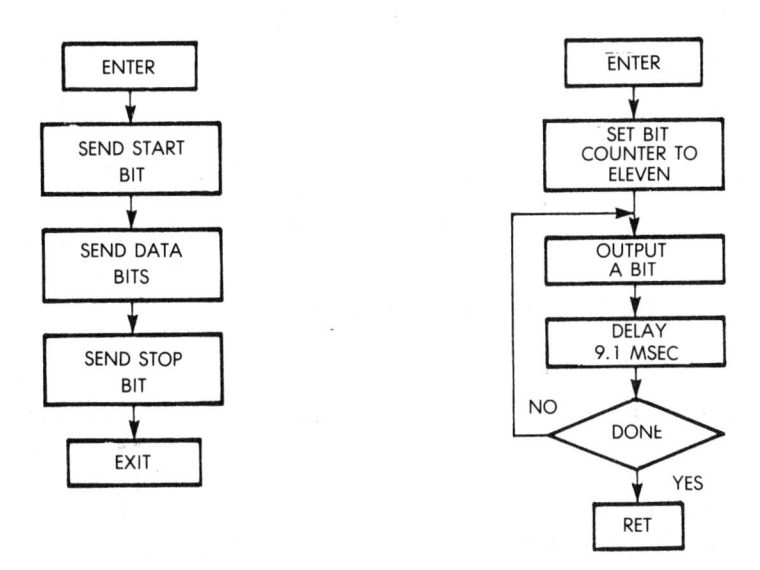

Fig. 6-16: Teletype Output

Exercise 6.19: *Using the example of the program developed above, write a PRINTC program which will print on the Teletype the contents of memory location CHAR.*

Exercise 6.20: *Modify the program so that it waits for a START bit instead of a STATUS bit.*

Printing a String of Characters

We will assume that the PRINTC routine (see Exercise 6-18) takes care of printing a character on our printer, display, or any output device. We will here print the contents of memory locations START N to START .

We will naturally use the indexed addressing mode and the program is straight-forward:

```
PSTRING   LDX   #N         NUMBERS OF WORDS
NEXT      LDA   START + N
          JSR   PRINTC
          DEX
          BPL   NEXT
```

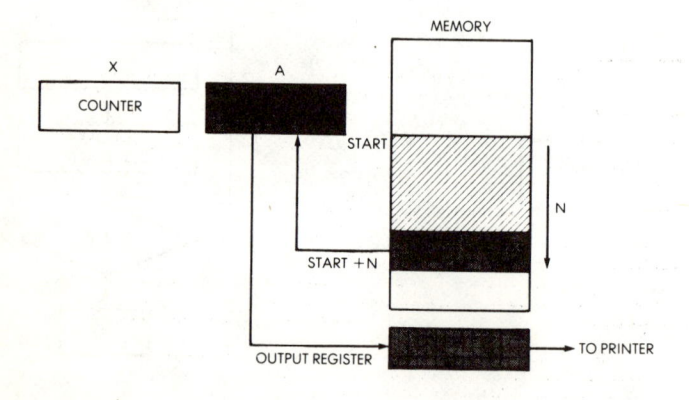

Fig. 6-17: Print a Memory Block

PERIPHERAL SUMMARY

We have now described the basic programming techniques used to communicate with typical input/output devices. In addition to the data transfer, it will be necessary to condition one or more

INPUT/OUTPUT TECHNIQUES

control registers within each I/O device in order to condition correctly the transfer speeds, the interrupt mechanism, and the various other options. The manual for each device should be consulted. (For more details on the specific algorithms to exchange information with all the usual peripherals, the reader is referred to our book,"C207, Microprocessor Interfacing Techniques.")

We have now learned to manage single devices. However, in a real system, all peripherals are connected to the busses, and may request service simultaneously. How are we going to schedule the processor's time?

INPUT/OUTPUT SCHEDULING

Since input/output requests may occur simultaneously, a scheduling mechanism must be implemented in every system to determine in which order service will be granted. Three basic input/output techniques are used, which can be combined. They are: polling, interrupt, DMA. Polling and interrupts will be described here. DMA is purely a hardware tech-

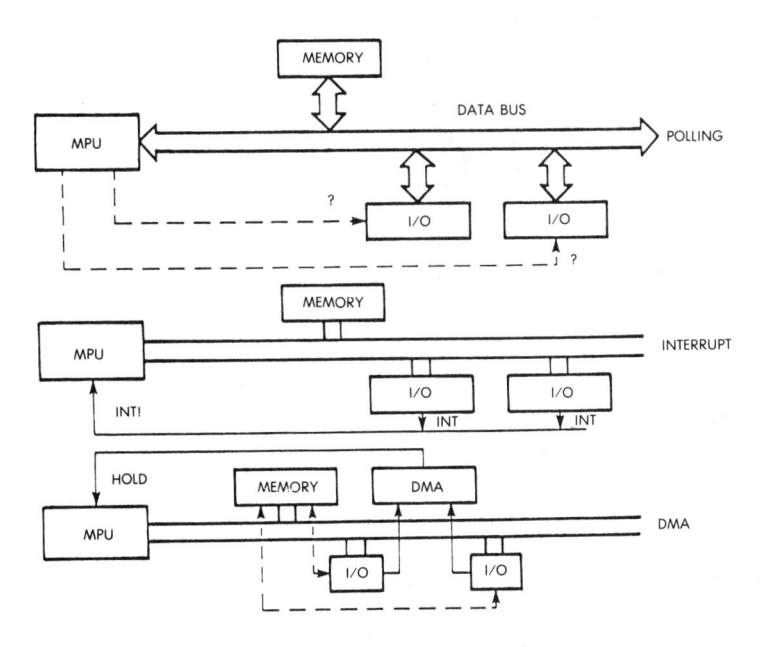

Fig. 6-18: Three Methods of I/O Control

nique, and as such will not be described here. (It is covered in the reference books C201 and C207).

Polling

Conceptually, polling is the simplest method for managing multiple peripherals. With this strategy, the processor interrogates the devices connected to the busses in turn. If a device requests service, the service is granted. If it does not request service, the next peripheral is examined. Polling is not just used for the devices, but for *any device service routine.*

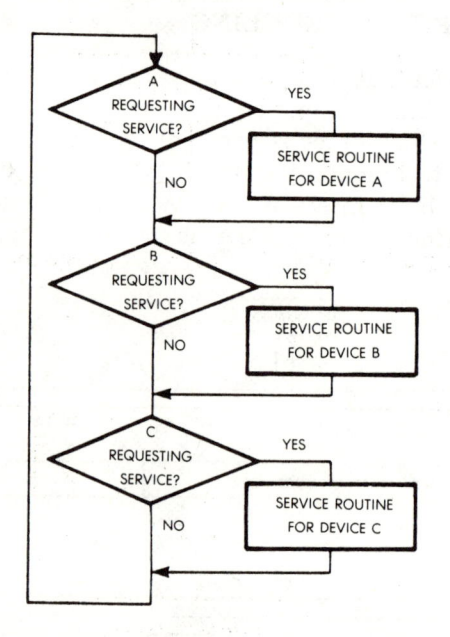

Fig. 6-19: Polling Loop Flow-chart

As an example, if the system is equipped with a Teletype, a tape recorder, and a CRT display, the polling routine would interrogate the Teletype: "Do you have a character to transmit?" It would interrogate the Teletype *output routine,* asking: "Do you have a character to send?" Then, assuming that the answers are negative so far, it would interrogate the tape recorder routines, and finally the CRT display. In the case that only one device is connected to a system, polling will be used as

INPUT/OUTPUT TECHNIQUES

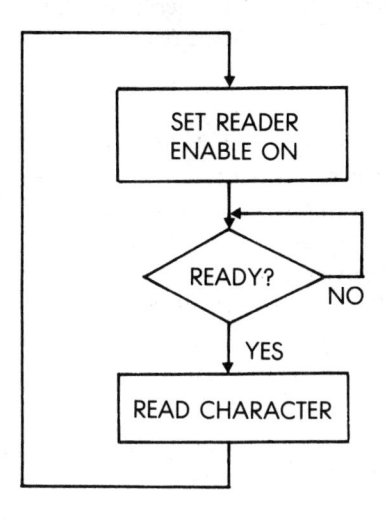

Fig. 6-20: Reading from a Paper-Tape Reader

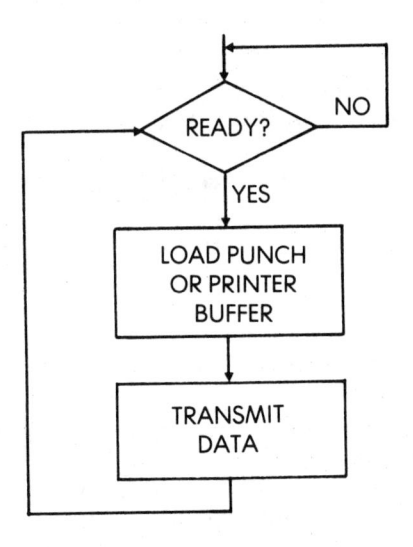

Fig. 6-21: Printing on a Punch or Printer

well to determine whether it needs service. As an example, the flow-charts for reading from a paper-tape reader and for printing on a printer appear in Figures 6-20 and 6-21.

Example: a polling loop for devices 1, 2, 3, 4, (see Fig. 6-18):

```
POLL4   LDA  STATUS1    SERVICE REQUEST IS BIT 7
        BMI  ONE
        LDA  STATUS2    DEVICE2?
        BMI  TWO
        LDA  STATUS3    DEVICE3?
        BMI  THREE
        LDA  STATUS4    DEVICE4
        BMI  FOUR
        JMP  POLL4      TEST AGAIN
```

Bit 7 of the status register for each device is "1" when it wants service. When a request is sensed, this program branches to the device handler, at address ONE for device 1, TWO for device 2, etc.

The advantages of polling are obvious: it is simple, does not require any hardware assistance, and keeps all input/output synchronous with the program operation. Its disadvantage is just as obvious: most of the processor's time is wasted looking at devices that do not need service. In addition, the processor might give service to a device too late, by wasting so much time.

Another mechanism is, therefore, desirable which guarantees that the processor's time can be used to perform useful computations, rather than polling devices needlessly all the time. However, let us stress that polling is used extensively whenever a microprocessor has nothing better to do, as it keeps the overall organization simple. Let us now examine the essential alternative to polling: interrupts.

Interrupts

The concept of interrupts is illustrated in Figure 6-18. A special hardware line is available, the interrupt line, which is connected to a specialized pin of the microprocessor. Multiple input/output devices may be connected to this interrupt line. When any one of them needs service, it sends a level or a pulse on this line. An interrupt signal is the service request from an input/output

INPUT/OUTPUT TECHNIQUES

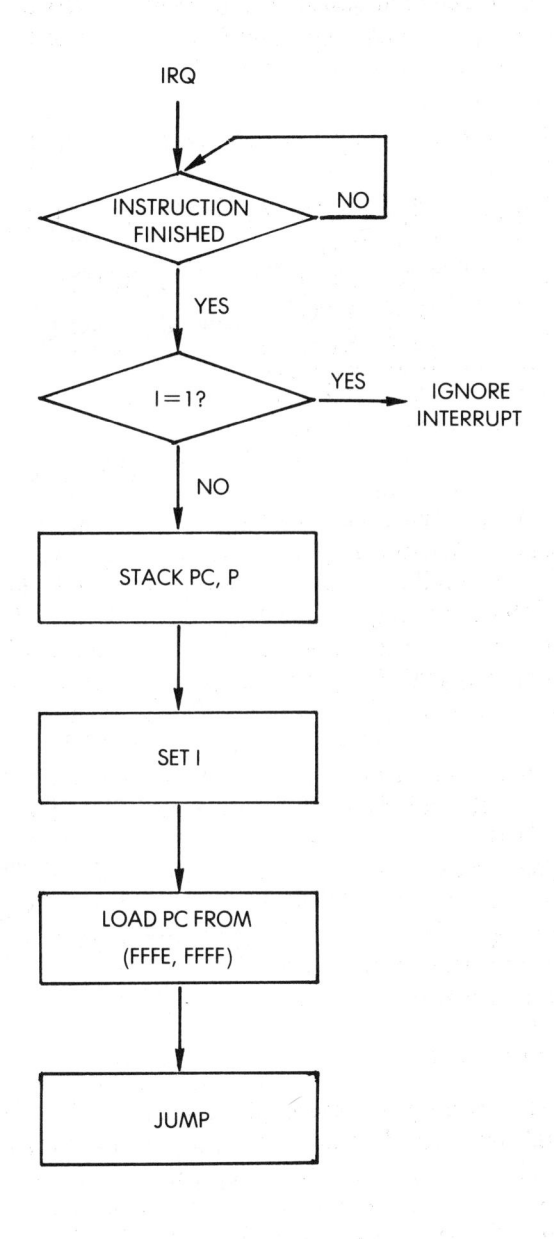

Fig. 6-22: Interrupt Processing

device to the processor. Let us examine the response of the processor to this interrupt.

In any case, the processor completes the instruction that it was currently executing, or else this would create chaos inside the microprocessor. Next, the microprocessor should branch to an interrupt handling routine which will process the interrupt. Branching to such a subroutine implies that the contents of the program counter must be saved on the stack. *An interrupt must, therefore, cause the automatic preservation of the program counter on the stack.* In addition, the status register (P) should also be automatically preserved, as its contents will be altered by any subsequent instruction. Finally, if the interrupt handling routine should modify any internal registers, these internal registers should also be preserved on the stack.

After all these registers have been preserved, one can branch to the appropriate interrupt handling address. At the end of this routine, all the registers should be restored, and a special interrupt return should be executed so that the main program will resume execution. Let us examine in more detail the two interrupt lines of the 6502.

6502 Interrupts

The 6502 is equipped with two interrupt lines, IRQ and NMI. IRQ is the regular interrupt line, while NMI is a higher priority non-maskable interrupt. Let us examine their operation.

IRQ is the level-activated interrupt. The status of the IRQ line will be sensed or ignored by the microprocessor depending upon the value of its internal flag I (interrput-mask flag). We will initially assume that interrupts are enabled. Whenever IRQ is activated, the interrupt will be sensed by the microprocessor. As soon as the interrupt is accepted (upon completion of the instruction currently executing), the internal I flag is automatically set. This will prevent the microprocessor from being interrupted again at a time when it is manipulating internal registers. The 6502 then automatically preserves the contents of PC (the program counter) and P (the status register) into the stack. The aspect of the stack after an interrupt has been processed is illustrated by Figure 6-23.

Next, the 6502 will automatically fetch the content of memory locations "FFFE" and "FFFF." This 16-bit memory location will

INPUT/OUTPUT TECHNIQUES

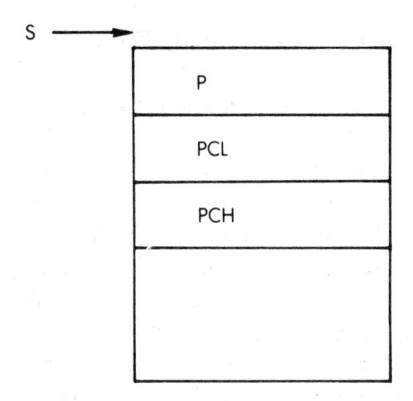

Fig. 6-23: 6502 Stack After Interrupt

contain the *interrupt-vector*. The 6502 will fetch the contents of this address, then branch to the specified 16-bit vector. The user is responsible for depositing this vectoring address at "FFFE"-"FFFF". However, several devices may be connected to the IRQ line. In this case, we are branching to a single interrupt handling routine. How are we going to differentiate between the various devices? This will be studied in the next section.

The NMI interrupt is essentially identical to IRQ except that it

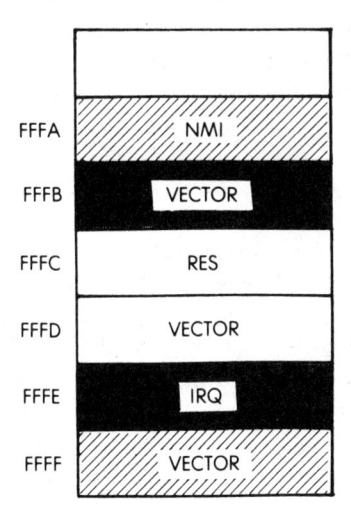

Fig. 6-24: Interrupt Vectors

cannot be masked by the I bit. It is a higher priority interrupt, typically used for power failures. Its operation is otherwise identical except that the processor branches automatically to the contents of "FFFA"-"FFFB". This is illustrated in Figure 6-24.

The return from an interrupt is accomplished by instruction RTI. This instruction transfers back into the microprocessor the top three words of the stack which contains P and PC (the 16-bit program counter). The program which had been interrupted can then resume. The internal state of the machine is exactly identical to the one at the time that the interrupt occurred. The effect has been to introduce a delay in the execution of the program.

Prior to returning from an interrupt, the programmer is responsible for clearing the interrupt that it has now serviced, and restoring the interrupt disable flag. In addition, should the interrupt handling routine modify the contents of any register, such as X or Y, the programmer is specifically responsible for preserving these registers in the stack prior to executing the interrupt handling routine. Otherwise, the contents of these registers will be modified, and when the interrupted program resumes execution, it will not be correct.

Assuming that the interrupt handling routine will use registers A, X, and Y, five instructions will be necessary within the interrupt handler to preserve these registers. They are:

```
SAVAXY    PHA    PUSH A IN THE STACK
          TXA    TRANSFER X TO A
          PHA    PUSH IT
          TYA    TRANSFER Y TO A
          PHA    PUSH IT
```

Unfortunately, the 6502 may only directly push the contents of A or P on the stack. As a result, preserving X and Y is time-consuming; it requires 4 instructions. This is illustrated in Figure 6-25.

Upon the completion of the interrupt handling routine, these registers must be restored and the interrupt handler must terminate with the sequence of six instructions:

INPUT/OUTPUT TECHNIQUES

PLA	PULL Y FROM STACK
TAY	RESTORE Y
PLA	PULL X
TAX	RESTORE X
PLA	RESTORE A
RTI	EXIT

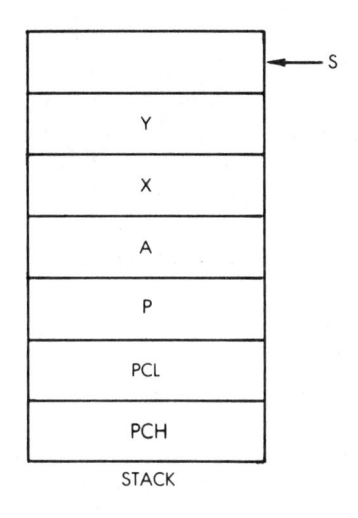

```
        ┌─────────┐
        │         │ ←── S
        ├─────────┤
        │    Y    │
        ├─────────┤
        │    X    │
        ├─────────┤
        │    A    │
        ├─────────┤
        │    P    │
        ├─────────┤
        │   PCL   │
        ├─────────┤
        │   PCH   │
        └─────────┘
           STACK
```

Fig. 6-25: Saving all the Registers

Exercise 6.21: *Using the table indicating the number of cycles per instruction, in the Appendix, compute how much time will be lost by saving and then restoring registers A, X, and Y.*

For a graphic comparison of the polling process vs. the interrupt process, refer to Figure 6-18, where the polling process is illustrated on the top, and the interrupt process underneath. It can be seen that in the polling technique, the program wastes a lot of time waiting. Using interrupts, the program is interrupted, the interrupt is serviced, then the program resumes. However, the obvious disadvantage of an interrupt is to introduce several additional instructions at the beginning and at the end, resulting in a delay before the first instruction of the device handler can be executed. This is additional overhead.

PROGRAMMING THE 6502

Having clarified the operation of the two interrupt lines, let us now consider two important problems remaining:

1. How do we resolve the problem of multiple devices triggering an interrupt at the same time?
2. How do we resolve the problem of an interrupt occurring while another interrupt is being serviced?

Multiple Devices Connected to a Single Interrupt Line

Whenever an interrupt occurs, the processor automatically branches to an address contained at "FFFE-FFFF" (for an IRQ), or at "FFFA-FFFB" (for an NMI). Before it can do any effective processing, the interrupt handling routine must determine which device triggered the interrupt. Two methods are available to identify the device, as usual: a software method and a hardware method.

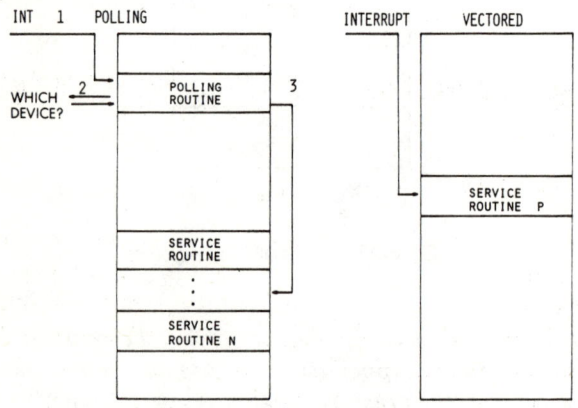

Fig. 6-26: Polled vs. Vectored Interrupt

In the software method, polling is used: the microprocessor interrogates each of the devices in turn and asks them, "Did you trigger the interrupt?" If not, it interrogates the next one. This process is illustrated in Figure 6-26. A sample program is:

```
        LDA     STATUS 1
        BMI     ONE
        LDA     STATUS 2
        BMI     TWO
```

INPUT/OUTPUT TECHNIQUES

The hardware method uses additional components but provides the address of the interrupting device simultaneously with the interrupt request. The device now universally used to provide this facility is called a "PIC," or priority-interrupt-controller. Such a PIC will automatically place on the data bus the actual required branching address for the interrupting peripheral. When the 6502 goes to "FFFE"-"FFFF," it will fetch this vectoring address. This concept is illustrated in Figure 6-26.

In most cases, the speed of reaction to an interrupt is not crucial, and a polling approach is used. If response time is a primary consideration, a hardware approach must be used.

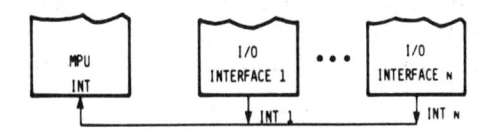

Fig. 6-27: Several Devices May Use the Same Interrupt Line

Multiple Interrupts

The next problem which may occur is that a new interrupt can be triggered during the execution of an interrupt handling routine. Let us examine what happens and how the stack is used to solve the problem. We have indicated in Chapter 2 that this was another essential role of the stack, and the time has come now to demonstrate its use. We will refer to Figure 6-28 to illustrate multiple interrupts. Time elapses from left to right in the illustration. The contents of the stack are shown at the bottom of the illustration. Looking at the left, at time T0, program P is in execution. Moving to the right, at time T1, interrupt I1 occurs. We will assume that the interrupt mask was enabled, authorizing I1. Program P will be suspended. This is shown at the bottom of the illustration. The stack will contain the program counter and the status register of Program P, at least, plus any optional registers that might be saved by the interrupt handler or I1 itself.

At time T1, interrupt I1 starts executing until time T2. At time T2, interrupt I2 occurs. We will assume that interrupt I2 is considered to have a higher priority than interrupt I1. If it had a

PROGRAMMING THE 6502

```
TIME            T₀   T₁      T₂          T₃      T₄      T₅   T₆
PROGRAM P       ├──┤ ─ ─ ─ ─ ─ ─ ─ ─ ─ ─ ─ ─ ─ ─ ─ ─ ─ ─ ─ ─ ┤├──
INTERRUPT 1₁         ├──────┤ ─ ─ ─ ─ ─ ─┤──────┤ ─ ─ ─ ─┤──
INTERRUPT 1₂                 ├──────────┤
INTERRUPT 1₃                                      ├──────┤
```

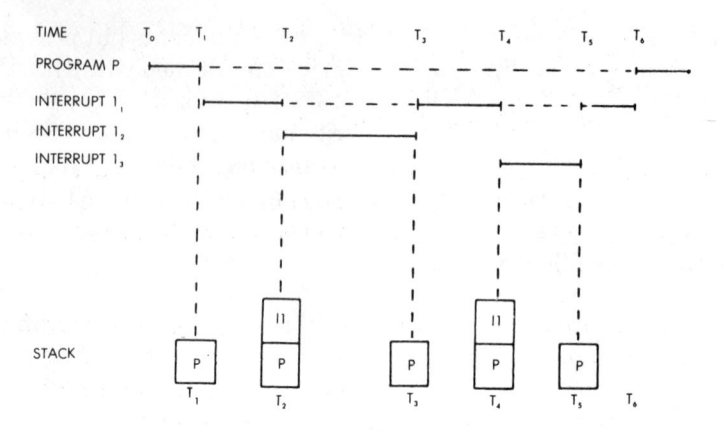

Fig. 6-28: Stack During Interrupts

lower priority, it would be ignored until I1 had been completed. At time T2, the registers for I1 are stacked, and this appears at the bottom of the illustration. Again, the contents of the program counter and P are pushed into the stack. In addition, the routine for I2 might decide to save an additional few registers. I2 will now execute to completion at time T3.

When I2 terminates, the contents of the stack are automatically popped back into the 6502, and this is illustrated at the bottom of Figure 6-28. Automatically, interrupt I1 thus resumes execution. Unfortunately, at time T4, an interrupt I3 of higher priority occurs again. We can see at the bottom of the illustration that **the registers for I1 are again pushed into the stack.** Interrupt I3 executes from T4 to T5 and terminates at T5. At that time, the contents of the stack are popped into 6502, and interrupt I1 resumes execution. This time it runs to completion and terminates at T6. At T6, the remaining registers that have been saved in the stack are popped into the 6502, and program P may resume execution. The reader will verify that the stack is empty at this point. In fact, the number of dashed lines indicating program suspension indicates at the same time the number of levels there are in the stack.

Exercise 6.22: *If we assume that every time an interrupt occurs the program counter PC, the register P, and the accumulator will be saved, this will be a minimum of four locations. (In practice, X*

INPUT/OUTPUT TECHNIQUES

and Y may be saved as well, resulting in six locations used). Assuming, therefore, that three registers only are saved in the stack, how many interrupt levels does the 6502 allow? (Remember that the stack is limited to 256 locations with Page 1).

Exercise 6.23: *Assuming this time that 5 registers may be preserved in the stack, what is the maximum number of simultaneous interrupts that can be handled? Will any other factor reduce even further the number of simultaneous interrupts?*

It must be stressed, however, that, in practice, microprocessor systems are normally connected to a small number of devices using interrupts. It is, therefore, unlikely that a high number of simultaneous interrupts will occur in such a system.

We have now solved all the problems normally associated with interrupts. Their use is, in fact, simple and they should be used to advantage even by the novice programmer. Let us complete our analysis of the 6502 resources by introducing one more instruction whose effect is identical to that of a synchronous interrupt:

Break

The BRK command in the 6502 is the equivalent of a software interrupt. It can be inserted in a program and results, just as in the case of IRQ, in the automatic preservation of PC and P, and an indirect branch to "FFFE"-"FFFF." This instruction can be used to advantage to generate programmed interrupts during the debugging of a program. This will result in creating a breakpoint, halting the program at a predetermined location, and branching to a routine which will typically allow the user to analyze the program. Since the net effect of the break and an interrupt are identical after they have occurred, a means must be provided for the programmer to determine whether it was an interrupt or a break. The 6502 will set a B-flag in register P (saved in the stack) to "1" if it was a break and to "0" if it was an interrupt. Testing the status of this bit may be accomplished by the following simple program:

```
BTEST   PLA             READ TOP OF STACK INTO A
        PHA             WRITE IT BACK
        AND #$10        MASK B-BIT
        BNE BRKPRG      GO TO BREAK PROGRAM
```

This test program is normally inserted at the end of the polling sequence which determines the nature of the device that triggered the interrupt.

Caution: A feature of the break is to preserve the contents of the program counter *plus* 2 automatically. Since the break is only a 1-byte instruction, the programmer may sometimes have to adjust the contents of the program counter in the stack by using an incrementing or decrementing instruction in order to resume execution of the correct address. In particular, the break is extensively used during debugging by writing it over another instruction in the program. If the program is reassembled prior to execution, the contents of the program counter which have been saved will normally have to be decremented by 1.

SUMMARY

We have presented in this chapter the range of techniques used to communicate with the outside world. From elementary input/output routines to more complex programs to communicate with actual peripherals, we have learned to develop all the usual programs and have even examined the efficiency of benchmark programs in the case of a parallel transfer and a parallel-to-serial conversion. Finally, we have learned to schedule the operation of multiple peripherals by using polling and interrupts. Naturally, many other exotic input/output devices might be connected to a system. With the array of techniques which have been presented so far, and with an understanding of the peripherals involved, it should be possible to solve most usual problems.

In the next chapter, we will examine the actual characteristics of the input/output interface chips usually connected to a 6502. Then, we will consider the basic data structures that the programmer may consider using.

EXERCISES

Exercise 6.24: *A 7-segment LED display can also display digits other than the hex alphabet. Compute the codes for $H, I, J, L, O, P, S, U, Y, g, h, i, j, l, n, o, p, r, t, u, y$.*

INPUT/OUTPUT TECHNIQUES

Exercise 6.25: *The flow-chart for interrupt management appears in Figure 6-29 below. Answer the following questions:*
a- What is done by hardware, what is done by software?
b- What is the use of the mask?
c- How many registers should be preserved?
d- How is the interrupting device identified?
e- What does the RTI instruction do? How does it differ from a subroutine return?
f- Suggest a way to handle a stack overflow situation.
g- What is the overhead ("lost time") introduced by the interrupt mechanism?

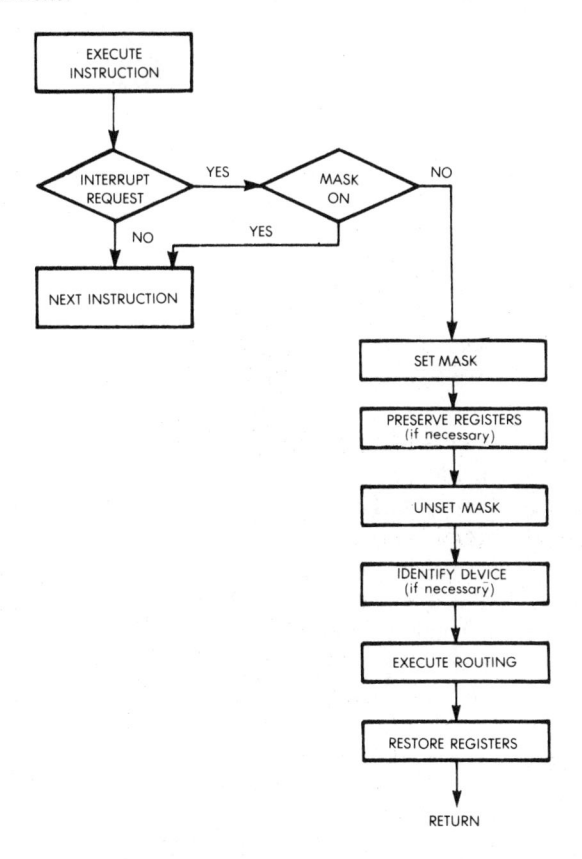

Fig. 6-29: Interrupt Logic

7
INPUT/OUTPUT DEVICES

INTRODUCTION

We have learned how to program the 6502 microprocessor in most usual situations. However, we should make a special mention of the input/output chips normally connected to the microprocessor. Because of the progress in LSI integration, new chips have been introduced which did not exist before. As a result, programming a system requires, naturally, first programming a microprocessor itself, but also *programming the input/output chips*. In fact, it is often more difficult to remember how to program the various control options of an input/output chip than to program the microprocessor itself! This is not because the programming in itself is more difficult, but because each of these devices has its own idiosyncrasies. We are going to examine here first the most general input/output device, the programmable input/output chip (in short a "PIO"), then "improvements" over this standard PIO, now frequently used with the 6502: the 6520, 6530, 6522 and 6532. The complete details are presented in reference D302.

The Standard PIO (6520)

There is no "standard PIO." However, the 6520 device is essentially analogous in function to all similar PIOs produced by other manufacturers for the same purpose. The purpose of a PIO is to provide a multiport connection for input/output devices. (A "port" is simply a set of 8 input/output lines). Each PIO provides at least

INPUT-OUTPUT DEVICES

two sets of 8-bit lines for I/O devices. Each I/O device needs a *data buffer* in order to stabilize the contents of the data bus on output at least. Our PIO will, therefore, be equipped at a minimum with a buffer for each port.

In addition, we have established that the microcomputer will use a *handshaking* procedure, or else *interrupts* to communicate with the I/O device. The PIO will also use a similar procedure to communicate with the peripheral. Each PIO must, therefore, be equipped with at least *two control lines per port* to implement the handshaking function.

The microprocessor will also need to be able to read the status of each port. Each port must be equipped with one or more *status bits*. Finally, a number of options will exist within each PIO to configure its resources. The programmer must be able to access a special register within the PIO to specify the programming options. This is the *control register*. In the case of the 6520, the status information is part of the control register.

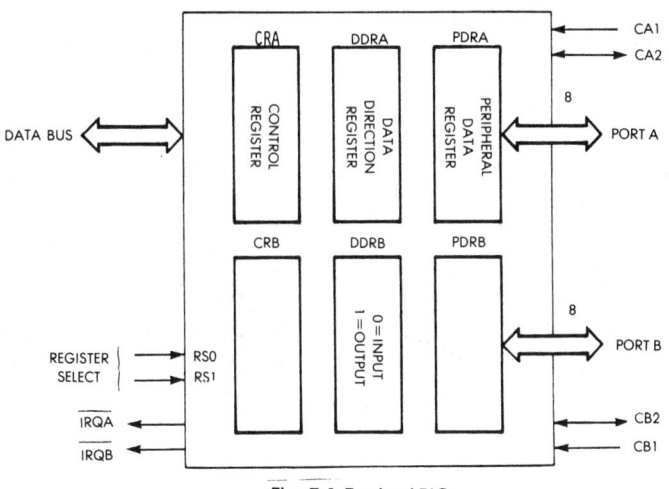

Fig. 7-1: Typical PIO

One essential faculty of the PIO is the fact that each line may be configured as either an input or an output line. The diagram of a PIO appears in illustration 7-1. The programmer may specify whether any line will be input or output. In order to program the direction of the lines, a *data direction register* is provided for each port. A "0" in a bit position of the data direction register specifies an input. A "1" specifies an output.

255

It may be surprising to see that a "0" is used for input and a "1" for output when really "0" should correspond to Output and "1" to Input. This is quite deliberate: whenever power is applied to the system, it is of great importance that all the I/O lines be configured as *input*. Otherwise, if the microcomputer is connected to some dangerous peripheral, it might activate it by accident. When a reset is applied, all registers are normally zeroed and that will result in configuring all input lines of the PIO as inputs. The connection to the microprocessor appears on the left of the illustration. The PIO naturally connects to the 8-bit data bus, the microprocessor address bus, and the microprocessor control bus. The programmer will simply specify the address of any register that it wishes to access within the PIO. The 6520, which is compatible with Motorola's 6820, has inherited one of its peculiarities: it is equipped with 6 internal registers. However, one can specify only one out of *four* registers! The way this problem is solved is by switching bit position 2 of the control register. When this bit is a "0," the corresponding data direction register may be selected. When it is a "1," the data register may be selected. Therefore, whenever the programmer wants to write data into the data direction register, he will first have to make sure that bit 2 of the appropriate control register is zero, before he can select this register. This is somewhat awkward to program, but it is important to remember in order to avoid painful difficulties.

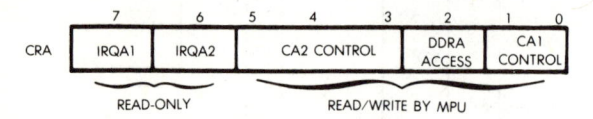

	7	6	5	4	3	2	1	0
CRA	IRQA1	IRQA2	CA2 CONTROL			DDRA ACCESS	CA1 CONTROL	
	READ-ONLY		READ/WRITE BY MPU					

Fig. 7-2: PIA Control Word Format

RS1	RS0	CRA 2	CRB 2	REGISTER SELECTED
0	0	1	—	PERIPHERAL REGISTER A
0	0	0	—	DATA DIRECTION REGISTER A
0	1	—	—	CONTROL REGISTER A
1	0	—	1	PERIPHERAL REGISTER B
1	0	—	0	DATA DIRECTION REGISTER B
1	1	—	—	CONTROL REGISTER B

Fig. 7-3: Addressing PIA Registers

INPUT-OUTPUT DEVICES

To clarify the effect of the address selection on the 6520, the address selection table appears above. RS0 and RS1 are two register-selection signals which are derived from the address bus. In other words, they represent two bits of the address specified by the programmer. CRA is the control register for port A. CRA (2) is bit 2 of this register. CRB is the control register for port B.

The Internal Control Register

The Control Register of the 6520 specifies, as we have seen, in bit position 2, a selection mode for the internal registers of the port. In addition, it provides a number of options for generating or sensing interrupts, or for implementing automatic handshake functions. The complete description of the facilities provided is not necessary here. Simply, the user of any practical system which uses the 6520 will have to refer to the data sheet showing the effect of setting the various bits of the control register. Whenever the system is initialized, the programmer will have to load the control register of the 6520 with the correct contents for the expected application.

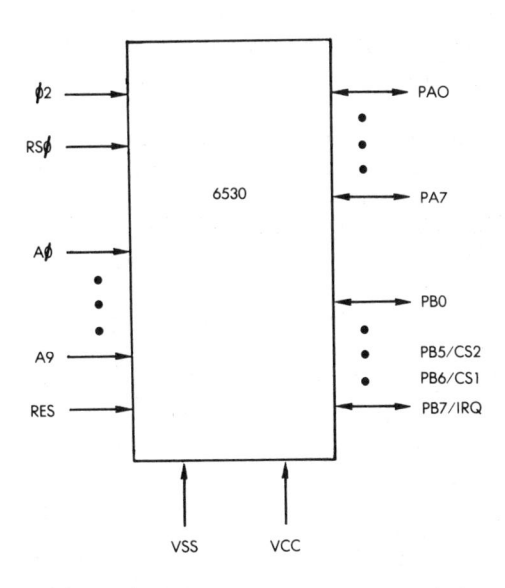

Fig. 7-4: 6530 Pinout

The 6530

The 6530 implements a combination of four functions, RAM, ROM, PIO, and TIMER. The RAM is a 64x8 memory. The ROM is a 1Kx8 memory. The timer provides the programmer with multiple interval timing facilities. The PIO section is essentially analogous to the 6520, which we have described: There are two ports, each with a data register and a data direction register. A "0" in a given bit position of the direction register specifies an input, while a "1" specifies an output.

The programmable interval timer can be programmed to count up to 256 intervals (it has 8 bits internally). The programmer may specify the time period to be 1, 8, 64, or 1024 times the system clock. Whenever the count is reached, the interrupt flag of the chip will be set to a logic "1". The contents of the timer are set by means of the data bus. The four possible time intervals must be specified on lines A0 and A1 of the address bus.

Three pins of port B have a dual role: PB5, PB6, and PB7 may be used for control functions. Pin PB7, for example, may be programmed as an interrupt input.

This chip is used, in particular, on the KIM board. (Note: on the KIM, PB6 is not available.)

Programming a PIO

As an example, here is a program to use a 6520 or a 6522. (We assume that the control register has already been set).

```
LDA   #FF        SET DATA DIRECTION
STA   DDRB       CONFIGURE B FOR OUTPUT
LDA   #00
STA   IORB       GENERATE ZERO OUTPUT
```

DDRB is the address of the Data Direction Register of port B for this PIO. IORB is the Input/Output or data register for port B; "FF" hexadecimal is "11111111" binary = all outputs.

The 6522

The 6522, also called "versatile interface adapter" (VIA), is an improved version of the 6520. In addition to the capabilities of the

INPUT-OUTPUT DEVICES

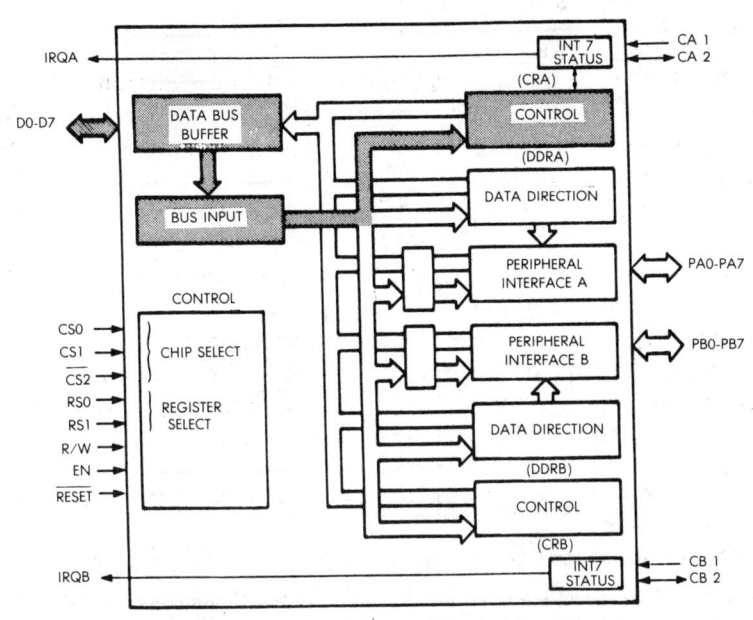

Fig. 7-5: Using a PIA: Load Control Register

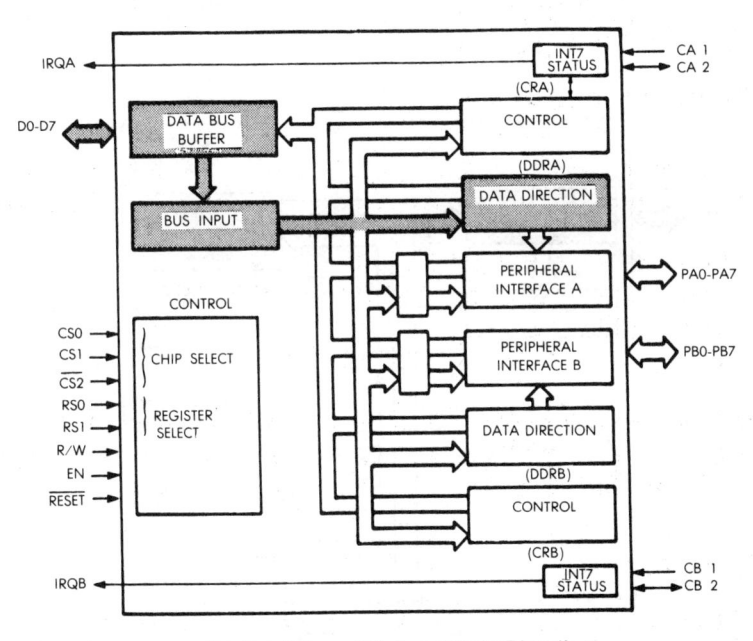

Fig. 7-6: Using a PIA: Load Data Direction

PROGRAMMING THE 6502

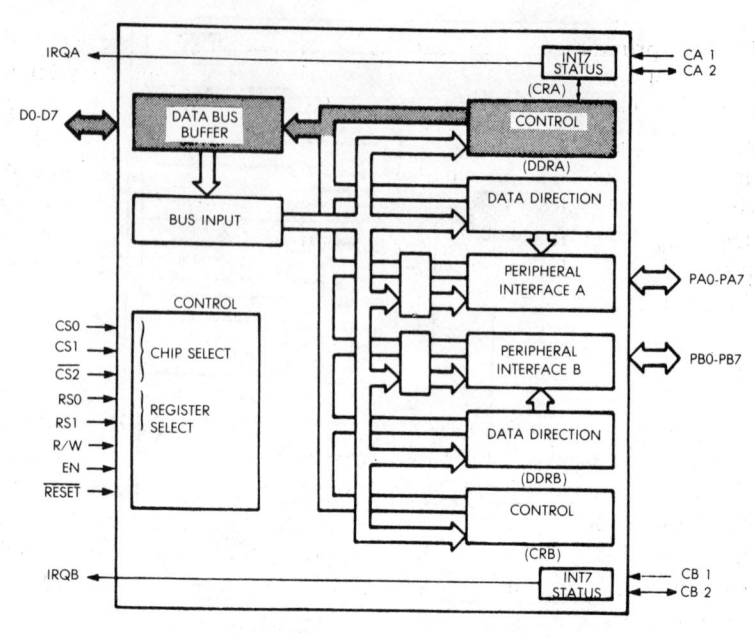

Fig. 7-7: Using a PIA: Read Status

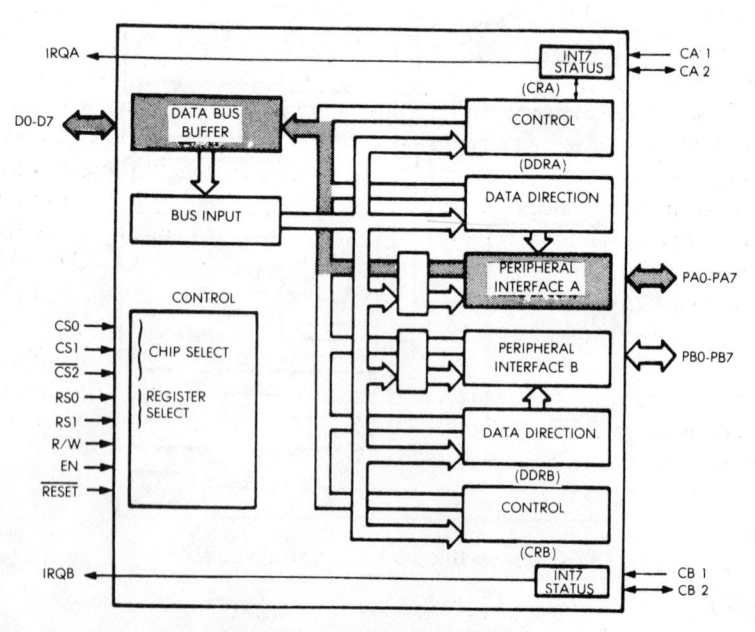

Fig. 7-8: Using a PIA: Read Input

INPUT-OUTPUT DEVICES

6520, it provides two programmable interval timers and a serial-to-parallel, plus parallel-to-serial converter, plus input data latching. The detailed hardware description of this component is beyond the scope of this book. Simply, with the description which has been provided for the previous components, it should be simple for the programmer to familiarize himself with the addressing of the internal registers of this component as well as its programming. This information is supplied in the manufacturer's data sheets.

The 6532

The 6532 is a combination chip which includes one 128×8 RAM, a PIO with two bi-directional ports, and a programmable interval timer. It is used on the SYM board, manufactured by Synertek Systems, which is analogous to the KIM board, manufactured by MOS Technology and by Rockwell. Again, the user should carefully examine the data sheets for this component in order to learn how to address and use the various internal registers.

SUMMARY

Unfortunately, in order to make effective use of such components, it will be necessary to understand in detail the function of every bit, or group of bits, within the various control registers. These complex new chips automate a number of procedures that had to be carried out by software or special logic before. In particular, many of the handshaking procedures are automated within components such as a 6522. Also, some interrupt handling and detection may be internal. With the information that has been presented in the preceding chapter, the reader should be able to read the corresponding data sheets and understand what the functions of the various signals and registers are. Naturally, still new components are going to be introduced which will offer a hardware implementation of still more complex algorithms. For a comprehensive description of I/O devices and techniques, the reader is referred to the companion volume D302.

8
APPLICATION EXAMPLES

INTRODUCTION

This chapter is designed to test your new programming skills by presenting a collection of utility programs. These programs, or "routines," are frequently encountered in applications and are generally called "utility routines." They will require a synthesis of the knowledge and techniques presented so far.

We are going to fetch characters from an I/O device and process them in various ways. But first, let us clear an area of the memory (this may not be necessary; each of these programs is only presented as a programming example).

CLEAR A SECTION OF MEMORY

We want to clear (zero) the contents of the memory from address BASE + 1 to address BASE + LENGTH, where length is less than 256.

The program is:

APPLICATION EXAMPLES

```
ZEROM      LDX #LENGTH
           LDA #0
CLEAR      STA BASE, X
           DEX
           BNE CLEAR
           RTS
```

Note that register X is used as an index to point to the current location of the memory section to be zeroed.

The accumulator A is loaded only once with the value 0 (all 0's), then written at successive memory locations:
BASE + LENGTH, BASE + LENGTH - 1, etc., until X decrements to zero. When X=0, the program returns.

In a memory test for example, this program could be used to zero a block, then verify its contents.

Exercise 8.1: *Write a memory test program which will zero a 256-word block and verify that each location is 0. Then, it will write all 1's and verify the contents of the block. Next, it will write 01010101 and verify the contents. Finally, it will write 10101010 and verify the contents.*

Let us now poll our I/O devices to find which one needs service.

POLLING I/O DEVICES

We will assume that 3 I/O devices are connected to our system. Their status registers are located at addresses IOSTATUS1, IOSTATUS2, and IOSTATUS3.

If their status bits are in bit position 7, we will just read the status registers, and test their sign bits. If the status bits are anywhere else, we will take advantage of the BIT instruction of the 6502:

263

```
TEST        LDA     MASK
            BIT     IOSTATUS1
            BNE     FOUND1
            BIT     IOSTATUS2
            BNE     FOUND 2
            BIT     IOSTATUS3
            BNE     FOUND3
            (failure exit)
```

The MASK will contain, for example, "00100000" if we test bit position 5. As a result of the BIT instruction, the Z bit of the status flags will be set to 0 if "MASK AND IOSTATUS" is non-zero i.e. if the corresponding bit of IOSTATUS matches the one in MASK. The BNE instruction (branch if non-equal to zero) will then result in a branch to the appropriate FOUND routine.

GETTING CHARACTERS IN

Assume we have just found that a character is ready at the keyboard. Let us accumulate characters in a memory area called buffer until we encounter a special character called SPC, whose code has been previously defined.

The subroutine GETCHAR will fetch one character from the keyboard (see Chapter 6 for more details) and leave it in the accumulator. We assume that a maximum of 256 characters will be fetched before an SPC character is found.

```
STRING  LDX     #0              INITIALIZE INDEX TO ZERO
NEXT    JSR     GETCHAR
        CMP     #SPC            IS IT THE BRK CHAR?
        BEQ     OUT             IF SO, FINISHED
        STA     BUFFER, X       NO: SAVE CHAR
        INX                     INCREMENT POINTER
        JMP     NEXT            GET NEXT CHAR
OUT     RTS
```

APPLICATION EXAMPLES

Exercise 8.2: *Let us improve this basic routine:*
a-Echo the character back to the device (for a Teletype, for example)
b-Check that the input string is no longer than 256 characters

We now have a string of characters in a memory buffer. Let us process them in various ways.

TESTING A CHARACTER

Let us determine if the character at memory location LOC is equal to 0, 1, or 2:

ZOT	LDA	LOC
	CMP	#$00
	BEQ	ZERO
	CMP	#$01
	BEQ	ONE
	CMP	#$02
	BEQ	TWO
	JMP	NOTFND

We simply read the character, then use the CMP instruction to check its value.

Let us run a different test now.

BRACKET TESTING

Let us determine if the ASII character at memory location LOC is a digit between 0 and 9:

BRACK	LDA	#$40	
	ADC	#$40	FORCE OVERFLOW
	LDA	LOC	
	ORA	#$80	SET BIT 7=1
	CMP	#$B0	ASCII 0
	BCC	TOOLOW	
	CMP	#$B9	ASCII 9
	BEQ	OUT	9 EXACTLY
	BCS	TOOHIGH	
OUT	CLC		
	CLV		
	RTS		

265

```
TOOLOW    SEC                           SET C TO ONE
          CLV
          RTS
TOOHIGH   RTS                           (C IS ONE)
```

ASCII 0 is represented in hexadecimal by "B0"
ASCII 9 is represented in hexadecimal by "B9"

Remember that when using a CMP instruction, the carry bit will be set if the value of the literal that follows is less than or equal to the accumulator. It will be reset (0) if greater.

If B0 is greater than the character, our character is too low, and a branch occurs.

We then compare it against B9. If it is less than or equal to 9, all is well, and we exit. Otherwise, we go to TOOHIGH.

When we exit from this program, we want to know if the number is TOOLOW, TOOHIGH, or else between 0 and 9. This will be indicated by the flags C and V. V is not altered by CMP, whereas Z, N and C are.

When returning from the subroutine, a "0" in V indicates "too high," a "1" in C indicates "too low," and a "0" in C indicates a correct digit between 0 and 9.

Naturally, other conventions could be used, such as loading a digit in the accumulator to indicate the result of the tests.

Exercise 8.3: *Simplify the above program by testing against the ASCII character which follows "9" instead of testing against 9 exactly.*

Exercise 8.4: *Determine if an ASCII character contained in the accumulator is a letter of the alphabet.*

APPLICATION EXAMPLES

When using an ASCII table, you will notice that *parity* is often used. (The example above does not use parity.) For example, the ASCII for "0" is "0110000," a 7-bit code. However, if we use odd parity,(for example we guarantee that the total number of ones in a word is odd), then the code becomes "10110000." An extra "1" is added to the left. This is "B0" in hexadecimal. Let us therefore develop a program to generate parity.

PARITY GENERATION

This program will generate an even parity in bit position 7:

PARITY	LDX	#$07	BIT COUNT
	LDA	#$00	
	STA	ONECNT	COUNT OF 1'S
	LDA	CHAR	READ CHARACTER
	ROL	A	DISCARD BIT 7
NEXT	ROL	A	NEXT BIT
	BCC	ZERO	IS IT A 1?
ONE	INC	ONECNT	
ZERO	DEX		DECREMENT BIT COUNT
	BNE	NEXT	LAST BIT?
	ROL	A	RESTORE BIT 0
	ROL	A	DISCARD BIT
	LSR	ONECNT	RIGHTMOST BIT IS PARITY
	ROR	A	PUT IT IN A
	RTS		

Register X is used to count bits as they are shifted left from the accumulator. Every time that a "1" is shifted off the left of A (it is tested by BCC), the one-counter is incremented. When 8 bits have shifted (the program ignores bit 7 which will be the parity bit), A is shifted left two more times so that bit 6 is on the left of A.

The correct parity bit is the right-most bit of ONECNT; it is installed into the carry bit by LSR and becomes bit 7 of A. Another ROR A copies this bit back into position 7 of A, and we are finished.

PROGRAMMING THE 6502

Exercise 8.5: *Using the above program as an example, verify the parity of a word. You must compute the correct parity, then compare it to the one expected.*

CODE CONVERSION: ASCII to BCD

Converting ASCII to BCD is very simple. We will observe that the hexadecimal representations of ASCII characters 0 to 9 are B0 to B9 with parity, or 30 to 39 without parity. The BCD representation is simply obtained by dropping the "B"; that is, by masking off the left nibble (4 bits):

```
LDA     CHAR
AND     #$0F      MASK OFF LEFT NIBBLE
STA     BCDCHAR
```

Exercise 8.6: *Write a program to convert BCD to ASCII.*

Exercise 8.7: *(more difficult) Write a program to convert BCD to binary.*

Hint: $N_3 N_2 N_1 N_0$ in BCD is $(((N_3 \times 10) + N_2) \times 10 + N_1) \times 10 + N_0$ in binary.
To multiply by 10, use a left shift (=x2), another left shift (=x4), an ADC (=x5), and another left shift (=x10).
In full BCD notation, the first word may contain the count of BCD digits, the next nibble may contain the sign, and every successive nibble may contain a BCD digit. (We assume no decimal point.) The last nibble of the block may be unused.

FIND THE LARGEST ELEMENT OF A TABLE

The beginning address of the table is contained at memory address BASE in page zero. The first entry of the table is the number of bytes it contains. This program will search for the largest element of the table. Its value will be left in A, and its position will be stored in memory location INDEX.

APPLICATION EXAMPLES

This program uses registers A and Y, and will use indirect addressing, so that it can search any table anywhere in the memory.

MAX	LDY	#0	THIS IS OUR INDEX TO TABLE
	LDA	(BASE), Y	ACCESS ENTRY 0=LENGTH
	TAY		SAVE IT IN Y
	LDA	#0	MAX VALUE INITIALIZED TO ZERO
	STA	INDEX	INITIALIZE INDEX TO ZERO
LOOP	CMP	(BASE), Y	IS CURRENT MAX ELEMENT?
	BCS	NOSWITCH	YES?
	LDA	(BASE), Y	LOAD NEW MAX
	STY	INDEX	LOCATION OF MAX
NOSWITCH	DEY		POINT TO NEXT ELEMENT
	BNE	LOOP	KEEP TESTING?
	RTS		FINISH IF Y=0

This program tests the Nth entry first. If it is greater than 0, it goes in A, and its location is remembered into INDEX. The (N-1)st entry is then tested, etc.

This program works for positive integers.

Exercise 8.8: *Modify the program so that it works also for negative numbers in two's complement.*

Exercise 8.9: *Will this program also work for ASCII characters?*

Exercise 8.10: *Write a program which will sort N numbers in ascending order.*

Exercise 8.11: *Write a program which will sort N names (3 characters each) into alphabetical order.*

SUM OF N ELEMENTS

This program will compute the 16-bit sum of N entries of a table. The starting address of the table is contained at memory address BASE in page zero. The first entry of the table contains the number of elements N. The 16-bit sum will be left in memory locations SUMLO and SUMHI. If the sum should require more than 16 bits, only the lower 1t will be kept. (The high-order bits are said to be truncated.)

PROGRAMMING THE 6502

This program will modify registers A and Y. It assumes 256 elements maximum.

```
            LDA     #0              INITIALIZE SUM
            STA     SUMLO           INITIALIZE SUM
            STA     SUMHI           INITIALIZE SUM
            TAY                     INITIALIZE Y TO ZERO
            LDA     (BASE), Y       GET N
            TAY                     INTO Y
            CLC                     CLEAR CARRY FOR ADC
ADLOOP      LDA     (BASE), Y       GET NEXT ELEMENT
            ADC     SUMLO           ADD IT TO SUMLO
            STA     SUMLO           SAVE RESULT
            BCC     NOCARRY         CARRY?
            INC     SUMHI           ADD IT TO SUMHI
            CLC                     FOR NEXT SUM
NOCARRY     DEY                     NEXT ELEMENT
            BNE     ADLOOP          AGAIN IF Y NOT ZERO
            RTS
```

This program is straightforward and should be self-explanatory.

Exercise 8.12: *Modify this program to compute:*
a) a 24-bit sum,
b) a 32-bit sum,
c) to detect any overflow.

A CHECKSUM COMPUTATION

A checksum is a digit, or set of digits, computed from a block of successive characters. The checksum is computed at the time the data is stored and put at the end. In order to verify the integrity of the data, the data is read and the checksum is recomputed and compared against the stored value. A discrepancy indicates an error or a failure.

APPLICATION EXAMPLES

Several algorithms are used. Here, we will exclusive-OR all bytes in a table of N elements, and leave the result in the accumulator. As usual, the base of the table is stored at the address BASE in page zero. The first entry of the table is its number of elements N. The program modifies A and Y. N must be less than 256.

CHECKSUM	LDY	#0	POINT TO FIRST ENTRY
	LDA	(BASE), Y	GET N
	TAY		STORE IT IN Y
	LDA	#0	INITIALIZE CHECKSUM
CHLOOP	EOR	(ADDR), Y	EOR NEXT ENTRY
	DEY		POINT TO NEXT
	BNE	CHLOOP	KEEP GOING
	RTS		

COUNT THE ZEROES

This program will count the number of zeroes in our usual table, and leave it in register X.
It modifies A,X,Y:

ZEROES	LDY	#0	POINT TO FIRST ENTRY
	LDA	(ADDR), Y	GET N
	TAY		STORE IT IN Y
	LDX	#0	INITIALIZE NO. OF ZEROES
ZLOOP	LDA	(ADDR), Y	GET NEXT ENTRY
	BNE	NOTZ	IS IT ZERO?
	INX		YES. COUNT IT
NOTZ	DEY		POINT TO NEXT
	BNE	ZLOOP	KEEP GOING
	RTS		

Exercise 8.13: *Modify this program to count:*
a-the number of stars (the character "")*
b-the number of letters of the alphabet
c-the number of digits between 0 and 9

A STRING SEARCH

A string of characters is stored in the memory, as indicated in Fig. 8-1. We will search the string for the occurrence of a shorter one, called a template (TEMPLT), of length TPTLEN. The length of the original string is STRLEN, and the program will return

PROGRAMMING THE 6502

with register X containing the location where the TEMPLT was found, and FF hexadecimal otherwise. The flowchart for the program is shown in Fig. 8-2. The string is first scanned for the occurrence of the first character in TEMPLT. If this first character is never found, the program will exit with a failure. If this first character is found, the second character will be matched against the next one in the string. If that fails, the search is restarted for the first character since there might be another occurrence of this first character within the original string. If the first and the second one match, the search will proceed with the following characters of TEMPLT in the same manner. The corresponding program is shown in Fig. 8-3. Note that Register X is used as the running pointer during the search pointing to the current element of string. Indexed addressing is naturally used to retrieve the current element of string.

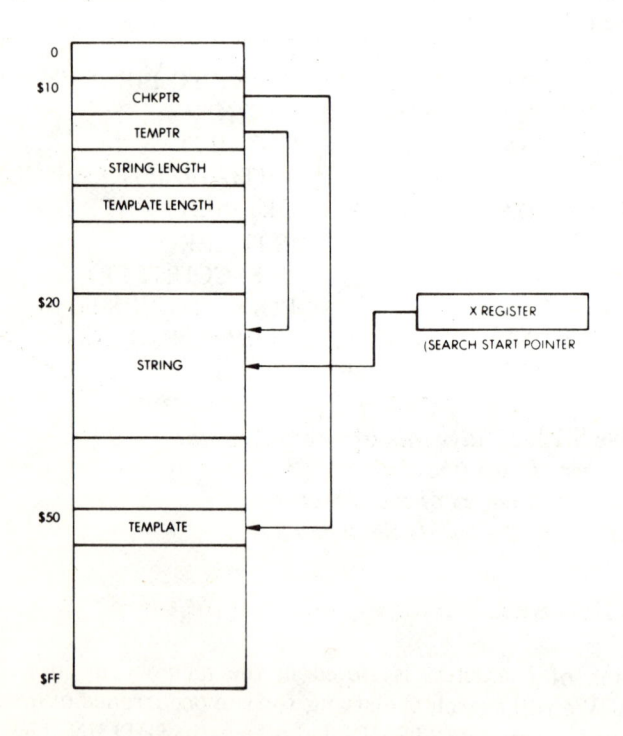

Fig: 8-1: String Search: The Memory

APPLICATION EXAMPLES

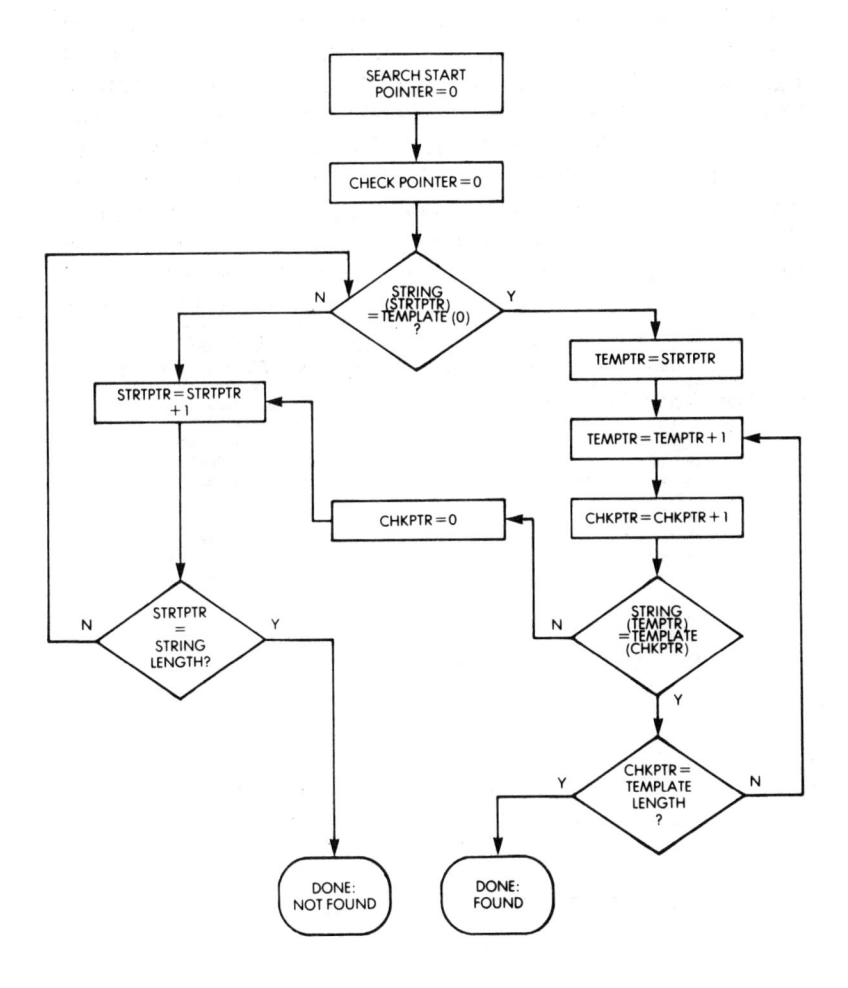

Fig. 8-2: Program Flowchart: String Search

PROGRAMMING THE 6502

```
LINE # LOC    CODE       LINE

0002  0000               ;STRING SEARCH.
0003  0000               ;FINDS LOCATION IN STRING OF LENGTH 'STRLEN'
0004  0000               ;STARTING AT 'STRING' OF A TEMPLATE OF
0005  0000               ;LENGTH 'TPTLEN' STARTING AT 'TEMPLT', AND
0006  0000               ;RETURNS WITH X=LOCATION OF TEMPLATE
0007  0000               ;IN STRING IF FOUND, OR X=$FF IF NOT FOUND.
0008  0000               ;
0009  0000               STRING = $20       ;1ST LOCATION OF STRING.
0010  0000               TEMPLT = $50       ;1ST LOCATION OF TEMPLATE.
0011  0000               * = $10
0012  0010               CHKPTR *=*+1
0013  0011               TEMPTR *=*+1
0014  0012               STRLEN *=*+1       ;LENGTH OF STRING.
0015  0013               TPTLEN *=*+1       ;LENGTH OF TEMPLATE.
0016  0014               * = $200
0017  0200  A2 00                LDX #0     ;RESET SEARCH START POINTER.
0018  0202  A5 50        NXTPOS  LDA TEMPLT ;IS FIRST ELEMENT OF TEMPLATE...
0019  0204  D5 20                CMP STRING,X ;= CURRENT STRING ELEMENT?
0020  0206  F0 08                BEQ CHECK  ;IF YES, CHECK FOR REST OF MATCH.
0021  0208  E8           NXTSTR  INX        ;INCREMENT SEARCH START COUNTER.
0022  0209  E4 12                CPX STRLEN ;IS IT EQUAL TO STRING LENGTH?
0023  020B  D0 F5                BNE NXTPOS ;NO, CHECK NEXT STRING POSITION.
0024  020D  A2 FF                LDX #$FF   ;YES, SET 'NOT FOUND' INDICATOR.
0025  020F  60                   RTS        ;RETURN: ALL CHRS CHECKED.
0026  0210  86 11        CHECK   STX TEMPTR ;LET TEMPORARY POINTER=
0027  0212                                  ;CURRENT STRING POINTER.
0028  0212  A9 00                LDA #0
0029  0214  85 10                STA CHKPTR ;RESET TEMPLATE POINTER.
0030  0216  E6 11        CHKLP   INC TEMPTR ;INCREMENT TEMPORARY POINTER.
0031  0218  E6 10                INC CHKPTR ;INCREMENT TEMPLATE POINTER.
0032  021A  A4 10                LDY CHKPTR
0033  021C  C4 13                CPY TPTLEN ;DOES TEMPLATE POINTER=TEMPLATE LENGTH?
0034  021E  F0 0C                BEQ FOUND  ;IF YES, TEMPLATE MATCHED.
0035  0220  B9 50 00             LDA TEMPLT,Y ;LOAD TEMPLATE ELEMENT.
0036  0223  A4 11                LDY TEMPTR
0037  0225  D9 20 00             CMP STRING,Y ;COMPARE TO STRING CHR.
0038  0228  D0 DE                BNE NXTSTR ;IF NO MATCH, CHECK NEXT STRING CHR.
0039  022A  F0 EA                BEQ CHKLP  ;IF MATCH, CHECK NEXT CHR.
0040  022C  60           FOUND   RTS        ;DONE.
0041  022D                       .END
```

Fig. 8-3: String Search Program

SUMMARY

In this chapter, we have presented common utility routines which use combinations of the techniques described in previous chapters. These routines should now allow you to start designing your own programs. Many of them have used a special data structure, the table. However, other possibilities exist for structuring data, and these will now be reviewed.

9
DATA STRUCTURES
PART I: DESIGN CONCEPTS

INTRODUCTION

The design of a good program involves two tasks: *algorithm design and data structures design.* In most simple programs, no significant data structures are involved, so the main problem that must be surmounted to learn programming is learning how to design algorithms and code them efficiently in a given machine language. This is what we have accomplished here. However, designing more complex programs also requires an understanding of data structures. Two data structures have already been used throughout the book: the table, and the stack. The purpose of this chapter is to present other, more general, data structures that you may want to use. This chapter is completely independent from the microprocessor, or even the computer, selected. It is theoretical and involves logical organization of data in the system. Specialized books exist on the topic of data structures, just like specialized books exist on the subject of efficient multiplication, division or other usual algorithms. This single chapter, therefore, should be considered as an overview, and it will be necessarily limited to the essentials only. It does not claim to be exhaustive.

Let us now review the most common data structures:

POINTERS

A pointer is a number which is used to designate the location of the actual data. Every pointer is an address. However, every address is not necessarily called a pointer. An address is a pointer only if it points at some type of data or at structured information. We have already encountered a typical pointer, the stack pointer, which points to the top of the stack (or usually just over the top of the stack). We will see that the stack is a common data structure, called a LIFO structure.

As another example, when using indirect addressing, the indirect address is always a pointer to the data that one wishes to retrieve.

Exercise 9.1: *Examine Figure 9-1. At address 15 in the memory, there is a pointer to Table T. Table T starts at address 500. What are the actual contents of the pointer to T?*

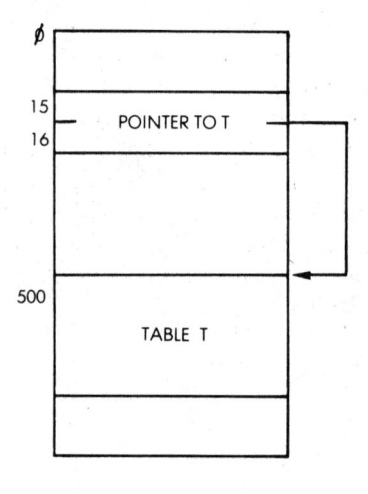

Fig 9-1: An Indirection Pointer

LISTS

Almost all data structures are organized as lists of various kinds.

Sequential Lists

A sequential list, or table, or block, is probably the simplest data structure, and one that we have already used. Tables are normally

DATA STRUCTURES

ordered in function of a specific criterion, such as, for example, alphabetical ordering, or numerical ordering. It is then easy to retrieve an element in a table, using, for example, indexed addressing, as we have done. A block normally refers to a group of data which has definite limits but whose contents are not ordered. It may, for example, contain a string of characters. Or it may be a sector on a disk. Or it may be some logical area (called segment) of the memory. In such cases, it may not be easy to access a random element of the block.

In order to facilitate the retrieval of blocks of information, diretories are used:

Directories

A directory is a list of tables, or blocks. For example, the file system will normally use a directory structure. As a simple example, the master directory of the system may include a list of the users' names. This is illustrated in Figure 9-2. The entry for user "John" points to John's file directory. The file directory is a table which contains the names of all of John's files and their location. This is, again, a table of pointers. In this case, we have just designed a two-level directory. A flexible directory system will allow the inclusion of additional intermediate directories, as may be found convenient by the user.

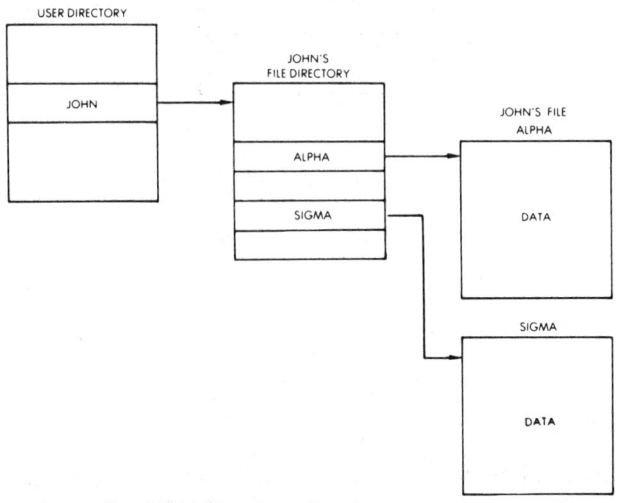

Fig. 9-2: A Directory Structure

Linked List

In a system there are often blocks of information which represent data, or events, or other structures, which cannot be easily moved. If they could be easily moved, we would probably assemble them in a table in order to sort them or structure them. The problem now is that we wish to leave them where they are and still establish an ordering between them such as first, second, third, and fourth. A linked list will be used to solve this problem. The concept of a linked list is illustrated by Figure 9-3. IN the illustration, we see that a list pointer, called FIRSTBLOCK, points to the beginning of the first block. A dedicated location within Block 1, such as, perhaps, the first or the last word of it, contains a pointer to Block 2, called PTR1. The process is then repeated for Block 2 and Block 3. Since Block 3 is the last entry in the list, PTR3, by convention, contains a special "nil" value, or else points to itself, so that the end of the list can be detected. This structure is economical as it requires only a few pointers (one per block) and prevents the user from having to physically move the blocks in the memory.

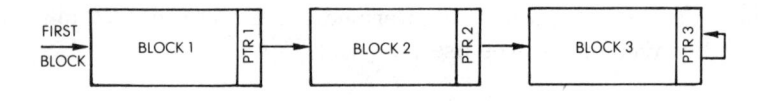

Fig. 9-3: A Linked List

Let us examine, for example, how a new block will be inserted. This is illustrated by Figure 9-4. Let us assume that the new block is at address NEWBLOCK, and is to be inserted between Block 1 and Block 2. Pointer PTR1 is simply changed to the value NEWBLOCK, so that it now points to Block X. PTRX will contain the former value of PTR1 (i.e., it will point to Block 2). The other pointers in the structure are left unchanged. We can see that the insertion of a new block has simply required updating two pointers in the structure. This is clearly efficient.

Exercise 9.2: *Draw a diagram showing how Block 2 would be removed from this structure.*

Several types of lists have been developed to facilitate specific

DATA STRUCTURES

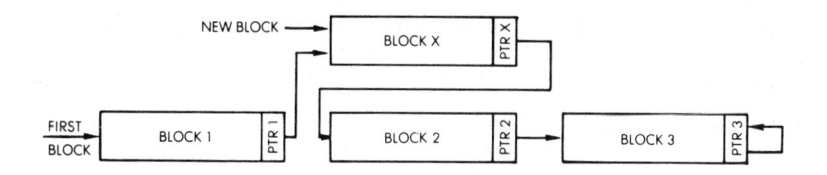

Fig. 9-4: Inserting a New Block

types of access or insertions or deletions to or from the list. Let us examine some of the most frequently used types of linked lists:

Queue

A queue is formally called a FIFO, or first-in-first-out list. A queue is illustrated in Figure 9-5. To clarify the diagram, we can assume, for example, that the block on the left is a service routine for an output device, such as a printer. The blocks appearing on the right are the request blocks from various programs or routines, to print characters. The order in which they will be serviced is the

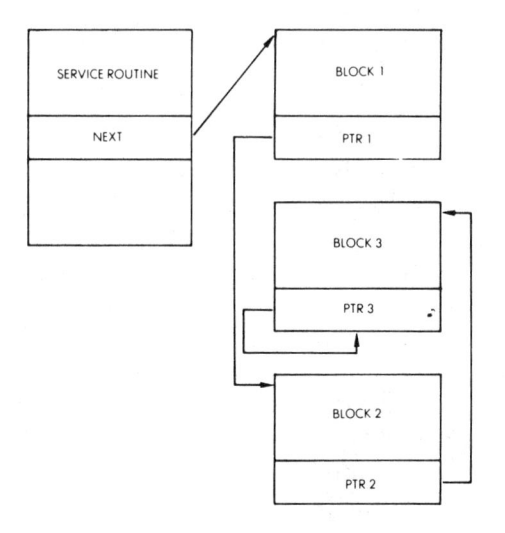

Fig. 9-5: A Queue

279

order established by the waiting queue. It can be seen that the next event which will obtain service is Block 1, then Block 2, and finally Block 3. In a queue, the convention is that any new event arriving in the queue will be inserted at the end of it. Here it will be inserted after PTR3. This guarantees that the first block to have been inserted in the queue will be the first one to be serviced. It is quite common in a computer system to have waiting queues for a number of events whenever they must wait for a scarce resource, such as the processor or some input/output device.

Stack

The stack structure has already been studied in detail throughout the book. It is a last-in-first-out structure (LIFO). The last element deposited on top of it is the first one to be removed. A stack may be implemented as a sorted block, or else it may be implemented as a list. Because most stacks in microprocessors are used for high speed events, such as subroutines and interrupts, a continuous block is usually allocated to the stack rather than using a linked list.

Linked List vs. Block

Similarly, the queue could be implemented as a block of reserved locations. The advantage of using a continuous block is fast retrieval and the elimination of the pointers. The disadvantage is that it is usually necessary to dedicate a fairly large block to accommodate the worst-case size of the structure. Also, it makes it difficult or impractical to insert or remove elements from within the block. Since memory is traditionally a scarce resource, blocks have been traditionally reserved for fixed-size structures or else structures requiring the maximum speed of retrieval, such as the stack.

Circular List

"Round robin" is a common name for a circular list. A circular list is a linked list where the last entry points back to the first one. This is illustrated in Figure 9-6. In the case of a circular list, a current-block pointer is often kept. In the case of events or programs waiting for service, the current-event pointer will be moved by one position to the left or to the right every time. A round-robin usually corresponds to a structure where all blocks are assumed to

DATA STRUCTURES

have the same priority. However, when performing a search a circular list may also be used as a subcase of other structures simply to facilitate the retrieval of the first block after the last one.

As an example of a circular list, a polling program usually goes around in a round-robin fashion, interrogating all peripherals and then coming back to the first one.

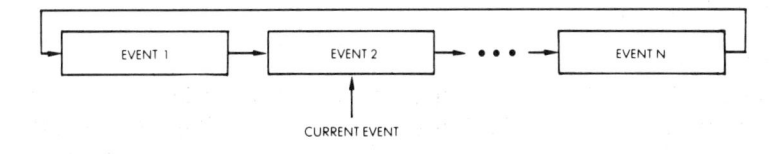

Fig. 9-6: Round-Robin is Circular List

Trees

Whenever a logical relationship exists between all elements of a structure (this is usually called a syntax), a tree structure may be used. A simple example of a tree structure is a descendant tree or a genealogical tree. This is illustrated in Figure 9-7. It can be seen that Smith has two children: a son, Robert, and a daughter, Jane. Jane, in turn, has three children: Liz, Tom and Phil. Tom, in turn has two more children: Max and Chris. However, Robert, on the left of the illustration, has no descendants.

This is a structured tree. We have, in fact, already encountered an example of a simple tree in Figure 9-2. The directory structure is a two-level tree. Trees are used to advantage whenever elements may be classified according to a fixed structure. This facilitates insertion and retrieval. In addition, trees may establish groups of information in a structured way. Such information may be required for later processing, such as in a compiler or interpreter design.

Doubly-Linked Lists

Additional links may be established between elements of a list. The simplest example is the doubly-linked list. This is illustrated in Figure 9-8. We can see that we have the usual sequence of links from left to right, plus another sequence of links from right to left.

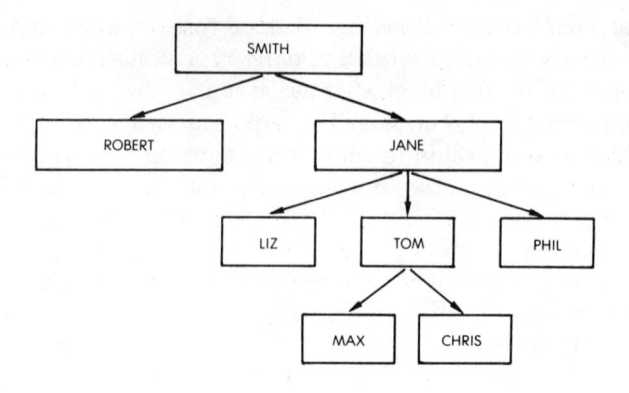

Fig. 9-7: Genealogical Tree

The goal is to allow easy retrieval of the element just before the one which is being processed, as well as the one just after it. This costs an extra pointer per block.

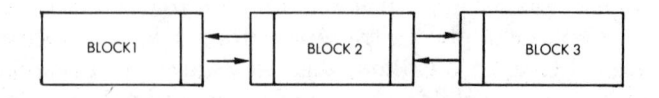

Fig. 9-8: Doubly-Linked List

SEARCHING AND SORTING

Searching and sorting elements of a list depend directly on the type of structure which has been used for the list. Many searching algorithms have been developed for the most frequently used data structures. We have already used indexed addressing. This is possible whenever the elements of a table are ordered in function of a known criterion. Such elements may then be retrieved by their numbers.

Sequential searching refers to the linear scanning of an entire block. This is clearly inefficient but, for lack of a better technique, may have to be used whenever the elements are not ordered.

DATA STRUCTURES

Binary, or logarithmic searching, attempts to find an element in a sorted list by dividing the search interval in half at every step. Assuming, for example, that we are searching an alphabetical list, one might start in the middle of a table and determine if the name for which we are looking is before or after this point. If it is after this point, we will eliminate the first half of the table and look at the middle element of the second half. We again compare this entry to the one for which we are looking, and restrict our search to one of the two halves, and so on. The maximum length of a search is then guaranteed to be $\log_2 n$, where n is the number of elements in the table.

Many other search techniques exist.

SUMMARY

This section was intended as only a brief presentation of typical data structures which may be used by a programmer. Although most common data structures have been rationalized in types and given a name, the overall organization of data in a complex system may use any combination of them, or require the programmer to invent more appropriate structures. The array of possibilities is limited only by the imagination of the programmer. Similarly, a number of well-known sorting and searching techniques have been developed to cope with the usual data structures. A comprehensive description is beyond the scope of this book. The contents of this section were intended to stress the importance of designing appropriate data structures for the data to be manipulated and to provide the basic tools to that effect.

9

DATA STRUCTURES
PART II: DESIGN EXAMPLES

INTRODUCTION

Actual design examples will be presented here for typical data structures: table, linked list, sorted tree. Practical sorting, searching and insertion algorithms will be programmed for these structures. Additional advanced techniques such as hashing and merging will also be described.

The reader interested in these advanced programming techniques is encouraged to analyze in detail the programs presented in this section. However, the beginning programmer may skip this section initially, and come back to it when he feels ready for it.

A good understanding of the concepts presented in the first part of this chapter is necessary to follow the design examples. Also, the programs will use all the addressing modes of the 6502, and integrate many of the concepts and techniques presented in the previous chapters.

Four structures will now be introduced: a simple list, an alphabetical list, a linked list plus directory, and a tree. For each structure, three programs will be developed: search, enter and delete.

In addition, three specialized algorithms will be described separately at the end of the section: hashing, bubble-sort, and merging.

DATA STRUCTURES

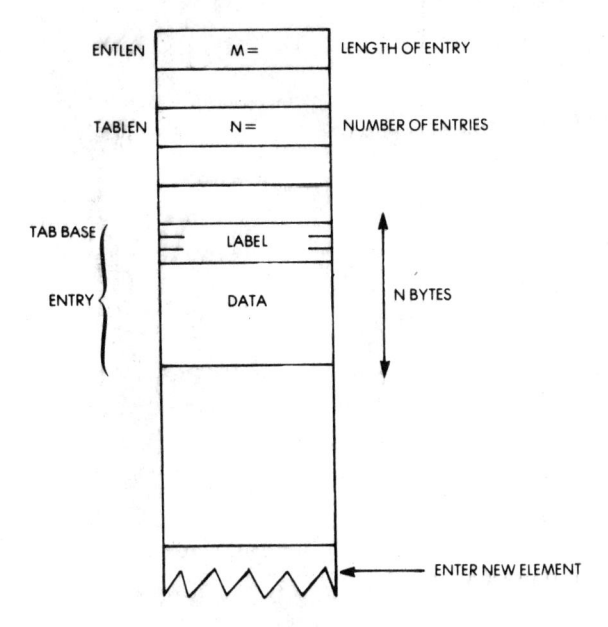

Fig. 9-9: The Table Structure

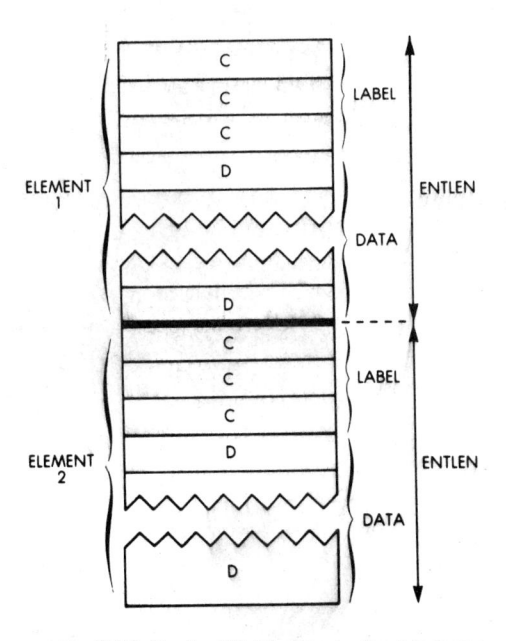

Fig 9-10: Typical List Entries in the Memory

DATA REPRESENTATION FOR THE LIST

Both the simple list and the alphabetic list will use a common representation for each list element:

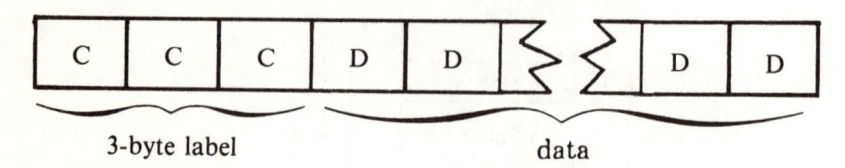

| C | C | C | D | D | ≈ ≈ | D | D |

⎵⎵⎵⎵⎵⎵⎵⎵⎵⎵⎵⎵   ⎵⎵⎵⎵⎵⎵⎵⎵⎵⎵⎵⎵
  3-byte label   data

Each element or "entry" includes a 3-byte label and an n-byte block of data with n between 1 and 253. Thus, each entry uses, at most, one page (256 bytes). Within each list, all elements have the same length (see Fig. 9-10). The programs operating on these two simple lists use some common variable conventions:

ENTLEN is the length of an element. For example, if each element has 10 bytes of data, ENTLEN = 3 + 10 = 13 bytes
TABASE is the base of the list or table in the memory
POINTR is a running pointer to the current element
OBJECT is the current entry to be inserted or deleted
TABLEN is the number of entries

All labels are assumed to be distinct. Changing this convention would require a minor change in the programs.

A SIMPLE LIST

The simple list is organized as a table of n elements. The elements are not sorted (see Fig. 9-11).

When searching, one must scan through the list until an entry is found or the end of the table is reached. When inserting, new entries are appended to the existing ones. When an entry is deleted, the entries in higher memory locations, if any, will be shifted down to keep the table continuous.

Searching

A serial search technique is used. Each entry's label field is compared in turn to the OBJECT's label, letter by letter.

The running pointer POINTR is initialized to the value of TABASE.

The index register X is initialized to the number of entries contained in the list (stored at TABLEN).

DATA STRUCTURES

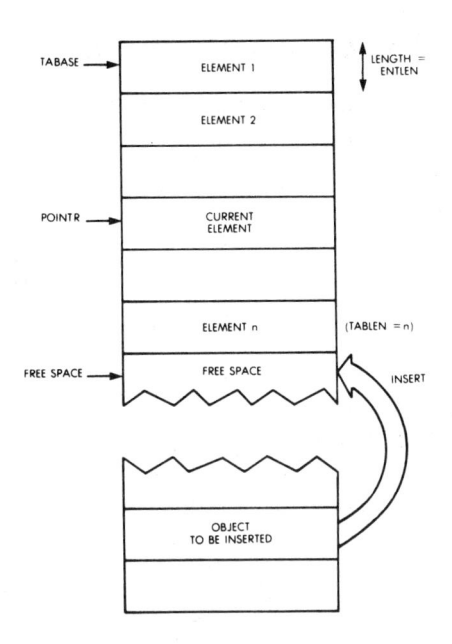

Fig. 9-11: The Simple List

The search proceeds in the obvious way, and the corresponding flowchart is shown in Fig. 9-12. The program appears in Fig. 9-16 at the end of this section (program "SEARCH").

Element Insertion

When inserting a new element, the first available memory block of (ENTLEN) bytes at the end of the list is used (see Fig. 9-11).
The program first checks that the new entry is not already in the list (all labels are assumed to be distinct in this example). If not, it increments the list length TABLEN, and moves the OBJECT to the end of the list. The corresponding flowchart is shown on Fig. 9-13.
The program is shown on Fig. 9-16 at the end of this section. It is called "NEW" and resides at memory locations 0636 to 0659.

Element Deletion

In order to delete an element from the list, the elements following it at higher addresses are merely moved up by one element position. The length of the list is decremented. This is illustrated in Fig. 9-14.

287

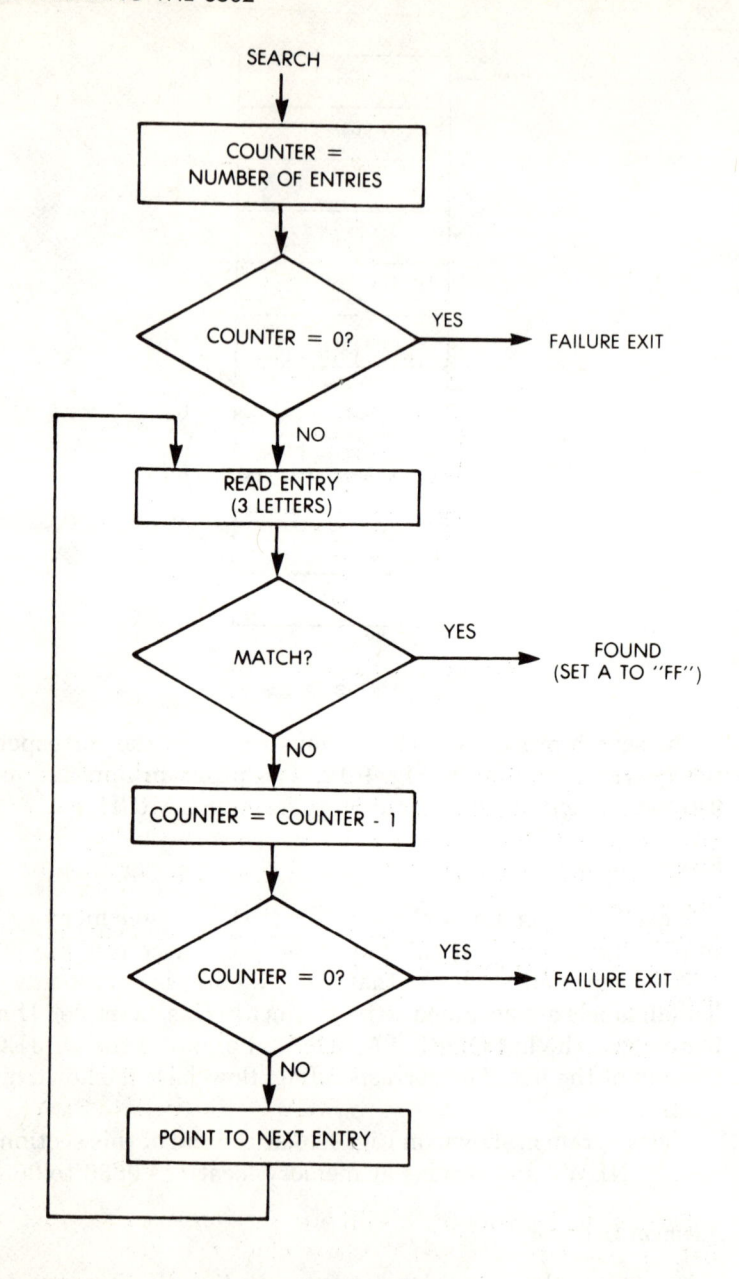

Fig. 9-12: Table Search Flowchart

DATA STRUCTURES

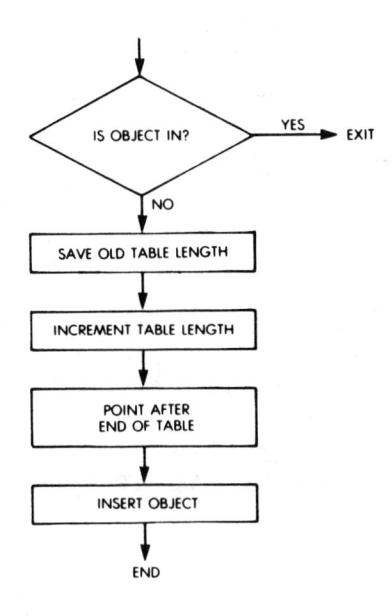

```
                    │
                    ▼
              ╱IS OBJECT IN?╲──YES──▶ EXIT
               ╲            ╱
                ╲          ╱
                    │NO
                    ▼
          ┌─────────────────────┐
          │ SAVE OLD TABLE LENGTH│
          └─────────────────────┘
                    │
                    ▼
          ┌─────────────────────┐
          │INCREMENT TABLE LENGTH│
          └─────────────────────┘
                    │
                    ▼
          ┌─────────────────────┐
          │    POINT AFTER      │
          │    END OF TABLE     │
          └─────────────────────┘
                    │
                    ▼
          ┌─────────────────────┐
          │    INSERT OBJECT    │
          └─────────────────────┘
                    │
                    ▼
                   END
```

Fig. 9-13: Table Insertion Flowchart

The corresponding program is straightforward and appears in Fig. 9-16. It is called "DELETE" and resides at memory addresses 0659 to 0686. The flowchart is shown in Fig. 9-15.

Memory location TEMPTR is used as a temporary pointer pointing to the element to be moved up.

Index register Y is set to the length of a list element, and used to automate block transfers. Note that indirect indexed addressing is used:

(0672)	LOOPE	DEY	
		LDA	(TEMPTR), Y
		STA	(POINTR), Y
		CPY	#0
		BNE	LOOPE

During the transfer, POINTR always points to the "hole" in the list, i.e. the destination of the next block transfer.

The Z flag is used to indicate a successful deletion upon exit.

289

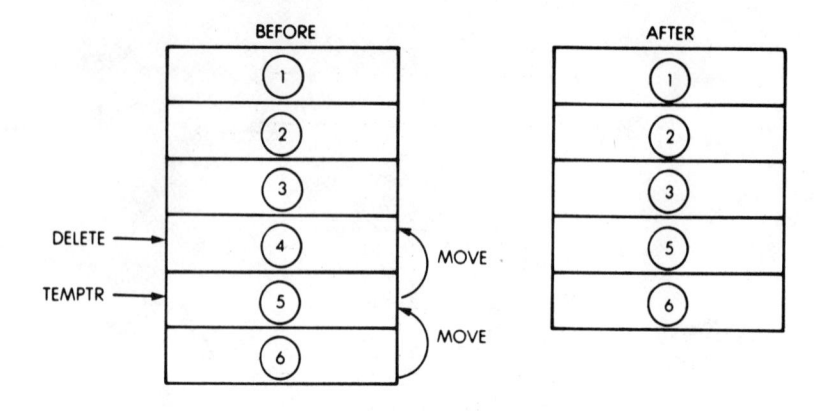

Fig. 9-14: Deleting An Entry (Simple List)

ALPHABETIC LIST

The alphabetic list, or "table" unlike the previous one, keeps all its elements sorted in alphabetic order. This allows the use of faster search techniques then the linear one. A binary search is used here.

Searching

The search algorithm is a classical binary search. Let us recall that the technique is essentially analogous to the one used to find a name in a telephone book. One usually starts somewhere in the middle of the book, and then, depending on the entries found there, goes either backwards or forwards to find the desired entry. This method is fast, and it is reasonably simple to implement.

The binary search flowchart is shown in Fig. 9-17, and the program is shown in Fig. 9-22.

This list keeps the entries in alphabetical order and retrieves them by using a binary or "logarithmic" search. An example is shown in Fig. 9-18.

DATA STRUCTURES

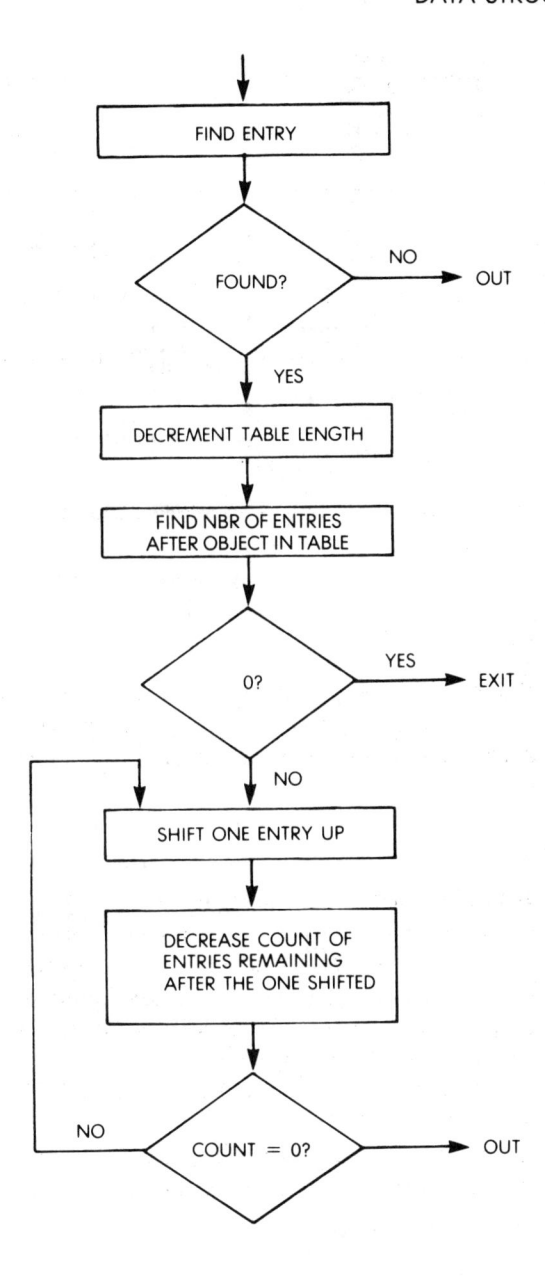

Fig. 9-15: Table Deletion Flow Chart

PROGRAMMING THE 6502

```
LINE # LOC    CODE           LINE
0002   0000                  TABASE = $10
0003   0000                  POINTR = $12
0004   0000                  TABLEN = $14
0005   0000                  OBJECT = $15
0006   0000                  ENTLEN = $17
0007   0000                  TEMPTR = $18
0008   0000                  ;
0009   0000                  *=$600
0010   0600                  ;
0011   0600   A5 10   SEARCH LDA TABASE      ;INITIALIZE POINTER
0012   0602   85 12          STA POINTR
0013   0604   A5 11          LDA TABASE+1
0014   0606   85 13          STA POINTR+1
0015   0608   A6 14          LDX TABLEN      ;STORE TABLEN AS A VARIABLE
0016   060A   F0 29          BEQ OUT         ;CHECK FOR 0 TABLE
0017   060C   A0 00   ENTRY  LDY #0          ;COMPARE FIRST LETTERS
0018   060E   B1 15          LDA (OBJECT),Y
0019   0610   D1 12          CMP (POINTR),Y
0020   0612   D0 0E          BNE NOGOOD
0021   0614   C8             INY             ;COMPARE SECOND LETTERS
0022   0615   B1 15          LDA (OBJECT),Y
0023   0617   D1 12          CMP (POINTR),Y
0024   0619   D0 07          BNE NOGOOD
0025   061B   C8             INY             ;COMPARE THIRD LETTERS
0026   061C   B1 15          LDA (OBJECT),Y
0027   061E   D1 12          CMP (POINTR),Y
0028   0620   F0 11          BEQ FOUND
0029   0622   CA      NOGOOD DEX             ;SEE HOW MANY ENTRIES ARE LEFT
0030   0623   F0 10          BEQ OUT
0031   0625   A5 17          LDA ENTLEN      ;ADD ENTLEN TO POINTER
0032   0627   18             CLC
0033   0628   65 12          ADC POINTR
0034   062A   85 12          STA POINTR
0035   062C   90 DE          BCC ENTRY
0036   062E   E6 13          INC POINTR+1
0037   0630   4C 0C 06       JMP ENTRY
0038   0633   A9 FF   FOUND  LDA #$FF        ;CLEAR Z FLAG IF FOUND
0039   0635   60      OUT    RTS
0040   0636                  ;
0041   0636                  ;
0042   0636                  ;
0043   0636   20 00 06 NEW   JSR SEARCH      ;SEE IF OBJECT IS THERE
0044   0639   D0 1D          BNE OUTE
0045   063B   A6 14          LDX TABLEN      ;CHECK FOR 0 TABLE
0046   063D   F0 0B          BEQ INSERT
0047   063F   A5 12          LDA POINTR      ;POINTER IS AT LAST ENTRY
0048   0641   18             CLC             ;..MUST MOVE IT TO END OF TABLE
0049   0642   65 17          ADC ENTLEN
0050   0644   85 12          STA POINTR
0051   0646   90 02          BCC INSERT
0052   0648   E6 13          INC POINTR+1
0053   064A   E6 14   INSERT INC TABLEN      ;INCREMENT TABLE LENGTH
0054   064C   A0 00          LDY #0          ;MOVE OBJECT TO END OF TABLE
0055   064E   A6 17          LDX ENTLEN
0056   0650   B1 15   LOOP   LDA (OBJECT),Y
0057   0652   91 12          STA (POINTR),Y
0058   0654   C8             INY
0059   0655   CA             DEX
0060   0656   D0 F8          BNE LOOP
0061   0658   60      OUTE   RTS             ;Z SET IF WAS DONE
0062   0659                  ;
0063   0659                  ;
0064   0659                  ;
0065   0659   20 00 06 DELETE JSR SEARCH     ;FIND WHERE OBJECT IS
0066   065C   F0 2D          BEQ OUTS        ;EXIT IF NOT FOUND
0067   065E   C6 14          DEC TABLEN      ;DECREMENT TABLE LENGTH
0068   0660   CA             DEX             ;SEE HOW MANY ENTRIES ARE
```

Fig. 9-16: Simple List Programs: Search, Enter, Delete

DATA STRUCTURES

```
0069  0661  F0 26            BEQ DONE        ;..AFTER ONE TO BE DELETED
0070  0663  A5 12     ADDEN  LDA POINTR      ;ADD ENTLEN TO POINTER AND
0071  0665  18               CLC             ;..SAVE AT TEMP STORAGE
0072  0666  65 17            ADC ENTLEN
0073  0668  85 18            STA TEMPTR
0074  066A  A9 00            LDA #0
0075  066C  65 13            ADC POINTR+1    ;ADD CARRY TO HIGH BYTE
0076  066E  85 19            STA TEMPTR+1
0077  0670  A4 17            LDY ENTLEN
0078  0672  88        LOOPE  DEY
0079  0673  B1 18            LDA (TEMPTR),Y  ;SHIFT ONE ENTRY OF MEMORY DOWN
0080  0675  91 12            STA (POINTR),Y
0081  0677  C0 00            CPY #0
0082  0679  D0 F7            BNE LOOPE
0083  067B  CA               DEX             ;DECREMENT ENTRY COUNTER
0084  067C  F0 0B            BEQ DONE
0085  067E  A5 18            LDA TEMPTR      ;MOVE TEMP TO POINTER
0086  0680  85 12            STA POINTR
0087  0682  A5 19            LDA TEMPTR+1
0088  0684  85 13            STA POINTR+1
0089  0686  4C 63 06         JMP ADDEN
0090  0689  A9 FF     DONE   LDA #$FF        ;CLEAR Z FLAG IF IT WAS DONE
0091  068B  60        OUTS   RTS
0092  068C                   ;
0093  068C                   ;
0094  068C                   .END

ERRORS = 0000 <0000>



SYMBOL TABLE

SYMBOL   VALUE

ADDEN    0663    DELETE  0659    DONE     0689    ENTLEN   0017
ENTRY    060C    FOUND   0633    INSERT   064A    LOOP     0650
LOOPE    0672    NEW     0636    NOGOOD   0622    OBJECT   0015
OUT      0635    OUTE    0658    OUTS     068B    POINTR   0012
SEARCH   0600    TABASE  0010    TABLEN   0014    TEMPTR   0018

END OF ASSEMBLY
```

Fig. 9-16: Simple List Programs: Search, Enter, Delete (cont.)

PROGRAMMING THE 6502

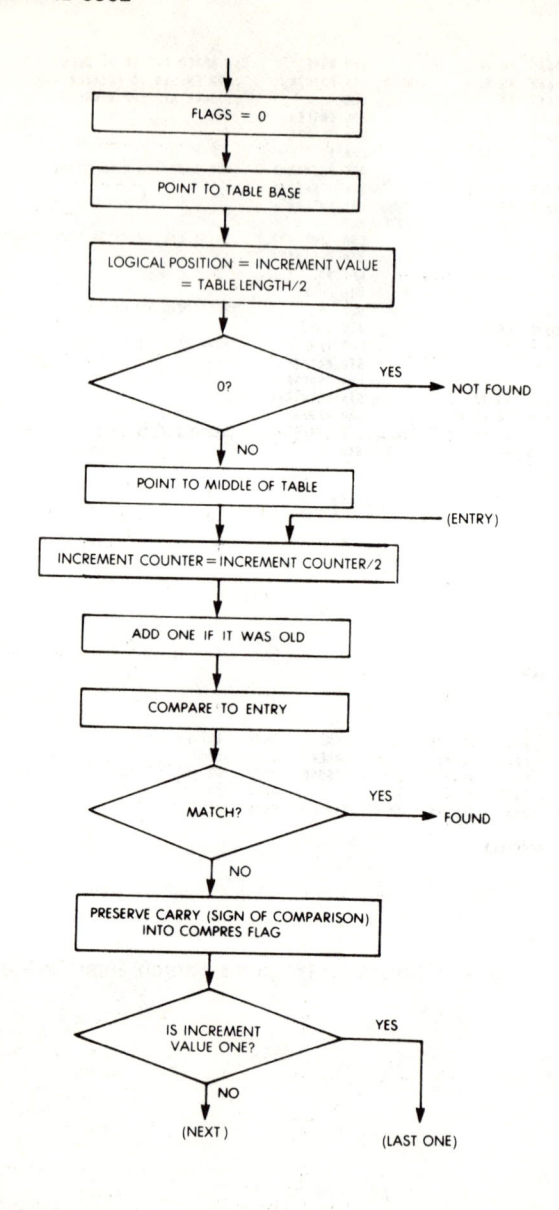

Fig. 9-17: Binary Search Flowchart

DATA STRUCTURES

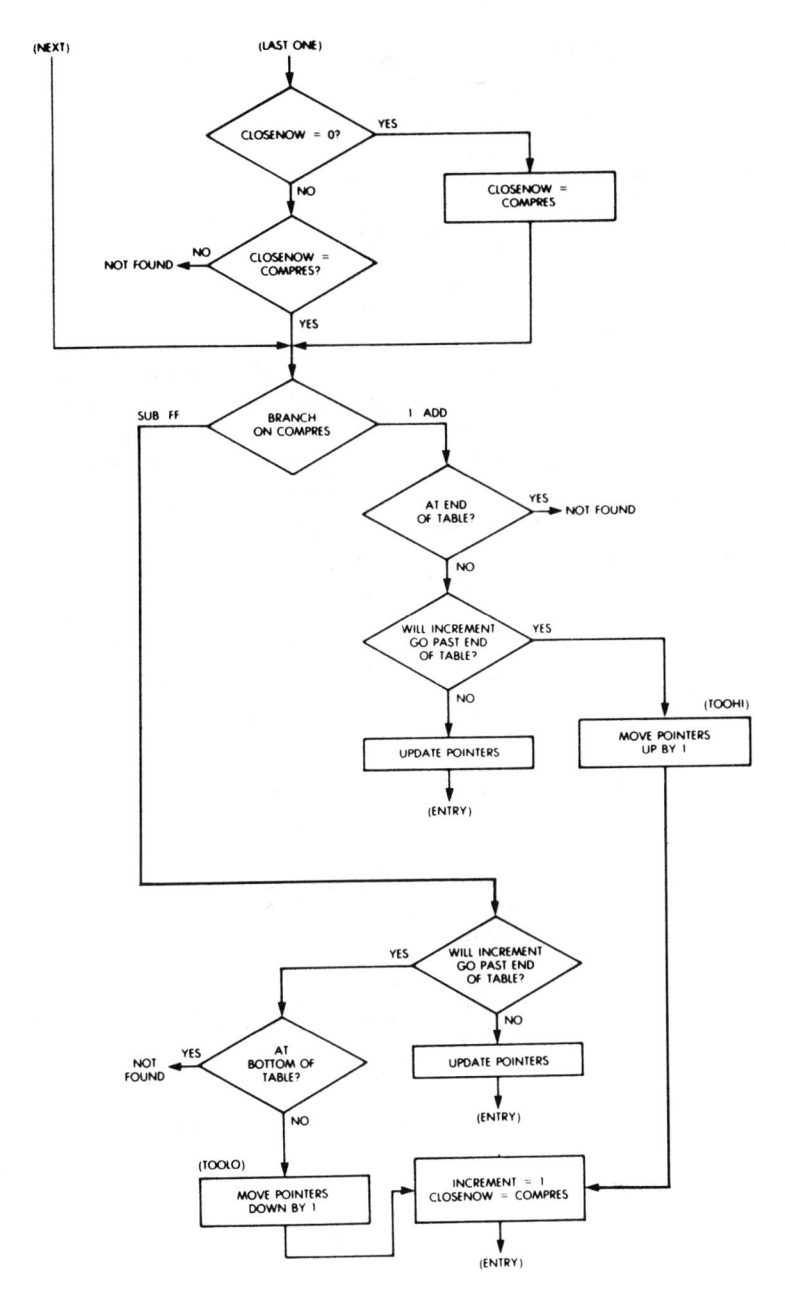

Fig. 9-17: Binary Search Flow Chart (cont.)

PROGRAMMING THE 6502

The search is somewhat complicated by the need to keep track of several conditions. The major problem to be avoided is searching for an object that is not there. In such a case, the entries with the immediately higher and lower alphabetic values could be alternately tested forever. To avoid this, a flag is maintained in the program to preserve the value of the carry flag after an unsuccessful comparison. When the INCMNT value, which shows by how much the pointer will next be incremented, reaches a value of "1", another flag called "CLOSE" is set to the value of the CMPRS flag. Thus, since all further increments will be "1," if the pointer goes past the point where the object should be, CMPRES will not longer equal CLOSE, and the search will terminate. This feature also enables the NEW routine to determine where the logical and physical pointers are located, relative to where the object will go.

Thus, if the OBJECT searched for is not in the table, and the running pointer is incremented by one, the CLOSE flag will be set. On the next pass of the routine, the result of the comparison will be opposite to the previous one. The two flags will no longer match, and the program will exit indicating "not found."

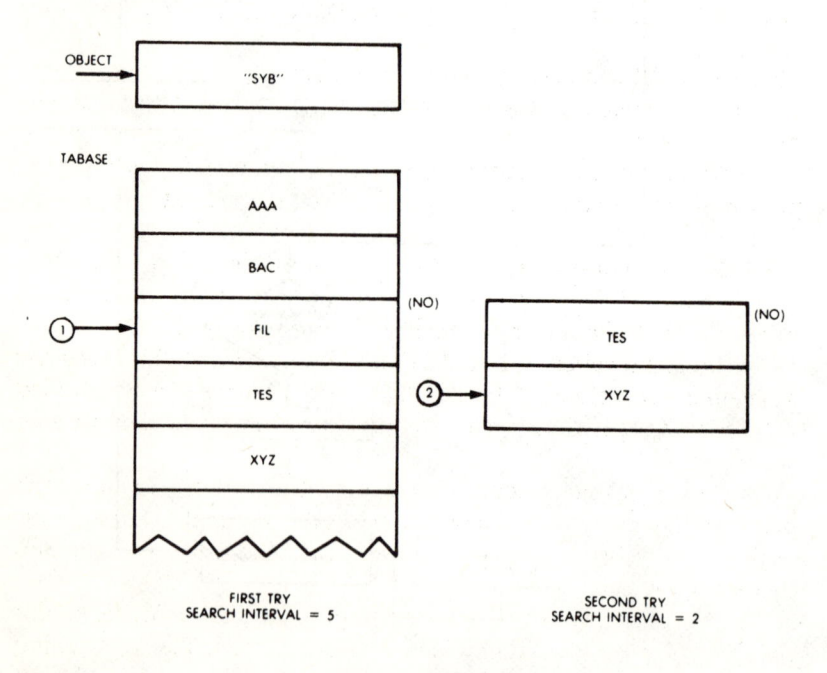

Fig. 9-18: A Binary Search

DATA STRUCTURES

The other major problem that must be dealt with is the possibility of running off one end of the table when adding or subtracting the increment value. This is solved by performing an "add" or "subtract" test using the logical pointer and length value to determine the actual number of entries, rather than using physical pointers to determine their mere physical positions.

In summary, two flags are used by the program to memorize information: CMPRES and CLOSE. The CMPRES flag is used to preserve the fact that the carry was either "0" or "1" after the most recent comparison. This determines if the element under test was larger or smaller than the one to which it was compared. Whenever the carry C is "1," the entry is smaller than the object, and CMPRES is set to "1." Whenever the carry C is "0," the entry is greater than the object, and CMPRES will be set to "FF."

Also note that when the carry is "1", the running pointer will point to the entry below the OBJECT.

The second flag used by the program is CLOSE. This flag is set equal to CMPRES when the search increment INCMNT becomes equal to "1." It will detect the fact that the element has not been found if CMPRES is not equal to CLOSE the next time around.

Other variables used by the program are:

LOGPOS, which indicates the logical position in the table (element number).

INCMNT, which represents the value by which the running pointer will be incremented or decremented if the next comparison fails.

TABLEN represents, as usual, the total length of the list. LOGPOS and INCMNT will be compared to TABLEN in order to ascertain that the limits of the list are not exceeded.

The program called "SEARCH" is shown in Fig. 9-22. It resides at memory locations, 0600 to 06E3, and deserves to be studied with care, as it is much more complex than in the case of a linear search.

An additional complication is due to the fact that the search interval may at times be either even or odd. When it is even, a correction must be introduced. It cannot, for instance, point to the middle element of a 4-element list.

When it is odd, a "trick" is used to point to the middle element: the division by 2 is accomplished by a right shift. The bit "falling out" into the carry after the LSR instruction will be "1" if the interval was odd. It is merely added back to the pointer:

```
(0615)   DIV   LSR   A           DIVIDE BY TWO
               ADC   #0          PICK UP CARRY
               STA   LOGPOS      NEW POINTER
```

The OBJECT is then matched against the entry in the middle of the new search interval. If the comparison succeeds, the program exits. Otherwise ("NOGOOD"), the carry is set to 0 if the OBJECT is less than the entry. Whenever the INCMNT becomes "1", the CLOSE flag (which had been initialized to "0") is then checked to see if it was set. If it was not, it gets set. If it was set, a check is run to determine whether we passed the location where the OBJECT should have been but was not found.

Element Insertion

In order to insert a new element, a binary search is conducted. If the element is found in the table, it does not need to be inserted. (We assume here that all elements are distinct). If the element was not found in the table, it must be inserted. The value of the CMPRES flag after the search indicates whether this element should be inserted immediately before or immediately after the last element to which it was compared. All the elements following the new location where it is going to be placed are then moved down by one block position, and the new element is inserted.

The insertion process is illustrated in Figure 9-19 and the corresponding program appears on Figure 9-22.

The program is called "NEW", and resides at memory locations 06E3 to 075E.

Note that indirect indexed addressing is used again for block transfers:

```
(072A)                  LDY    ENTLEN
         ANOTHR         DEY
                        LDA    (POINTR), Y
                        STA    (TEMP), Y
                        CPY    #0
                        BNE    ANOTHR
```

Observe the same at memory location 0750.

DATA STRUCTURES

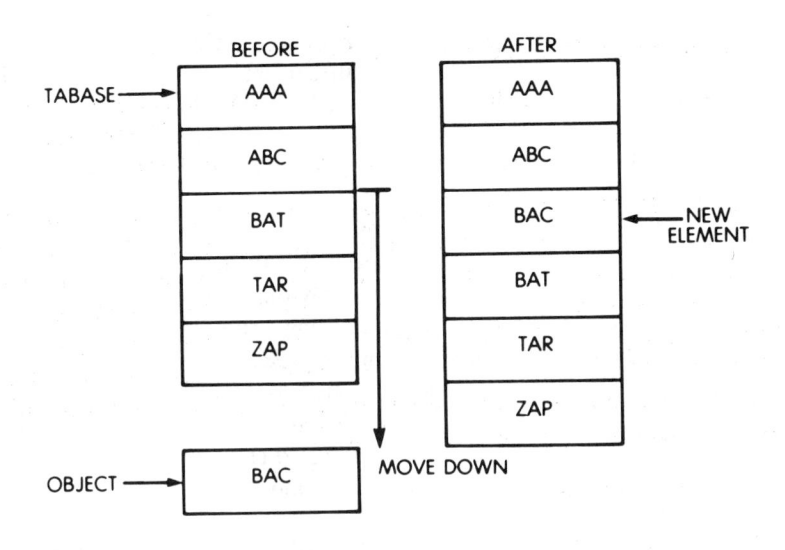

```
              BEFORE              AFTER
            ┌────────┐         ┌────────┐
TABASE ───► │  AAA   │         │  AAA   │
            ├────────┤         ├────────┤
            │  ABC   │         │  ABC   │
            ├────────┤         ├────────┤
            │  BAT   │         │  BAC   │ ◄── NEW ELEMENT
            ├────────┤         ├────────┤
            │  TAR   │         │  BAT   │
            ├────────┤         ├────────┤
            │  ZAP   │         │  TAR   │
            └────────┘         ├────────┤
                               │  ZAP   │
            ┌────────┐         └────────┘
OBJECT ───► │  BAC   │   MOVE DOWN
            └────────┘
```

Fig. 9-19: Insert: "BAC"

Element Deletion

Similarly, in order to delete an element, a binary search is conducted to find the object. If the search fails, it does not need to be deleted. If the search succeeds, the element is deleted, and all the following elements are moved up by one block position. A corresponding example is shown in Fig. 9-20, and the program appears in Figure 9-22. The flowchart is shown in Fig. 9-21.

It is called "DELETE," and resides at memory addresses 075F to 0799.

LINKED LIST

The linked list is assumed to contain, as usual, the three alphanumeric characters for the label, followed by 1 to 250 bytes of data, followed by a 2-byte pointer which contains the starting address of the next entry, and lastly followed by a 1-byte marker. Whenever this 1-byte marker is set to "1," it will prevent the insert-routine from substituting a new entry in the place of the existing one.

PROGRAMMING THE 6502

Further, a directory contains a pointer to the first entry for each letter of the alphabet, in order to facilitate retrieval. It is assumed in the program that the labels are ASCII alphabetic characters. All pointers at the end of the list are set to a NIL value which has been chosen here to be equal to the table base, as this value should never occur within the linked list.

The insertion and the deletion program perform the obvious pointer manipulations. They use the flag INDEXD to indicate if a pointer pointing to an object came from a previous entry in the list or from the directory table. The corresponding programs are shown in Fig. 9-27. the data structure is shown in Fig. 9-23.

An application for this data structure would be a computerized address book, where each person is represented by a unique 3-letter code (perhaps the usual initials) and the data field contains a simplified address, plus the telephone number (up to 250 characters).

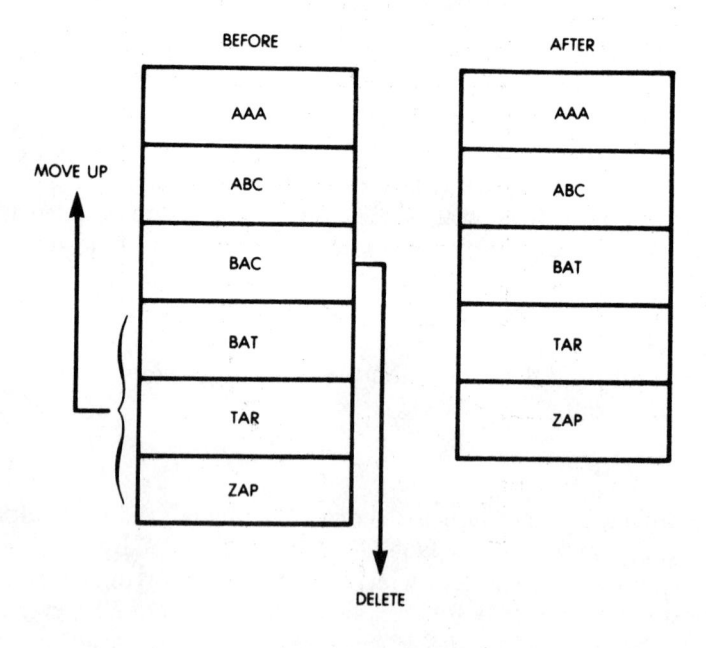

Fig. 9-20: Delete: "BAC"

DATA STRUCTURES

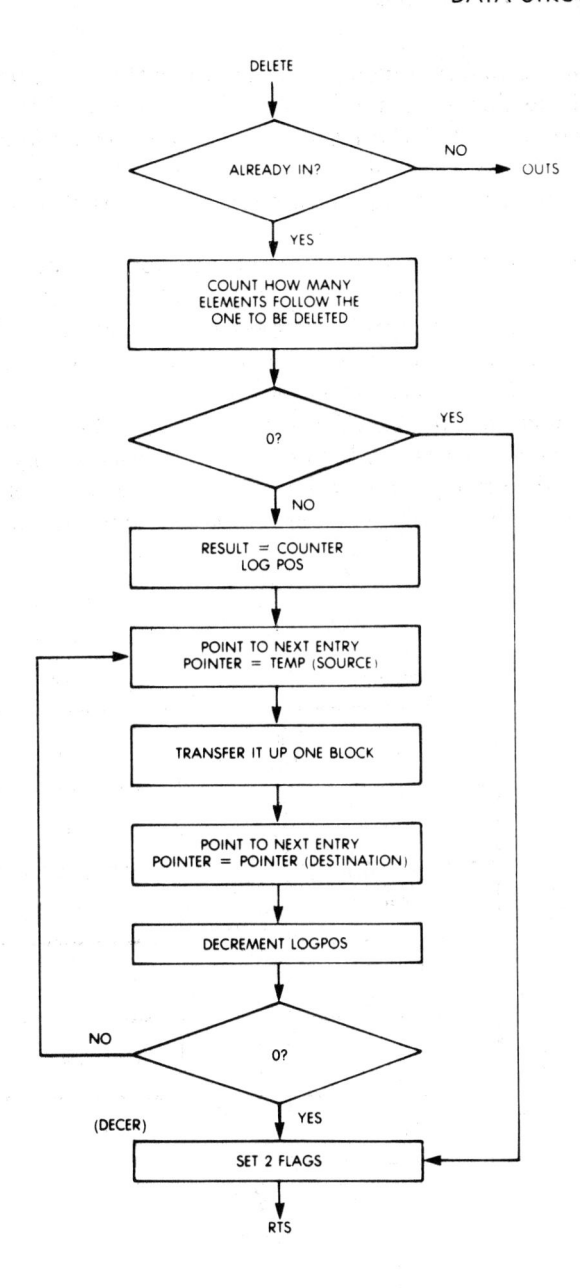

Fig. 9-21: Deletion Flowchart (Alphabetic List)

```
LINE # LOC    CODE        LINE
0002  0000                CLOSE   = $10
0003  0000                CMPRES  = $11
0004  0000                TABASE  = $12
0005  0000                POINTR  = $14
0006  0000                TABLEN  = $16
0007  0000                LOGPOS  = $17
0008  0000                INCMNT  = $18
0009  0000                TEMP    = $19
0010  0000                ENTLEN  = $1B
0011  0000                OBJECT  = $1C
0012  0000                ;
0013  0000                * = $600
0014  0600                ;
0015  0600  A9 00    SEARCH LDA #0            ;ZERO FLAGS
0016  0602  85 10           STA CLOSE
0017  0604  85 11           STA CMPRES
0018  0606  A5 12           LDA TABASE       ;INITIALIZE POINTER
0019  0608  85 14           STA POINTR
0020  060A  A5 13           LDA TABASE+1
0021  060C  85 15           STA POINTR+1
0022  060E  A5 16           LDA TABLEN       ;GET TABLE LENGTH
0023  0610  D0 03           BNE DIV
0024  0612  4C E0 06        JMP OUT
0025  0615  4A       DIV    LSR A            ;DIVIDE IT BY 2
0026  0616  69 00           ADC #0           ;ADD BACK IN 1'S BIT
0027  0618  85 17           STA LOGPOS       ;STORE AS LOGICAL POSITION
0028  061A  85 18           STA INCMNT       ;STORE AS INCREMENT VALUE
0029  061C  A6 17           LDX LOGPOS       ;MULTIPLY ENTLEN BY LOGPOS
0030  061E  CA              DEX              ;..ADDING RESULT TO POINTER
0031  061F  F0 0E           BEQ ENTRY
0032  0621  A5 1B    LOOP   LDA ENTLEN
0033  0623  18              CLC
0034  0624  65 14           ADC POINTR
0035  0626  85 14           STA POINTR
0036  0628  90 02           BCC LOPP
0037  062A  E6 15           INC POINTR+1
0038  062C  CA       LOPP   DEX
0039  062D  D0 F2           BNE LOOP
0040  062F  A5 18    ENTRY  LDA INCMNT       ;DIVIDE INCREMENT VALUE BY 2
0041  0631  4A              LSR A
0042  0632  69 00           ADC #0
0043  0634  85 18           STA INCMNT
0044  0636  A0 00           LDY #0           ;COMPARE FIRST LETTERS
0045  0638  B1 1C           LDA (OBJECT),Y
0046  063A  D1 14           CMP (POINTR),Y
0047  063C  D0 11           BNE NOGOOD
0048  063E  C8              INY              ;COMPARE 2ND LETTERS
0049  063F  B1 1C           LDA (OBJECT),Y
0050  0641  D1 14           CMP (POINTR),Y
0051  0643  D0 0A           BNE NOGOOD
0052  0645  C8              INY              ;COMPARE 3RD LETTERS
0053  0646  B1 1C           LDA (OBJECT),Y
0054  0648  D1 14           CMP (POINTR),Y
0055  064A  D0 03           BNE NOGOOD
0056  064C  4C E2 06        JMP FOUND
0057  064F  A0 FF    NOGOOD LDY #$FF         ;SET COMPARE RESULT FLAG
0058  0651  90 02           BCC TESTS        ;IF OBJ < POINTR : C=0
0059  0653  A0 01           LDY #1
0060  0655  84 11    TESTS  STY CMPRES
0061  0657  A4 18           LDY INCMNT       ;IS INCR. VALUE A 1?
0062  0659  88              DEY
0063  065A  D0 10           BNE NEXT
0064  065C  A5 10           LDA CLOSE        ;CHECK CLOSE FLAG IF IT WAS
0065  065E  F0 08           BEQ MAKCLO       ;IF CLOSE FLAG NOT SET, GO DO IT
0066  0660  38              SEC
0067  0661  E5 11           SBC CMPRES       ;SEE IF GAVE PASSED WHERE OBJ.
0068  0663  F0 07           BEQ NEXT         ;..SHOULD BE BUT ISNT
```

Fig. 9-22: Alphabetic List Programs: Binary Search, Delete, Insert

DATA STRUCTURES

```
0069  0665  4C E0 06            JMP OUT
0070  0668  A5 11      MAKCLO   LDA CMPRES     ;SET CLOSE FLAG TO CMPRES
0071  066A  85 10               STA CLOSE
0072  066C  24 11      NEXT     BIT CMPRES
0073  066E  30 35               BMI SUBIT
0074  0670  A5 16               LDA TABLEN     ;SEE IF ADDITIION OF INCMNT
0075  0672  38                  SEC            ;..WILL RUN PAST END OF TABLE
0076  0673  E5 17               SBC LOGPOS
0077  0675  F0 69               BEQ OUT        ;CHECK TO SEE IF AT END OF TABLE ALREADY
0078  0677  E5 18               SBC INCMNT
0079  0679  90 1A               BCC TOOHI
0080  067B  A6 18               LDX INCMNT     ;IS ALL RIGHT, INC POINTER BY
0081  067D  A5 1B      ADDER    LDA ENTLEN     ;..PROPER AMOUNT
0082  067F  18                  CLC
0083  0680  65 14               ADC POINTR
0084  0682  85 14               STA POINTR
0085  0684  90 02               BCC AD1
0086  0686  E6 15               INC POINTR+1
0087  0688  CA         AD1      DEX
0088  0689  D0 F2               BNE ADDER
0089  068B  A5 17               LDA LOGPOS     ;INCREMENT LOGICAL POSITION
0090  068D  18                  CLC
0091  068E  65 18               ADC INCMNT
0092  0690  85 17               STA LOGPOS
0093  0692  4C 2F 06            JMP ENTRY
0094  0695  E6 17      TOOHI    INC LOGPOS     ;INCR. LOGICAL POSITION
0095  0697  A5 1B               LDA ENTLEN     ;MOVE POINTER UP ONE ENTRY
0096  0699  18                  CLC
0097  069A  65 14               ADC POINTR
0098  069C  85 14               STA POINTR
0099  069E  90 35               BCC SETCLO
0100  06A0  E6 15               INC POINTR+1
0101  06A2  4C D5 06            JMP SETCLO
0102  06A5  A5 17      SUBIT    LDA LOGPOS     ;SEE IF INC WILL GO OFF BOTTOM
0103  06A7  38                  SEC            ;.. OF TABLE
0104  06A8  E5 18               SBC INCMNT
0105  06AA  F0 17               BEQ TOOLOW
0106  06AC  90 15               BCC TOOLOW
0107  06AE  85 17               STA LOGPOS     ;SAVE NEW LOGICAL POSITION
0108  06B0  A6 18               LDX INCMNT
0109  06B2  A5 14      SUBLOP   LDA POINTR     ;SUBTRACT PROPER AMT. FROM POINTER
0110  06B4  38                  SEC
0111  06B5  E5 1B               SBC ENTLEN
0112  06B7  85 14               STA POINTR
0113  06B9  B0 02               BCS SUB0
0114  06BB  C6 15               DEC POINTR+1
0115  06BD  CA         SUB0     DEX
0116  06BE  D0 F2               BNE SUBLOP
0117  06C0  4C 2F 06            JMP ENTRY
0118  06C3  A6 17      TOOLOW   LDX LOGPOS     ;SEE IF POS IS ALREADY 1
0119  06C5  CA                  DEX
0120  06C6  F0 18               BEQ OUT
0121  06C8  C6 17               DEC LOGPOS
0122  06CA  A5 14               LDA POINTR     ;SUB 1 ENTRY FROM POINTER
0123  06CC  38                  SEC
0124  06CD  E5 1B               SBC ENTLEN
0125  06CF  85 14               STA POINTR
0126  06D1  B0 02               BCS SETCLO
0127  06D3  C6 15               DEC POINTR+1
0128  06D5  A9 01      SETCLO   LDA #1
0129  06D7  85 18               STA INCMNT
0130  06D9  A5 11               LDA CMPRES
0131  06DB  85 10               STA CLOSE
0132  06DD  4C 2F 06            JMP ENTRY
0133  06E0  A2 FF      OUT      LDX #$FF       ;Z SET IF FOUND
0134  06E2  60         FOUND    RTS
0135  06E3                      ;
0136  06E3                      ;
0137  06E3                      ;
0138  06E3  20 00 06   NEW      JSR SEARCH     ;SEE IF OBJECT IS ALREADY THERE
```

Fig. 9-22: Alphabetic List Programs: Binary Search, Delete, Insert (cont.)

PROGRAMMING THE 6502

```
0139  06E6  F0 76              BEQ OUTE
0140  06E8  A5 16              LDA TABLEN      ;CHECK FOR 0 TABLE
0141  06EA  F0 62              BEQ INSERT
0142  06EC  24 11              BIT CMPRES      ;TEST LAST COMPARE RESULT
0143  06EE  10 05              BPL LOSIDE
0144  06F0  C6 17              DEC LOGPOS      ;SET LOGICAL POSITION SO
0145  06F2  4C 00 07           JMP SETUP       ;..SUB WORKS LATER
0146  06F5  A5 1B       LOSIDE LDA ENTLEN      ;SET POINTER ABOVE WHERE
0147  06F7  18                 CLC             ;..OBJECT WILL GO
0148  06F8  65 14              ADC POINTR
0149  06FA  85 14              STA POINTR
0150  06FC  90 02              BCC SETUP
0151  06FE  E6 15              INC POINTR+1
0152  0700  A5 16       SETUP  LDA TABLEN      ;SEE HOW MANY ENTRIES THERE
0153  0702  38                 SEC             ;..ARE AFTER WHERE OBJ. WILL GO
0154  0703  E5 17              SBC LOGPOS
0155  0705  F0 47              BEQ INSERT
0156  0707  AA                 TAX
0157  0708  A8                 TAY
0158  0709  88                 DEY             ;SEE IF ALREADY POINTING TO
0159  070A  F0 0E              BEQ SETEMP      ;..LAST ENTRY
0160  070C  A5 1B       UPLOOP LDA ENTLEN      ;MOVE POINTER TO LAST ENTRY
0161  070E  18                 CLC
0162  070F  65 14              ADC POINTR
0163  0711  85 14              STA POINTR
0164  0713  90 02              BCC SET0
0165  0715  E6 15              INC POINTR+1
0166  0717  88          SET0   DEY
0167  0718  D0 F2              BNE UPLOOP
0168  071A  A5 14       SETEMP LDA POINTR      ;ADD ENTLEN TO POINTER
0169  071C  18                 CLC             ;..STORE AT TEMP
0170  071D  65 1B              ADC ENTLEN
0171  071F  85 19              STA TEMP
0172  0721  90 01              BCC SET1
0173  0723  C8                 INY             ;T WAS ALREADY 0
0174  0724  98          SET1   TYA
0175  0725  18                 CLC
0176  0726  65 15              ADC POINTR+1
0177  0728  85 1A              STA TEMP+1
0178  072A  A4 1B       MOVER  LDY ENTLEN      ;SET Y FOR SHIFT
0179  072C  88          ANOTHR DEY
0180  072D  B1 14              LDA (POINTR),Y  ;MOVE A BYTE
0181  072F  91 19              STA (TEMP),Y
0182  0731  C0 00              CPY #0
0183  0733  D0 F7              BNE ANOTHR
0184  0735  A5 14              LDA POINTR      ;DECR. POINTER AND TEMP
0185  0737  38                 SEC             ;..BY ENTLEN
0186  0738  E5 1B              SBC ENTLEN
0187  073A  85 14              STA POINTR
0188  073C  B0 02              BCS M1
0189  073E  C6 15              DEC POINTR+1
0190  0740  CA          M1     DEX
0191  0741  D0 D7              BNE SETEMP
0192  0743  A5 1B              LDA ENTLEN      ;MOVE POINTER BACK TO
0193  0745  18                 CLC             ;WHERE OBJ. WILL GO
0194  0746  65 14              ADC POINTR
0195  0748  85 14              STA POINTR
0196  074A  90 02              BCC INSERT
0197  074C  E6 15              INC POINTR+1
0198  074E  A0 00       INSERT LDY #0          ;MOVE OBJECT INTO TABLE
0199  0750  A6 1B              LDX ENTLEN
0200  0752  B1 1C       INNER  LDA (OBJECT),Y
0201  0754  91 14              STA (POINTR),Y
0202  0756  C8                 INY
0203  0757  CA                 DEX
0204  0758  D0 F8              BNE INNER
0205  075A  E6 16              INC TABLEN      ;INCREMENT TABLE LENGTH
0206  075C  A2 FF              LDX #$FF
```

Fig. 9-22: Alphabetic List Programs: Binary Search, Delete, Insert (cont.)

DATA STRUCTURES

```
0207   075E   60                 OUTE    RTS                ;Z SET IF NOT DONE
0208   075F                              ;
0209   075F                              ;
0210   075F                              ;
0211   075F   20 00 06           DELETE  JSR SEARCH         ;GET ADDR OF OBJECT IN TABLE
0212   0762   D0 35                      BNE OUTS           ;SEE IF IT IS THERE
0213   0764   A5 16                      LDA TABLEN         ;SEE HOW MANY ENTRIES ARE
0214   0766   38                         SEC                ;..LEFT AFTER OBJ. IN TABLE
0215   0767   E5 17                      SBC LOGPOS
0216   0769   F0 2A                      BEQ DECER
0217   076B   85 17                      STA LOGPOS         ;STORE RESULT AS A COUNTER
0218   076D   A5 1B              BIGLOP  LDA ENTLEN         ;SET TEMP & ENTRY ABOVE 1 ENTRY ABOVE OBJ.
0219   076F   18                         CLC
0220   0770   65 14                      ADC POINTR
0221   0772   85 19                      STA TEMP
0222   0774   A9 00                      LDA #0
0223   0776   65 15                      ADC POINTR+1
0224   0778   85 1A                      STA TEMP+1
0225   077A   A6 1B                      LDX ENTLEN         ;SET COUNTERS
0226   077C   A0 00                      LDY #0
0227   077E   B1 19              BYTE    LDA (TEMP),Y       ;MOVE A BYTE
0228   0780   91 14                      STA (POINTR),Y
0229   0782   C8                         INY                ;IS BLOCK MOVED YET?
0230   0783   CA                         DEX
0231   0784   D0 F8                      BNE BYTE
0232   0786   A5 1B                      LDA ENTLEN
0233   0788   18                         CLC
0234   0789   65 14                      ADC POINTR
0235   078B   85 14                      STA POINTR
0236   078D   90 02                      BCC D2
0237   078F   E6 15                      INC POINTR+1
0238   0791   C6 17              D2      DEC LOGPOS
0239   0793   D0 D8                      BNE BIGLOP
0240   0795   C6 16              DECER   DEC TABLEN
0241   0797   A9 00                      LDA #0             ;Z SET IF WAS DONE
0242   0799   60                 OUTS    RTS
0243   079A                              .END

ERRORS = 0000 <0000>


SYMBOL TABLE

SYMBOL   VALUE

AD1      0688    ADDER    067D   ANOTHR   072C   BIGLOP   076D
BYTE     077E    CLOSE    0010   CMPRES   0011   D2       0791
DECER    0795    DELETE   075F   DIV      0615   ENTLEN   001B
ENTRY    062F    FOUND    06E2   INCMNT   0018   INNER    0752
INSERT   074E    LOGPOS   0017   LOOP     0621   LOPP     062C
LOSIDE   06F5    M1       0740   MAKCLO   0668   MOVER    072A
NEW      06E3    NEXT     066C   NOGOOD   064F   OBJECT   001C
OUT      06E0    OUTE     075E   OUTS     0799   POINTR   0014
SEARCH   0600    SET0     0717   SET1     0724   SETCLO   06D5
SETEMP   071A    SETUP    0700   SUB0     06BD   SUBIT    06A5
SUBLOP   06B2    TABASE   0012   TABLEN   0016   TEMP     0019
TESTS    0655    TOOHI    0695   TOOLOW   06C3   UPLOOP   070C

END OF ASSEMBLY

<
```

Fig. 9-22: Alphabetic List Programs: Binary Search, Delete, Insert (cont.)

Let us examine the structure in more detail in Fig. 9-23.
The entry format is:

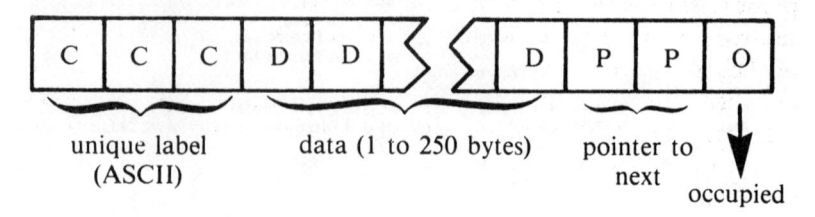

```
| C | C | C | D | D |>< D | P | P | O |
  _____/   _____/    \___/
  unique label  data (1 to 250 bytes)  pointer to      ↓
  (ASCII)                               next        occupied
```

As usual the conventions are:

ENTLEN: total element length (in bytes)
TABASE: address of base of list
TABLEN: number of entries (1 to 256)

Here, REFBASE points to the base address of the directory, or "reference table."

Each two-byte address within this directory points to the first occurrence of the letter to which it corresponds in the list. Thus each group of entries with an identical first letter in their labels actually form a separate list within the whole structure. This feature facilitates searching and is analogous to an address book. Note that no data are moved during an insert or a delete. Only pointers are changed, as in every well-behaved linked list structure.

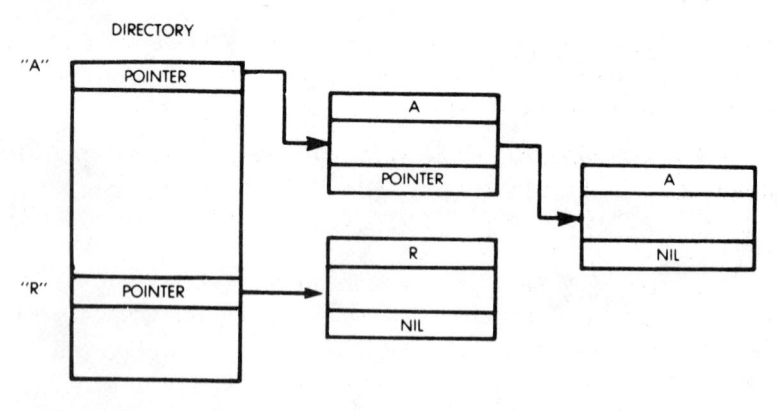

```
          DIRECTORY
  "A"  |  POINTER  |─────┐
       |           |     │     ┌─────────┐
       |           |     │     │    A    │
       |           |     └────▶├─────────┤      ┌─────────┐
       |           |           │ POINTER │─────▶│    A    │
       |           |           └─────────┘      ├─────────┤
       |           |                            │   NIL   │
       |           |           ┌─────────┐      └─────────┘
       |           |           │    R    │
  "R"  |  POINTER  |──────────▶├─────────┤
       |           |           │   NIL   │
                               └─────────┘
```

Fig. 9-23: Linked List Structure

If no entry starting with a specific letter is found, or if there is no entry alphabetically following an existing one, their pointers will point to the beginning of the table (= "NIL"). At the bottom of the table, by convention, a value is stored such that the absolute value of the difference between it and "Z" is greater than the difference between "A" and "Z." This represents an End Of Table (EOT) marker. The EOT value is assumed here to occupy the same amount of memory as a normal entry but could be just one byte if desired.

The letters are assumed here to be alphabetic letters in ASCII code. Changing this would require changing the constant at the PRETAB routine.

The End Of Table marker is set to the value of the beginning of the table ("NIL").

By convention, the "NIL pointers," found either at the end of a string or within a directory location which does not point to a string, are set to the value of the table base to provide a unique identification. Another convention could be used. In particular, a different marker for EOT would result in some space savings, as no NIL entries need be kept for nonexisting entries.

Insertion and deletion are performed in the usual way (see Part I of this chapter) by merely modifying the required pointers. The INDEXD flag is used to indicate if the pointer to the object is in the reference table or another string element.

Searching

The SEARCH program resides at memory locations 0600 to 0650. In addition, it uses subroutine PRETAB at address 06F8.

The search principle is straightforward:

1— Get the directory entry corresponding to the letter of the alphabet in the first position of the OBJECT's label.

2— Get the pointer out of the directory. Access the element. If NIL, the entry does not exist.

3— If not NIL, match the element against the OBJECT. If a match is found, the search has succeeded. If not, get the pointer to the next entry down the list.

4— Go back to 2.

An example is shown in Fig. 9-24.

PROGRAMMING THE 6502

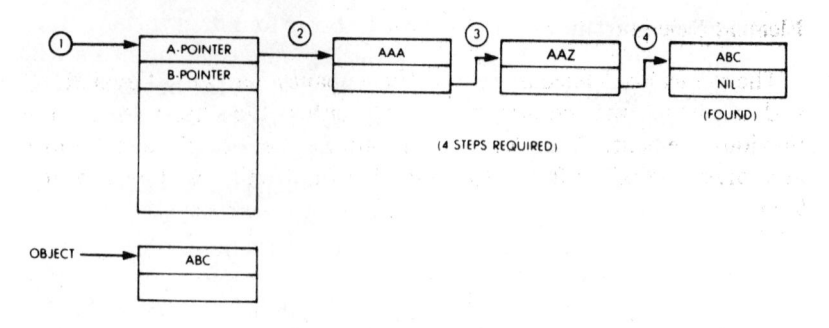

Fig. 9-24: Linked List: A Search

Element Insertion

The insertion is essentially a search followed by an insertion once a "NIL" has been found. A block of storage for the new entry is allocated past the EOT marker by looking for an occupancy marker set at "available". The program is called "NEW" and resides at addresses 0651 to 06BD. An example is shown in Fig. 9-25.

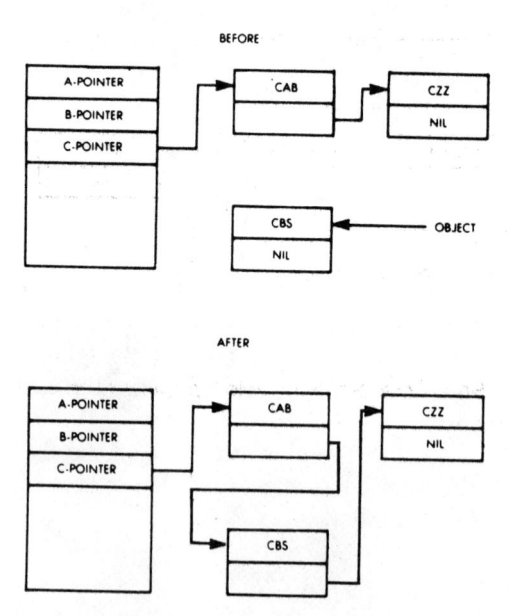

Fig. 9-25: Linked List: Example of Insertion

DATA STRUCTURES

Element Deletion

The element is deleted by setting its occupancy marker to "available" and adjusting the pointer text from either the directory or the previous element. The program is called "DELETE" and resides at addresses 06BE to 06F7. An example of a deletion is shown in Fig. 9-26.

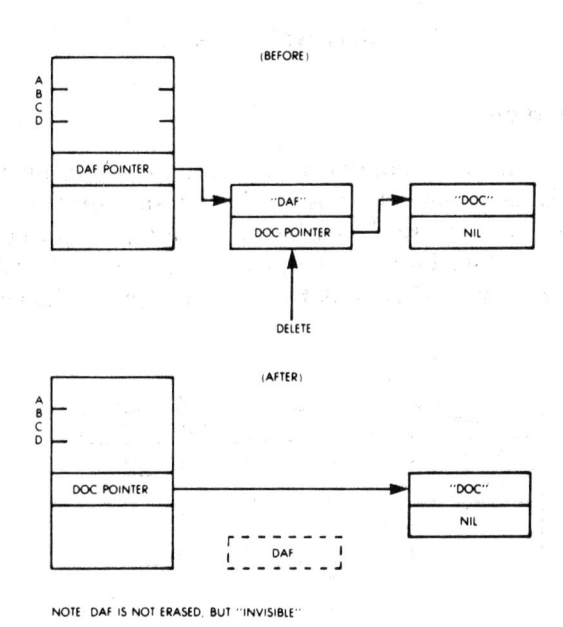

Fig. 9-26: Example of Deletion (Linked List)

PROGRAMMING THE 6502

```
LINE # LOC    CODE         LINE
0002  0000                 INDEXD = $10
0003  0000                 INDLOC = $11
0004  0000                 POINTR = $13
0005  0000                 OBJECT = $15
0006  0000                 TEMP   = $17
0007  0000                 REFBAS = $19
0008  0000                 OLD    = $1B
0009  0000                 TABASE = $1D
0010  0000                 ENTLEN = $1F
0011  0000                 ;
0012  0000                        * = $600
0013  0600                 ;
0014  0600  A9 01          SEARCH LDA #1            ;INITIALIZE FLAGS
0015  0602  85 10                 STA INDEXD
0016  0604  20 F8 06              JSR PRETAB        ;GET REF. POINTER FOR START
0017  0607  B1 11                 LDA (INDLOC),Y    ;PUT IT IN POINTR
0018  0609  85 13                 STA POINTR
0019  060B  C8                    INY
0020  060C  B1 11                 LDA (INDLOC),Y
0021  060E  85 14                 STA POINTR+1
0022  0610  A0 00          ENTRY  LDY #0            ;SEE IF ENTRY IS EOT VALUE
0023  0612  B1 13                 LDA (POINTR),Y
0024  0614  C9 7C                 CMP #$7C
0025  0616  F0 36                 BEQ NOTFND
0026  0618  B1 15                 LDA (OBJECT),Y    ;COMPARE FIRST LETTERS
0027  061A  D1 13                 CMP (POINTR),Y
0028  061C  90 30                 BCC NOTFND
0029  061E  D0 12                 BNE NOGOOD
0030  0620  C8                    INY               ;COMPARE SECOND LETTERS
0031  0621  B1 15                 LDA (OBJECT),Y
0032  0623  D1 13                 CMP (POINTR),Y
0033  0625  90 27                 BCC NOTFND
0034  0627  D0 09                 BNE NOGOOD
0035  0629  C8                    INY               ;COMPARE THIRD LETTERS
0036  062A  B1 15                 LDA (OBJECT),Y
0037  062C  D1 13                 CMP (POINTR),Y
0038  062E  90 1E                 BCC NOTFND
0039  0630  F0 1E                 BEQ FOUND
0040  0632  A5 14          NOGOOD LDA POINTR+1      ;SAVE POINTR FOR POSSIBLE REF.
0041  0634  85 1C                 STA OLD+1
0042  0636  A5 13                 LDA POINTR
0043  0638  85 1B                 STA OLD
0044  063A  A4 1F                 LDY ENTLEN        ;GET POINTER FROM ENTRY AND
0045  063C  B1 13                 LDA (POINTR),Y    ;..LOAD IT INTO POINTR
0046  063E  AA                    TAX
0047  063F  C8                    INY
0048  0640  B1 13                 LDA (POINTR),Y
0049  0642  85 14                 STA POINTR+1
0050  0644  8A                    TXA
0051  0645  85 13                 STA POINTR
0052  0647  A9 00                 LDA #0
0053  0649  85 10                 STA INDEXD        ;RESET FLAG
0054  064B  4C 10 06              JMP ENTRY
0055  064E  A9 FF          NOTFND LDA #$FF
0056  0650  60             FOUND  RTS               ;Z SET IF FOUND
0057  0651                 ;
0058  0651                 ;
0059  0651                 ;
0060  0651  20 00 06       NEW    JSR SEARCH        ;SEE IF OBJ. IS ALREADY THERE
0061  0654  F0 67                 BEQ OUTE
0062  0656  A5 1D                 LDA TABASE        ;LOOK FOR UNOCCUPIED ENTRY
0063  0658  18                    CLC               ;..BLOCK
0064  0659  69 01                 ADC #1            ;JUMP PAST EOT VALUE
0065  065B  85 17                 STA TEMP
0066  065D  A9 00                 LDA #0
0067  065F  65 1E                 ADC TABASE+1
0068  0661  85 18                 STA TEMP+1
0069  0663  A4 1F                 LDY ENTLEN        ;SET Y TO POINT TO OCCUPANCY
```

Fig. 9-27: Linked List Program

DATA STRUCTURES

```
0070  0665  C8                      INY           ;..MARKER OF AN ENTRY
0071  0666  C8                      INY
0072  0667  A9 01        LOOP       LDA #1        ;TEST FOR OCCUPANCY MARKER
0073  0669  D1 17                   CMP (TEMP),Y
0074  066B  D0 16                   BNE INSERT
0075  066D  A5 17                   LDA TEMP      ;IF IS USED, MOVE TEMP TO NEXT
0076  066F  18                      CLC           ;..ENTRY BLOCK
0077  0670  65 1F                   ADC ENTLEN
0078  0672  90 02                   BCC MORE
0079  0674  E6 18                   INC TEMP+1
0080  0676  69 03        MORE       ADC #3
0081  0678  85 17                   STA TEMP
0082  067A  A9 00                   LDA #0
0083  067C  65 18                   ADC TEMP+1
0084  067E  85 18                   STA TEMP+1
0085  0680  4C 67 06                JMP LOOP
0086  0683  88           INSERT     DEY           ;SET Y BACK TO POINTING TO
0087  0684  88                      DEY           ;..TOP OF DATA
0088  0685  88           LOPE       DEY           ;MOVE OBJECT INTO SPACE
0089  0686  B1 15                   LDA (OBJECT),Y
0090  0688  91 17                   STA (TEMP),Y
0091  068A  C0 00                   CPY #0
0092  068C  D0 F7                   BNE LOPE
0093  068E  A4 1F                   LDY ENTLEN    ;PUT THE VALUE OF POINTR, THE
0094  0690  A5 13                   LDA POINTR    ;ENTRY AFTER OBJECT, INTO
0095  0692  91 17                   STA (TEMP),Y  ;POINTER AREA OF OBJECT
0096  0694  C8                      INY
0097  0695  A5 14                   LDA POINTR+1
0098  0697  91 17                   STA (TEMP),Y
0099  0699  C8                      INY
0100  069A  A9 01                   LDA #1        ;SET OCCUPANCY MARKER
0101  069C  91 17                   STA (TEMP),Y
0102  069E  A5 10                   LDA INDEXD    ;TEST TO SEE IF REF. TABLE
0103  06A0  D0 0D                   BNE SETINX    ;..NEEDS READJUSTING
0104  06A2  88                      DEY
0105  06A3  A5 18                   LDA TEMP+1    ;NO, CHANGE PREVIOUS ENTRY'S
0106  06A5  91 1B                   STA (OLD),Y   ;..POINTER
0107  06A7  88                      DEY
0108  06A8  A5 17                   LDA TEMP
0109  06AA  91 1B                   STA (OLD),Y
0110  06AC  4C BB 06                JMP DONE
0111  06AF  20 F8 06     SETINX     JSR PRETAB    ;GET ADDRESS OF WHATS TO BE CHANGED
0112  06B2  A5 17                   LDA TEMP      ;LOAD ADDR. OF OBJ. THERE
0113  06B4  91 11                   STA (INDLOC),Y
0114  06B6  C8                      INY
0115  06B7  A5 18                   LDA TEMP+1
0116  06B9  91 11                   STA (INDLOC),Y
0117  06BB  A9 FF        DONE       LDA #$FF
0118  06BD  60           OUTE       RTS           ;Z CLEAR IF DONE
0119  06BE               ;
0120  06BE               ;
0121  06BE               ;
0122  06BE  20 00 06     DELETE     JSR SEARCH    ;GET ADDR OF OBJ.
0123  06C1  D0 34                   BNE OUTS
0124  06C3  A4 1F                   LDY ENTLEN    ;STORE POINTER AT END
0125  06C5  B1 13                   LDA (POINTR),Y ;..OF OBJECT
0126  06C7  85 17                   STA TEMP
0127  06C9  C8                      INY
0128  06CA  B1 13                   LDA (POINTR),Y
0129  06CC  85 18                   STA TEMP+1
0130  06CE  C8                      INY
0131  06CF  A9 00                   LDA #0        ;CLEAR OCCUPANCY MARKER
0132  06D1  91 13                   STA (POINTR),Y
0133  06D3  A5 10                   LDA INDEXD    ;SEE IF REF. TABLE NEEDS
0134  06D5  F0 06                   BEQ PREINX    ;..READJUSTING
0135  06D7  20 F8 06                JSR PRETAB
0136  06DA  4C EA 06                JMP MOVEIT
0137  06DD  A5 1B        PREINX     LDA OLD       ;SET FOR CHANGING PREVIOUS
0138  06DF  18                      CLC           ;..ENTRY
```

Fig. 9-27: Linked List Program (cont.)

```
0139  06E0  65 1F              ADC ENTLEN
0140  06E2  85 11              STA INDLOC
0141  06E4  A9 00              LDA #0
0142  06E6  65 1C              ADC OLD+1
0143  06E8  85 12              STA INDLOC+1
0144  06EA  A5 17       MOVEIT LDA TEMP        ;CHANGE WHAT NEEDS CHANGING
0145  06EC  A0 00              LDY #0
0146  06EE  91 11              STA (INDLOC),Y
0147  06F0  C8                 INY
0148  06F1  A5 18              LDA TEMP+1
0149  06F3  91 11              STA (INDLOC),Y
0150  06F5  A9 00              LDA #0
0151  06F7  60          OUTS   RTS             ;Z SET IF DONE
0152  06F8                     ;
0153  06F8                     ;
0154  06F8                     ;
0155  06F8  A0 00       PRETAB LDY #0
0156  06FA  B1 15              LDA (OBJECT),Y
0157  06FC  38                 SEC             ;REMOVE ASCII LEADER FROM
0158  06FD  E9 41              SBC #$41        ;..FIRST LETTER IN OBJECT
0159  06FF  0A                 ASL A           ;MULTIPLY BY 2
0160  0700  18                 CLC
0161  0701  65 19              ADC REFBAS      ;INDEX INTO REF. TABLE
0162  0703  85 11              STA INDLOC
0163  0705  A9 00              LDA #0
0164  0707  65 1A              ADC REFBAS+1
0165  0709  85 12              STA INDLOC+1
0166  070B  60                 RTS
0167  070C                     .END

ERRORS = 0000 <0000>


SYMBOL TABLE

SYMBOL     VALUE

DELETE     06DE    DONE     06BB    ENTLEN   001F    ENTRY    061B
FOUND      0650    INDEXD   0010    INDLOC   0011    INSERT   0683
LOOP       0667    LOPE     0685    MORE     0676    MOVEIT   06EA
NEW        0651    NOGOOD   0632    NOTFND   064E    OBJECT   0015
OLD        001B    OUTE     06BD    OUTS     06F7    POINTR   0013
PREINX     06DD    PRETAB   06F8    REFBAS   0019    SEARCH   0600
SETINX     06AF    TABASE   001D    TEMP     0017
END OF ASSEMBLY
```

Fig. 9-27: Linked List Program (cont.)

DATA STRUCTURES

BINARY TREE

We will now develop typical tree management routines. Our simple structure is shown in Fig. 9-28. It is a binary tree, and the nodes are names of persons. Names will be internally sorted by "tags" which will be the first three letters of every name. The memory representation of this tree structure is shown in Fig. 9-29. The contents of the nodes are shown, as well as the two links. The first link, to the left of the name, is the "left sibling" and the next link, to its right, is the "right sibling." For example, the entry for Jones contains two links: "2" and "4". This indicates that its left sibling is entry number 2 (Anderson), and its right sibling is entry number 4 (Smith). A "0" in the link field indicates no sibling. A left sibling's tag comes alphabetically before its parent. A right sibling's tag comes after.

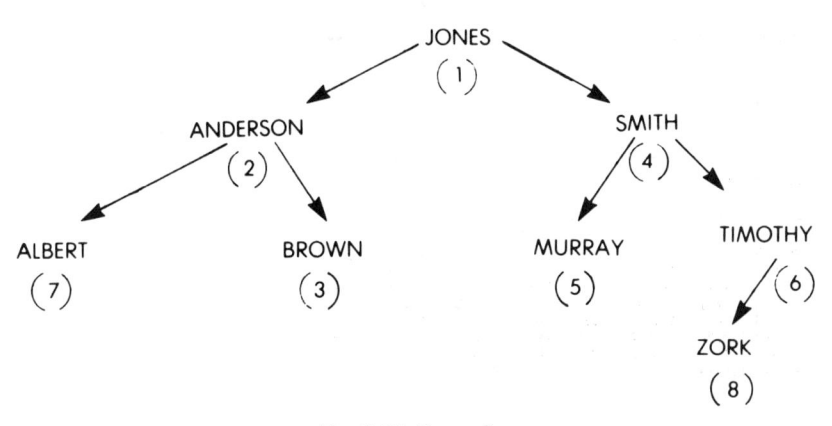

Fig. 9-28: Binary Tree

The two main routines for tree management are the *tree builder* and the *tree traverser*. The element to be inserted will be placed in a buffer. The tree builder will insert the content of the buffer into the tree at the appropriate node. The tree traverser is said to traverse the tree recursively, and prints the contents of each of its nodes in alphanumeric order. The flowchart for the tree builder is shown in Fig. 9-30, and the flowchart for the tree traverser is shown in Fig. 9-31.

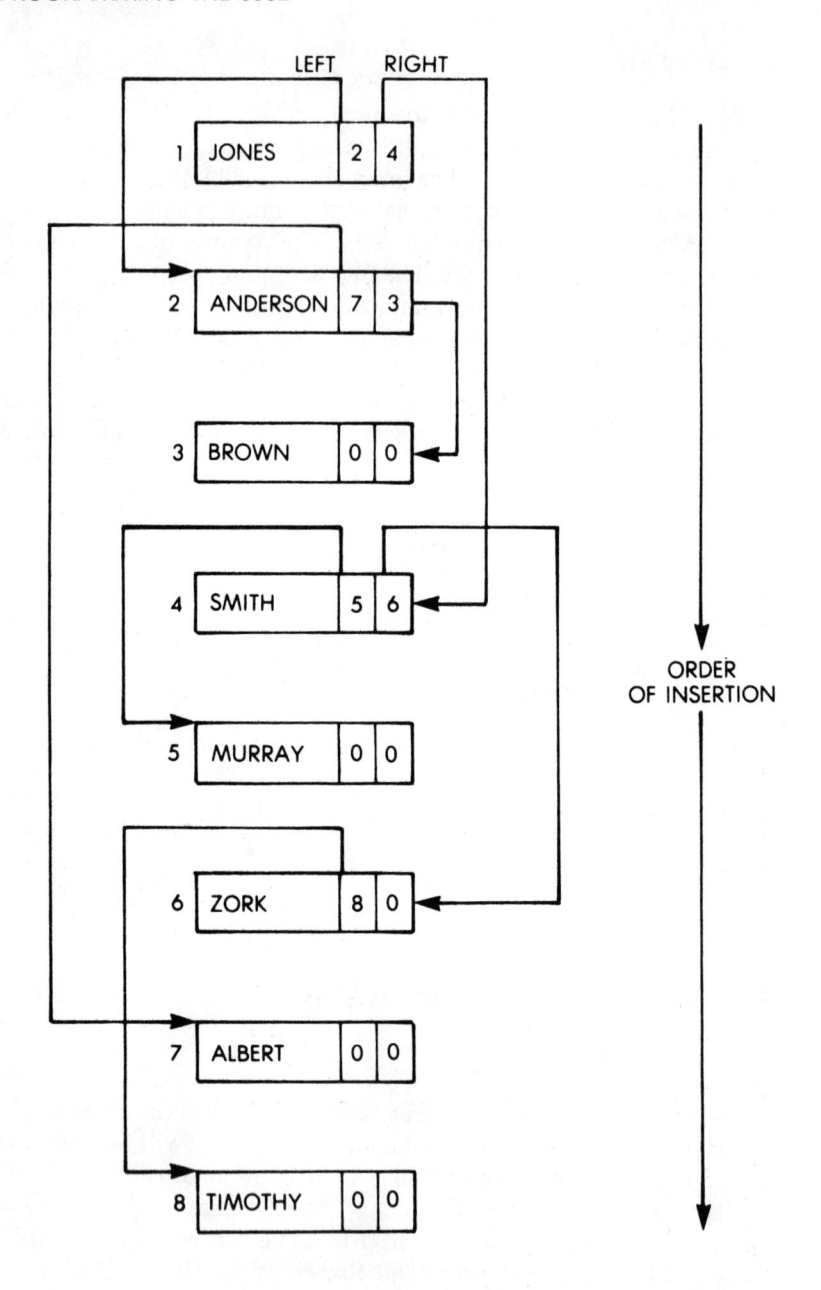

	LEFT	RIGHT
1 JONES	2	4
2 ANDERSON	7	3
3 BROWN	0	0
4 SMITH	5	6
5 MURRAY	0	0
6 ZORK	8	0
7 ALBERT	0	0
8 TIMOTHY	0	0

ORDER OF INSERTION →

Fig. 9-29: Representation in Memory

DATA STRUCTURES

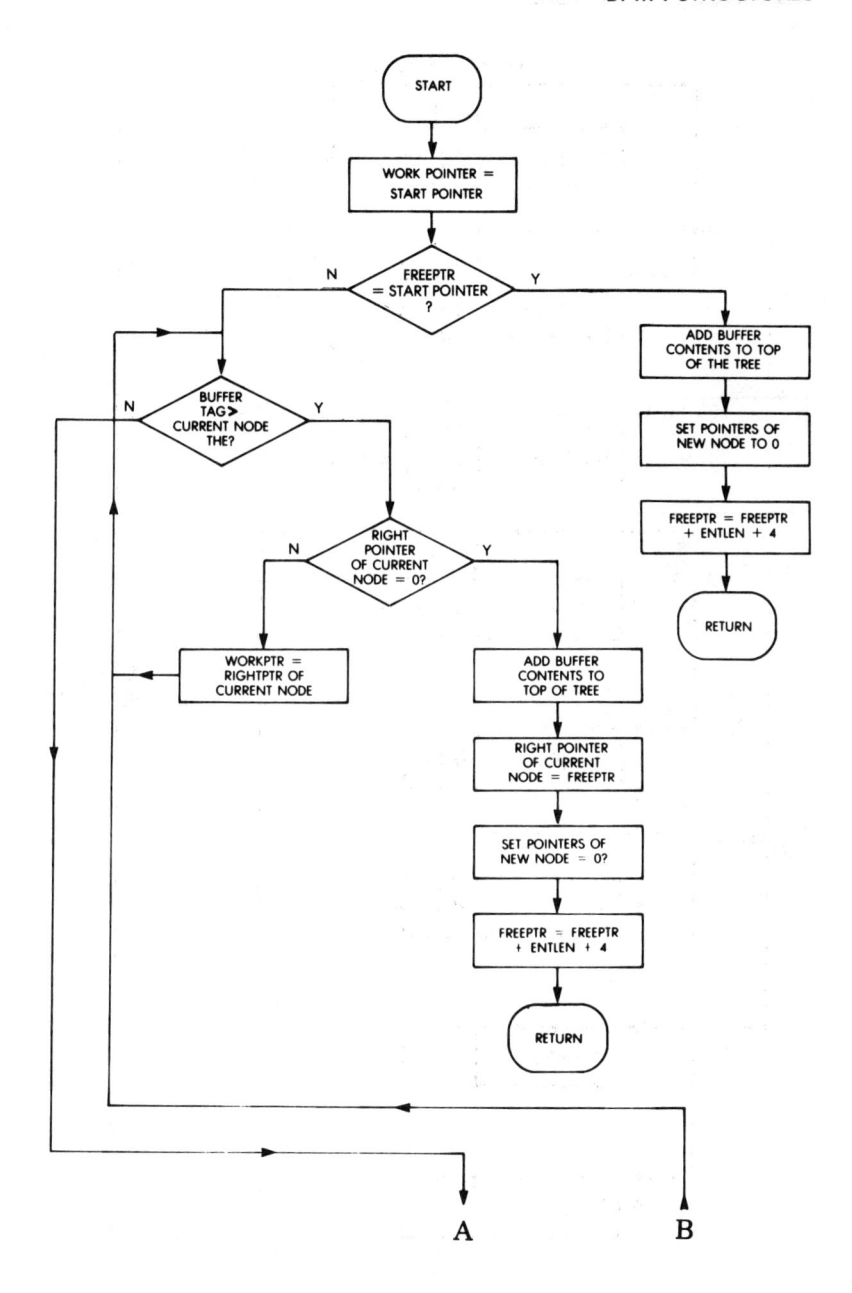

Fig. 9-30: The Tree Builder Flowchart

PROGRAMMING THE 6502

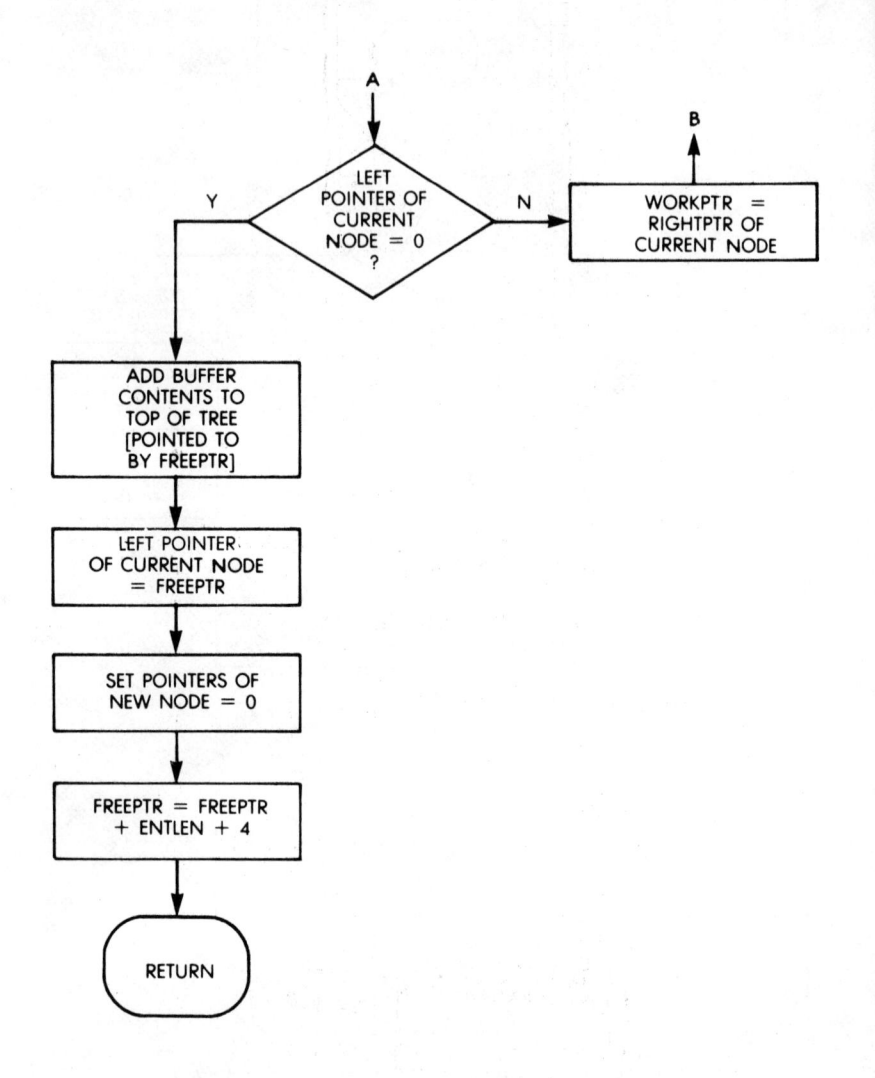

Fig. 9-30: The Tree Builder Flowchart (cont.)

DATA STRUCTURES

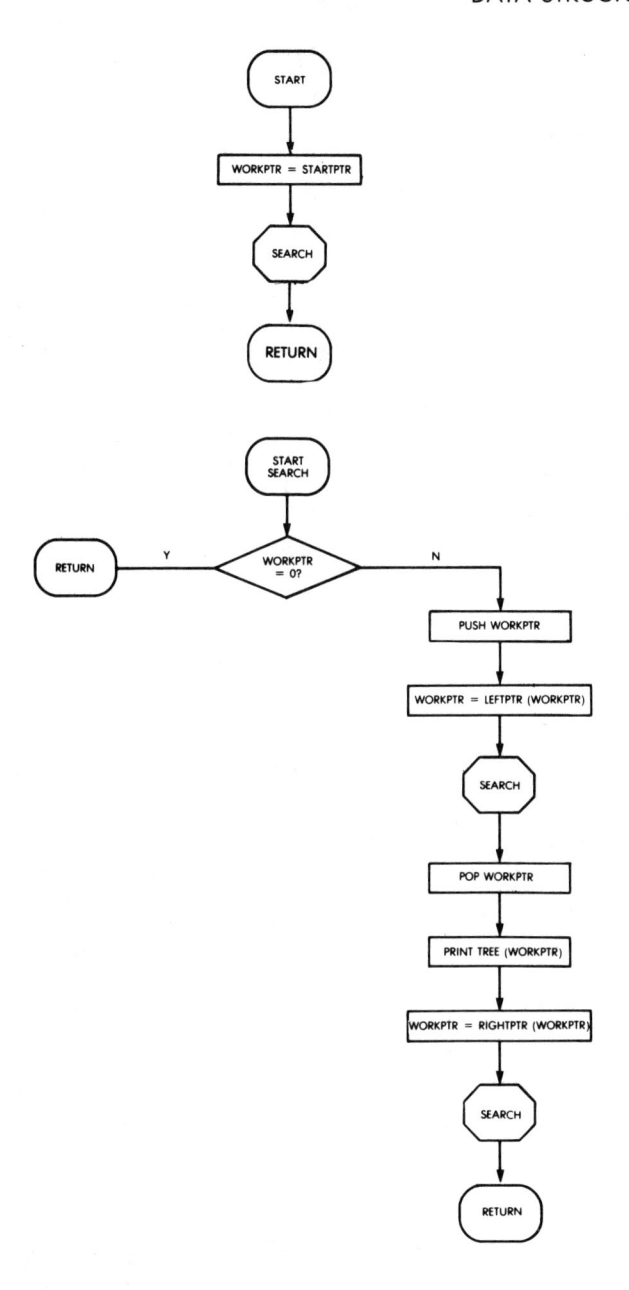

Fig. 9-31: Tree Traverser Flowchart

Since the routine for the traversal is recursive, it does not lend itself well to flowchart representation. Another description of the routine in a high-level format is therefore shown in Fig. 9-32. An actual node of the tree is shown in Fig. 9-33. It contains data of length ENTLEN, then two 16-bit pointers (the right pointer and the left pointer). In order to avoid a possible confusion, note that the representation of Fig. 9-29 has been simplified and that the right pointer appears to the left of the left pointer in the memory. The memory allocation used by this program is shown in Fig. 9-34, and the actual program appears in Fig. 9-37.

The INSERT routine resides at addresses 0200 to 0282. The tag of the object to be inserted is compared to that of the entry. If greater, one moves to the right. If smaller, to the left, down by one position. The process is then repeated until either an empty link is found or a suitable "bracket" is found for the new node (i.e., one node is greater and the next one smaller, or vice versa). The new node is then inserted by merely setting the appropriate links.

```
PROGRAM TREETRAVERSER;
BEGIN
      CALL SEARCH (STARTPOINTER);
END.

ROUTINE SEARCH (WORKPOINTER);
BEGIN
      IF WORKPOINTER = 0 THEN RETURN;
      SEARCH [LEFTPTR (WORKPOINTER)];
      PRINT TREE (WORKPOINTER);
      SEARCH [RIGHTPTR (WORKPTR)];
      RETURN;
END.
```

Fig. 9-32: Tree Traversal Algorithm

DATA STRUCTURES

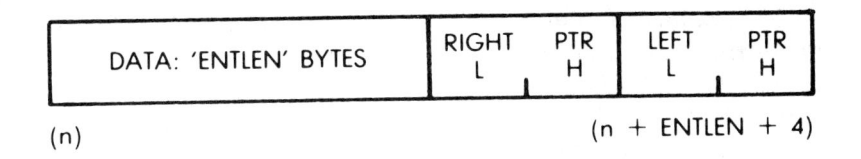

DATA: 'ENTLEN' BYTES	RIGHT PTR L H	LEFT PTR L H

(n)   (n + ENTLEN + 4)

Fig. 9-33: Data Units, or "Nodes" of Tree

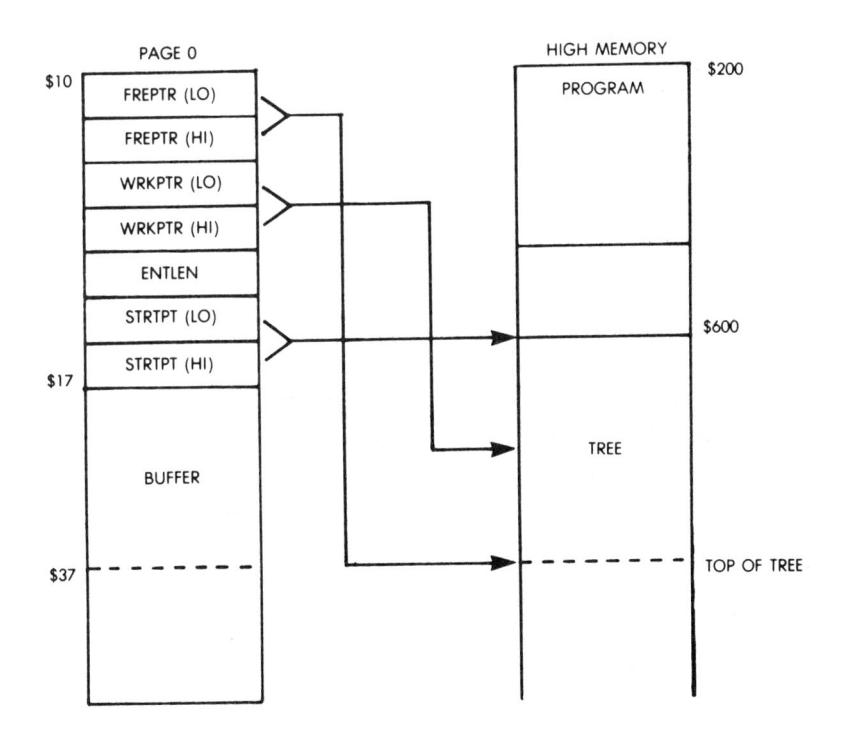

PAGE 0:
- $10: FREPTR (LO)
- FREPTR (HI)
- WRKPTR (LO)
- WRKPTR (HI)
- ENTLEN
- STRTPT (LO)
- STRTPT (HI)
- $17
- BUFFER
- $37

HIGH MEMORY:
- $200: PROGRAM
- $600: TREE
- TOP OF TREE

Fig. 9-34: Memory Maps

PROGRAMMING THE 6502

The TRAVERSE routine resides at addresses 0285 to 02D6. The utility routines OUT, ADD and CLRPTR reside at addresses 0207 to 02FE (see Fig. 9-37).

An example of a tree insertion is shown in Fig. 9-35, and an example of a tree traversal in Fig. 9-36.

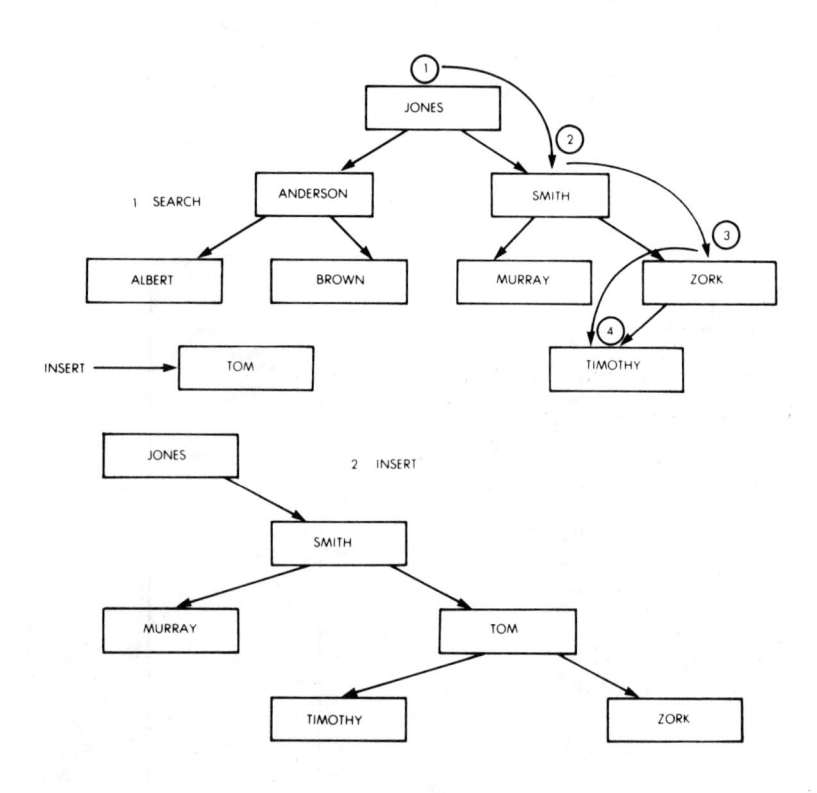

Fig. 9-35: Inserting an Element in the Tree

DATA STRUCTURES

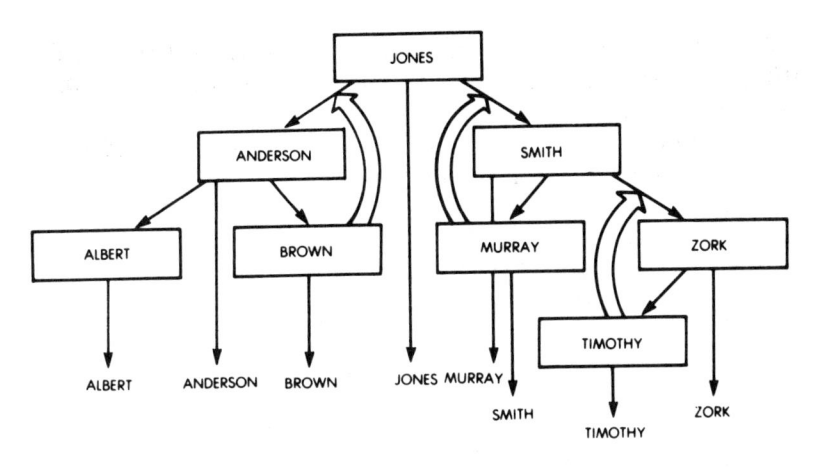

Fig. 9-36: Listing the Tree

Note on Trees

Binary trees may be constructed and traversed in many ways. For example, another representation for our tree could be:

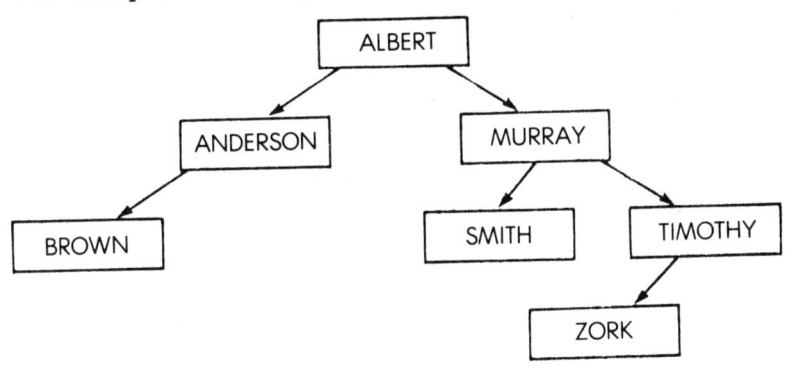

Fig. 9-38 : Tree in Preorder

It would then have to be traversed in "preorder":

1— list the root
2— traverse left subtree
3— traverse right subtree

Many other techniques and conventions exist.

PROGRAMMING THE 6502

```
0002  0000              ;TREE MANAGEMENT PROGRAM.
0003  0000              ;2 ROUTINES: ONE, WHEN CALLED, PLACES
0004  0000              ;THE CONTENTS OF THE BUFFER INTO THE
0005  0000              ;TREE; AND THE SECOND TRAVERSES
0006  0000              ;THE TREE RECURSIVELY, PRINTING ITS
0007  0000              ;NODE CONTENTS IN ALPHANUMERIC ORDER.
0008  0000              ;NOTE: 'ENTLEN' MUST BE INITIALIZED
0009  0000              ;AND 'FREPTR' MUST BE SET EQUAL TO
0010  0000              ;'STRTPTR' BEFORE EITHER ROUTINE IS USED.
0011  0000              ;
0012  0000                      * = $10
0013  0010              FREPTR  *=*+2           ;FREE SPACE POINTER: POINTS TO
0014  0012                      ;NEXT FREE LOCATION IN MEMORY.
0015  0012              WRKPTR  *=*+2           ;WORKING POINTER, POINTS TO CURRENT NODE
0016  0014              ENTLEN  *=*+1           ;TREE ENTRY LENGTH, IN BYTES.
0017  0015  00 06       STRTPT  .WORD $600
0018  0017              BUFFER  *=*+20          ;I/O BUFFER.
0019  002B              ;
0020  002B                      * = $200
0021  0200              ;
0022  0200              ;ROUTINE TO BUILD TREE: ADDS ONE DATA UNIT,
0023  0200              ;OR NODE, TO TREE. MUST BE CALLED
0024  0200              ;WITH DATA UNIT TO BE ADDED IN 'BUFFER'.
0025  0200              ;
0026  0200  A5 15       INSERT  LDA STRTPT      ;WORKPOINTER (= FREEPOINTER.
0027  0202  85 12               STA WRKPTR
0028  0204  A5 16               LDA STRTPT+1
0029  0206  85 13               STA WRKPTR+1
0030  0208  A5 10               LDA FREPTR      ;IF FREEPOINTER <>
0031  020A  C5 15               CMP STRTPT      ;STARTING LOCATION POINTER,
0032  020C  D0 0D               BNE INLOOP      ;GOTO INSERTION LOOP.
0033  020E  A5 11               LDA FREPTR+1
0034  0210  C5 16               CMP STRTPT+1
0035  0212  D0 07               BNE INLOOP
0036  0214  20 D7 02            JSR ADD         ;LOAD BUFFER INTO CURRENT POSITION.
0037  0217  20 E4 02            JSR CLRPTR      ;SET POINTERS OF CURRENT NODE TO 0.
0038  021A  60                  RTS             ;DONE ADDING 1ST NODE.
0039  021B  A0 00       INLOOP  LDY #0          ;COMPARE BUFFER TAG TO TAG OF CURRENT
0040  021D  B9 17 00    CMPLP   LDA BUFFER,Y    ;LOCATION...
0041  0220  D1 12               CMP (WRKPTR),Y
0042  0222  90 33               BCC LESSTN      ;BUFR TAG LOWER: ADD BUFFER TO
0043  0224                      ;LEFT SIDE OF TREE.
0044  0224  F0 02               BEQ NXT         ;TAGS EQUAL, TRY NEXT CHR. IN TAGS.
0045  0226  B0 05               BCS GRTNEQ      ;BUFR TAG GREATER, ADD BUFR TO
0046  0228                      ;RIGHT SIDE OF TREE.
0047  0228  C8          NXT     INY
0048  0229  C9 04               CMP #4          ;3 CHRS. COMPARED?
0049  022B  D0 F0               BNE CMPLP       ;NO, CHECK NEXT CHR.
0050  022D  A4 14       GRTNEQ  LDY ENTLEN      ;DOES
0051  022F  B1 12               LDA (WRKPTR),Y  ;RIGHT POINTER OF CURRENT NODE = 0 ?
0052  0231  D0 15               BNE NXRNOD      ;IF NOT, MOVE DOWN/RIGHT IN TREE.
0053  0233  C8                  INY
0054  0234  B1 12               LDA (WRKPTR),Y
0055  0236  D0 10               BNE NXRNOD
0056  0238  A5 11               LDA FREPTR+1    ;SET RIGHT POINTER OF CURRENT
0057  023A  91 12               STA (WRKPTR),Y  ;NODE = FREEPOINTER.
0058  023C  88                  DEY
0059  023D  A5 10               LDA FREPTR
0060  023F  91 12               STA (WRKPTR),Y
0061  0241  20 D7 02            JSR ADD         ;ADD BUFFER TO TREE.
0062  0244  20 E4 02            JSR CLRPTR      ;CLEAR POINTERS OF NEW NODE.
0063  0247  60                  RTS             ;DONE, NEW RIGHT NODE ADDED.
0064  0248  A4 14       NXRNOD  LDY ENTLEN      ;SET WORKING POINTER =
0065  024A  B1 12               LDA (WRKPTR),Y  ;RIGHT POINTER OF CURRENT NODE.
0066  024C  AA                  TAX
0067  024D  C8                  INY
0068  024E  B1 12               LDA (WRKPTR),Y
0069  0250  85 13               STA WRKPTR+1
0070  0252  86 12               STX WRKPTR
0071  0254  4C 1B 02            JMP INLOOP      ;TRY NEW CURRENT NODE.
```

Fig. 9-37: Tree Search Programs

DATA STRUCTURES

```
0072  0257  A4 14      LESSTN LDY ENTLEN       ;DOES LEFT POINTER OF
0073  0259  C8                INY              ;CURRENT NODE = 0 ?
0074  025A  C8                INY
0075  025B  B1 12             LDA (URKPTR),Y
0076  025D  D0 15             BNE NXLNOD       ;IF SO, MOVE DOWN/LEFT IN TREE.
0077  025F  C8                INY
0078  0260  B1 12             LDA (URKPTR),Y
0079  0262  D0 10             BNE NXLNOD
0080  0264  A5 11             LDA FREPTR+1     ;SET LEFT POINTER OF CURRENT NODE TO
0081  0266  91 12             STA (URKPTR),Y   ;POINT TO NEW NODE.
0082  0268  88                DEY
0083  0269  A5 10             LDA FREPTR
0084  026B  91 12             STA (URKPTR),Y
0085  026D  20 D7 02          JSR ADD          ;ADD NEW NODE CONTENTS.
0086  0270  20 E4 02          JSR CLRPTR       ;CLEAR POINTERS OF NEW NODE.
0087  0273  60                RTS              ;DONE, NEW LEFT NODE ADDED.
0088  0274  A4 14      NXLNOD LDY ENTLEN       ;SET WORKING POINTER =
0089  0276  C8                INY              ;LEFT POINTER OF CURRENT NODE.
0090  0277  C8                INY
0091  0278  B1 12             LDA (URKPTR),Y
0092  027A  AA                TAX
0093  027B  C8                INY
0094  027C  B1 12             LDA (URKPTR),Y
0095  027E  85 13             STA URKPTR+1
0096  0280  86 12             STX URKPTR
0097  0282  4C 1B 02          JMP INLOOP       ;TRY NEW CURRENT NODE.
0098  0285              ;
0099  0285              ;TREE TRAVERSER : LISTS NODES OF TREE
0100  0285              ;IN ALPHANUMERICAL ORDER.
0101  0285              ;OUTPUT ROUTINE TO XFER BUFFER TO OUTPUT
0102  0285              ;DEVICE IS NEEDED.
0103  0285              ;
0104  0285  A5 15      TRVRSE LDA STRTPT       ;WORKING POINTER <= START POINTER.
0105  0287  85 12             STA URKPTR
0106  0289  A5 16             LDA STRTPT+1
0107  028B  85 13             STA URKPTR+1
0108  028D  A5 13      SEARCH LDA URKPTR+1
0109  028F  A6 12             LDX URKPTR       ;IF WORKING POINTER <> 0,
0110  0291  D0 07             BNE OK           ;CONTINUE;
0111  0293  A4 13             LDY URKPTR+1
0112  0295  D0 03             BNE OK
0113  0297  4C C6 02          JMP RETN         ;ELSE, RETURN.
0114  029A  48         OK     PHA              ;PUSH WORKING POINTER
0115  029B  8A                TXA              ;ONTO STACK.
0116  029C  48                PHA
0117  029D  A4 14             LDY ENTLEN       ;SET WORKING POINTER =
0118  029F  C8                INY              ;LEFT POINTER OF CURRENT NODE.
0119  02A0  C8                INY
0120  02A1  B1 12             LDA (URKPTR),Y
0121  02A3  AA                TAX
0122  02A4  C8                INY
0123  02A5  B1 12             LDA (URKPTR),Y
0124  02A7  85 13             STA URKPTR+1
0125  02A9  86 12             STX URKPTR
0126  02AB  20 8D 02          JSR SEARCH       ;SEARCH NEW NODE, RECURSIVELY.
0127  02AE  68                PLA              ;POP OLD CURRENT NODE INTO WORKING POINTER.
0128  02AF  85 12             STA URKPTR
0129  02B1  68                PLA
0130  02B2  85 13             STA URKPTR+1
0131  02B4  20 C7 02          JSR OUT          ;OUTPUT CURRENT NODE CONTENTS.
0132  02B7  A4 14             LDY ENTLEN       ;SET WORKING POINTER =
0133  02B9  B1 12             LDA (URKPTR),Y   ;CURRENT NODE'S RIGHT POINTER.
0134  02BB  AA                TAX
0135  02BC  C8                INY
0136  02BD  B1 12             LDA (URKPTR),Y
0137  02BF  85 13             STA URKPTR+1
0138  02C1  86 12             STX URKPTR
0139  02C3  20 8D 02          JSR SEARCH       ;SEARCH NEW NODE.
0140  02C6  60         RETN   RTS              ;DONE, RETURN.
```

Fig. 9-37: Tree Search Programs (cont.)

```
0141   02C7                   ;
0142   02C7                   ;BUFFER OUTPUT ROUTINE.
0143   02C7                   ;
0144   02C7  A0 00      OUT    LDY #0
0145   02C9  B1 12      XFR    LDA (WRKPTR),Y   ;GET CHR. FROM CURRENT NODE.
0146   02CB  99 17 00          STA BUFFER,Y     ;PUT IN BUFFER.
0147   02CE  C8                INY              ;REPEAT UNTIL...
0148   02CF  C4 14             CPY ENTLEN       ;ALL CHARACTERS XFERRED.
0149   02D1  D0 F6             BNE XFR
0150   02D3  EA                NOP              ;INSERT CALL TO SUBROUTINE
0151   02D4  EA                NOP              ;WHICH OUTPUTS BUFFER HERE.
0152   02D5  EA                NOP
0153   02D6  60                RTS              ;DONE.
0154   02D7                   ;
0155   02D7                   ;ROUTINE WHICH PLACES BUFFER
0156   02D7                   ;CONTENTS IN NEW NODE.
0157   02D7                   ;
0158   02D7  A0 00      ADD    LDY #0
0159   02D9  B9 17 00   MOV    LDA BUFFER,Y     ;GET CHR. FROM BUFFER.
0160   02DC  91 10             STA (FREPTR),Y   ;STORE IN NEW NODE.
0161   02DE  C8                INY              ;REPEAT UNTIL...
0162   02DF  C4 14             CPY ENTLEN       ;ALL CHRS XFERRED.
0163   02E1  D0 F6             BNE MOV
0164   02E3  60                RTS              ;DONE.
0165   02E4                   ;
0166   02E4                   ;ROUTINE TO CLEAR POINTERS OF NEW NODE,
0167   02E4                   ;AND UPDATE FREE SPACE POINTER.
0168   02E4                   ;
0169   02E4  A4 14      CLRPTR LDY ENTLEN       ;SET UP INDEX TO POINT
0170   02E6                                     ;TO TOP OF POINTER LOCATIONS.
0171   02E6  A9 00             LDA #0
0172   02E8  A2 04             LDX #4           ;LOOP 4X TO CLEAR POINTERS
0173   02EA  91 10      CLRLP  STA (FREPTR),Y   ;CLEAR POINTER LOCATION.
0174   02EC  C8                INY              ;POINT TO NEXT POINTER LOCATION.
0175   02ED  CA                DEX
0176   02EE  D0 FA             BNE CLRLP        ;LOOP IF NOT DONE.
0177   02F0  A5 14             LDA ENTLEN       ;GET ENTRY LENGTH,
0178   02F2  18                CLC              ;AND ADD 4 FOR POINTER SPACE.
0179   02F3  69 04             ADC #4
0180   02F5  65 10             ADC FREPTR       ;ADD TO FREE SPACE POINTER TO
0181   02F7  90 02             BCC CC           ;UPDATE IT.
0182   02F9  E6 11             INC FREPTR+1     ;TAKE CARE OF OVERFLOWS.
0183   02FB  85 10      CC     STA FREPTR       ;RESTORE UPDATED FREE SPACE PTR.
0184   02FD  60                RTS              ;DONE.
0185   02FE                   .END

ERRORS = 0000 <0000>
END OF ASSEMBLY
```

Fig. 9-37: Tree Search Programs (cont.)

A HASHING ALGORITHM

A common problem when creating data structures is how to place identifiers within a limited amount of memory space in a systematic way so that they can be retrieved easily. Unfortunately, unless identifiers are distinct sequential numbers (without gaps), they do not lend themselves to placement in the memory without gaps. In particular, if names were to be placed in the memory so that they could be most easily retrieved (i.e., if they were placed alphabetically), this would require a huge amount of memory; a single memory block would have to be reserved for every possible name. This is clearly not acceptable. To solve this problem, a hashing algorithm can be used to allocate a unique (or almost unique) number to every name which has to be entered into memory. The mathematical function used to perform the hashing should be simple so that the algorithm can be fast, yet sophisticated enough to randomize the distribution of the possible names over the available memory space. The resulting number can then be used as an index to the actual location, and fast retrieval will be possible. It is for this reason that hashing is commonly used for directives of alphabetic names.

Since no algorithm can guarantee that two names will not hash into the same memory location (a "collision") a technique must be devised to resolve the problem of collisions. A good hashing algorithm will spread names evenly over the available memory space, and will allow efficient retrieval of their values once they have been stored in a table. The hashing algorithm used here is a very simple one, where we perform the exclusive OR of all the bytes of the key. A rotation is performed after every addition to improve the randomization.

The technique used to resolve collisions is a simple sequential one. It is technically called a "sequential open addressing technique;" the next sequentially available block in the table is allocated to the entry. This can be compared to a pocket address book. Let us assume that a new entry must be entered for SMITH. However, the "S" page is full in our small address book. We will use the next sequential page ("T" here). Note that there will not necessarily be another collision with a new entry starting with a "T"; the entry for "S" may be removed ("whited out," in our comparison) before a "T" ever needs to be entered.

Also note that there could be a chain of collisions. If the chain is long, and the table is not full, the hashing algorithm is a bad design.

PROGRAMMING THE 6502

Since it is convenient to use a power of two for the data format, the length of the data is eight characters; six are allocated to the key, and two to the data. This is a typical situation when creating, for example, the symbol table for an assembler. Up to six hexadecimal symbols are allocated to the symbol, and two are allocated to the address it represents (2 bytes).

When retrieving elements from the hashing table, the time required by the search does not depend on the table size, but on the degree to which the table has been filled. Typically, keeping the table less than 80% full will insure a high access time (one or two tries). It is the responsibility of the calling routine to keep track of the degree of fullness of the table and prevent overflow.

The increase of the access time versus table fullness is shown in Fig. 9-39. The main routines used by the program are the initialize subroutine (INIT), shown in Fig. 9-40; the store routine, shown in Fig. 9-41; the retrieve routine, shown in Fig. 9-42; and the hash routine, shown in Fig. 9-43. The memory allocation is shown in Fig. 9-44, and the program is given in Fig. 9-45. The program is intended to demonstrate all the main algorithms used in an actual hashing mechanism. If these programs are to be imbedded in an actual implementation, it is strongly suggested that the usual housekeeping

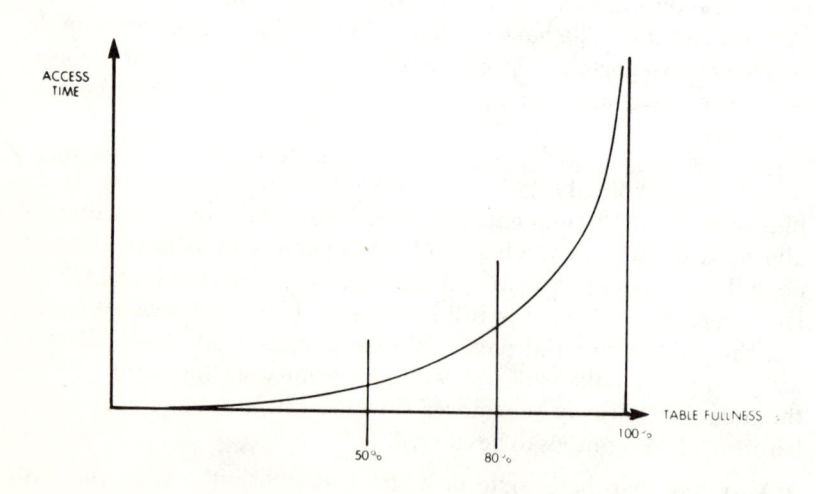

Fig. 9-39: Access Time vs. Relative Fullness

DATA STRUCTURES

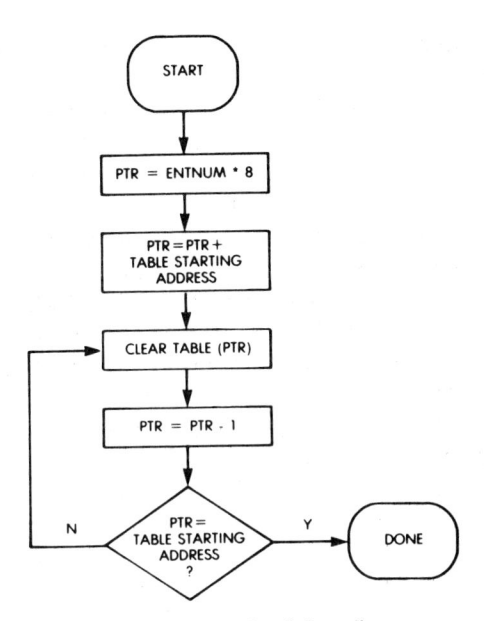

Fig. 9-40: Initialize Subroutine

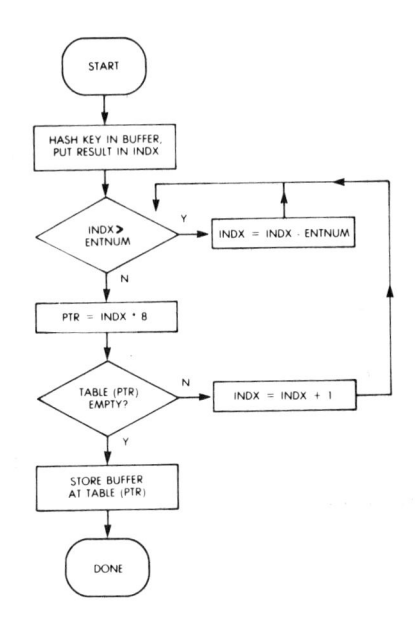

Fig. 9-41: "Store" Routine

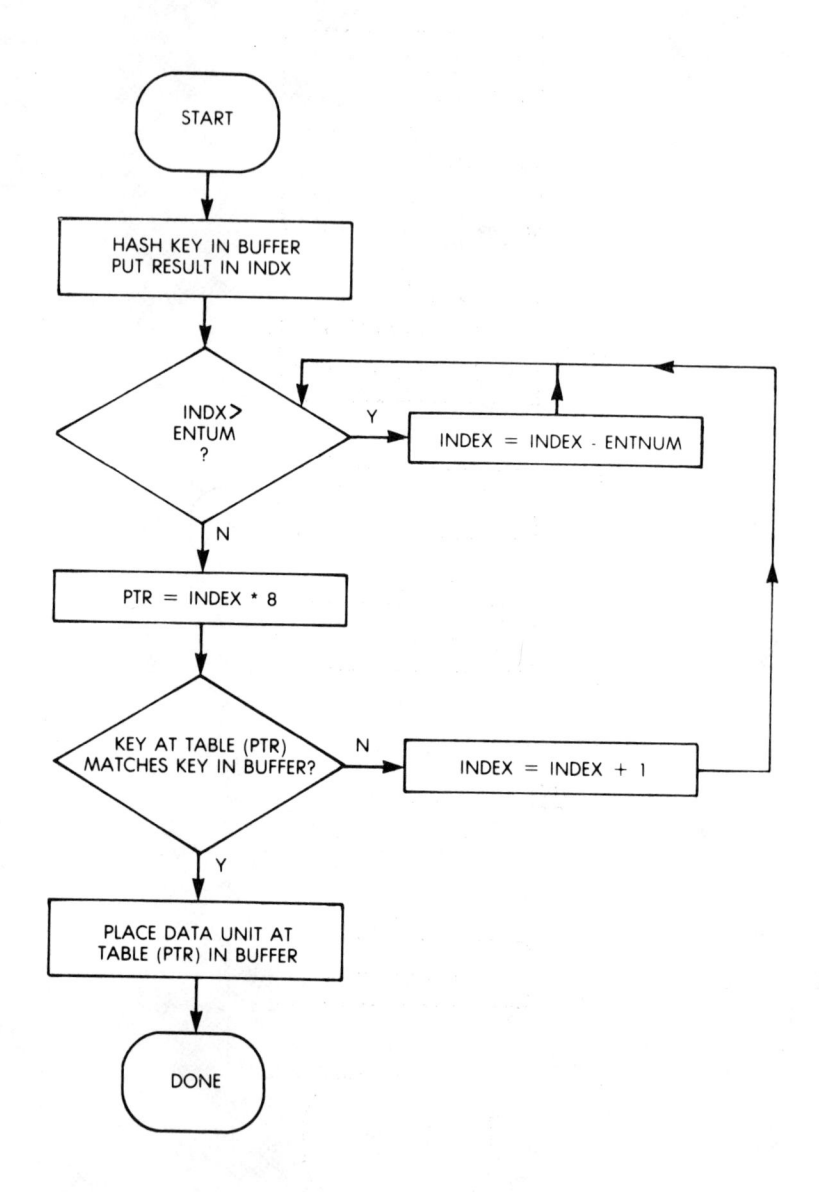

Fig. 9-42: Retrieve Routine, "Find"

DATA STRUCTURES

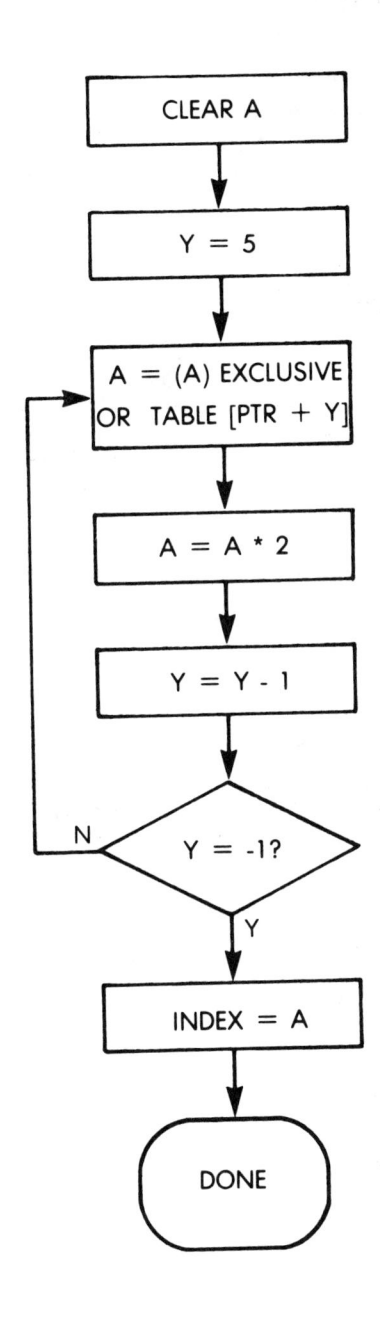

```
          ┌─────────┐
          │ CLEAR A │
          └────┬────┘
               ↓
          ┌─────────┐
          │  Y = 5  │
          └────┬────┘
               ↓
    ┌──────────────────────┐
    │ A = (A) EXCLUSIVE    │
───→│ OR TABLE [PTR + Y]   │
│   └──────────┬───────────┘
│              ↓
│        ┌──────────┐
│        │ A = A * 2│
│        └────┬─────┘
│             ↓
│       ┌──────────┐
│       │ Y = Y - 1│
│       └────┬─────┘
│            ↓
│        ╱ Y = -1? ╲ ──N──┘
│        ╲         ╱
│             │ Y
│             ↓
│       ┌──────────┐
│       │ INDEX = A│
│       └────┬─────┘
│            ↓
│          ( DONE )
```

Fig. 9-43: Hash Routine

PROGRAMMING THE 6502

functions required to prevent unexpected situations be added. In particular, one should guard against the possibility of a full table or of an incorrect key since these might cause infinite loops to occur in the program. The reader is strongly encouraged to study this program. Not only will it demystify a hashing algorithm, but it will also solve an important practical problem encountered when designing an assembler, or any other structure where tables of names with their equivalent values must be kept in an efficient way.

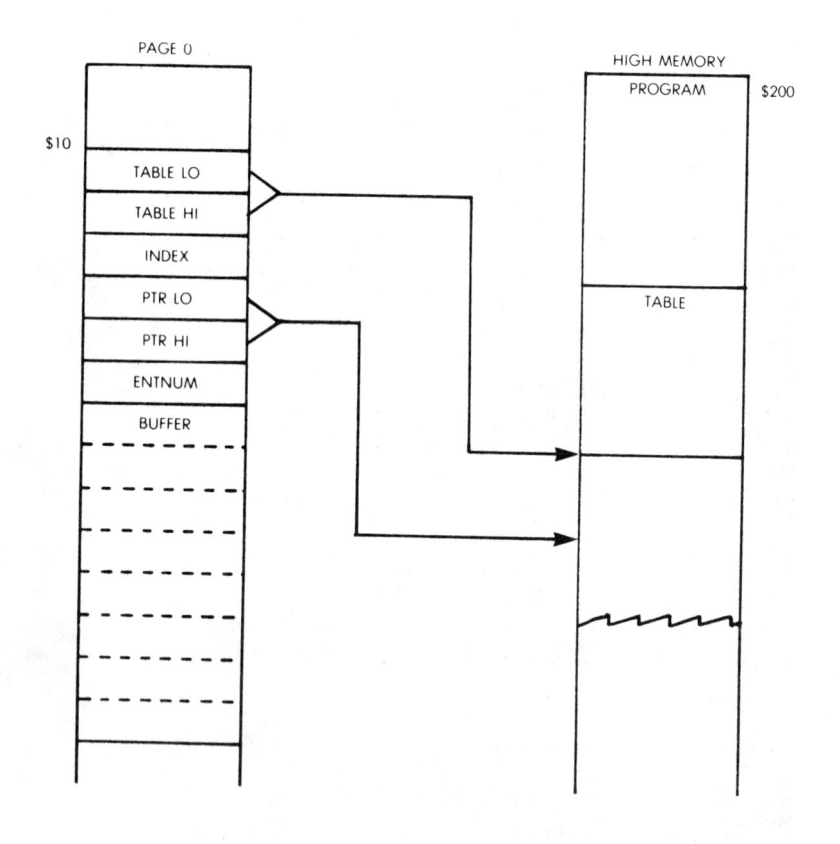

Fig. 9-44: Hash Store/Retrieve: Memory Maps

DATA STRUCTURES

```
LINE # LOC     CODE        LINE
0002   0000                ;PROGRAM TO STORE ASSEMBLER SYMBOLS IN A
0003   0000                ;TABLE, ACCESSED BY HASHING. THE SYMBOLS
0004   0000                ;ARE 6 CHRS, DATA 2. THE MAXIMUM NUMBER OF
0005   0000                ;8-BYTE UNITS TO BE STORED IN THE TABLE
0006   0000                ;SHOULD BE IN 'ENTNUM', BEGINNING ADDRESS OF
0007   0000                ;TABLE SHOULD BE IN 'TABLE'. NOTE THAT
0008   0000                ;TABLE MUST BE INITIALIZED WITH ROUTINE
0009   0000                ;'INIT' PRIOR TO USE.
0010   0000                ;IT IS THE RESPONSIBILITY OF THE CALLING
0011   0000                ;PROGRAM NO TO EXCEED THE TABLE SIZE.
0012   0000                ;
0013   0000                       * = $10
0014   0010   00 06        TABLE  .WORD $600    ;STARTING ADDRESS OF TABLE.
0015   0012                INDX   *=*+1         ;NUMBER OF DATA UNIT TO BE ACCESSED.
0016   0013                PTR    *=*+2         ;POINTER TO DATA UNIT IN TABLE.
0017   0015                ENTNUM *=*+1         ;NUMBER OF ENTRIES IN TABLE (256 MAX)
0018   0016                BUFFER *=*+8         ;INPUT/ OUTPUT BUFFER.
0019   001E                ;
0020   001E                       * = $200
0021   0200                ;
0022   0200                ;ROUTINE 'INIT' : INITIALIZES TABLE
0023   0200                ;TO ZEROES.
0024   0200                ;
0025   0200   A5 15        INIT   LDA ENTNUM
0026   0202   85 13               STA PTR       ;STORE # OF ENTRIES IN POINTER
0027   0204   20 72 02            JSR SHADD     ;MULTIPLY PTR*8, ADD TABLE POINTER.
0028   0207   A2 00               LDX #0        ;CLEAR X FOR INDIRECT ADDRESSING.
0029   0209   A9 00        CLRLP  LDA #0        ;GET CLEARING CONSTANT
0030   020B   A4 13               LDY PTR
0031   020D   D0 02               BNE DECR      ;IF PTR <> 0, DON'T DECREMENT HI BYTE.
0032   020F   C6 14               DEC PTR+1     ;DECREMENT HI BYTE OF POINTER.
0033   0211   C6 13        DECR   DEC PTR       ;DECREMENT LO BYTE.
0034   0213   81 13               STA (PTR,X)   ;CLEAR LOCATION.
0035   0215   A5 13               LDA PTR       ;CHECK IF POINTER = TABLE POINTER,
0036   0217   C5 10               CMP TABLE     ;IF UNEQUAL, CLEAR NEXT LOCATION.
0037   0219   D0 EE               BNE CLRLP
0038   021B   A5 14               LDA PTR+1
0039   021D   C5 11               CMP TABLE+1
0040   021F   D0 E8               BNE CLRLP
0041   0221   60                  RTS
0042   0222                ;
0043   0222                ;ROUTINE 'STORE': PLACES BUFFER CONTENTS IN
0044   0222                ;TABLE, USING 1ST 6 CHRS. OF BUFFER AS A
0045   0222                ;'KEY' TO DETERMINE HASHED ADDRESS IN
0046   0222                ;TABLE.
0047   0222                ;
0048   0222   A2 00        STORE  LDX #0        ;CLEAR X FOR INDEXED ADDRESSING.
0049   0224   20 90 02            JSR HASH      ;GET HASHED INDEX..
0050   0227   20 62 02     CMPR1  JSR LIMIT     ;MAKE SURE INDEX IS WITHIN BOUNDS.
0051   022A   A1 13               LDA (PTR,X)   ;CHECK DATA UNIT...
0052   022C   F0 05               BEQ EMPTY     ;JUMP IF EMPTY.
0053   022E   E6 12               INC INDX      ;TRY NEXT UNIT.
0054   0230   4C 27 02            JMP CMPR1     ;CHECK FOR NEXT UNIT INDEX VALID.
0055   0233   A0 07        EMPTY  LDY #7        ;LOOP 8X TO LOAD DATA UNIT.
0056   0235   B9 16 00     FILL   LDA BUFFER,Y  ;GET CHR FROM BUFFER,
0057   0238   91 13               STA (PTR),Y   ;PLACE IT IN BUFFER.
0058   023A   88                  DEY
0059   023B   10 F8               BPL FILL      ;XFER NEXT CHR.
0060   023D   60                  RTS           ;ADDITION DONE.
0061   023E                ;
0062   023E                ;ROUTINE 'FIND' :
0063   023E                ;FINDS ENTRY WHOSE KEY IS IN BUFFER.
0064   023E                ;ENTRY, WHEN FOUND, IS COPIED INTO
0065   023E                ;BUFFER, ALONG WITH 2 BYTES OF DATA.
0066   023E                ;
0067   023E   A2 00        FIND   LDX #0        ;CLEAR X FOR INDIRECT ADDRESSING.
0068   0240   20 90 02            JSR HASH      ;GET HASH PRODUCT.
0069   0243   20 62 02     CMPR2  JSR LIMIT     ;MAKE SURE RESULT IS WITHIN LIMITS
```

Fig. 9-45: Hashing Program

PROGRAMMING THE 6502

```
0070  0246  A0 05              LDY #5          ;LOOP 6X TO COMPARE BUFFER TO DATA ITEM.
0071  0248  B1 13        CHKLP LDA (PTR),Y     ;GET CHR FROM TABLE.
0072  024A  D9 16 00           CMP BUFFER,Y    ;IS IT = BUFFER CHR?
0073  024D  D0 0E              BNE BAD         ;IF NOT, TRY NEXT DATA UNIT.
0074  024F  88                 DEY
0075  0250  10 F6              BPL CHKLP       ;CHECK NEXT CHRS.
0076  0252  A0 07        MATCH LDY #7          ;LOOP 8X TO XFER CHRS TO BUFFER.
0077  0254  B1 13        XFER  LDA (PTR),Y     ;GET CHR. FROM TABLE.
0078  0256  99 16 00           STA BUFFER,Y    ;STORE IN BUFFER.
0079  0259  88                 DEY
0080  025A  10 F8              BPL XFER        ;LOOP TO XFER CHRS.
0081  025C  60                 RTS             ;DONE :DATA UNIT FOUND, IN BUFFER.
0082  025D  E6 12        BAD   INC INDX        ;NOT FOUND, TRY NEXT DATA UNIT.
0083  025F  4C 43 02           JMP CMPR2       ;VALIDATE NEW DATA UNIT INDEX.
0084  0262               ;
0085  0262               ;ROUTINE TO MAKE SURE DATA INDEX IS WITHIN
0086  0262               ;BOUNDS SET BY ENTNUM, THEN MULTIPLY INDEX
0087  0262               ;BY 8, AND ADD IT TO TABLE POINTER. THE
0088  0262               ;RESULT IS PLACED IN 'PTR' AS DATA UNIT ADDRESS.
0089  0262               ;
0090  0262  A5 12        LIMIT LDA INDX        ;GET INDEX.
0091  0264  C5 15        TEST  CMP ENTNUM      ;INDEX > NUMBER OF DATA ITEMS?
0092  0266  90 06              BCC OK          ;JUMP IF NOT.
0093  0268  38                 SEC             ;YES -
0094  0269  E5 15              SBC ENTNUM      ;SUBTRACT # OF ITEMS UNTIL
0095  026B  4C 64 02           JMP TEST        ;INDEX WITHIN BOUNDS.
0096  026E  85 13        OK    STA PTR         ;STORE GOOD INDEX IN POINTER.
0097  0270  85 12              STA INDX        ;SAVE UPDATED INDEX.
0098  0272  A9 00        SHADD LDA #0          ;CLEAR UPPER POINTER FOR SHIFT.
0099  0274  85 14              STA PTR+1
0100  0276  06 13              ASL PTR         ;SHIFT PTR 3X LEFT - MULTIPLY BY 8.
0101  0278  26 14              ROL PTR+1
0102  027A  06 13              ASL PTR
0103  027C  26 14              ROL PTR+1
0104  027E  06 13              ASL PTR
0105  0280  26 14              ROL PTR+1
0106  0282  18                 CLC
0107  0283  A5 10              LDA TABLE       ;ADD POINTER AND TABLE START
0108  0285  65 13              ADC PTR         ;ADDRESS AND PLACE RESULT IN POINTER.
0109  0287  85 13              STA PTR
0110  0289  A5 11              LDA TABLE+1
0111  028B  65 14              ADC PTR+1
0112  028D  85 14              STA PTR+1
0113  028F  60                 RTS
0114  0290               ;
0115  0290               ;ROUTINE TO GENERATE DATA UNIT INDEX IN TABLE
0116  0290               ;BY HASHING 'KEY', OR CHRS OF LABEL.
0117  0290               ;
0118  0290  A9 00        HASH  LDA #0          ;CLEAR LOCATION FOR INDEX.
0119  0292  18                 CLC             ;PREPARE TO ADD.
0120  0293  A0 05              LDY #5          ;LOOP 6X FOR EXCLUSIVE ORS.
0121  0295  59 16 00     EXOR  EOR BUFFER,Y    ;EXCLUSIVE-OR ACCUM. WITH BUFFER CHR.
0122  0298  2A                 ROL A           ;MULTIPLY ACCUM. BY 2.
0123  0299  88                 DEY             ;COUNT DOWN CHRS.
0124  029A  10 F9              BPL EXOR        ;GET NEXT CHR.
0125  029C  85 12              STA INDX SAVE HASH PRODUCT AS INDEX.
0126  029E  60                 RTS             ;DONE.
0127  029F               .END
```

ERRORS = 0000 <0000>

SYMBOL TABLE

SYMBOL   VALUE

```
BAD      025D    BUFFER   0016    CHKLP    0248    CLRLP    020F
CMPR1    0227    CMPR2    0243    DECR     0211    EMPTY    0233
ENTNUM   0015    EXOR     0295    FILL     0235    FIND     023E
HASH     0290    INDX     0012    INIT     0200    LIMIT    0262
MATCH    0252    OK       026E    PTR      0013    SHADD    0272
STORE    0222    TABLE    0010    TEST     0264    XFER     0254
```

END OF ASSEMBLY

Fig. 9-45: Hashing Program (cont.)

BUBBLE-SORT

Bubble-sort is a sorting technique used to arrange the elements of a table in ascending or descending order. The bubble-sort technique derives its name from the fact that the smallest element "bubbles up" to the top of the table. Every time it "collides" with a "heavier" element, it jumps over it.

A practical example of bubble-sort is shown in Fig. 9-46. The list to be sorted contains: 10, 5, 0, 2, and 100, and must be sorted in descending order ("0" on top). The algorithm is simple, and the flowchart is shown in Fig. 9-47.

The top two (or bottom two) elements are compared. If the lower one is less ("lighter") than the top one they are exchanged. Otherwise, they remain the same. For practical purposes, the exchange, if it occurs, will be noted for future use. Then, the next pair of elements will be compared, etc., until all elements have been compared two by two.

This first pass is illustrated by steps 1, 2, 3, 4, 5, and 6 in Fig. 9-47, going from the bottom up. (Equivalently, we would go from the top down.)

If no elements have been exchanged in one pass, the sort is complete. If an exchange has occurred, we start all over again.

Looking at Fig. 9-47, it can be seen that four passes are necessary in this example.

The process described above is simple, and is widely used.

One additional complication resides in the actual mechanism of the exchange. When exchanging A and B, one may not write:

$$A = B$$
$$B = A$$

as this would result in the loss of the previous value of A. (try it on an example.)

The correct solution is to use a temporary variable or location to preserve the value of A:

$$TEMP = A$$
$$A\quad = B$$
$$B\quad = TEMP$$

It works. (Again, try it on an example.) This is called a circular permutation., and it is the way all programs implement the exchange. The technique is illustrated in the flowchart of Fig. 9-47.

PROGRAMMING THE 6502

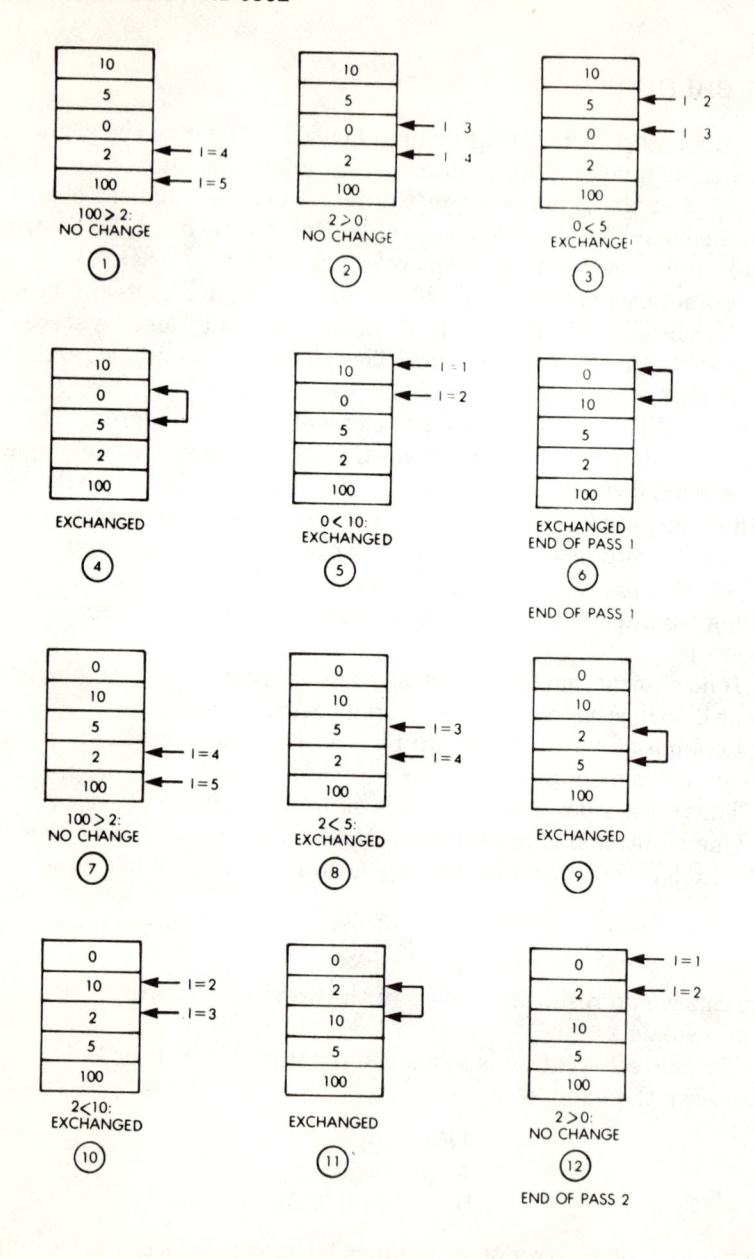

Fig. 9-46: Bubble-Sort Example

DATA STRUCTURES

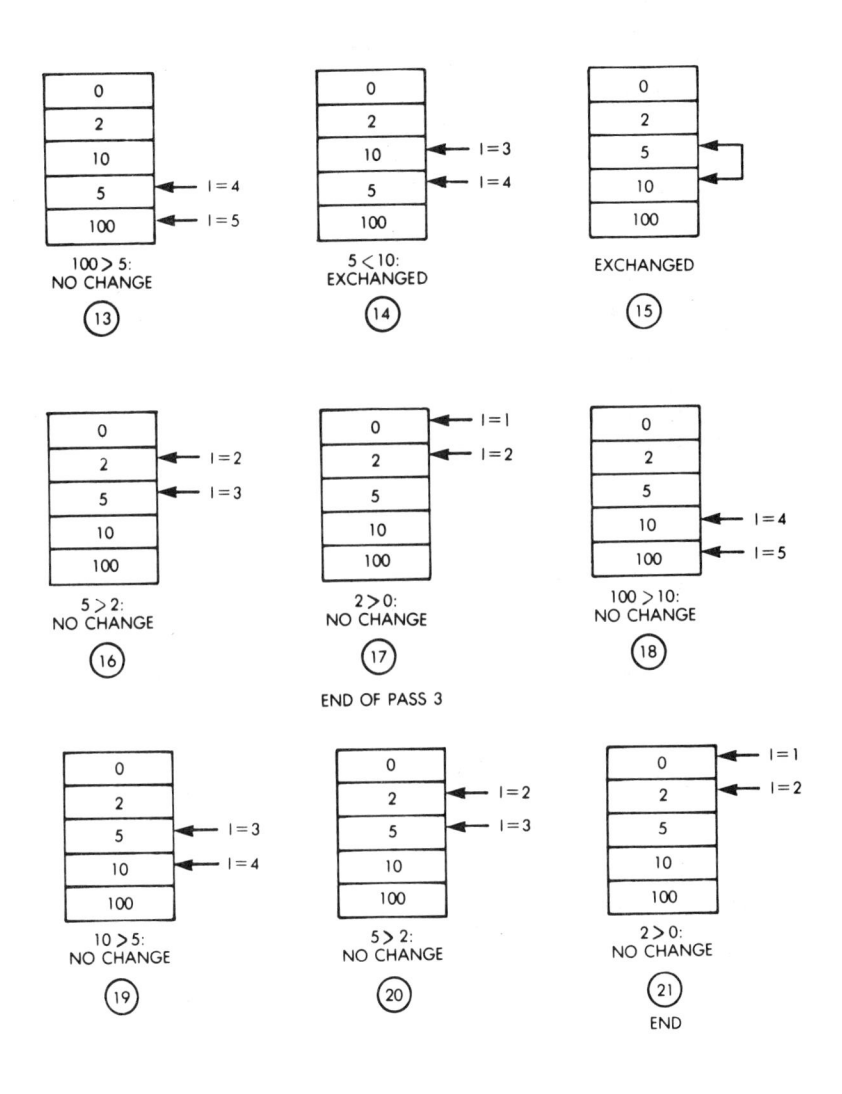

Fig. 9-46: Bubble-Sort Example (cont.)

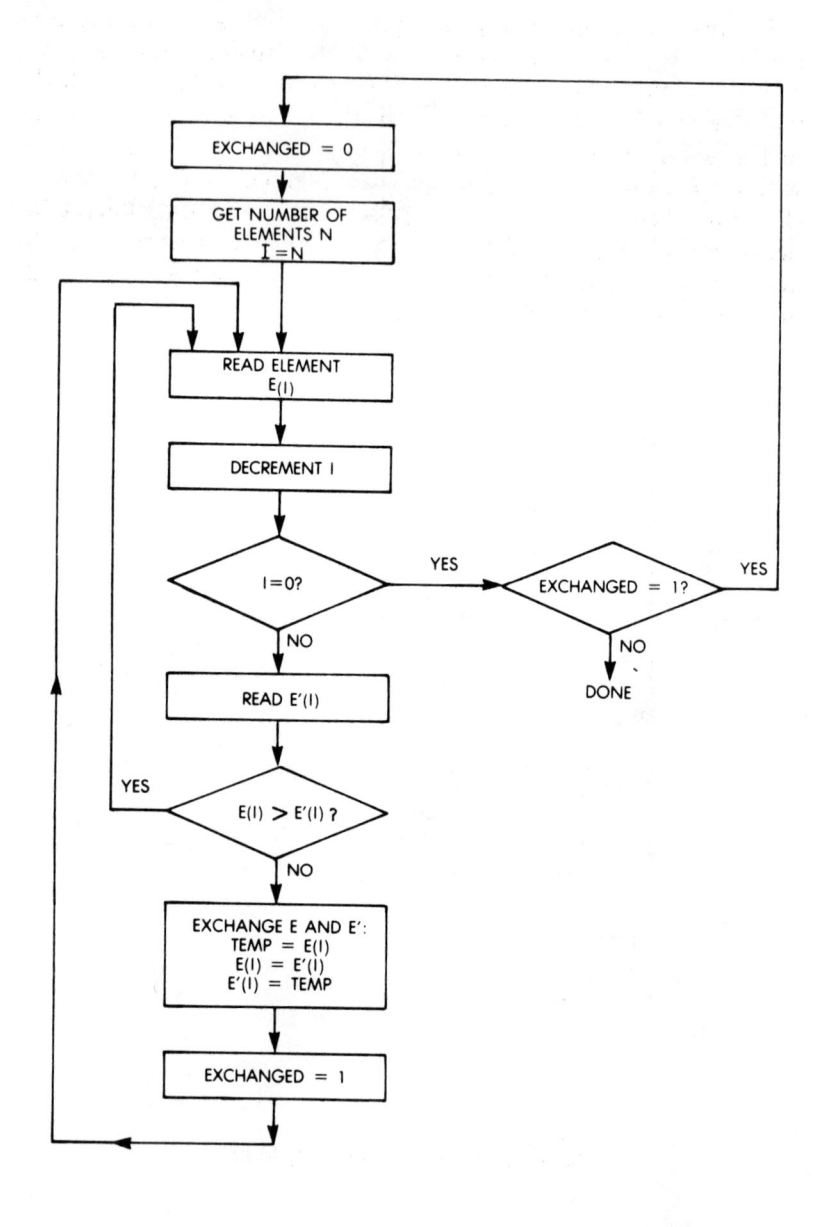

Fig. 9-47: Bubble-Sort

DATA STRUCTURES

The memory map corresponding to the bubble-sort program is shown in Fig. 9-48. In this program, every element will be an 8-bit positive number. The program resides at addresses 200 and following. Register X is used to memorize the fact that an exchange has or has not occurred, while register Y is used as the running pointer within the table. TAB is assumed to be the beginning address of the table. The actual program appears in Fig. 9-49. Indirect indexed addressing is used throughout for efficient accessing. Note how short the program is, due to the efficiency of the indirect addressing mode of the 6502.

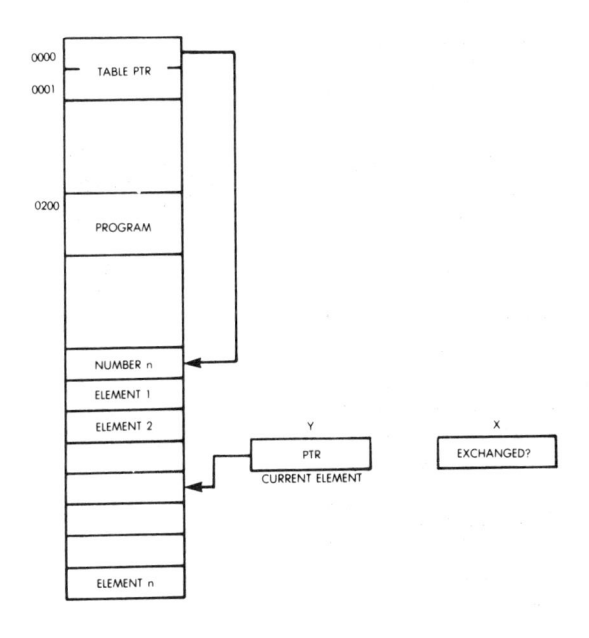

Fig. 9-48: Bubble-Sort: Memory Map

337

PROGRAMMING THE 6502

```
SORT......PAGE 0001

LINE # LOC     CODE        LINE
0002  0000                  ;       BUBBLE SORT PROGRAM
0003  0000                  ;
0004  0000                          * = $0
0005  0000                  ;
0006  0000    00 06    TAB          .WORD $600
0007  0002                  ;
0008  0002                          * = $200
0009  0200                  ;
0010  0200    A2 00    SORT         LDX #0           ;SET 'EXCHANGED' TO 0
0011  0202    A1 00                 LDA (TAB,X)
0012  0204    A8                    TAY              ;NUMBER OF ELEMENTS IS IN Y
0013  0205    B1 00    LOOP         LDA (TAB),Y      ;READ ELEMENT E(I)
0014  0207    88                    DEY              ;DECREMENT NUMBER OF ELEMENTS TO READ.
0015  0208    F0 12                 BEQ FINISH       ;END IF NO MORE ELEMENTS
0016  020A    D1 00                 CMP (TAB),Y      ;COMPARE TO E'(I)
0017  020C    B0 F7                 BCS LOOP         ;GET NEXT ELEMENT IF E(I)>E'(I)
0018  020E    AA       EXCH         TAX              ;EXCHANGE ELEMENTS
0019  020F    B1 00                 LDA (TAB),Y
0020  0211    C8                    INY
0021  0212    91 00                 STA (TAB),Y
0022  0214    8A                    TXA
0023  0215    88                    DEY
0024  0216    91 00                 STA (TAB),Y
0025  0218    A2 01                 LDX #1           ;SET 'EXCHANGED' TO 1
0026  021A    D0 E9                 BNE LOOP         ;GET NEXT ELEMENT
0027  021C    8A       FINISH       TXA              ;SHIFT 'EXCHANGED' TO A REG. FOR COMPARE...
0028  021D    D0 E1                 BNE SORT         ;IF SOME EXCHANGES MADE, DO ANOTHER PASS.
0029  021F    60                    RTS
0030  0220                          .END

ERRORS = 0000 <0000>




SYMBOL TABLE

SYMBOL   VALUE

EXCH     020E    FINISH   021C    LOOP    0205    SORT    0200
TAB      0000
END OF ASSEMBLY

<
<
```

Fig. 9-49: Bubble-Sort Program

DATA STRUCTURES

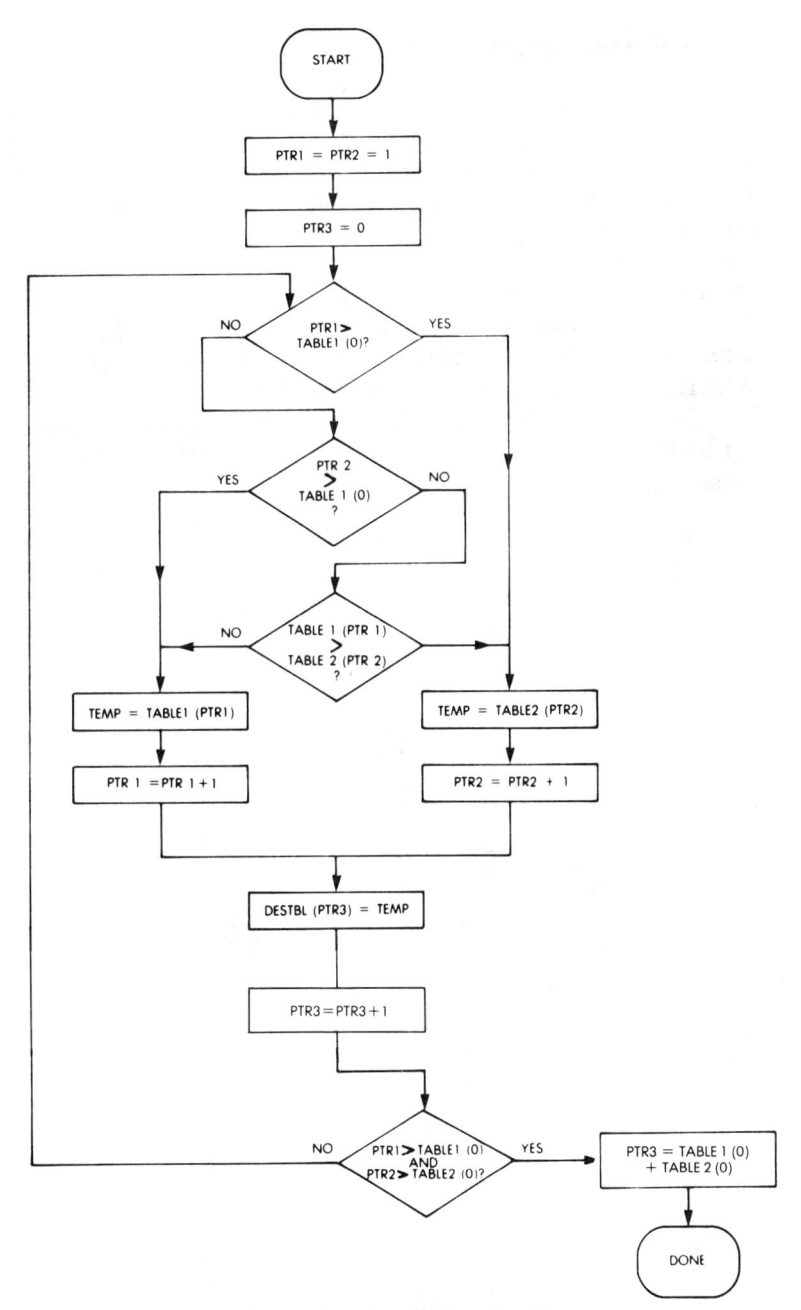

Fig. 9-50: Merge Flowchart

PROGRAMMING THE 6502

A MERGE ALGORITHM

Another common problem consists in merging two sets of data into a third one. We will assume here that two tables of data have been previously sorted, and we want to merge them into a third table. The length of each of the two original tables will be limited to 256 bytes (one page). The first entry of every table contains the length of the table. of the table.

The algorithm for merging two tables is shown in Fig. 9-50. The corresponding memory organization is shown in Fig. 9-51, and the program appears in Fig. 9-52. Remember to set "TABLE1", "TABLE2," and "DESTBL" before using it.

The algorithm itself is straightforward. Two running pointers PTR1 and PTR2, point to the two source tables. PTR3 points to the resulting table.

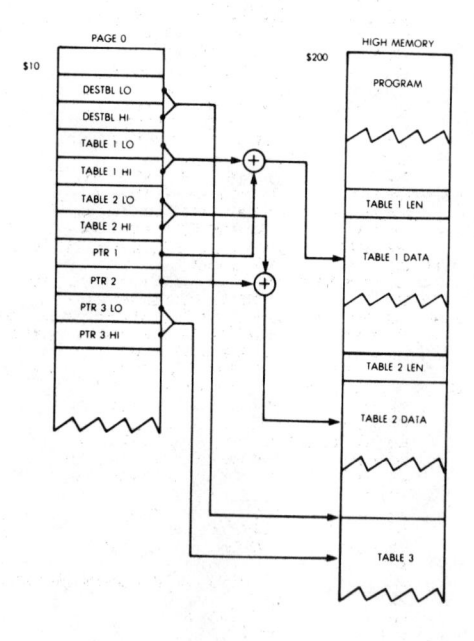

Fig. 9-51: Merge Memory Map

DATA STRUCTURES

```
LINE # LOC    CODE       LINE

0002   0000              ;2-PAGE MERGE.
0003   0000              ;TAKES 2 DATA TABLES PREVIOUSLY SORTED,
0004   0000              ;AND MERGES THEM INTO A THIRD TABLE.
0005   0000              ;EACH SOURCE TABLE CAN BE UP TO ONE
0006   0000              ;PAGE (256 BYTES) IN LENGTH.
0007   0000              ;THE FIRST ELEMENT OF THE SOURCE
0008   0000              ;TABLES MUST CONTAIN THE TABLE LENGTH.
0009   0000              ;'PTR3' CONTAINS THE LENGTH OF THE
0010   0000              ;DESTINATION TABLE AT RETURN.
0011   0000              ;
0012   0000                         * = $10
0013   0010              DESTBL *=*+2        ;POINTER TO BEGINNING OF DESTINATION TABLE.
0014   0012              TABLE1 *=*+2        ;POINTER TO SOURCE TABLE 1.
0015   0014              TABLE2 *=*+2        ;POINTER TO SOURCE TABLE 2.
0016   0016              PTR1   *=*+1        ;TABLE 1 INDEX.
0017   0017              PTR2   *=*+1        ;TABLE 2 INDEX.
0018   0018              PTR3   *=*+2        ;DESTINATION TABLE INDEX.
0019   001A              ;
0020   001A                         * = $200
0021   0200              ;
0022   0200  A5 11              LDA DESTBL+1    ;PTR3 = TABLE3
0023   0202  85 19              STA PTR3+1
0024   0204  A5 10              LDA DESTBL
0025   0206  85 18              STA PTR3
0026   0208  A9 01              LDA #1          ;SET SOURCE TABLE POINTERS TO BEGINNING,
0027   020A  85 16              STA PTR1        ;SKIPPING TABLE LENGTHS.
0028   020C  85 17              STA PTR2
0029   020E  A2 00              LDX #0          ;CLEAR X FOR INDIRECT ADDRESSING.
0030   0210  A1 14       COMPR  LDA (TABLE2,X)  ;IS TABLE 2 LENGTH <
0031   0212  C5 17              CMP PTR2        ;TABLE 2 POINTER?
0032   0214  90 19              BCC TKTB1       ;IF YES, GET BYTE FROM TABLE 1.
0033   0216  A1 12              LDA (TABLE1,X)  ;IS TABLE 1 LENGTH <
0034   0218  C5 16              CMP PTR1        ;TABLE 1 POINTER?
0035   021A  90 0A              BCC TKTB2       ;IF YES, GET BYTE FROM TABLE 2
0036   021C  A4 16              LDY PTR1        ;GET POINTER FOR TABLE 1.
0037   021E  B1 12              LDA (TABLE1),Y  ;USE IT TO FETCH BYTE.
0038   0220  A4 17              LDY PTR2        ;GET POINTER FOR TABLE 2,
0039   0222  D1 14              CMP (TABLE2),Y  ;USE IT TO FIND BYTE TO COMPARE
0040   0224                                     ;TO TABLE 1 BYTE.
0041   0224  90 09              BCC TKTB1       ;IF TABLE 1 BYTE LESS, TAKE IT.
0042   0226  A4 17       TKTB2  LDY PTR2        ;GET POINTER FOR TABLE 2.
0043   0228  B1 14              LDA (TABLE2),Y  ;GET NEXT BYTE FROM TABLE 2.
0044   022A  E6 17              INC PTR2        ;INCREMENT POINTER FOR TABLE 2.
0045   022C  4C 35 02           JMP STORE       ;GO STORE BYTE IN DESTINATION TABLE.
0046   022F  A4 16       TKTB1  LDY PTR1        ;GET POINTER 1...
0047   0231  B1 12              LDA (TABLE1),Y  ;AND USE IT TO GET BYTE FROM TABLE.
0048   0233  E6 16              INC PTR1        ;INCREMENT POINTER FOR TABLE 1.
0049   0235  81 18       STORE  STA (PTR3,X)    ;STORE BYTE AT NEXT LOCATION IN TABLE 3
0050   0237  E6 18              INC PTR3        ;INCREMENT LO ORDER TABLE 3 POINTER.
0051   0239  D0 02              BNE CC          ;IF NO OVERFLOW, SKIP
0052   023B  E6 19              INC PTR3+1      ;INCREMENT HI ORDER TABLE 3 POINTER.
0053   023D  A1 12       CC     LDA (TABLE1,X)  ;IS TABLE 1 LENGTH GREATER
0054   023F  C5 16              CMP PTR1        ;THAN OR EQUAL TO POINTER 1?
0055   0241  B0 CD              BCS COMPR       ;IF YES, GET NEXT BYTE.
0056   0243  A1 14              LDA (TABLE2,X)  ;IS TABLE 2 LENGTH GREATER
0057   0245  C5 17              CMP PTR2        ;THAN OR EQUAL TO POINTER 2?
0058   0247  B0 C7              BCS COMPR       ;IF YES, GET NEXT BYTE.
0059   0249  A9 00              LDA #0
0060   024B  85 19              STA PTR3+1      ;CLEAR PTR3 HI ORDER.
0061   024D  18                 CLC             ;MERGE DONE, NOW..
0062   024E  A1 12              LDA (TABLE1,X)  ;ADD TABLE 1 AND 2 LENGTHS.
0063   0250  61 14              ADC (TABLE2,X)
0064   0252  85 18              STA PTR3        ;STORE SUM IN TABLE 3 TEMPORARY POINTER.
0065   0254  90 04              BCC CCC         ;AND..
0066   0256  A9 01              LDA #1          ;OVERFLOW IN...
0067   0258  85 19              STA PTR3+1      ;HI BYTE.
0068   025A  60          CCC    RTS
0069   025B                     .END

ERRORS = 0000 <0000>
END OF ASSEMBLY
```

Fig. 9-52: Merge Program

The current entries in TABLE1 and TABLE2 are compared two at a time. The smaller one is copied into TABLE3 and the corresponding running pointer is incremented. The process is repeated and terminates when both PTR1 and PTR2 have reached the bottom of their respective tables.

SUMMARY

The basic concepts relative to common data structures, as well as actual implementation examples have been presented.

Because of its powerful addressing modes, the 6502 lends itself well to the management of complex data structures. Its efficiency is demonstrated by the terseness of the programs shown.

In addition, special techniques have been presented for hashing, sorting and merging, which are typical of those required to solve complex problems involving actual data structures.

The beginning programmer need not concern himself yet with the details of data structures implementation and management. However, for efficient programming of non-trivial algorithms, a good understanding of data structures is required. The actual examples presented in this chapter should help the reader achieve such an understanding and solve all the common problems encountered with reasonable data structures.

10
PROGRAM DEVELOPMENT

INTRODUCTION

All the programs we have studied and developed so far have been developed by hand without the aid of any software or hardware resources. The only improvement we have used over straight binary coding has been the use of mnemonic symbols, those of the assembly language. For effective software development, it is necessary to understand the range of hardware and software development aids. It is the purpose of this chapter to present and evaluate these aids.

BASIC PROGRAMMING CHOICES

Three basic alternatives exist: writing a program in binary or hexadecimal, writing it in assembly-level language, or writing it in a high-level language. Let us review these alternatives.

1. Hexadecimal Coding

The program will normally be written using assembly language mnemonics. However, most low-cost, one-board computer systems do not provide an assembler. The assembler is the program which will automatically translate the mnemonics used for the program into the required binary codes. When no assembler is available, this translation from mnemonics into binary must be performed by hand. Binary is unpleasant to use and error-prone, so that hexadecimal is normally used. It has been shown in Chapter 1 that one hexadecimal digit will represent 4 binary bits. Two hexadecimal digits will, therefore, be used to represent the contents of every byte. As an example, the table showing the hexadecimal equivalent of the 6502 instructions appears in the Appendix.

In short, whenever the resources of the user are limited and no assembler is available, he will have to translate the program by hand into hexadecimal. This can reasonably be done for a small number of instructions, such as, perhaps, 10 to 100. For larger **programs, this process is tedious and error-prone, so that it tends not to be used.** However, nearly all single-board microcomputers require the entry of programs in hexadecimal mode. They are not equipped with an assembler and are not equipped with a full alphanumeric keyboard, in order to limit their cost.

In summary, hexadecimal coding is not a desirable way to enter a program in a computer. It is simply an economical one. The cost of an assembler and the required alphanumeric keyboard is traded-off against increased labor to enter the program in the memory. However, this does not change the way the program itself is written. The program is still written in assembly-level language so that it can be not only meaningful, but also capable of inspection and examination by the human programmer.

2. Assembly Language Programming

Assembly-level programming covers programs that may be entered in hexadecmial, as well as those that may be entered in symbolic assembly- level form, in the system. Let us now directly examine the entry of a program, in its assembly language representation. An assembler program must be available. The assembler will read each of the mnemonic instructions of the program and translate it into the required bit pattern using 1, 2 or 3 bytes, as specified by the encoding of the instructions. In addition, a good assembler will offer a number of additional facilities for writing the program. These will be reviewed in the section on the assembler below. In particular, *directives* are available which will modify the value of symbols. Symbolic addressing may be used, and a branch to a symbolic location may be specified. During the

PROGRAM DEVELOPMENT

debugging phase where a user may remove instructions or add instructions, it will not be necessary to re-write the entire program if an extra instruction is inserted between a branch and the

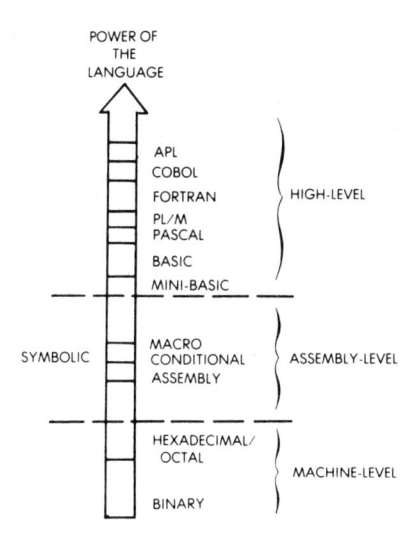

```
                    POWER OF
                      THE
                    LANGUAGE
                       ↑
                    ┌──┴──┐
                    │     │
                    ├─────┤  APL
                    ├─────┤  COBOL
                    ├─────┤  FORTRAN      ⎫
                    ├─────┤  PL/M         ⎬  HIGH-LEVEL
                    ├─────┤  PASCAL       ⎪
                    ├─────┤  BASIC        ⎭
                    ├─────┤  MINI-BASIC
      ──────────    ├─────┤  ─────────────
                    │     │
                    ├─────┤  MACRO        ⎫
   SYMBOLIC         ├─────┤  CONDITIONAL  ⎬  ASSEMBLY-LEVEL
                    ├─────┤  ASSEMBLY     ⎭
      ──────────    ├─────┤  ─────────────
                    │     │
                    ├─────┤  HEXADECIMAL/ ⎫
                    ├─────┤  OCTAL        ⎬  MACHINE-LEVEL
                    ├─────┤  BINARY       ⎭
                    └─────┘
```

Fig. 10-1: Programming Levels

point to which it branches, as long as symbolic labels are used. The assembler will automatically adjust all of the labels during the translation process. In addition, an assembler allows the user to debug his/her program in symbolic form. A *disassembler* may be used to examine the contents of a memory location and reconstruct the assembly-level instruction that it represents. The various software resources normally available on a system will be reviewed below. Let us now examine the third alternative.

3. High-Level Language

A program may be written in a high-level language such as BASIC, APL, PASCAL, or others. Techniques for programming in these various languages are covered by specific books and will not be reviewed here. We will, therefore, only briefly review this mode of programming. A high-level language offers powerful instructions which make programming much easier and faster. These instructions must then be translated by a complex program into the final binary representation that a microcomputer can execute. Typically, each high-level instruction will be translated into a large number of individual binary instructions. The program which performs this automatic translation is called a *compiler* or an *interpreter*. A compiler will translate all the instructions of a program in sequence into object code. In a separate phase, the resulting code will then be executed. By contrast, an interpreter will interpret a single instruction and execute it, then "translate" the next one and execute it. An interpreter offers the advantage of interactive response, but results in low efficiency compared to a compiler. These topics will not be studied further here. Let us revert to the programming of an actual microprocessor at the assembly-level language.

SOFTWARE SUPPORT

We will review here the main software facilities which are (or should be) available in the complete system for convenient software development. Some of the programs have already been introduced, and definitions of these will be summarized below. Definitions of other important programs will also be provided before we proceed.

The *assembler* is the program which translates the mnemonic representation of instructions into their binary equivalent. It normally translates one symbolic instruction into one binary instruction (which may occupy 1, 2, or 3 bytes). The resulting binary code is called *object code*. It is directly executable by the microcomputer. As a side effect, the assembler will also produce a complete symbolic listing of the program, as well as the equivalence tables to be used by the programmer and the symbol occurrence list in the program. Examples will be presented later in this chapter.

A *compiler* is the program which translates high-level language instructions into their binary form.

An *interpreter* is a program similar to a compiler. It also translates high-level instructions into their binary form, but instead of keeping the intermediate representations, it executes the instructions immediately. In fact, if often does not even generate any intermediate code, but rather executes the high-level instructions directly.

A *monitor* is an indispensable program for using the hardware resources of this system. It continuously monitors the input devices for input and also manages the rest of the devices. As an example, a minimal monitor for a single-board microcomputer, equipped with a keyboard and with LEDs, must continuously scan the keyboard for user input and display the specified contents on the light-emitting-diodes. In addition, it must be capable of understanding a number of limited commands from the keyboard, such as START, STOP, CONTINUE, LOAD MEMORY, and EXAMINE MEMORY. On a large system, the monitor is often qualified as the *executive* program. When complex file management or task scheduling is also provided, the overall set of facilities is called an *operating system*. In the case in which files may be resident on a disk, the operating system is qualified as the *disk operating system,* or DOS.

An *editor* is the program designed to facilitate the entry and the modification of text or programs. It allows the user to conveniently enter characters, append them, insert them, add lines, remove lines, and search for characters or strings. It is an important resource for convenient and effective text entry.

A *debugger* is a facility necessary for debugging programs. Typically, when a program does not work correctly, there may be no indication whatsoever of the cause. The programmer, therefore, wishes to insert break-points in his program in order to suspend the execution of the program at specified addresses and to be able to examine the contents of registers or memory at these points. This is the primary function of a debugger. The debugger allows for the possibility of suspending a program, resuming execution, examining, displaying and modifying the contents of registers or memory. A good debugger will be equipped with a number of additional facilities, such as the possibility of examining data in symbolic form, hex, binary, or other usual representations, as well as entering data in this format.

A *loader*, or *linking loader*, will place various blocks of object code at specified positions in the memory and adjust their respective symbolic pointers so that they can reference each other. It is used to relocate programs or blocks in various memory areas.

A *simulator,* or an *emulator* program is used to simulate the operation of a device, usually the microprocessor, in its absence, when developing a program on a simulated processor prior to placing it on the actual board. Using this approach, it becomes possible to suspend the program, modify it, and keep it in RAM memory. The disadvantages of a simulator are that:

1. It usually simulates only the processor itself, not input/output devices.
2. The execution speed is slow, and one must operate in simulated time. It is therefore impossible to test real-time devices, which may result in synchronization problems even though the logic of the program may be found to be correct.

An *emulator* is actually a simulator in real time. It uses one processor to simulate another one, and simulates it in complete detail.

Utility routines are essentially all of the routines that the user wishes the manufacturer had provided! They may include multiplication, division and other arithmetic operations, block move routines, character tests, input/output device handlers (or "drivers"), and more.

THE PROGRAM DEVELOPMENT SEQUENCE

We will now examine a typical sequence for developing an assembly-level program. In order to demonstrate their value, we will assume that all the usual software facilities are available. If all of them should not be available in a particular system, it would still be possible to develop programs, but the convenience would be decreased, and therefore, the amount of time necessary to debug the program would most likely be increased.

PROGRAM DEVELOPMENT

The normal approach is to first design an algorithm and define the data structures for the problem to be solved. Next, a comprehensive set of flow-charts is developed which represents the program flow. Finally, the flow-charts are translated into the assembly-level language for the microprocessor; this is the coding phase.

Next, the program has to be entered on the computer. We will examine in the following section the hardware options to be used in this phase.

The program is entered in RAM memory of the system under the control of the editor. Once a section of the program, such as a subroutine, has been entered, it will be tested.

First, the assembler will be used. If the assembler does not already reside in the system, it will be loaded from an external memory, such as a disk. Then, the program will be assembled, i.e., translated into a binary code. This results in the object program, ready to be executed.

One does not normally expect a program to work correctly the first time. To verify its correct operation, a number of breakpoints will normally be set at crucial locations where it is easy to test whether the intermediate results are correct. The debugger will be used for this purpose. Breakpoints will be specified at selected locations. A "Go" command will then be issued so that program execution is started. The program will automatically stop at each of the specified breakpoints. The programmer can then verify, by examining the contents of the registers, or memory, that the data so far is correct. If it is correct, we proceed until the next breakpoint. Whenever we find incorrect data, an error in the program has been found. At this point the programmer normally refers to his program listing and verifies whether his coding has been correct. If no error can be found in the programming, the error might be a logical one that refers back to the flowchart. We will assume here that the flow-charts have been checked by hand and are assumed to be reasonably correct. The error is likely to come from the coding. It will, therefore, be necessary to modify a section of the program. If the symbolic representation of the program is still in the memory, we will simply re-enter the editor and modify the required lines, then go through the preceding sequence again. In some systems, the memory available may not be large enough, so that it is necessary to flush out the symbolic representation of the program onto a disk or cassette prior to executing the object code. Naturally, in such a case, one would have to reload the symbolic representation of the program from its support medium prior to entering the editor again.

The above procedure will be repeated as long as necessary until the results of the program are correct. Let us stress that prevention is much more effective than cure. A correct design will typi**cally result very quickly in a program which runs correctly once the usual typing mistakes or obvious coding errors have been** removed. However, sloppy design may result in programs which will take an extremely long time to be debugged. The debugging time is generally considered to be much longer than the actual design time. In short, it is always worth investing more time in the design in order to shorten the debugging phase.

Although using this approach makes it possible to test the overall organization of the program, it does not lend itself to testing the program in terms of real time and input/output devices. If input/output devices are to be tested, the direct solution consists of transferring the program onto EPROMs and installing it on the board where it can be watched to see whether it works or not.

There is an even better solution, and that is the use of an *in-circuit emulator*. An in-circuit emulator uses the 6502 microprocessor (or any other microprocessor) to emulate a 6502 in (almost) real time. It emulates the 6502 physically. The emulator is equipped with a cable terminated by a 40-pin connector, exactly identical to the pin-out of a 6502. This connector can be inserted on the real application board that one **is developing. The signals generated by the emulator will be** exactly those of the 6502, only perhaps a little slower. The essential advantage is that the program under test will still reside in the RAM memory of the development system. It will generate the real signals which will communicate with the real input/output devices that one wishes to use. As a result, it becomes possible to keep developing the program using all the resources of the development system (editor, debugger, symbolic facilities, file system) while testing input/output in real time.

In addition, a good emulator will provide special facilities, such as a *trace*. A trace is a recording of the last instructions or status

PROGRAM DEVELOPMENT

of various data busses in the system prior to a breakpoint. In short, a trace provides the film of the events that occurred prior to the breakpoint or the malfunction. It may even trigger a scope at a specified address or upon the occurrence of a specified combination of bits. Such a facility is of great value, since when an error is found it is usually too late. The instruction, or the data, which caused the error has occured prior to the detection. The availability of a trace allows the user to find which segment of the program caused the error to occur. If the trace is not long enough, we can simply set an earlier breakpoint.

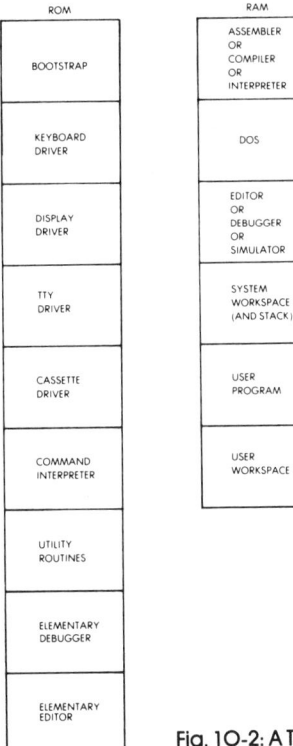

```
            ROM                        RAM
    ┌──────────────────┐       ┌──────────────────┐
    │                  │       │    ASSEMBLER     │
    │                  │       │       OR         │
    │    BOOTSTRAP     │       │    COMPILER      │
    │                  │       │       OR         │
    │                  │       │    INTERPRETER   │
    ├──────────────────┤       ├──────────────────┤
    │     KEYBOARD     │       │                  │
    │     DRIVER       │       │       DOS        │
    │                  │       │                  │
    ├──────────────────┤       ├──────────────────┤
    │                  │       │     EDITOR       │
    │     DISPLAY      │       │       OR         │
    │     DRIVER       │       │    DEBUGGER      │
    │                  │       │       OR         │
    │                  │       │    SIMULATOR     │
    ├──────────────────┤       ├──────────────────┤
    │                  │       │     SYSTEM       │
    │      TTY         │       │    WORKSPACE     │
    │     DRIVER       │       │    (AND STACK)   │
    │                  │       │                  │
    ├──────────────────┤       ├──────────────────┤
    │     CASSETTE     │       │      USER        │
    │     DRIVER       │       │    PROGRAM       │
    │                  │       │                  │
    ├──────────────────┤       ├──────────────────┤
    │     COMMAND      │       │      USER        │
    │   INTERPRETER    │       │    WORKSPACE     │
    │                  │       └──────────────────┘
    ├──────────────────┤
    │     UTILITY      │
    │     ROUTINES     │
    │                  │
    ├──────────────────┤
    │    ELEMENTARY    │
    │    DEBUGGER      │
    │                  │
    ├──────────────────┤
    │    ELEMENTARY    │
    │     EDITOR       │
    └──────────────────┘
```

Fig. 10-2: A Typical Memory Map

This completes our description of the usual sequence of events involved in developing a program. Let us now review the hardware alternatives available for developing programs.

THE HARDWARE ALTERNATIVES

1. Single-Board Microcomputer

The single-board microcomputer offers the lowest cost approach to program development. It is normally equipped with a hexadecimal keyboard, some function keys, and 6 LEDs which can display address and data. Since it is equipped with a small amount of memory, no assembler is usually available. At best, it has a small monitor and no editing or debugging facilities, except for a very few commands. All programs must, therefore, be entered in hexadecimal form. They will also be displayed in hexadecimal form on the LEDs. A single-board microcomputer has, in theory, the same hardware power as any other computer. However, because of its restricted memory size and keyboard, it does not support all the usual facilities of a larger system, and this makes program development much longer. The tediousness of developing programs in hexadecimal format makes a single-board microcomputer best suited for educational and training purposes where programs of limited length are desirable. Single-boards are probably the cheapest way to learn programming by doing. However, they cannot be used for complex program development, unless additional memory boards are attached and the usual software aids are made available.

2. The Development System

A development system is a microcomputer system equipped with a significant amount of RAM memory **(32K - 48K)** as well as the required input/output devices, such as a CRT display, a printer, disks, and usually a PROM programmer, as well as, perhaps, an in-circuit emulator. A development system is specifically designed to facilitate program development in an industrial environment. It normally offers all, or most, of the **software facilities that we have mentioned in the preceding section. In principle, it is the ideal software development tool.**

The limitation of a microcomputer development system is that it may not be capable of supporting a compiler or an interpreter.

PROGRAM DEVELOPMENT

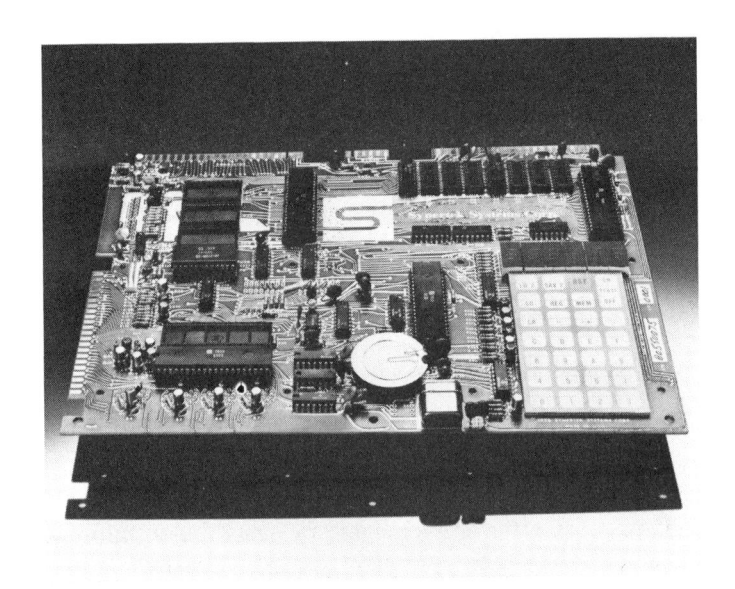

Fig. 10-3: SYM 1 is a Typical Microcomputer Board

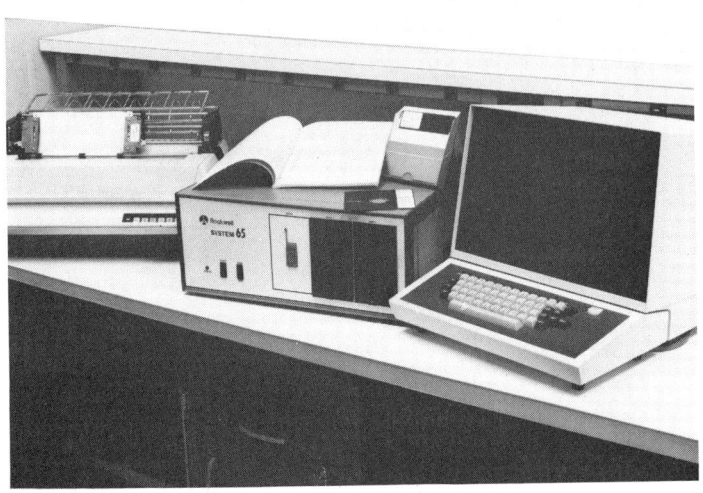

Fig. 10-4: Rockwell System 65 is a Development System

This is because a compiler typically requires a very large amount of memory, often more than is available in the system. However, for developing programs in assembly-level language, the development system offers all the required facilities. Unfortunately, because development systems sell in relatively small numbers compared to hobby computers, their cost is significantly higher.

3. Hobby-Type Microcomputers

The hobby-type microcomputer hardware is analogous to that of a development system. The main difference lies in the fact that the hobby-type microcomputer is normally not equipped with the sophisticated software development aids which are available on an industrial development system. As an example, many hobby-type microcomputers offer only elementary assemblers, minimal editors, minimal file systems, no facilities to attach a PROM programmer, no in-circuit emulator, no powerful debugger. They represent, therefore, an intermediate step between the single-board microcomputer and the full microprocessor development system. For a user who wishes to develop programs of modest complexity, they are probably the best compromise since they offer the advantage of low cost and a reasonable array of software development tools, even though they are quite limited as to their convenience.

4. Time-Sharing Systems

Several companies rent terminals that can be connected to time-sharing computer networks. These terminals share the time of the larger computer and benefit from all the advantages of large installations. *Cross assemblers* are available for all microcomputers in virtually all commercial time-sharing systems. A cross assembler is simply an assembler for, say, a 6502, which resides, for example, in an IBM370. Formally, a cross assembler is an assembler for microprocessor X, which resides on processor Y. The nature of the computer being used is irrelevant. The user still writes a program in 6502 assembly-level language, and the cross assembler translates it into the appropriate binary pattern. The only difficulty lies in the fact that this program cannot be executed immediately. It can be executed by a simulated processor, if one is available, but only if the program does not use any input/output resources. Because of this drawback, therefore, time-sharing is practical only in industrial environments.

5. **In-House Computer**

Whenever a large in-house computer is available, cross assemblers may also be available to facilitate program development. If such a computer offers time-sharing service, this option is essentially analogous to the one above. If it offers only batch service, this is probably one of the most inconvenient methods of program development, since submitting programs in batch mode at the assembly level for a microprocessor results in a very long development time.

Front Panel or No Front Panel?

The front panel is a hardware accessory often used to facilitate program debugging. It has been the traditional tool for displaying the binary contents of a register, or of memory, conveniently. However, most of the functions of the control panel may now be accomplished from a terminal through a CRT display. The CRT, with its ability to display the binary value of bits, thus offers a service almost equivalent to the control panel. The additional advantage of using the CRT display is that one can switch at will from binary representation to hexadecimal, to symbolic, to decimal (if the appropriate conversion routines are available, naturally). The main disadvantage of the CRT is that instead of turning a knob, one must hit several keys to obtain the appropriate display. However, since the cost of providing a control panel is quite substantial, most recent microcomputers have abandonned this debugging tool in favor of the CRT. The value of the control panel, then, is often evaluated more in function of emotional arguments based on one's own past experience rather than by a rational choice. It is not indispensable.

SUMMARY OF HARDWARE RESOURCES

Three broad cases may be distinguished. If you have only a minimal budget, and if you wish to learn how to program, buy a one-board microcomputer. Using it, you will be able to develop all the simple programs of this book and many more. Eventually, however, when you want to develop programs of more than a few hundred instructions, you will feel the limitations of this approach.

If you are an industrial user, you will need a full development system. Any solution short of the full development system will cause a significantly longer development time. The trade-off is clear: hardware resources *vs.* programming time. Naturally, if the programs to be developed are quite simple, a less expensive approach may be used. However, if complex programs are to be developed, it is difficult to justify any hardware savings when buying a development system; the resultant programming costs will far exceed any such savings.

For a personal computerist, a hobby-type microcomputer will typically offer sufficient, although minimal, facilities. Good development software is still to come for most of the hobby computers. The user will have to evaluate his system in view of the comments presented in this chapter.

Let us now analyze in more detail the most indispensable resource: the assembler.

THE ASSEMBLER

We have used assembly-level language throughout this book without presenting the formal syntax or definitions of assembly-level language. The time has come to present these definitions. An assembler is designed to provide a convenient symbolic representation of the user program, while at the same time providing a simple means of converting these mnemonics into their binary representation.

Assembler Fields

When typing in a program for the assembler, we have seen that fields are used. They are:

The label field, optional, which may contain a symbolic address for the instruction that follows.

The instruction field, which includes the opcode and any operands. (A separate operand field may be distinguished.)

The comment field, to the far right, which is optional and is intended to clarify the program.

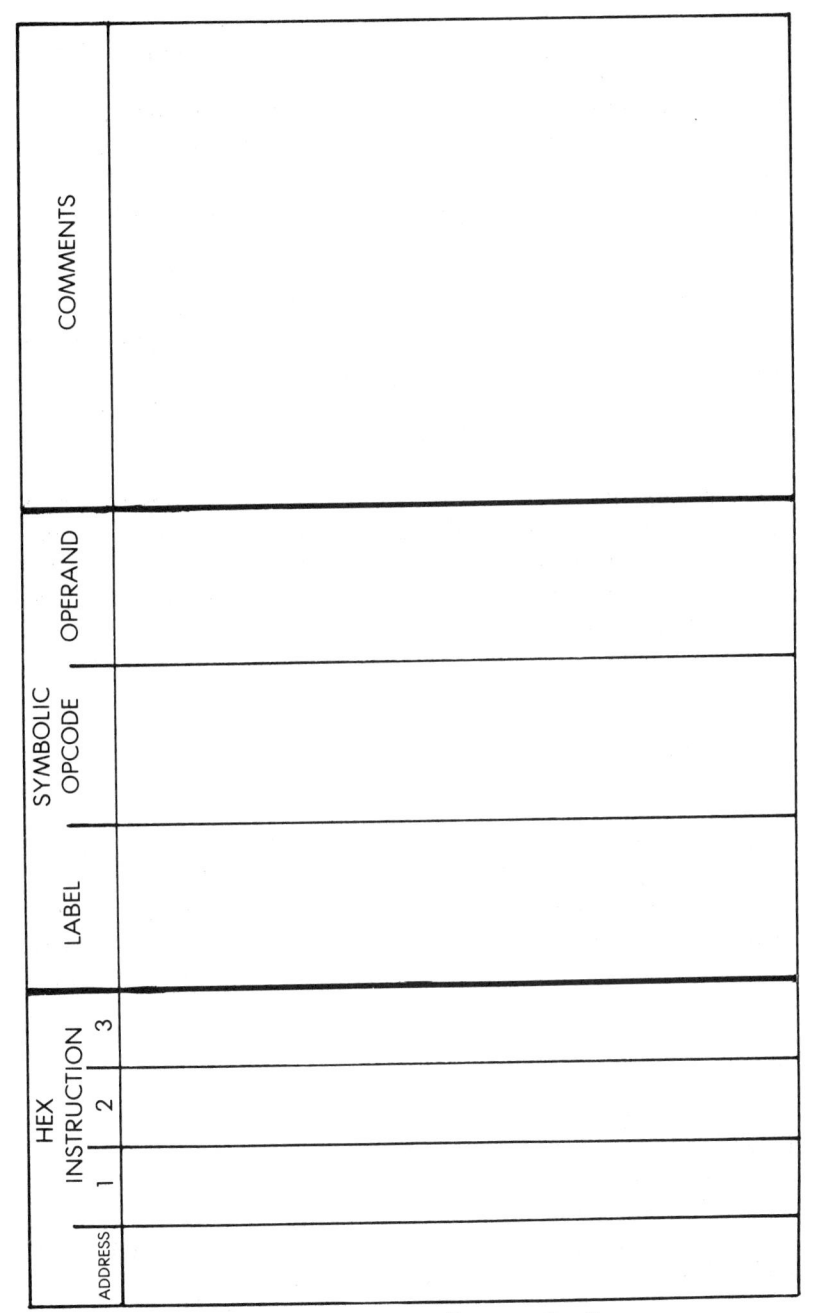

Fig. 10-5: Microprocessor Programming Form

Once the program has been fed to the assembler, the assembler will produce a *listing* of it. When generating a listing, the assembler will provide three additional fields, usually on the left of the page. An example appears in Fig. 10-6. On the far left is the line number. Each line which has been typed by the programmer is assigned a symbolic line number.

The next field to the right is the actual address field, which shows in hexadecimal the value of the program counter which will point to that instruction.

The next field to the right is the hexadecimal representation of the instruction.

This shows one of the possible uses of an assembler. Even if we are designing programs for a single-board microcomputer which accepts only hexadecimal, we can still write the programs in assembly-level language, providing we have access to a system equipped with an assembler. We can then run the programs on the system, using the assembler. The assembler will automatically generate the correct hexadecimal codes, which we can simply type in on our system. This shows, in a simple example, the value of additional software resources.

Tables

When the assembler translates the symbolic program into its binary representation, it performs two essential tasks:

1. It translates the mnemonic instructions into their binary encoding.
2. It translates the symbols used for constants and addresses into their binary representation.

In order to facilitate program debugging, the assembler shows at the end of the listing each symbol used and its equivalent hexadecimal value. This is called the symbol table.

Some symbol tables will not only list the symbol and its value, but also the line numbers where the symbol occurs, an additional facility.

Error Messages

During the assembly process, the assembler will detect syntax errors and list them as part of the final listing. Typical diagnostics include: undefined symbols, label already defined, illegal op-

PROGRAM DEVELOPMENT

code, illegal address, illegal addressing mode. Many more detailed diagnostics are naturally desirable and usually provided. They vary with each assembler.

The Assembly Language

Opcodes have already been defined. We will define here the symbols, constants and operators which may be used as part of the assembler syntax.

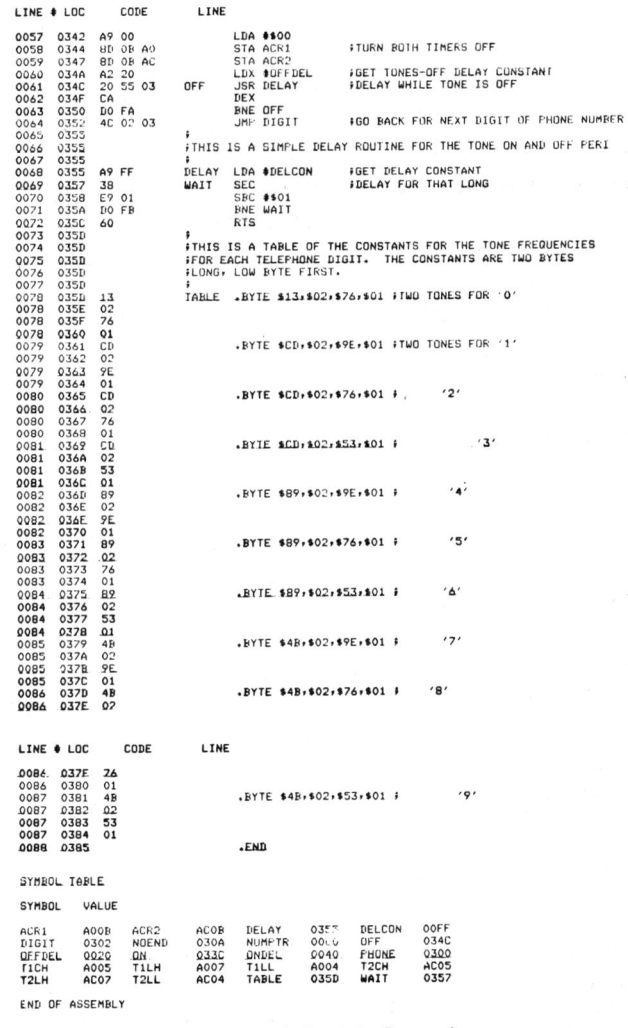

```
LINE # LOC    CODE         LINE
0057  0342  A9 00                LDA #$00
0058  0344  8D 0B A0             STA ACR1        ;TURN BOTH TIMERS OFF
0059  0347  8D 0B AC             STA ACR2
0060  034A  A2 20                LDX #OFFDEL     ;GET TONES-OFF DELAY CONSTANT
0061  034C  20 55 03     OFF     JSR DELAY       ;DELAY WHILE TONE IS OFF
0062  034F  CA                   DEX
0063  0350  D0 FA                BNE OFF
0064  0352  4C 02 03             JMP DIGIT       ;GO BACK FOR NEXT DIGIT OF PHONE NUMBER
0065  0355                ;
0066  0355                ;THIS IS A SIMPLE DELAY ROUTINE FOR THE TONE ON AND OFF PERI
0067  0355                ;
0068  0355  A9 FF        DELAY   LDA #DELCON     ;GET DELAY CONSTANT
0069  0357  38           WAIT    SEC             ;DELAY FOR THAT LONG
0070  0358  E9 01                SBC #$01
0071  035A  D0 FB                BNE WAIT
0072  035C  60                   RTS
0073  035D                ;
0074  035D                ;THIS IS A TABLE OF THE CONSTANTS FOR THE TONE FREQUENCIES
0075  035D                ;FOR EACH TELEPHONE DIGIT.  THE CONSTANTS ARE TWO BYTES
0076  035D                ;LONG, LOW BYTE FIRST.
0077  035D                ;
0078  035D  13           TABLE   .BYTE $13,$02,$76,$01  ;TWO TONES FOR '0'
0078  035E  02
0078  035F  76
0078  0360  01
0079  0361  CD                   .BYTE $CD,$02,$9E,$01  ;TWO TONES FOR '1'
0079  0362  02
0079  0363  9E
0079  0364  01
0080  0365  CD                   .BYTE $CD,$02,$76,$01 ;    '2'
0080  0366  02
0080  0367  76
0080  0368  01
0081  0369  CD                   .BYTE $CD,$02,$53,$01 ;    '3'
0081  036A  02
0081  036B  53
0081  036C  01
0082  036D  89                   .BYTE $89,$02,$9E,$01 ;    '4'
0082  036E  02
0082  036E  9E
0082  0370  01
0083  0371  89                   .BYTE $89,$02,$76,$01 ;    '5'
0083  0372  02
0083  0373  76
0083  0374  01
0084  0375  89                   .BYTE $89,$02,$53,$01 ;    '6'
0084  0376  02
0084  0377  53
0084  0378  01
0085  0379  4B                   .BYTE $4B,$02,$9E,$01 ;    '7'
0085  037A  02
0085  037B  9E
0085  037C  01
0086  037D  4B                   .BYTE $4B,$02,$76,$01 ;    '8'
0086  037E  02

LINE # LOC    CODE         LINE
0086  037E  76
0086  0380  01
0087  0381  4B                   .BYTE $4B,$02,$53,$01 ;    '9'
0087  0382  02
0087  0383  53
0087  0384  01
0088  0385                       .END

SYMBOL TABLE

SYMBOL    VALUE
ACR1      A00B    ACR2    ACOB    DELAY   0355    DELCON  00FF
DIGIT     0302    NOEND   030A    NUMPTR  00C0    OFF     034C
OFFDEL    0020    ON      033C    ONDEL   0040    PHONE   0300
T1CH      A005    T1LH    A007    T1LL    A004    T2CH    AC05
T2LH      AC07    T2LL    AC04    TABLE   035D    WAIT    0357

END OF ASSEMBLY
```

Fig. 10-6: Assembler Output: An Example

PROGRAMMING THE 6502

Symbols

Symbols are used to represent numerical values, either data or addresses. Traditionally, symbols may include 6 characters, the first one being alphabetical. One more restriction exists: the 56 opcodes utilized by the 6502 and the names of the registers i.e., A, X, Y, S, P may not be used as symbols.

Assigning a Value to a Symbol

Labels are special symbols whose values need not be defined by the programmer. They will automatically correspond to the line number where they appear. However, other symbols used for constants or memory addresses must be defined by the programmer prior to their use. The equal sign is used for that purpose, or else a special "directive." It is an instruction to the assembler which will not be translated into an executable statement; it is called an *assembler directive*.

As an example, the constant ALPHA will be defined as:

ALPHA = $A000

This assigns the value "A000" hexadecimal to variable ALPHA. The assembler directives will be examined in a later section.

Constants or Literals

Constants are traditionally expressed in either decimal, hexadecimal, octal or binary. Except in the case of a decimal number, a prefix is used to differentiate between a constant and the base used to represent a number. To load 18 into the accumulator we will simply write:

LDA #18 (where # denotes a literal)

A hexadecimal number will be preceded by the symbol $.
An octal symbol will be preceded by the symbol @
A binary symbol will be preceded by %.

For example, to load the value "11111111" into the accumulator, we will write:

LDA #%11111111.

Literal ASCII characters may also be used in a literal field. In older assemblers, it was traditional to enclose the ASCII symbol in quotes. In more recent assemblers, in order to have fewer characters to type in, the alphanumeric type is indicated by a single quote that precedes the symbol.

For example, to load the symbol "S" in the accumulator (in ASCII) we will write:

LDA #'S

In order to be able to load the quote symbol itself, the convention is:

LDA #'"

Exercise 10.1: *Will the following two instructions load the same value in the accumulator:* LDA #'5 *and* LDA #$5?

Operators

In order to further facilitate the writing of symbolic programs, assemblers allow the use of operators. At a minimum they should allow plus and minus so that one can specify, for example:
LDA ADR1, and
LDX ADR1+1

It is important to understand that the expression ADR1+1 will be computed by the assembler in order to determine what is the actual memory address which must be inserted as the binary equivalent. It will be computed *at assembly-time,* not at program execution time.

In addition, more operators may be available, such as multiply and divide, a convenience when accessing tables in memory. More specialized operators may also be available, such as, greater than and less than, which truncate a 2-byte value respectively into its high and low byte.

Naturally, an expression must evaluate to a positive value. Negative numbers are not usually used and should be expressed in a hexadecimal format.

Finally, a special symbol is traditionally used to represent the current value of the address of the line:*. This symbol should be interpreted as "current location" (value of PC).

Exercise 10.2: *What is the difference between the following instructions?*
LDA %10101010
LDA #%10101010

Exercise 10.3: *What is the effect of the following instruction?* BMI* −2?

Assembler Directives

Directives are special orders given by the programmer to the assembler. Some of these orders result in the storage of values in symbols or in the memory. Others are used to control the execution or printing modes of the assembler.

To provide a specific example, let us review here the nine assembler directives available on the Rockwell Development System ("System 65"). They are: =, .BYT, .WOR, .GBY, .PAGE, .SKIP, .OPT, .FILE and .END.

Equate Directive

An equal sign is used to assign a numeric value to a symbol. For example:

BASE = $1111
* = $1234

The effect of the first directive is to assign the value 1111 hexadecimal to BASE.

The effect of the second instruction is to force the line address to the hexadecimal value "1234." In other words, the next executable instruction encountered will be stored at memory location 1234.

Exercise 10.4: *Write a directive which will cause the program to reside at memory location 0 and up.*

Directives to Initialize Memory

Three directives are available for this purpose: .BYT, .WOR, .GBY.

.BYT will assign the characters or values that follow in consecutive memory bytes.

Example: RESERV .BYT 'SYBEX.'

This will result in storing the letters "SYBEX" in consecutive memory locations.

.WOR is used to store 2-byte addresses in the memory, low byte first.

Example: .WOR $1234, $2345

.GBY is identical to .WOR, except that it will store a 16-bit

PROGRAM DEVELOPMENT

value, high byte first. It is normally used for 16-bit data rather than 16-bit addresses.

The next three directives are used to control the input/output:

Input/Output Directives

The input/output directives are: .PAGE, .SKIP, .OPT.

PAGE causes the assembler to finish the page, i.e., move to the top of the next page. In addition a title may be specified for the page. For example: .PAGE "page title."

SKIP is used to insert blank lines in the listing. The number of lines to be skipped may be specified. For example: .SKIP 3.

OPT specifies four options: list, generate, errors, symbol. *List* will generate a list. *Generate* is used to print object code for strings with the .BYT directive. *Error* specifies whether error diagnostics should be printed. *Symbol* specifies whether the symbol table should be listed.

The last two directives control the assembler listing format:

.FILE and .END Directives

In the development of a large program, several portions of the program will typically be written and debugged separately. At some point it will be necessary to assemble these files together. The last statement of the first file will then include the directive .FILE NAME/1, where 1 is the number of the disk unit, and NAME is the name of the next file. The next file may be linked, in turn, to more files. At the end of the last file, there will be the directive: .END NAME/1, which is a pointer back to the first one.

Finally, a facility exists for inserting additional comments with the listing: ";"

";" may be used to enter comments at will within a line rather than enter an instruction. This is an important facility if programs are to be correctly documented.

MACROS

A macro facility is currently not available on most existing 6502 assemblers. However, we will define a macro here and explain its benefits. It is hoped that a macro facility will

Fig. 10-7: AIM65 is a Board with Mini-Printer and Full Keyboard

Fig. 10-8: Ohio Scientific is a Personal Microcomputer

soon be available on most 6502 assemblers.

A macro is simply a name assigned to a group of instructions. It is essentially a convenience to the programmer. For example, if a group of five instructions is used several times in a program, we could define a macro instead of always having to write these five instructions. As an example, we could write:

```
SAVREG MACRO PHA
              TXA
              PHA
              TYA
              PHA
       ENDM
```

Thereafter, we could write the name SAVREG instead of the above instructions.

Any time that we write SAVREG, the five corresponding lines will get substituted instead of the name. An assembler equipped with a macro facility is called a macro assembler. When the macro assembler encounters SAVREG, it will perform a mere physical substitution of the equivalent lines.

Macro or Subroutine?

At this point, a macro may seem to operate in a way analogous to a subroutine. This is not the case. When the assembler is used to produce the object code, any time that a macro name is encountered, it will be replaced by the actual instructions that it stands for. At execution time, the group of instructions will appear as many times as the name of the macro did.

By contrast, a subroutine is defined only once, and then it can be used repeatedly: the program will jump to the subroutine address. A macro is called an *assembly-time* facility. A subroutine is an *execution-time* facility. Their operation is quite different.

Macro Parameters

Each macro may be equipped with a number of parameters. As an example, let us consider the following macro:

```
SWAP  MACRO  M, N, T
      LDA    M
      STA    T
      LDA    N
      STA    M
```

```
    LDA    T
    STA    N
    ENDM
```

This macro will result in swapping (exchanging) the contents of memory locations M and N. A swap between two registers, or two memory locations, is an operation which is not provided by the 6502. A macro may be used to implement it. "T", in this instance, is simply the name for a temporary storage location required by the program. As an example, let us swap the contents of memory locations ALPHA and BETA. The instruction which does this appears below:

```
SWAP  ALPHA, BETA, TEMP
```

In this instruction, TEMP is the name of some temporary storage location which we know to be available and which can be used by the macro. The resulting expansion of the macro appears below:

```
    LDA   ALPHA
    STA   TEMP
    LDA   BETA
    STA   ALPHA
    LDA   TEMP
    STA   BETA
```

The value of a macro should now be apparent: it is a tremendous convenience for the programmer to be able to use pseudo-instructions which have been defined with macros. In this way, the apparent instruction set of the 6502 can be expanded at will. Unfortunately, one must bear in mind that each macro directive will expand into whatever number of instructions were used. A macro will, therefore, run more slowly than any single instruction. Because of its convenience for the development of any long program, a macro facility is highly desirable for such an application.

Additional Macro Facilities

Many other directives and syntactic facilities may be added to a simple macro facility. For instance, macros may be *nested,* i.e., a macro-call may appear within a macro definition. Using this facility, a macro may modify itself with a nested definition! A first call will produce one expansion, whereas subsequent calls will produce a modified expansion of the same macro.

CONDITIONAL ASSEMBLY

Conditional assembly is another assembler facility which is so far lacking on most 6502 assemblers. A conditional assembler facility allows the programmer to use the special instructions "IF," followed by an expression, then (optionally) "ELSE," and terminated by "ENDIF." Whenever the expression following the IF is true, then the instructions between the IF and the ELSE, or the IF and the ENDIF (if there is no ELSE), will be assembled. In the case in which IF followed by ELSE is used, either one of the two blocks of instructions will be assembled, depending on the value of the expression being tested.

With a conditional assembler facility, the programmer can devise programs for a variety of cases, and then conditionally assemble the segments of codes required by a specific application. As an example, an industrial user might design programs to take care of any number of traffic lights at an intersection for a variety of control algorithms. He/she will then receive the specifications from the local traffic engineer, who specifies how many traffic lights there should be, and which algorithms should be used. The programmer will then simply set parameters in his/her program, and assemble conditionally. The conditional assembly will result in a "customized" program which will retain only those routines which are necessary for the solution to the problem.

Conditional assembly is, therefore, of specific value to industrial program generation in an environment where many options exist and where the programmer wishes to assemble portions of programs quickly and automatically in response to external parameters.

SUMMARY

This chapter has presented an explanation of the techniques and the hardware and software tools required to develop a program, along with the various trade-offs and alternatives.

These range at the hardware level from the single-board microcomputer to the full development system. At the software level they range from binary coding to high-level programming. You will have to select from these tools and techniques in accordance with your goals and budget.

CHAPTER 11

CONCLUSION

We have now covered all important aspects of programming, including the definitions and basic concepts, the internal manipulations of the 6502 registers, the management of input/output devices, and the characteristics of software development aids. What is the next step? Two views can be offered, the first one relating to the development of technology, the second one relating to the development of your own knowledge and skill. Let us address these two points.

TECHNOLOGICAL DEVELOPMENT

The progress of integration in MOS technology makes it possible to implement more and more complex chips. The cost of implementing the processor function itself is constantly decreasing. The result is that many of the input/output chips, as well as the peripheral-controller chips, used in a system, now incorporate a simple processor. This means that most LSI chips now used in the system are becoming *programmable*. An interesting conceptual dilemma is thus developing. In order to simplify the software design task as well as to reduce the component count, the new I/O chips now incorporate sophisticated programmable capabilities: many programmed algorithms are now integrated within the chip. However, as a result, the development of programs is complicated by the fact that all these input/output chips are very different and need to be studied in detail by the programmer! *Programming the system is no longer programming the micro-*

Fig. 11-1: PET is an Integrated Unit

Fig. 11-2: APPLE II uses a conventional TV

processor alone, but also programming all the various other chips attached to it. The learning time for every chip can be significant.

Naturally, this is only an apparent dilemma. If these chips were not available, the complexity of the interface to be realized, as well as the corresponding programs, would be still greater. The new complexity that is introduced is that one has to program more than just a processor, and learn the various features of the different chips in a system to make effective use of them. However, it is hoped that the techniques and concepts presented in this book should make this a reasonably easy task.

THE NEXT STEP

You have now learned the basic techniques required in order to program simple applications on paper. This was the goal of this book. The next step is to actually practice. There is no substitute for it. It is impossible to learn programming completely on paper, and experience is required. You should now be in a position to start writing your own programs. It is hoped that this journey will be a pleasant one.

For those who feel they would benefit from the guidance of additional books, the companion volume to this one in the series is the "6502 Applications Book" (ref D302), which presents a range of actual applications which can be executed on a real microcomputer. Next is the "6502 Games Book" (ref G402), which presents programming techniques for complex algorithms. A 6502 assembler, written in standard Microsoft BASIC is also available.

APPENDIX A

HEXADECIMAL CONVERSION TABLE

HEX	0	1	2	3	4	5	6	7	8	9	A	B	C	D	E	F	00	000
0	0	1	2	3	4	5	6	7	8	9	10	11	12	13	14	15	0	0
1	16	17	18	19	20	21	22	23	24	25	26	27	28	29	30	31	256	4096
2	32	33	34	35	36	37	38	39	40	41	42	43	44	45	46	47	512	8192
3	48	49	50	51	52	53	54	55	56	57	58	59	60	61	62	63	768	12288
4	64	65	66	67	68	69	70	71	72	73	74	75	76	77	78	79	1024	16384
5	80	81	82	83	84	85	86	87	88	89	90	91	92	93	94	95	1280	20480
6	96	97	98	99	100	101	102	103	104	105	106	107	108	109	110	111	1536	24576
7	112	113	114	115	116	117	118	119	120	121	122	123	124	125	126	127	1792	28672
8	128	129	130	131	132	133	134	135	136	137	138	139	140	141	142	143	2048	32768
9	144	145	146	147	148	149	150	151	152	153	154	155	156	157	158	159	2304	36864
A	160	161	162	163	164	165	166	167	168	169	170	171	172	173	174	175	2560	40960
B	176	177	178	179	180	181	182	183	184	185	186	187	188	189	190	191	2816	45056
C	192	193	194	195	196	197	198	199	200	201	202	203	204	205	206	207	3072	49152
D	208	209	210	211	212	213	214	215	216	217	218	219	220	221	222	223	3328	53248
E	224	225	226	227	228	229	230	231	232	233	234	235	236	237	238	239	3584	57344
F	240	241	242	243	244	245	246	247	248	249	250	251	252	253	254	255	3840	61440

5		4		3		2		1		0	
HEX	DEC	HEX	DEC	HEX	DEC	HEX	DEC	HEX	DEC	HEX	DEC
0	0	0	0	0	0	0	0	0	0	0	0
1	1,048,576	1	65,536	1	4,096	1	256	1	16	1	1
2	2,097,152	2	131,072	2	8,192	2	512	2	32	2	2
3	3,145,728	3	196,608	3	12,288	3	768	3	48	3	3
4	4,194,304	4	262,144	4	16,384	4	1,024	4	64	4	4
5	5,242,880	5	327,680	5	20,480	5	1,280	5	80	5	5
6	6,291,456	6	393,216	6	24,576	6	1,536	6	96	6	6
7	7,340,032	7	458,752	7	28,672	7	1,792	7	112	7	7
8	8,388,608	8	524,288	8	32,768	8	2,048	8	128	8	8
9	9,437,184	9	589,824	9	36,864	9	2,304	9	144	9	9
A	10,485,760	A	655,360	A	40,960	A	2,560	A	160	A	10
B	11,534,336	B	720,896	B	45,056	B	2,816	B	176	B	11
C	12,582,912	C	786,432	C	49,152	C	3,072	C	192	C	12
D	13,631,488	D	851,968	D	53,248	D	3,328	D	208	D	13
E	14,680,064	E	917,504	E	57,344	E	3,584	E	224	E	14
F	15,728,640	F	983,040	F	61,440	F	3,840	F	240	F	15

APPENDIX B

6502 INSTRUCTIONS—ALPHABETIC

ADC	Add with carry	JSR	Jump to subroutine
AND	Logical AND	LDA	Load accumulator
ASL	Arithmetic shift left	LDX	Load X
BCC	Branch if carry clear	LDY	Load Y
BCS	Branch if carry set	LSR	Logical shift right
BEQ	Branch if result = 0	NOP	No operation
BIT	Test bit	ORA	Logical OR
BMI	Branch if minus	PHA	Push A
BNE	Branch if not equal to 0	PHP	Push P status
BPL	Branch if plus	PLA	Pull A
BRK	Break	PLP	Pull P status
BVC	Branch if overflow clear	ROL	Rotate left
BVS	Branch if overflow set	ROR	Rotate right
CLC	Clear carry	RTI	Return from interrupt
CLD	Clear decimal flag	RTS	Return from subroutine
CLI	Clear interrupt disable	SBC	Subtract with carry
CLV	Clear overflow	SEC	Set carry
CMP	Compare to accumulator	SED	Set decimal
CPX	Compare to X	SEI	Set interrupt disable
CPY	Compare to Y	STA	Store accumulator
DEC	Decrement memory	STX	Store X
DEX	Decrement X	STY	Store Y
DEY	Decrement Y	TAX	Transfer A to X
EOR	Exclusive OR	TAY	Transfer A to Y
INC	Increment memory	TSX	Transfer SP to X
INX	Increment X	TXA	Transfer X to A
INY	Increment Y	TXS	Transfer X to SP
JMP	Jump	TYA	Transfer Y to A

APPENDIX C

BINARY LISTING OF 6502 INSTRUCTIONS

ADC	011bbb01	LDX	101bbb10
AND	001bbb01	LDY	101bbb00
ASL	000bbb10	LSR	01bbbb10
BCC	10110000	NOP	01bbb110
BEQ	11110000	ORA	000bbb01
BIT	0010b100	PHP	01001000
BMI	00110000	PHA	00001000
BNE	11010000	PLA	01101000
BPL	00010000	PLP	00101000
BRK	01010000	ROL	001bbb10
CLC	00011000	ROR	011bbb10
CLD	11011000	RTI	01000000
CLI	01011000	RTS	01100000
CMP	110bbb01	SBC	111bbb01
CPX	1110bb00	SEC	00111000
CPY	1100bb00	SED	11111000
DEC	110bb110	SEI	01111000
DEX	11001010	STA	100bbb01
DEY	10001000	STX	100bb110
EOR	010bbb01	STY	100bb100
INC	111bb110	TAX	10101010
INX	11101000	TAY	10101000
INY	11001000	TSX	10111010
JMP	01b01100	TXA	10001010
JSR	00100000	TXS	10011010
LDA	101bbb01	TYA	10011000

See Chapter 4 for definition of "bb" field.

APPENDIX D

6502—INSTRUCTION SET: HEX AND TIMING

MNEMONIC		IMPLIED			ACCUM.			ABSOLUTE			ZERO PAGE			IMMEDIATE			ABS. X			ABS. Y		
		OP	n	#	OP	n	#	OP	n	#	OP	n	#	OP	n	#	OP	n	#	OP	n	#
A D C	(1)							6D	4	3	65	3	2	69	2	2	7D	4	3	79	4	3
A N D	(1)							2D	4	3	25	3	2	29	2	2	3D	4	3	39	4	3
A S L					0A	2	1	0E	6	3	06	5	2				1E	7	3			
B C C	(2)																					
B C S	(2)																					
B E Q	(2)																					
B I T								2C	4	3	24	3	2									
B M I	(2)																					
B N E	(2)																					
B P L	(2)																					
B R K		00	7	1																		
B V C	(2)																					
B V S	(2)																					
C L C		18	2	1																		
C L D		D8	2	1																		
C L I		58	2	1																		
C L V		B8	2	1																		
C M P								CD	4	3	C5	3	2	C9	2	2	DD	4	3	D9	4	3
C P X								EC	4	3	E4	3	2	E0	2	2						
C P Y								CC	4	3	C4	3	2	C0	2	2						
D E C								CE	6	3	C6	5	2				DE	7	3			
D E X		CA	2	1																		
D E Y		88	2	1																		
E O R	(1)							4D	4	3	45	3	2	49	2	2	5D	4	3	59	4	3
I N C								EE	6	3	E6	5	2				FE	7	3			
I N X		E8	2	1																		
I N Y		C8	2	1																		
J M P								4C	3	3												
J S R								20	6	3												
L D A	(1)							AD	4	3	A5	3	2	A9	2	2	BD	4	3	B9	4	3
L D X	(1)							AE	4	3	A6	3	2	A2	2	2				BE	4	3
L D Y	(1)							AC	4	3	A4	3	2	A0	2	2	BC	4	3			
L S R					4A	2	1	4E	6	3	46	5	2				5E	7	3			
N O P		EA	2	1																		
O R A								0D	4	3	05	3	2	09	2	2	1D	4	3	19	4	3
P H A		48	3	1																		
P H P		08	3	1																		
P L A		68	4	1																		
P L P		28	4	1																		
R O L					2A	2	1	2E	6	3	26	5	2				3E	7	3			
R O R					6A	2	1	6E	6	3	66	5	2				7E	7	3			
R T I		40	6	1																		
R T S		60	6	1																		
S B C	(1)							ED	4	3	E5	3	2	E9	2	2	FD	4	3	F9	4	3
S E C		38	2	1																		
S E D		F8	2	1																		
S E I		78	2	1																		
S T A								8D	4	3	85	2	2				9D	5	3	99	5	3
S T X								8E	4	3	86	2	2									
S T Y								8C	4	3	84	2	2									
T A X		AA	2	1																		
T A Y		A8	2	1																		
T S X		BA	2	1																		
T X A		8A	2	1																		
T X S		9A	2	1																		
T Y A		98	2	1																		

(1) Add 1 to n if crossing page boundary

APPENDIX

(IND, X)			(IND)Y			Z. PAGE, X			RELATIVE			INDIRECT			Z. PAGE, Y			PROCESSOR STATUS CODES							MNEMONIC
OP	n	#	OP	n	#	OP	n	#	OP	n	#	OP	n	#	OP	n	#	N	V	B	D	I	Z	C	
61	6	2	71	5	2	75	4	2										●	●				●	●	A D C
21	6	2	31	5	2	35	4	2										●					●		A N D
						16	6	2										●					●	●	A S L
									90	2	2														B C C
									B0	2	2														B C S
									F0	2	2														B E Q
																		M₇	M₆				●		B I T
									30	2	2														B M I
									D0	2	2														B N E
									10	2	2														B P L
																				1		1			B R K
									50	2	2														B V C
									70	2	2														B V S
																								0	C L C
																					0				C L D
																						0			C L I
																			0						C L V
C1	6	2	D1	5	2	D5	4	2										●					●	●	C M P
																		●					●	●	C P X
																		●					●	●	C P Y
						D6	6	2										●					●		D E C
																		●					●		D E X
																		●					●		D E Y
41	6	2	51	5	2	55	4	2										●					●		E O R
						F6	6	2										●					●		I N C
																		●					●		I N X
																		●					●		I N Y
												6C	5	3											J M P
A1	6	2	B1	5	2	B5	4	2										●					●		J S R
															B6	4	2	●					●		L D A
						B4	4	2										●					●		L D X
						56	6	2										0					●	●	L D Y
																									L S R
																									N O P
01	6	2	11	5	2	15	4	2										●					●		O R A
																									P H A
																									P H P
																		●	●	●	●	●	●	●	P L A
																		●	●	●	●	●	●	●	P L P
						36	6	2										●					●	●	R O L
						76	6	2										●					●	●	R O R
																		●	●	●	●	●	●	●	R T I
																									R T S
E1	6	2	F1	5	2	F5	4	2										●	●				●	●	S B C
																								1	S E C
																					1				S E D
																						1			S E I
81	6	2	91	6	2	95	4	2																	S T A
															96	4	2								S T X
						94	4	2																	S T Y
																		●					●		T A X
																		●					●		T A Y
																		●					●		T S X
																		●					●		T X A
																									T X S
																		●					●		T Y A

(2) Add 2 to n if branch within page
Add 3 to n if branch to another page

APPENDIX E

ASCII CONVERSION TABLE

HEX LSD	MSD BITS	0 000	1 001	2 010	3 011	4 100	5 101	6 110	7 111
0	0000	NUL	DLE	SPACE	0	@	P	‑	p
1	0001	SOH	DC1	!	1	A	Q	a	q
2	0010	STX	DC2	"	2	B	R	b	r
3	0011	ETX	DC3	#	3	C	S	c	s
4	0100	EOT	DC4	$	4	D	T	d	t
5	0101	ENQ	NAK	%	5	E	U	e	u
6	0110	ACK	SYN	&	6	F	V	f	v
7	0111	BEL	ETB	'	7	G	W	g	w
8	1000	BS	CAN	(	8	H	X	h	x
9	1001	HT	EM	)	9	I	Y	i	y
A	1010	LF	SUB	*	:	J	Z	j	z
B	1011	VT	ESC	+	;	K	[	k	{
C	1100	FF	FS	,	<	L	\	l	‑‑
D	1101	CR	GS	‑	=	M	]	m	}
E	1110	SO	RS	.	>	N	^	n	~
F	1111	SI	US	/	?	O	←	o	DEL

THE ASCII SYMBOLS

NUL — Null
SOH — Start of Heading
STX — Start of Text
ETX — End of Text
EOT — End of Transmission
ENQ — Enquiry
ACK — Acknowledge
BEL — Bell
BS — Backspace
HT — Horizontal Tabulation
LF — Line Feed
VT — Vertical Tabulation
FF — Form Feed
CR — Carriage Return
SO — Shift Out
SI — Shift In

DLE — Data Link Escape
DC — Device Control
NAK — Negative Acknowledge
SYN — Synchronous Idle
ETB — End of Transmission Block
CAN — Cancel
EM — End of Medium
SUB — Substitute
ESC — Escape
FS — File Separator
GS — Group Separator
RS — Record Separator
US — Unit Separator
SP — Space (Blank)
DEL — Delete

APPENDIX F

RELATIVE BRANCH TABLES

FORWARD RELATIVE BRANCH

MSD\LSD	0	1	2	3	4	5	6	7	8	9	A	B	C	D	E	F
0	0	1	2	3	4	5	6	7	8	9	10	11	12	13	14	15
1	16	17	18	19	20	21	22	23	24	25	26	27	28	29	30	31
2	32	33	34	35	36	37	38	39	40	41	42	43	44	45	46	47
3	48	49	50	51	52	53	54	55	56	57	58	59	60	61	62	63
4	64	65	66	67	68	69	70	71	72	73	74	75	76	77	78	79
5	80	81	82	83	84	85	86	87	88	89	90	91	92	93	94	95
6	96	97	98	99	100	101	102	103	104	105	106	107	108	109	110	111
7	112	113	114	115	116	117	118	119	120	121	122	123	124	125	126	127

BACKWARD RELATIVE BRANCH TABLE

MSD\LSD	0	1	2	3	4	5	6	7	8	9	A	B	C	D	E	F
8	128	127	126	125	124	123	122	121	120	119	118	117	116	115	114	113
9	112	111	110	109	108	107	106	105	104	103	102	101	100	99	98	97
A	96	95	94	93	92	91	90	89	88	87	86	85	84	83	82	81
B	80	79	78	77	76	75	74	73	72	71	70	69	68	67	66	65
C	64	63	62	61	60	59	58	57	56	55	54	53	52	51	50	49
D	48	47	46	45	44	43	42	41	40	39	38	37	36	35	34	33
E	32	31	30	29	28	27	26	25	24	23	22	21	20	19	18	17
F	16	15	14	13	12	11	10	9	8	7	6	5	4	3	2	1

PROGRAMMING THE 6502

APPENDIX G:

HEX OPCODE LISTING

LSD MSD	0	1	2	3	4	5	6	7
0	BRK	ORA-I, X				ORA-∅-P	ASL-∅-P	
1	BPL	ORA-I, Y				ORA-∅-P, X	ASL-∅-P, X	
2	JSR	AND-I, X			BIT-∅-P	AND-∅-P	ROL-∅-P	
3	BMI	AND-I, Y				AND-∅-P, X	ROL-∅-P, X	
4	RTI	EOR-I, X				EOR-∅-P	LSR-∅-P	
5	BVC	EOR-I, Y				EOR-∅-P, X	LSR-∅-P, X	
6	RTS	ADC-I, X				ADC-∅-P	ROR-∅-P	
7	BVS	ADC-I, Y				ADC-∅-P, X		
8		STA-I, X			STY-∅-P	STA-∅-P	STX-∅-P	
9	BCC	STA-I, Y			STY-∅-P, X	STA-∅-P, X	STX-∅-P, Y	
A	LDY-IMM	LDA-I, X	LDX-IMM		LDY-∅-P	LDA-∅-P	LDX-∅-P	
B	BCS	LDA-I, Y			LDY-∅-P, X	LDA-∅-P, X	LDX-∅-P, Y	
C	CPY-IMM	CMP-I, X			CPY-∅-P	CMP-∅-P	DEC-∅-P	
D	BNE	CMP-I, Y				CMP-∅-P, X	DEC-∅-P, X	
E	CPX-IMM	SBC-I, X			CPX-∅-P	SBC-∅-P	INC-∅-P	
F	BEQ	SBC-I, Y				SBC-∅-P, X	INC-∅-P, X	

8	9	A	B	C	D	E	F	LSD MSD
PHP	ORA-IMM	ASL-A			ORA	ASL		0
CLC	ORA, Y				ORA, X	ASL, X		1
PLP	AND-IMM	ROL-A		BIT	AND	ROL		2
SEC	AND, Y				AND, X	ROL, X		3
PHA	EOR-IMM	LSR-A		JMP	EOR	LSR		4
CLI	EOR, Y				EOR, X	LSR, X		5
PLA	ADC-IMM	ROR-A		JMP-I	ADC	ROR		6
SEI	ADC, Y				ADC, X			7
DEY		TXA		STY	STA	STX		8
TYA	STA, Y	TXS			STA, X			9
TAY	LDA-IMM	TAX		LDY	LDA	LDX		A
CLV	LDA, Y	TSX		LDY, X	LDA, X	LDX, Y		B
INY	CMP-IMM	DEX		CPY	CMP	DEC		C
CLD	CMP, Y				CMP, X	DEC, X		D
INX	SBC-IMM	NOP		CPX	SBC	INC		E
SED	SBC, Y				SBC, X	INC, X		F

I = indirect
∅-P = zero page

APPENDIX H:

DECIMAL TO BCD CONVERSION

DECIMAL	BCD	DEC	BCD	DEC	BCD
0	0000	10	00010000	90	10010000
1	0001	11	00010001	91	10010001
2	0010	12	00010010	92	10010010
3	0011	13	00010011	93	10010011
4	0100	14	00010100	94	10010100
5	0101	15	00010101	95	10010101
6	0110	16	00010110	96	10010110
7	0111	17	00010111	97	10010111
8	1000	18	00011000	98	10011000
9	1001	19	00011001	99	10011001

INDEX

A

A 187
abbreviations 112
absolute 197
absolute addressing 66, 190, 191, 195
accumulator 41, 48, 55, 110, 122, 133, 143,
 152, 165, 178, 182, 183, 185, 190, 263
ADC 62, 113
addition 54, 59, 67
address 39, 149, 188, 189, 191, 192, 306
address bus 39, 44, 45, 49
address field 358
addressing 188, 189
addressing modes 188, 200
addressing techniques 188
algorithm 7, 8, 69, 275, 318, 320, 340
alphabetic list 290, 301, 302, 303, 304, 305
alphabetical order 269, 372
alphanumeric 31
ALU 39, 41
AND 87, 104, 110, 115
APL 345
arithmetic 41, 67, 100, 103, 117
arithmetic logical unit 39, 41
arithmetic operation 41, 100
arithmetic programs 54
ASCII 31, 32, 267, 268, 360, 376
ASL 106, 117
assembler 55, 343, 345, 346, 356, 358, 359
assembler directives 362
assembly level language 344, 356, 358, 359
assembly time 361, 365
asynchronous 216, 221, 228

B

BASIC 16, 345
basic concepts 7
baud 235
BCC 74, 109, 119
BCD 26, 27, 64, 65, 103, 268, 379
BCD addition 63, 66
BCD flags 67
BCD mode 67, 108
BCD subtraction 66
BCS 109, 120
benchmark 220
BEQ 109, 121
binary 12, 13, 14, 33, 34, 35, 36, 37, 64,
 343, 346, 358, 361, 373
binary digit 10, 12
binary division 86
binary mode 108
binary representation 12, 33, 358
binary searching 283, 290, 294, 295,
 296, 299
binary tree structure 313, 320
BIT 110, 122
bit 10, 12, 33, 54, 59, 100, 122, 167, 169
bit serial transfer 221, 223
block 203, 204, 205, 208, 276, 277, 279, 280
block transfer routine 203, 204, 205
BMI 109, 123, 208
BNE 77, 109, 124, 207, 208, 264
bootstrap 40
BPL 109, 125
bracket testing 265
branch 101, 119, 120, 121, 123, 124, 125,
 127, 128, 191, 196, 264
branches 196
branching 191
branching point 69
break 102, 108, 126, 251
break point 108, 251, 349
BRK 108, 111, 126, 251
bubble sort 333, 334, 335, 336, 337, 338
buffer 255
buffered 41
busses 39
BVC 109, 127
BVS 109, 128
byte 10, 11, 27, 62

INDEX

C

C	43
call	101
carry	19, 21, 22, 43, 57, 75, 109, 113, 119, 120, 129, 173, 175, 191
central processing unit	39
characters	31, 265, 266
checksum	270
chronological structure	47
circular list	280, 281
classes of instruction	99
CLC	57, 63, 67, 129
CLD	58, 130
clear	57, 58, 111, 119, 127, 129, 130, 131, 132, 191
CLI	131
clock	40, 45, 73
CLV	132
CMP	110, 133
code conversion	268
coding	8, 349
collision	321
combination chips	41
combinations	194
commands	8
comment field	55, 356
comparisons	106
compiler	346
complement	14, 30, 54
conditional assembly	367
constants	66, 360
control bus	39
control instructions	102, 111
control lines	255
control register	255, 257
control signals	51
control unit	39, 45
counter	71, 214
counting	213
CPU	39
CPX	111, 135
CPY	111, 137
cross assemblers	354
crystal	40
current location	361

D

D	58, 108
data	39, 255
data bus	39, 45
data direction register	255, 256, 259
data processing	100, 103
data representation	286
data structures	275, 284, 300
data transfer	67, 99, 102
data transfer rate	221
data units	319
debugger	347
debugging	10, 347
DEC	139
decimal	12, 13, 14, 35, 36, 58, 108, 130, 176, 379
decimal adjust	64
decimal mode	176
decoding logic	41, 45
decrement	100, 103, 139, 141, 142, 207, 214
delay	213, 214
deleting	287, 301, 309
design examples	284
destination	39
development system	352
device handler	248, 348
DEX	77, 141, 207
DEY	142, 207
direct addressing	82, 190, 191
direct binary	11, 37
directive	95, 360, 362
directories	277, 306
disassembler	345
disk operating system	347
displacement	110, 189, 191
division	86, 88, 89
DMA	239
documenting	55
DOS	347
doubly linked lists	281, 282
drivers	41
duration	217

E

EBCDIC	31
echo	234, 237
editor	347
element deletion	299
element insertion	298
emulator	348, 350

381

EOR	22, 87, 104, 105, 143
error messages	358, 363
executive	347, 360
execution speed	42, 45, 82, 348
exponent	28, 29
extended addressing	191
external device	39

F

fetch	44, 45, 46, 47
fields	356
FIFO	279
file system	277
flags	22, 102, 106, 130, 132, 297
flip-flop	42
floating point	28, 29, 31, 100
flow charting	8, 9, 10, 69, 86, 89, 214, 219, 223, 240, 273, 288, 289, 291, 294, 301, 315, 316, 317, 339
front panel	33, 355

G

generate a signal	212, 363

H

half carry	65
handshaking	228, 229, 255, 261
hardware concepts	38, 227, 239, 355
hardware delays	216
hardware stack	48
hashing algorithm	320, 321, 322, 329, 330, 331, 332
hexadecimal	33, 34, 35, 343, 358, 361, 371, 374, 375
hexadecimal coding	36, 343, 344
high level language	345
hobby type microcomputers	354

I

I	244
immediate addressing	66, 190, 195
implicit addressing	190
implied addressing	194
improved multiplication	82
INC	145, 207
incircuit emulator	350, 352
inclusive OR	161
increment	100, 103, 145, 147, 148
indexed addressing	191, 197, 238
indexed indirect addressing	198, 199, 209
index registers	47, 191, 200, 289
indirect addressing	193, 194, 198, 276
indirect indexed addressing	192, 199
indirection pointer	276
initialization	70
input/output	102, 211, 228, 239, 363
input/output devices	39, 102, 211, 228, 238, 239, 254, 263
input/output instructions	111
input ports	41
inserting	287, 298, 308, 320
instruction	11, 55, 112, 372, 373
instruction field	356
instruction register	45
instruction set	99, 374, 375
instruction types	67
interface chips	40
internal control register	190, 257
internal organization	10, 41, 42
interpreter	346
interrupt	48, 102, 108, 131, 171, 177, 216, 242, 243, 255
interrupt handling routine	249
interrupt levels	251
interrupt-mask	108, 244
interrupt request	51
interrupt vector	245, 248
INX	147
INY	148
IR	45
IRQ	51, 111, 244, 245
iteration	201

J

JMP	110, 149
JSR	95, 110, 151
jump	95, 101, 149, 151, 200

K

K	16, 49
keyboard	264
KIM	261

INDEX

L

label field	356
largest element	268
LDA	55, 67, 152, 268
LDX	154
LDY	156
LED	33, 230, 231
level activated	244
levels	95
LIFO	47, 276, 280
light emitting diode	230
line number	358
linked list	278, 280, 299, 306, 308, 309, 310, 311, 312
linking loader	347
listing	95, 322, 359, 378
lists	276, 285, 286, 287, 292, 293, 363
literal	65, 66, 189, 190, 360
load	55, 152, 154, 156, 257, 259
loader	347
location	73
logarithmic searching	283, 290
logical	41, 104, 115, 158
logical operations	41, 87, 100
long branch	200
longer delays	215
loops	53, 191, 240
LSR	106, 158

M

macros	363, 365, 366
macro parameters	365
main program	91
mantissa	28, 29, 31
masking	131
master directory	277
memory	39, 44, 45, 55, 57, 97, 122, 145, 178, 180, 181, 218, 272, 276, 285, 314
memory mapped I/O	102, 337, 351
memory test	263, 319
merge	339, 340, 341
mnemonics	343, 358
monitor	40, 347
MOS Technology	261
MPU	38, 39, 40
multiple interrupts	248, 249
multiple precision	59

multiplicand	75, 77, 81, 83
multiplication	68, 69, 80, 82

N

N	43, 107, 110
negative	16, 17, 18, 23, 43
nested	366
nested calls	93
next instruction	43, 46
nibble	10, 27, 100
NMI	51, 111, 244, 245
nodes	319
non-maskable interrupt	51, 244
NOP	111, 160
normalize	28
normalized mantissa	28

O

object code	346
octal	33, 34, 35, 36, 360
one K	49
one's complement	17, 19
one-shot	216
opcode	41, 189
operand	41, 54, 59, 61, 356
operand field	356
operating system	347
operators	361
ORA	87, 104, 161
oscillator	40
overflow	20, 21, 22, 23, 51, 107, 127, 128, 132
overhead	247, 253

P

P	60, 244
packed BCD	27, 63
page 0	49
paging	49, 50
parallel input/output chips	40
parallel word transfer	218, 219
parameters	365
parity	31, 32, 267
parity generation	267
partial product	71, 72
PASCAL	345

383

PC	43, 244, 361
PCH	43
PCL	43
PHA	163
PHP	164
physical address	75
PIA	256, 257, 259, 260
PIC	249
PIO	40, 254, 255, 256, 258
PIT	213
PLA	165
PLP	166
pointers	97, 194, 275, 276, 278, 297
polling	216, 219, 240, 247, 248, 263
pop	48
port	40, 254, 255
positional notation	12
positive	16, 17, 23, 269
post indexing	192
power failures	40
precision	27
pre-indexing	192
printer	35, 229, 241, 279
printing a string	238
priority	245, 246
priority interrupt controller	249
process control	40
program	8, 40
programming	7, 8, 81
program counter	43, 45, 47, 244, 358
program development	343, 348
program loop	70
programmable interval timer	213
programming alternative	81
programming form	357
programming hints	67
programming language	8, 345
programming techniques	53
PROM programmer	354
pseudo instructions	58
pull	48, 100, 165, 166
pulse counting	216
pulses	212, 213, 217
push	48, 100, 163, 164

Q

quartz	40
queue	279, 280

R

RAM	40, 41, 44, 349, 352
Random Access Memory	40
RDY	51
read only memory	40, 256
read write memory	40, 256
recursion	96
register	33, 39, 73, 75, 83, 96, 97, 106, 135, 154, 156, 190, 247, 256
register management	53
regular interrupt line	244
relative addressing	191, 196
relay	212
representation of information	33, 35
RES	51
reset	256
restoring method	86
retrieval	280, 328
return	90, 171, 172
Rockwell	261, 353
ROL	167
ROM	40, 44
ROR	169
rotate	72, 77, 101, 167, 169
rotation	77, 100
routines	262
round robin	280, 281
RTI	110, 171, 245, 246
RTS	95, 110, 172
RW	51

S

S	47, 184, 186
SBC	62, 173
scheduling	239
scope	351
searching and sorting	282
search techniques	283, 286, 290, 307
SEC	63, 175
SED	67, 176
SEI	177
sending a character	229
sensing pulses	216
sequencing	38, 46
sequential block access	200
sequential lists	276
sequential searching	282

INDEX

serial search	286
set	120, 128, 175, 176, 177
shift	71, 72, 76, 77, 100, 101, 117, 158
shift operations	106
short address	189, 195, 200
sign	107
signed binary	16, 17, 18
sign extension	100
simulator	348
simultaneous interrupts	249
simple list	286, 290
single board microcomputer	344, 352
6502	38, 194, 350, 372
6502 peculiarities	57
6522	258
6530	257, 258
6532	261
skew	100
skip	102
SO	51
software stack	48
software support	346
sort	269
source	39
STA	67, 103, 178, 207
stack	47, 97, 166, 244, 250, 275, 280
stack operations	49, 103
stack overflow	253
standard PIO	254
start bit	235, 236, 255
status flags	42
status manipulation	67
status register	244
stop bit	235
store	103, 178, 180, 181, 327
string	230, 271, 272
STX	180
STY	181
subroutines	48, 90, 92, 95, 96, 151, 172, 327, 365
subroutine call	91, 95
subroutine level	95, 96
subroutine library	98
subtract	62, 173
subtraction	14, 67
sum of n elements	269
SYM	261
symbol	360, 363
symbolic label	75, 345
symbolic representation	35, 356

symbol table	358
SYNC	51
synchronization	39, 102, 348
synchronous	221
Synertek Systems	261
syntax	281
system architecture	38
system 65	362

T

table	191, 197, 202, 276, 277, 285, 288, 289, 290, 291, 326, 358, 377
TAX	182
TAY	183
teletype input-output	233, 235, 236, 237
ten's complement	66
test and branch	102, 106, 109
testing	8
timer	216, 258
time sharing system	354
trace	350, 351
transfer	182, 183, 184, 185, 186, 187
translation	55
tree builder	313, 315, 316
tree search	323, 324, 325
trees	281, 282, 313, 319, 320, 321, 322
tree traverser	313, 317, 318, 320
truncations	25
TSX	184
two's complement	17, 18, 19, 29, 63, 100, 107
TXA	185
TXS	186
TYA	187

U

UART	227
unconditional jump	95
underflow	24
utility programs	262
utility routines	262, 348

V

versatile interface adapter	258
VIA	258
volatile	40

W

working registers   73, 195

X

X   47, 135, 141, 147, 154, 180, 182, 184
185, 186

Y

Y   47, 137, 142, 148, 156, 181, 183, 187, 207

Z

Z   43, 107, 108, 110
zero   43, 108, 121, 124, 271
zero page addressing   195

SYBEX BIBLIOGRAPHY

VIDEO COURSES

V1	Microprocessors (12 hours)
V3	Military Microprocessor Systems (6 hours)
V5	Bit-Slice (6 hours)
V7	Microprocessor Interfacing Techniques (6 hours)

AUDIO COURSES

S1	Introduction to Microprocessors (2½ hours)
S2	Programming Microprocessors (2½ hours)
S3	Designing a Microprocessor (2½ hours)
SB1	Microprocessors (12 hours)
SB2	Programming Microprocessors (10 hours)
SB3	Military Microprocessor Systems (6 hours)
SB5	Bit-Slice (6 hours)
SB6	Industrial Microprocessor Systems (4½ hours)
SB7	Microprocessor Interfacing Techniques (6 hours)
SB10	Introduction to Personal Computing (2½ hours)

REFERENCE TEXTS

C200	Introduction to Personal and Business Computing
C201	Microprocessors
C202	Programming the 6502
C207	Microprocessor Interfacing Techniques
C280	Programming the Z80
C281	Programming the Z8000
C300	CP/M Handbook (withMP/M)
D302	6502 Applications Book
G402	6502 Games
IMD	International Microprocessor Dictionary (10 languages)
X1	Microprocessor Lexicon
Z10	Microprogrammed APL Implementation

SOFTWARE

ASM 65	6502 Assembler (Microsoft BASIC)
S6580-KIM	8080 Simulator for KIM (Cassette Tape or 5'' Diskette)
S6580-APL	8080 Simulator for APPLE (Cassette Tape or 5'' Diskette)

SELF-STUDY SYSTEM

CPT	Computeacher™
CPTG	Games Board™

FOR A COMPLETE CATALOGUE
OF OUR PUBLICATIONS

U.S.A.
2344 Sixth Street
Berkeley, California 94710
Tel: (415) 848-8233
Telex: 336311

EUROPE
18 rue Planchat
75020 Paris, France
Tel: (1) 3703275
Telex: 211801

SYBEX